Keys to College Success

Keys to College Success:

Reading and Study Improvement

FOURTH EDITION

Minnette Lenier
Los Angeles Pierce College

Janet Maker
Los Angeles Trade Technical College

PRENTICE HALL, Upper Saddle River, New Jersey 07458

Library of Congress Cataloging-in-Publication Data

LENIER, MINNETTE.
    Keys to college success : reading and study improvement / Minnette
G. Lenier, Janet Maker. — 4th ed.
        p.   cm.
    Includes bibliographical references and index.
    ISBN 0–13–270935–X
    1. Study skills.   2. Reading (Higher education)   3. College
student orientation.   I. Maker, Janet.   II. Title.
LB2395.L447   1998
378.1′7028′1—dc21

                                        97–7828
                                        CIP

Acquisitions Editor: Maggie Barbieri
Editorial Assistant: Joan Polk
Project Manager: Judith Winthrop
Production Liaison: Fran Russello
Cover design: Bruce Kenselaar
Manufacturing buyer: Mary Ann Gloriande

This book was set in 10/12 Times Roman by Pine Tree Composition, Inc.
and was printed and bound by Courier Companies, Inc.
The cover was printed by Courier Companies, Inc.

Drawings on pages 1, 24, 47, 72, 105, 135, 163, 214, and 235 by
David Porter and Jules Lenier. Drawings on pages 48, 185, 193, 209, 271 and 295
by Bill Proctor and Jules Lenier. All other printed material used with permission.
Credits and information can be found in the text and the bibliography.

 © 1998, 1990, 1985, 1980 by Prentice-Hall, Inc.
Simon & Schuster/A Viacom Company
Upper Saddle River, New Jersey 07458

Printed in the United States of America

10   9   8   7   6   5   4   3   2   1

ISBN 0-13-270935-X

Prentice-Hall International (UK) Limited, *London*
Prentice-Hall of Australia Pty. Limited, *Sydney*
Prentice-Hall of Canada Inc., *Toronto*
Prentice-Hall Hispanoamericana, S.A., *Mexico*
Prentice-Hall of India Private Limited, *New Delhi*
Prentice-Hall of Japan, Inc., *Tokyo*
Simon & Schuster Asia Pte. Ltd., *Singapore*
Editora Prentice-Hall do Brasil, Ltda., *Rio de Janeiro*

Contents

Reading Critically   *47*

Reading Textbooks I: Preview, Question, Read   *72*

Reading Textbooks II: Write, Recall, Review   **105**

Reading Textbooks III: Working with Technical Material   *135*

7

Learning from Lectures   *163*

8

Improving Memory   *185*

Taking Tests

209

Using the Library

235

Improving Vocabulary

271

12

Varying Reading Rates

295

Appendix

Preface

A locksmith could pick a lock with certain tools, but it takes time and may or may not be successful. It is far more practical for him/her to have a set of master keys common to most locks. Similarly, the purpose of this user-friendly book is to give you keys to work the locks of the academic world.

When the authors of this book started college, no one talked about reading and study skills. It was expected that any reasonably intelligent high school graduate already knew how to take notes, memorize textbook material, and do well on tests. We found that this expectation was unrealistic: both of us had done very well in high school, yet we were sadly lacking in many skills needed for college-level work. For example, we reread our textbooks several times because we didn't know how to read them efficiently the first time. We stayed up half the night before each exam trying to memorize everything because we didn't know how to identify the important ideas likely to be on the test. Finally, as a result of painful experience, our study habits improved.

We see our present college students going through this same trial-and-error process. We wrote this book to give students a head start by helping them benefit from our experiences and those of other successful students. If you use the techniques taught, you will have all the skills needed to succeed in nearly any college course. You will have learned *how* to learn, and studying will be easier and more enjoyable.

This fourth edition of *Keys to College Success* reflects the several years of experience we and others have had using the book with students. As a result of comments by students and teachers, we have changed the book to further emphasize textbook and critical reading skills. We have now included over fifty new textbook selections from a wide variety of academic areas (from agriculture to zoology.) In addition, we have updated previous reading selections, added a new chapter on reading technical material and expanded the section on using and creating graphic organizers. This edition includes added information on identifying and using individual learning styles so that you can customize a study program most likely to lead you to college success. To aid comprehension, we have, for the first time, glossed (defined) key words in the margins next to where they appear in the reading selections. The glossed words are in **boldface type** in the readings so that you will know to look in the margins for definitions. (We do not intend these definitions to be the most common or best for each word. Instead, we've defined each glossed word as used in its reading selection.) If a word is not glossed, frequently it has been defined in the reading article itself. Finally, we have updated many other selections; for example, we have added new information on using library computer services. In conclusion, we believe that you will find this edition easier to read, more relevant and a master key for ensuring college success!

Organization

Keys to College Success is a practical guide to the most important reading and study skills students need in college: time management, identification of main ideas and supporting details, critical reading, study reading, memory, note-taking, test taking, using the library, writing term papers, vocabulary, and increasing reading efficiency.

Each chapter contains a skills section, exercises for practicing the skills, comprehension questions, and one or more reading selections. All reading selections were chosen for their relevance and interest to college students. All comprehension quizzes include both multiple choice and open-ended questions. Furthermore, longer reading selections were followed by general questions for discussion and writing. All answers to objective questions are in the **Answers** in the back of the book. Sample answers to PQ4R, outlines, study maps, lecture notes and a full textbook chapter for practice are in the **Appendix**

Acknowledgments

For their creative and/or editorial assistance, we wish to thank Jules Lenier, Shannon Lenier Moon and also Prentice-Hall.

Special thanks to Carolyn Taffel whose editorial assistance and fresh ideas helped change an excellent book into an even better one and to Marjorie Young, M.L.S., who gave invaluable assistance in preparing Chapter 10, "Using the Library." Chapter 6, "Reading Technical Material in Textbooks," could not have been as thorough without the input of Michael Goldfarb, Assistant Professor of Mechanical Engineering at Vanderbilt University, Steven Lenier, Managing Editor of *Neurosurgery* magazine, Edmont Katz, of the Microbiology Laboratory at Los Angeles Pierce College, Melissa Jordan Grey, Production Manager, Consumer Division, Microsoft Corporation and countless other technical experts who read, suggested, and reread the techniques and sample materials in this new chapter. The special cartoons that open each chapter and so ably capture the core of the material to come are the artwork of Bill Proctor and David Porter. The clever words of cartoon characters came from the pen of Jules Lenier.

Finally, this book would not exist without the help of Maggie Barbieri, Developmental English Editor for Prentice-Hall, the production work of Judith Winthrop of Dummy Smart and the following reviewers who gave of their time and wealth of knowledge to improve this edition: Dee Bostick, Midlands Technical College, Judith Schein Cohen, University of Illinois at Chicago, Michael Strumpf, Moorpark College, Charles R. Rogers, Pasco-Hernando Community College, and Eileen H. Schwartz, Purdue Calumet.

Minnette Lenier

Janet Maker

Keys to College Success

Adjusting to College Responsibilities

1

Adjusting to College Responsibilities

You can lead a boy to college but you cannot make him think.
Elbert Hubbard

Knowing What to Expect

Whether you have just finished high school, are beginning college while working or raising a family, or have just returned to college after a lengthy absence, you may find your first term of college confusing, even frustrating. Perhaps you are expecting things to be the same as they were in high school. Realizing the facts about college life will help you modify your expectations and increase your chances for success. Here are three of the most common false expectations:

Expectation

All I need to do to get decent grades in college is to keep a low profile. This means I need to attend classes regularly but avoid asking questions (so that the instructors won't notice me), and turn in all assignments, even if they're done incorrectly.

The Reality. This approach is guaranteed to get you low grades in most colleges. It is your responsibility not only to show up and turn in assignments, but to understand the material so that you can do assignments correctly and get high grades on exams. This usually means asking questions in class and/or during the instructor's office hours. It won't work to blame the instructor because you didn't understand a concept included in a test.

Expectation

If I read the assigned chapters at least twice, I should be able to remember the material when I take the test.

The Reality. Reading a chapter is a passive activity. In order to get good grades on a test, you usually don't have to read the chapter more than once, but you do have to decide what you think will be included in a test and then learn those concepts. Techniques for study reading and memorization will be discussed in Chapters 4, 5, 6, and 8.

Expectation

If I am absent, it is the instructor's responsibility to tell me what I missed.

The Reality. If you were absent, you have to find out three things: (1) whether any assignments were made; (2) whether any handouts were given; and (3) what was discussed in the lecture. You are responsible for obtaining the necessary information from your classmates and/or the instructor.

Getting Along with Instructors

College instructors have different expectations of their students than most high school teachers do. The way to get along with instructors is to act like a responsible adult. Here are some things you will want to do and avoid doing.

	Do	**Don't**
1.	Do come prepared to class and/or to the instructor's office during office hours. If you have missed class, get the lecture notes from another student before you ask questions.	Don't ask questions that show you haven't done the assigned reading or that you haven't been listening to the lecture.
2.	Do get another student's notes and have that student explain them to you. Ask the instructor questions about the lecture only when you can't get the answers from your classmates.	Don't expect the instructor to repeat a lecture for you privately if you were absent.
3.	Do read each assigned chapter and ask *specific* questions about those concepts that are giving you trouble.	Don't ask general questions such as "Could you explain Chapter 3?"
4.	Do ask the instructor during office hours.	Don't ask personal questions during class, such as "When can I take my makeup exam?"
5.	Do ask the instructor during office hours. If the question is relevant to the whole class, raise your hand and ask it in class.	Don't rush up to the instructor before, during, or after class to ask questions about assignments or parts of the lecture you didn't understand.
6.	Do find out from a classmate the title of the handout you need, then ask the instructor for it by title during office hours, or photocopy a classmate's copy.	Don't ask during class for any handouts that you missed because of an absence.

Do	Don't
7. Do turn in assignments on time. Instructors are not likely to accept your excuses more than once or twice. They've heard them all before.	Don't expect the instructor to accept your excuses for turning in late assignments, if you do so often.
8. Do type or print neatly. Copy over anything that is messy. If you cause an instructor to take twice as long to read your assignments because of sloppiness, your grades are likely to suffer.	Don't turn in messy assignments and expect the instructor to struggle to read them.
9. Do be courteous. Come to class on time and leave at the end. If you are too tired to stay awake, stay home. If you have to study for a test in another subject, don't come to class. If you have something to say to a classmate, make a note to yourself and tell that person at the break or after class. If you anger instructors by being discourteous, they will be much less likely to go out of their way to help you.	Don't offend your instructor or distract your classmates. Falling asleep or reading during a lecture or constantly coming late to class or leaving early is insulting to the instructor. Talking to a classmate during a lecture offends the instructor and distracts the members of the class who are trying to concentrate.

Organizing Your Time

Time management begins with your decision about which courses to take and when to take them. If you have already picked a major or a career goal, you will have a clearer idea of which classes to take. If you are not sure about your major, it's a good idea to begin by taking general courses that apply to several majors.

Setting Goals

If you're not sure about your career goal, you can profit from a visit to the counseling center at your college. The counselors have information about most occupations, and they can also test whether your interests, abilities, and personality fit your occupational goals.

In choosing a goal, you should consider the kinds of courses that will be required as well as other prerequisites. For example, did you know that a major in architecture requires knowledge of higher mathematics? Or that nursing requires knowledge of microbiology?

Assessing Your Skills, Aptitudes, and Learning Style

Before you can decide how many and what types of classes you can handle, you must consider what you know, the abilities with which you were born (aptitudes), and the methods by which you learn best (learning style).

Evaluating Your Basic Skills. Everybody has strengths and weaknesses. You have to assess realistically your reading, writing, math, and study skills. When you entered college, you may have been given an entrance test that included several of these skills. If so, use the results to evaluate what basic skills courses you may need before taking a full-time academic program. If you are unsure of your level, find out if the counseling office or learning center offers testing in this area. The results of the tests can help you decide when to take a class. For example, if you are a slow reader and are considering a class that requires a lot of reading, such as history or English, you may want to take that class when your overall reading load is lighter. If a course requires a term paper and writing is hard for you, you will have to spend more time on this course than on others and you should plan your course load accordingly. Another example is that if you are not competent in at least elementary algebra, you will need to build your math skills before taking chemistry courses, even if there are no prerequisites listed in the college catalog.

Becoming Aware of Your Aptitudes. It seems obvious that everyone is born with different strengths and weaknesses. You may have walked at a later age than did your brother or said your first word at an earlier age than did your sister. Some do well in spatial tasks such as reading blueprints or learning anatomy; others excel in learning languages or remembering technical terms; still others possess musical aptitudes, unusual athletic ability, or excellent manual dexterity (skill in the use of their hands). These are only a few examples of the many special abilities with which individuals are born. It may help you to learn about your own aptitudes to know that aptitudes are not only abilities—they are also appetites. Think about what you like to do in your free time; this will help you discover your natural abilities. If this kind of thinking doesn't help you uncover your native strengths, perhaps your college offers an aptitude test in its counseling department. In addition, you may find books in your library or bookstore that can help.

Fortunately, you don't have to be at the top of your class at note-taking or a gold medalist at textbook reading to do well in school. Just as the athlete improves his or her ability by lifting weights, you can strengthen your learning skills by practicing. Just as the athlete is better after learning some quick moves and new plays, you will be more effective after learning new study skills and shortcuts. The place to start is to assess where you are now. What are your strengths and weaknesses and how will they affect your college career? Identify your inborn talents.

Once you become aware of your own aptitudes, you are in a better position to determine your learning style.

Recognizing Your Learning Style.   Everyone has a different learning style. For example, one person may find it easier to remember what is heard while another remembers more of what is read. A third person may learn best from hands-on experience. As an example, some preschoolers learn the alphabet by running a finger over sandpaper letters while others learn by singing a song.

While your style may be based on natural abilities, you can strengthen your learning approach by knowing effective strategies with which to approach difficult tasks. By analyzing your current learning style, you can recognize situations that may require more time or effort on your part. In short, you can learn to capitalize on your strengths.

Remember, however, that as a college student, you must also learn to be flexible. For example, you may like to take objective tests more than essay tests, but you will still be expected to take both. Therefore, the aim of this section is to alert you to those skills in which you are weak so that you can pay special attention to them in the following chapters. You may not become an A student, but at least you will be able to strengthen all of your skills to the point where you can pass any class you need. Take the following self-test to identify your current learning style. Fill in the letter of each of your answers in the spaces provided. Then look on the next page to help you evaluate your answers.

Do you remember more from (a) what you read or (b) what you hear?

1. _____

Do you understand and remember more (a) when you read a process step by step or (b) when a diagram or the process is presented?

2. _____

Given that you have the time, do you prefer to (a) stay with one class assignment until it is done even if it takes three hours or (b) do small portions of assignments from several classes in the same amount of time?

3. _____

Do you prefer studying (a) alone or (b) with a group?

4. _____

Do you prefer to study (a) specific facts or (b) general concepts and theories?

5. _____

Do you prefer classes that have mainly (a) lectures or (b) participation in group discussions and/or other group activities?

6. _____

Would you probably get a higher grade on (a) an objective test or (b) an essay test?

7. _____

Are you better able to answer questions that require (a) memory or (b) problem solving?

8. _____

Do you prefer to read (a) science and technical material or (b) essays by famous writers?

9. _____

Do you prefer to (a) outline material or (b) summarize it?

10. _____

Now that you have completed the self test, read the following paragraph which will provide you with insights about your learning style.

If you answered mostly **a,** you are probably more systematic, structured, and organized and find it easier to work alone. If you answered mostly **b,** you are probably more creative, enjoy unstructured situations, find concepts easier to learn than facts and work well in groups.

Since a large portion of this book is devoted to giving you alternative ways to learn academic material, you should try the different techniques offered in each chapter and find which ones are most appropriate to your learning style. Sometimes, by asking students who have already taken a particular class and instructor, you can find an instructor who teaches in a manner compatible with your learning style. For example, there are English instructors who lecture on how to write a good essay and there are those who use group criticism of writing assignments more than lectures to teach writing techniques.

Of course, sometimes you can temporarily avoid classes that deal heavily in areas in which you think are weak. For example, you can delay taking classes that require essay tests until you have time to strengthen your essay writing. However, this is not always practical. For instance, you may need to take a math class next semester, but you are not good at problem solving. In this case try varying your learning techniques. How about organizing a study group? By working with people who understand how to do the problems, you will probably begin to understand their strategies. In other words, you can make up for your weaknesses until you can strengthen them. One of the authors of this book had to take an accounting class but was not good at problem solving involving math. Knowing of this weakness, she allotted extra time in the library to work the accounting problems. She made sure she asked in class about any problems she did not understand. She also realized that she could work with other classmates if she needed extra help. Furthermore, she made sure that she had telephone numbers of some students who seemed to understand the material. She also checked and found she could go to the learning center and sign up for tutoring if she began to have severe problems. In short, knowing she had a weakness in this area, she not only found alternative strategies, she found extra resources for help if she needed them. Being aware of her limitations gave her a better chance for success. She made sure, for example, that she took the course when she had extra time to devote to this kind of class. If she had been a full-time student, she would not have taken several of these challenging classes at one time.

Next, you will be exploring how to use your study time efficiently. Apply what you have learned about your basic skills, aptitudes, and learning style. Although our sample schedule, for example, is broken into one-hour blocks and is for a person who will study alone, after you have tried it for a week or two, you may wish to modify it to fit your individual needs. For instance, you may find you are not able to read the amount of material indicated on the sample schedule in a particular time block, or you may want to add time to study with one or more classmates each week. As long as you adjust the schedule to one where you finish all the work you must do, it will be a good schedule for you. Above all, be honest with yourself. A realistic assessment of your strengths and weaknesses will result in a more realistic schedule, thus increasing your chances for success.

Choosing Full-Time or Part-Time Study

Another major decision is whether to attend college full-time or part-time. If you have to work, you will have less time for study. By work, we mean not only a job, but also any responsibilities, such as child care, that you may have in addition to your course load. If you have extra responsibilities, you might consider attending school part-time.

Deciding How Many Classes to Take.   Be realistic about how many classes you can handle. Remember, some classes will be harder than others. A realistic schedule takes both strengths and weaknesses into account and increases chances for success. In general, we recommend that working students reduce their course loads by three semester units for every ten hours they work each week. In addition, the number of classes you should take depends on your academic strengths and weaknesses and on the difficulty of the classes you are considering. To find out how hard a class is, ask students who have taken the class before and go to the bookstore to survey the textbook and other required readings. Find out as much as you can before you commit yourself.

Breaking Tasks into Subgoals

Learning to manage time efficiently is key to succeeding in college. Time spent studying does not by itself guarantee high grades. The amount of time students need to study depends on their abilities, the difficulty of their classes, the grades they are trying for, and how efficiently they use their study time. Students who carry around their vocabulary flash cards and review them whenever they have a few minutes between classes will not need to spend hours studying vocabulary before every test. Students who review psychology notes soon after every class will not need to stay up all night memorizing them before the final exam.

Breaking tasks into realistic subgoals is a good way to combat the anxiety and guilt that often trouble students. For instance, if you know that you cannot read for two hours straight, break your reading assignments into shorter segments that you are able to handle. The rationale is that setting the goal of reading 10 pages will result in satisfaction at the end of those 10 pages rather than guilt for not having read 50.

Try to base your goals on the amount of work you want to accomplish rather than on the length of time you plan to study. If you assign yourself 10 pages of history, the time spent per page will probably be less than if you had assigned yourself one hour of studying history. This is because your concentration will improve when you have a clear goal. If you must plan your goals in terms of time units, set a timer or alarm clock to let you know when the study period is up. That way you won't waste your study time watching the clock.

Now take a few minutes to break a task into at least 10 smaller steps. Choose any familiar task, such as planning a trip, cleaning the house, or giving a party. Remember to include the earliest steps: getting maps; making sure you have the cleaning supplies; choosing a day for the party. List the task and the steps in the spaces that follow. (Answers will vary.)

1. _____
2. _____
3. _____
4. _____
5. _____

6. _____
7. _____
8. _____
9. _____
10. _____

Now break a school-related task into 10 smaller steps. Some examples are writing a composition, doing an art project, or studying for a test. Write the task and the steps in the spaces that follow. (Answers will vary.)

1. _____
2. _____
3. _____
4. _____
5. _____

6. _____
7. _____
8. _____
9. _____
10. _____

Scheduling

Scheduling begins with choosing your classes. Figure out the time of day when you are most alert and schedule your classes for that time, if possible. It often helps to schedule a break between classes so that you can review your notes both before and after class. If this is not possible, you can prepare for classes the night before and review notes later the same day.

Scheduling by the day and by the week also helps to organize your life. First, a written schedule helps you establish priorities and counteracts the natural tendency to avoid difficulty or unpleasant tasks. It's harder to overlook an assignment that's written down. Second, a schedule causes you to space your study time so that you review frequently and won't have to cram for exams. Third, a schedule allows you to enjoy your free time because you know that you are keeping up with your work.

Schedules should be realistic. All students need time for social activities, hobbies, and being by themselves. Students who don't allow time for these activities are setting themselves up for failure. Planning your time will save you a great deal of guilt, frustration, and anxiety.

Maintaining Flexibility.   Schedules should be flexible. Some things cannot be changed, such as the time you spend in class or, if you have a job, the time you are at work. However, many other things can be changed. If your schedule says that you will study on Thursday, and you are invited out on Thursday by the person of your dreams, you might study on Friday instead, as long as Friday is a free night on your schedule. The week an important paper is due, you may have to borrow time from other activities to write it. Some activities can safely be postponed, such as cleaning out your desk or doing laundry. It is even possible to exist for a few days on takeout foods if you haven't had time to do grocery shopping because you are studying for midterm exams. A realistic schedule includes enough flexibility to allow for unexpected changes. You may postpone study times when necessary as long as you make them up within the same week.

Sticking to a Schedule.

1. To avoid becoming tired, do your most difficult tasks when you are freshest. Similarly, save the more interesting work until last; having something to look forward to will help you stick to the jobs you don't like.
2. Reward yourself by doing something you like or by giving yourself a day off when you have earned it by sticking to your schedule.
3. Buy a pocket-sized notebook for your schedule and carry it with you. A schedule will not help you unless you can conveniently refer to it. Having your schedule in a pocket notebook also helps you look ahead to future weeks so that you can keep track of long-term assignments.
4. Think positively. Concentrate on what you have accomplished rather than on what you have failed to do.

Analyzing a Sample Schedule.   One student's weekly schedule follows. Look at it carefully. Note that the week's assignments are broken into subgoals that are realistic for her. Notice all the free time: she can watch her favorite television programs, which are on Thursday and Friday evenings. She can do her Sunday evening studying on Friday or Saturday if she prefers.

REVISED SCHEDULE

Long-Term Assignments		
class	assignment	due
Psych. Eng. Hist.	term paper book review Test Chaos. 1–3	May 3 wk. from Mon. wk. from Fri.

Top Priorities
Psych Quiz – Friday Art Project – next Tuesday Dentist Appt. – Tuesday I P.M.

	Mon.	Tues.	Wed.	Thurs.	Fri.	Sat.	Sun.
7	←—— woke up, breakfast, get ready ——→						
8	←——— go to school ———→ ←—— review Eng. & Psych. notes ——→						
9	ENGLISH	ART	ENGLISH	ART	ENGLISH		
10	PSYCH	MATH	PSYCH	MATH	PSYCH		
11	review Eng & Psych notes library		review Eng & Psych notes choose bk.		ck. Psych quiz		
12	LUNCH review hist. notes	LUNCH	LUNCH review hist. notes	LUNCH	LUNCH review hist. notes		
1	AM HIST	DENTIST	AM HIST		AM HIST		
2	review hist. notes	GO TO WORK	review hist. notes		review hist. notes Cards for Psych. paper		
3	←——— WORK ———→			Study history			
4	←——— WORK ———→						50 pages novel
5	go home						
6	←——— DINNER ———→						
7	read 1/2 Psych Chap. 3	read 1/2 Psych Chap. 3	math assign.	review for Psych. quiz	30 pgs. of novel		read 1/2 Eng. text Chap.
8	math assign.	read 1/2 Eng. Chap.	read 1/2 Hist. Chap.	finish art project	work on Psych. paper		30 pgs. novel
9	read 1/2 Hist. Chap. 2	art assign.	read 30 pgs. novel		review Hist. text		
10	prepare for school						prepare for school
11							

Total Hours		Mon.	Tues.	Wed.	Thurs.	Fri.	Sat.	Sun.	Totals per Week
	in class	3	3	3	3	3	0	0	15
	new assign.	3	3	3 1/2	1	4 1/4	0	3	17 3/4
	review	1 1/2	1/2	1 1/2	1 1/2	1 1/2	0	0	6 1/2

Analyzing a Sample Daily Schedule.   Here is one day taken from the weekly schedule on the preceding page. Notice the logic behind the way this day is organized.

	Wed.
7	wake up, breakfast, get ready
8	go to school / review Eng. & Psych notes
9	ENGLISH
10	PSYCH
11	review Eng. & Psych notes / choose books
12	LUNCH
12:45	rev. History notes
1	AMERICAN HISTORY
2	rev. History notes / go to work
3	WORK
4	WORK
5	go to work
6	DINNER
7	math assign.
8	read 1/2 chap. History
9	read 30 pages novel
10	10 min. to prepare for school / FREE
11	

travel time includes parking, walking to class.

allow time to eat breakfast and preview the day's activities.

this 15 minute review time allows you to organize for class and take better notes.

this is from the long-term assign-ments list.
        allow at least 30 minutes.

take 15 minutes to fill in ideas that you missed during the lectures as soon as possible.

allow enough time to leave campus so you won't have to rush in late.

15 minutes reviewing before class helps you to take better notes and participate in class.

take an hour to eat and digest food before studying.

allow time for relaxation before dinner.

this could take less than an hour for a student who is good at math. If this student liked math more than history, he could do his history first.

every study hour is 50 minute study/10 minute break.

this is part of a long-term assign-ment that must be continued through-out the next two weeks. The student can continue reading during his free time if he wishes. He plans to read one-half of the book this week.

allow 10 minutes to organize for the next day to make morning more relaxed.

allow at least a half hour to relax. This decreases the chance of toss-ing all night thinking about school.

TOTAL HRS.
        IN CLASS   3
        ON NEW ASSIGNMENTS   3 1/2
        REVIEW   1 1/2

Preparing a Trial Schedule. Now you are ready to prepare a schedule that you can try out for the next week. As you read the directions, fill out the blank schedule that follows.

Directions

1. Fill in the hours in the left-hand column. If you get up at 7 a.m., start with 7 a.m. If you get up at noon, start with noon.
2. Fill in class hours.
3. Block out other fixed hours, such as work, child care, meetings and appointments.
4. List priorities in the box in the upper right corner and put them on your schedule.
5. Write long-term assignments in the upper left box and allow time for them in the schedule.
6. Fill in when you plan to have your meals and when you plan to go to sleep. Stick to your normal patterns if possible. Be sure to allow enough time for sleep.
7. Allow 10 minutes for reviewing notes before classes.
8. Allow at least 15 minutes immediately after lecture classes (or as soon as possible) to review notes so that you can fill in any missing or confusing areas and reinforce concepts in your mind.
9. Allow half an hour to an hour to relax before you sleep so that you won't toss all night worrying about your classes.
10. Allow free time during the day to provide for the unexpected. If nothing unexpected happens, relax and enjoy yourself!
11. Start by planning two hours of study for every class hour. Later you can tailor the amount to the time you actually need. Allow less time only if you are sure that you will not have pressing assignments.
12. Schedule study in one-hour blocks with 50 minutes of studying and a 10-minute break.
13. Schedule work on assignments at least two days before they are due to allow for unexpected delays. It's better to be finished one day early than to lose a grade for turning an assignment in late.
14. Keep a list of optional tasks that can be fitted into unexpected gaps. Otherwise, you will waste small free periods. For example, an extra 10 minutes can be used for reviewing vocabulary flash cards.
15. Carry your schedule with you so that you won't have to guess what comes next.

TRAIL SCHEDULE

Long-Term Assignments			Top Priorities		
class	assignment	due			

	Mon.	Tues.	Wed.	Thurs.	Fri.	Sat.	Sun.	
								Totals per Week
Total Hours	in class							
	new assign.							
	review							

―――――――――――――― TRIAL SCHEDULE ――――――――――――――

Evaluating Your Schedule.   After you have lived with your schedule for a week, you probably will have found items that need to be changed. Evaluate it by answering the questions that follow.

1. What activities, if any, were not on your schedule that should have been included?
2. Were there any tasks on your schedule that you did not do? If so, what were they and why didn't you do them (lack of time, misuse of time, or decision that task was unimportant, etc.)?
3. Which activities on your schedule required more time than you allowed?
4. Which activities required less time than you allowed?
5. Is there anything else on your schedule that should be changed? If so, what?

After you have answered these questions, prepare your schedule for the next week. It may take several attempts before you can establish a realistic schedule. Most of us underestimate how long it will take to read a chapter or study lecture notes. If you have problems discovering where you are "losing time," create a daily schedule such as the one on p. 12. In the margin put the actual time each activity took and when the next activity on the schedule began. After three days, look at what you have been doing with your time. Make a brief list of the ways you lose time. Efficient use of small blocks of time—for example, reviewing your lecture notes while waiting in line at the bank—will reduce your study time tremendously. By learning your own patterns, you can better manage the time you have.

Using Support Services

Some students have problems or special needs that can affect their ability to study. Examples are financial problems, problems with basic skills, or family problems. Familiarity with the support services on campus will help such students. The college catalog and the counseling office can provide specific information on services available.

Counseling (sometimes includes testing)	Provides academic counseling; career advisement, including vocational interests and aptitude testing; personal and crisis counseling; and sometimes entrance testing.
Financial Aid Office	Has information and applications for grants, loans, and scholarships.
Placement Office	Assists students in finding full- and part-time jobs on and off campus. May offer services for graduates, such as keeping a file of references.

Learning Center	Offers tutoring and individualized instruction in study skill, basic skills, and some subject areas.
Student Health Office	May have a nurse or doctor available to handle illness or injury.
Student Center (also called Student Activities Office)	Provides a variety of services, including areas where students can relax. Sometimes provides recreational activities such as bowling and ping pong. Also has information on extracurricular social activities and club events. May provide off-campus housing lists.
Business Office (also called Bursar's Office)	Accepts tuition and fee payments. Has students' financial records.
Admissions Office (also called Registrar's or Student Records Office)	Receives applications to the college and keeps students' academic records.
Specially Funded Services	Offers state or federally funded service programs for special groups, such as veterans, returning students, economically disadvantaged students, and handicapped students.

Summary

Some students don't know what to expect from college life. Instructors expect students to be self-directed and to behave like responsible adults. Students who prepare for their classes, turn in assignments on time, and ask for specific help when they need it are likely to earn higher grades. Students must make realistic decisions concerning career goals, choice of major, courses to take, and course load. Since these decisions have important consequences, they should be based on a realistic evaluation of personal strengths and weaknesses. Efficient time management requires breaking tasks into realistic subgoals and setting up a flexible schedule that you can stick to. Finding a schedule that works for you requires trial and revision. Awareness of campus support services can help you solve problems.

Comprehension Check

Circle the letter preceding the correct answer. Then check your answers in the back of the book.

1. If you were absent from class, you should
   a. ask the instructor if there were any assignments.
   b. ask another student if there were any assignments.
   c. ask the instructor what was covered in his or her lecture.

    d. ask the instructor to bring the handouts you missed to the next class meeting.

2. A good study schedule includes
    a. four-hour study blocks every night.
    b. time for recreation.
    c. no time wasted for breaks.
    d. studying one subject each night.

3. The correct time to ask for an extension on an assignment is
    a. after class, as soon as the other students leave.
    b. during the break.
    c. in the instructor's office during office hours.
    d. in the hallway between classes.

4. The most important thing to do before coming to class is to
    a. read the assigned chapter.
    b. establish specific subgoals.
    c. find out what the instructor is planning to cover.
    d. make a study schedule.

5. The most important thing about a study schedule is that
    a. it be realistic
    b. it includes every subject every day.
    c. you limit free time to one hour a day.
    d. you stick to it no matter what.

6. Good study habits
    a. depend on a student's ability.
    b. depend on how much time a student spends studying.
    c. are impossible if you have children.
    d. can be developed.

7. Which question would an instructor be most likely to appreciate?
    a. "Did we do anything in class yesterday?"
    b. "Can you give me some examples of irregular Spanish verbs?"
    c. "Did I miss any handouts or assignments last week?"
    d. "I'm having trouble with my girlfriend; is it okay if I turn in my assignment late?"

8. If you have to take a course from a difficult instructor, the best thing to do is
    a. figure that the course is probably graded unfairly and don't spend much time on it.
    b. complain about the instructor to the department head.
    c. plan on doing more work on your own since you probably won't get much help from your instructor.
    d. argue with the instructor so that he or she can see how bright you are.

9. If in one evening you have to study sociology (which is your favorite subject), math (which you hate), and English (which you can take or leave), which is the best schedule? _____
_____   _____

10. Two of the advantages of breaking tasks into subgoals are _____
_____
and _____.

Reading Selection: Business Management

Time Management: A Guide for Personal Planning

by Stephen P. Robbins

Do any of the following describe you?

- You do interesting things before the uninteresting things.
- You do things that are easy before things that are difficult.
- You do things that are urgent before things that are important.
- You work on things in the order of their arrival.
- You wait until a deadline approaches before really moving on a project.

Time Management.   If you answered yes to one or more of these questions, you could benefit from time management. In this section, we'll present some suggestions to help you manage your time better. We'll show you that time management is actually a personal form of scheduling. Managers who use their time effectively know what activities they want to accomplish, the best order in which to take the activities, and when they want to complete those activities.

Time as a Scarce Resource

Time is a resource in that if it's wasted it can never be replaced. While people talk about saving time, the fact is that time can never actually be saved. It can't be stockpiled for use in some future period. If lost, it can't be **retrieved.** When a minute is gone, it is gone forever.

gotten back

The positive side of this resource is that all managers have it in equal abundance. While money, labor, and other resources are distributed equally in this world, thus putting some managers at a disadvantage, every manager is allotted 24 hours every day and 7 days every week. Some just use their allotments better than others.

Focusing on Discretionary Time

Managers can't control all of their time. They are routinely interrupted and have to respond to unexpected crises. It's necessary, therefore, to **differentiate** between response time and discretionary time.

note the differences between

The majority of a manager's time is spent responding to requests, demands, and problems initiated by others. We call this response time and treat it as uncontrollable. The portion that is under a manager's control is called discretionary time. Most of the suggestions offered to improve time management apply to its discretionary **component.** Why? Because only this part is manageable!

part

Unfortunately for most managers, particularly those in the lower and middle rank of the organization, discretionary time makes up only about 25 percent of their work hours. Moreover, discretionary time tends to become available in small pieces—five minutes here, five minutes there. Thus it is very difficult to use effectively. The challenge, then, is to know what time is discretionary and then to organize activities so as to accumulate discretionary time in blocks large enough to be useful. Managers who are good at identifying and organizing their discretionary time accomplish significantly more, and the things they accomplish are more likely to be high-priority activities.

The best log is a daily dairy or calendar broken into 15-minute intervals. To get enough information from which to generalize, you need about two weeks' worth of entries. During this two-week period, enter everything you do in the diary in 15-minute segments. To minimize memory loss, post the entries as you do them. Keep in mind that honesty is important. You want to record how you *actually* spent your time, not how you *wished* you had spent your time.

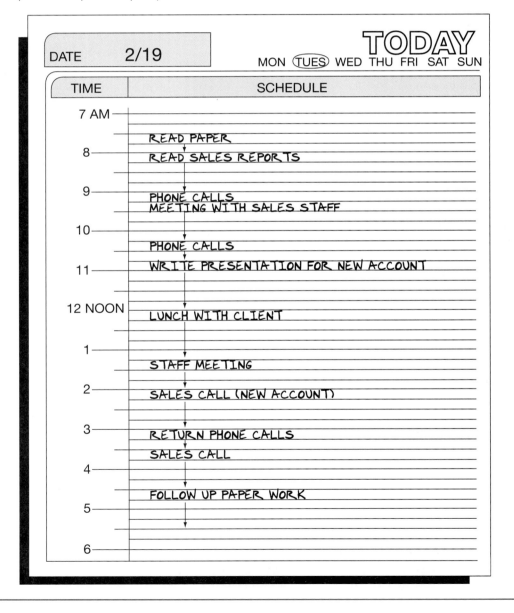

How Do You Use Your Time?

How do managers, or any individuals for that matter, determine how well they use their time? The answer is that they should keep a log or dairy or daily activities for a short period of time and then evaluate the data they gather.

Try keeping such a diary. When it is complete, you will have a detailed time and activity log. Then you can analyze how effectively you use your time. Rate each activity in terms of its importance and urgency. (See Table 9–4.) If you find that many activities received C's or D's, you'll find the next sections valuable. They provide detailed guidelines for better time management.

Rate Each Activity

For Importance
A. Very important: must be done
B. Important: should be done
C. Not so important: may be useful, but is not necessary
D. Unimportant: doesn't accomplish anything

For Urgency
A. Very urgent: must be done now
B. Urgent: should be done now
C. Not urgent: can be done sometime later
D. Time not a factor

Table 9–4
Analyzing Activities for Importance and Urgency

Five Steps to Better Time Management

The **essence** of time management is to use your time effectively. This requires that you know the objectives you want to accomplish, the activities that will lead to the accomplishment of those objectives, and the importance and urgency of each activity. We've translated this into a five-step process.

core

1. *Make a list of your objectives.* What specific objectives have you set for yourself and the unit you manage?
2. *Rank the objectives according to their importance.* Not all objectives are of equal importance. Given the limitations on your time, you want to make sure you give highest priority to the most important objectives.
3. *List the activities necessary to achieve your objectives.* What specific actions do you need to take to achieve your objectives?
4. *For each objective, assign priorities to the various activities required to reach the objective.* This step imposes a second set of priorities. Here, you need to emphasize both importance and urgency. If the activity

is not important, you should consider **delegating** it to someone below you. If it's not urgent, it can usually wait. This step will identify activities that you must do, those you should do, those you'll get to when you can, and those that can be delegated to others.

5. *Schedule your activities according to the priorities you've set.* The final step is to prepare a daily plan. Every morning, or at the end of the previous work day, make a list of the five or so most important things you want to do for the day. If the list grows to 10 or more activities, it becomes **cumbersome** and ineffective. Then set priorities for the activities listed on the basis of importance and urgency.

assigning

clumsy

Some Additional Points to Ponder

Follow the 10–90 Principle.   Most managers produce 90 percent of their results in only 10 percent of their time. It's easy for managers to get caught up in the activity trap and confuse actions with accomplishments. Those who use their time well make sure that the critical 10 percent gets highest priority.

Know Your Productivity Cycle.   Each of us has a daily cycle. Some of us are morning people, while others are late-afternoon or evening people. Managers who know their cycle and schedule their work accordingly can significantly increase their effectiveness. They handle their most demanding problems during the high part of their cycle, when they are most alert and productive. They **relegate** their routine and undemanding tasks to their low periods.

assign

Remember Parkinson's Law.   Parkinson's Law says that work expands to fill the time available. The **implication** for time management is that you can schedule too much time for a task. If you give yourself an excess amount of time to perform an activity, you're likely to pace yourself so that you use up the entire time **allocation.**

implied lesson

allotment

Group Less Important Activities Together.   Set aside a regular time period each day to make phone calls, do follow-ups, and perform other kinds of busywork. Ideally, this should be during your low cycle. This avoids duplication, waste, and **redundancy;** it also prevents **trivia** from intruding on high-priority tasks

repetition, unimportant details

Minimize Disruptions.   When possible, try to minimize disruptions by setting aside that part of the day when you are most productive as a block of discretionary time. Then, try to **insulate** yourself. During this time you should limit access to your work area and avoid interruptions. Refuse phone calls or visits during these hours. You can set aside other blocks of time each day when your door is open for unexpected visits and when you can initiate or return all your calls. The ability to insulate yourself depends on your organization's culture, your boss, and how much faith you have

protect

in your **subordinates.** But most critical is your level in the organization. Generally, the higher up you are in an organization, the less crucial it is that you be available for every emergency. In contrast, most supervisors can be out of touch with the work areas they oversee for only short periods of time.

people whom you manage

Beware of Wasting Time in Poorly Run Meetings. Meetings take up a large proportion of a manager's time. They also tend to run on at length. If you're running a meeting, you should set a time limit at the outset. You should prepare a written **agenda** for the meeting and stick to it. Another suggestion, which is a bit **bizarre** but works wonders for keeping meetings brief, is to require all members to remain standing. As soon as people sit down and get comfortable, they lose any motivation to keep discussion tightly focused on the issues. Some managers have no chairs in their office other than the one they occupy. Visitors are subtly encouraged to avoid wasting the manager's time. Managers usually move important meetings that demand long and thoughtful discussion to an adjoining conference room that has **an ample** supply of chairs.

schedule
odd

more than enough

Comprehension Check

Circle the letter preceding the correct answer to the question. Then check your answers in the back of the book.

1. The reason for writing the daily dairy is to
   a. remind you of what you need to do.
   b. help you evaluate how you have spent your time.
   c. avoid doing unimportant tasks before important ones.
   d. all of the above.

2. Which of the following is *not* true?
   a. Successful people set priorities.
   b. Successful people have better memories than others.
   c. Successful people make better use of their time than most people.
   d. Successful people keep daily diaries.

3. Which of the following activities would probably be labeled a D in your daily dairy?
   a. buy groceries
   b. read psychology chapter
   c. wash car
   d. think about term paper

4. Students who keep a daily dairy are likely to
   a. feel less stressed than those who don't.
   b. earn better grades than others.
   c. be successful in life.
   d. all of the above.

5. The 10–90 principle means that most managers
   a. produce 10 percent of their work every 90 minutes.
   b. produce 10 percent of their work in 90 percent of their time.
   c. produce 90 percent of their results in only 10 percent of their time.
   d. can delegate 90 percent of their work to others.

6. The main idea of this article is _____.

7. The five steps to better time management are:
   a. _____
   b. _____
   c. _____
   d. _____
   e. _____

8. Parkinson's law says that _____.

9. The difference between discretionary time and response time is _____ _____.

10. a. The ideal number of tasks you should put in a daily diary is _____.
    b. If you put _____ or more tasks in your daily dairy, it becomes ineffective.

Questions for Discussion and Writing

1. Keep a daily diary for two weeks. Then evaluate your rise of discretionary time. When is it available? What did you do with it? Are there ways you could use it more effectively? How?

2. Apply the 10–90 principle to your studying. When do you produce the most results now? What are you doing that reduces your efficiency? What can you do to better achieve the 90-percent output the article mentions?

Working with Paragraphs: Subject, Main Idea, and Support

2

Working with Paragraphs

I divide all readers into two classes: those who read to remember and those who read to forget.
William Lyon Phelps

Have you ever found yourself in the middle of a paragraph with no idea of what the author is trying to say? If you can't pick out the important ideas that might be on a test, you will have to try to memorize everything, an impossible task. You will save time and get higher grades if you can recognize the author's subject, main idea, and supporting details. The purpose of this chapter is to give you some techniques to help you quickly figure out the ideas to remember.

The Subject, the Main Idea, and Support

A paragraph is a group of sentences related to one central idea. Each paragraph has three necessary parts: a subject, a main idea, and support. To find these parts, you can ask six basic questions: *who, what, where, when, why,* and *how.* The subject is the general topic of the paragraph. If a title or heading precedes a paragraph, it likely reveals the subject. The main idea is the most important thing the author wants you to know about the subject. It limits the subject. Support consists of details supplied to strengthen the main idea. Support often answers the questions "where," "when," "why," or "how." An example of a subject of a paragraph is "failure in college." An example of a main idea is "Students sometimes fail in college because of poor time management." An example of support is the following: "Some students spend much of their available study time playing cards or chatting with friends."

Subject

The subject is the topic of the paragraph. To find the subject, ask *who* or *what* the whole paragraph is about.

Paragraph A

Among the great celebrities of the 1920s was the gangster Al Capone. He received fan mail from all over the world, including re-

lounging

quests to "rub out" irritating neighbors. The lucky visitor to Chicago might catch a glimpse of the "big fellow" **lolling** in his seven-ton, silk-upholstered limousine complete with bodyguard in the front seat nursing a machine gun on his lap. The extravagant Capone customarily wore a fifty-thousand-dollar diamond ring and carried fifty thousand in cash in

picky

his wallet. **Meticulous** and fond of personal luxury, Al slept between monogrammed silk sheets; his solid silver toilet seat also bore his initials.

Burner, Marcus, and Rosenberg, *America: A Portrait in History*, p. 492

What is the subject of Paragraph A?

a. gangsters
b. the roaring twenties
c. Al Capone
d. Capone's toilet seat

The subject is **c,** Al Capone. Most subjects can be stated in just a few words. Remember, though, that the subject must cover the entire paragraph. Answer **a** is too broad, **d** is too specific, and **b** is not on the subject.

Paragraph B

The controversy surrounding the issue of children's advertising has encouraged the advertising industry to regulate this practice carefully. In the 1970s the industry issued written guidelines for children's advertising and established the Children's Advertising Review Unit within the Council of Better Business Bureaus to oversee the self-regulatory process. The Unit revised the written guidelines in 1977 and again in 1983.

Wells, Burnett, and Moriarty, *Advertising Principles and Practices*, p. 58

What is the subject of Paragraph B?

a. government regulations
b. children's television shows
c. regulation of children's advertising
d. advertising

The subject is **c,** regulation of children's advertising. Answers **a** and **b** depart from the subject, and **d** is too broad.

Main Idea

The main idea of a paragraph is the main thing the author wants you to know about the subject.

What is the main idea of the paragraph about Al Capone?

a. Al Capone received fan mail.
b. Al Capone was a gangster.

c.   Al Capone was a celebrity in the 1920s.

d.   Visitors to Chicago hoped to catch a glimpse of Al Capone.

Sentence **c** is the main idea.

What is the main idea of Paragraph B?

a.   The advertising industry requires regulation.

b.   Advertising to children is carefully regulated.

c.   Advertising for children needs to be free of violence.

d.   Advertising is an effective way of influencing children.

Sentence **b** is the main idea.

Support

The author supports the main idea by giving details that clarify, develop, and justify it. The most common types of support for the main idea are examples, facts, reasons, and testimony. Examples of each type of support follow. Circle the main idea in each passage. Then underline the support.

Examples.   Examples illustrate the main idea.

Many origin myths deal with the origin of humans in the context of the origin of the universe. One **cosmological** tradition found in both ancient Greece and India teaches that life resulted from the opening of a cosmic egg that is the source of all life.

concerning the universe

Scupin, *Cultural Anthropology: A Global Perspective*, p. 2

In this example, you should have circled the first sentence and underlined the second.

Facts.   Data that support the main idea may be found in the form of historical facts, statistics, or scientific laws.

The highest mountain peak in North America is Mt. McKinley.
It is located in south-central Alaska in the Alaska Range.

You should have circled the first sentence and underlined the second.

Reasons.   Reasons are given to justify the main idea.

Myths are important to a society because they increase group **solidarity.** Furthermore they are important in communicating and helping a group sustain its values.

unity

Scupin, *Cultural Anthropology: A Global Perspective*, p. 18

You should have circled the first sentence and underlined the second.

Testimony.   Opinions of people other than the author are used to support the main idea.

Paragraph C

Concerns for the environment are also appearing in fashion collections. Fashion designer Adrienne Vittadini observes, "Fashion is a reflection of society and the concern for the earth is in the back of everyone's mind so it is only natural for designers to reveal our support through our clothes." "The use of natural fabrics and dyes to save our environment is more than a trend, it is a life style," agrees Marylou Marsh Sanders of Ecosport. "It has to be because we don't have a choice."

Frings, *Fashion: From Concept to Consumer*, p. 36

You should have circled the first sentence and underlined the last three.

Finding the Main Idea

In the preceding paragraphs the main idea was always stated in the first sentence. In most paragraphs the main idea will be in the first sentence, but it can appear anywhere in the paragraph. In the next two examples, read the paragraph and underline the sentence that best states the main idea.

Paragraph D

The many areas under investigation by chemists today reflect the explosion of interest in and understanding of chemical processes. Some of these processes have been known for a long time. For example, the ancient Egyptians and Chinese were well acquainted with the process of **fermentation** in the production of alcoholic beverages. Some of the foundations of modern chemistry trace back to the early Greeks and Arabs. Democritus (about 460–370 B.C.), a Greek, proposed a theory on the atomic structure of substances that preceded John Dalton's atomic theory by 2200 years. Al-Khowarizmi, an Arab mathematician, devised the number zero in about A.D. 825, providing the mathematical expression so essential to modern science. In the Medieval period, European alchemists experimented endlessly in a **fruitless** attempt to turn lead into gold.

breakdown of fruit or grain

unsuccessful

Daub and Seese, *Basic Chemistry*, p. 71

In this example the main idea is in the second sentence: "Some of these processes have been known for a long time."

Paragraph E

Cartier arrived in the Gulf of St. Lawrence in the late summer of 1541. He promptly set to work constructing a base. The Indians were suspicious of Cartier's failure to return with Donnacona and were not soothed by his story that the Indians taken captive in 1535 were great lords in France now and refused to return to their homeland. Consequently, over the winter, **friction** increased. Roberval did not arrive in the early spring, and Cartier began to suspect that the Kingdom of Saguenay was only a myth. In the meantime, the soldiers under his command were acting as if they had no need to go farther in the search of their treasure, and occupied themselves by gathering "precious stones" that lay conveniently all about. If Cartier suspected that such gems were less than they seemed, his doubts did not prevent him from allowing his men to barrel them up and load the cargo onboard ship. With nearly a dozen barrels of "treasure," he then set sail for France. In short, from the time he arrived in the New World to find the treasures in the Kingdom of Saguenay until the time he **abandoned** the project, everything went wrong.

tension

gave up

Finlay and Sprague, *The Structure of Canadian History*, pp. 10–11

In this example, the main idea is the last sentence: "In short, from the time he arrived in the New World to find the treasures in the Kingdom of Saguenay until the time he abandoned the project, everything went wrong."

Clues to Finding the Main Idea and Support

Authors try to write clearly, so that their ideas can be understood. They frequently give clues to their organization by means of headings, typographical clues, and signal words. Writers of textbooks tend to give more clues than do writers of other material.

Headings

Titles of books and articles, chapter headings, and subheadings help the reader understand what the author is trying to say. Headings provide important clues to main ideas. Read the following paragraph:

Paragraph F

The procedure is actually quite simple. First you arrange items into different groups. Of course one pile may be sufficient depending on how much there is to do. If you have to go somewhere else due to lack of facilities, that is the next step. Otherwise, you are pretty well set. It is important not to overdo things; that is, it is better to do too few things at once than too many. In the short run this may not seem important but complications can easily arise. A mistake can be expensive as well. At

aspect

first, the whole procedure will seem complicated. Soon, however, it will become just another **facet** of life. It is difficult to foresee any end to the necessity for this task in the immediate future, but then, one never can tell. After the procedure is completed one arranges the materials into different groups again. Then they can be put into their appropriate places. Eventually they will be used once and the whole cycle will then have to be repeated. However, this is a part of life.

Worchell and Shebilske, Psychology, p. 63

Now cover up the paragraph. Try to remember as much of the paragraph as you can. Place an **X** on the line to indicate the percentage you remembered.

0% ———————————————————————————————— 100%

The topic heading for this selection is "Washing Clothes." Now that you know its heading, reread the paragraph. Again place an **X** on the line to indicate the percentage you remembered. Didn't you find that the passage made more sense and was easier to recall than it was after you read it the first time? Headings make a significant difference!

Typographical Clues

You have probably noticed, especially in textbooks, that key ideas are often set off by different kinds of type—*italics*, CAPITALS, and **boldface.** All three kinds of type are meant to add emphasis to what the author is trying to say. Ideas that appear in these kinds of type generally are the main ideas. Numbers, letters, and Roman numerals in the text also give clues to the author's organization. Use typographical clues to help you understand the complex paragraph that follows.

Paragraph G

adjust

overly extreme

Sociologists use the term *culture shock* to describe the physical and mental strain that people from one culture experience when they must **reorient** themselves to the ways of a new culture. In particular, they must adjust to a new language and to the idea that the behaviors and responses they learned in their home culture and have come to take for granted do not apply in the foreign setting. The intensity of culture shock depends on several factors: (1) the extent to which the home and the foreign culture are different, (2) the level of preparation or knowledge about the new culture, and (3) the circumstances (vacation, job transfer, or war) surrounding the encounter. Some cases of culture shock are so intense and so unsettling that people become ill. Among the symptoms, according to David Lamb, author of *The Arabs,* are "**obsessive** concern with cleanliness, depression, compulsive eating and drinking, excessive sleeping, irritability, lack of self-confidence, fits of weeping, nausea."

Macionis, Sociology, p. 62

Circle the main idea.

a. People who experience culture shock may experience depression.

b. People experiencing culture shock must learn that behaviors they have come to take for granted do not apply in the foreign setting.

c. The intensity of culture shock—the strain experienced when people adapt to a new culture—depends on several factors.

d. Some cases of culture shock are so intense people become nauseated.

The correct answer is **c.** Sentence **b** may be true, but it is not the main point of the paragraph. Sentences **a** and **d** are true, but they're too narrow to be the main idea.

Signal Words

Just as authors use typefaces and enumeration (typographical clues) to set off key ideas, they also use *signal words* to give you clues to the relationship between the parts of a sentence, between sentences, and between paragraphs. These words are connections, or transitions from one idea to another. These transition words often signal the main idea or supporting details. For example, some words can show you that supporting material is about to be presented. The use of "for example" in the previous sentence served just that purpose. You knew a supporting detail would follow. Words such as *first, second,* and *finally,* when they come in the same paragraph, usually support a main idea. On the other hand, sentences starting with phrases such as *in summary, most importantly, in conclusion,* and *thus* often state the main idea. Here is an example:

Paragraph H

Performative elements (including dramatic and theatrical) are present in every society, no matter how complex or how **unsophisticated** a society may be. These elements are evident in our political campaigns, holiday celebrations, sports events, religious ceremonies, and children's make-believe, just as they are in the dances and rituals of primitive peoples. Nevertheless, most participants in these activities do not consider them to be primarily theatrical, even when **spectacle,** dialogue, and conflict play large roles. Consequently, it is usual to **acknowledge a distinction** between theatre (as a form of art and entertainment) and the presence of theatrical or performative elements in other activities. This distinction is **crucial** here, since it would be virtually impossible to write **a coherent** history of all the human activities that through the ages have made use of performative **conventions.** Therefore, this book is concerned primarily with the origin and **subsequent** development of the theatre as an **autonomous** activity.

performing
simple

display

note a difference

vital
consistent
traditions
later
independent

Brockett, *History of the Theatre,* p. 1

In this example, *therefore* gives us the clue that the main idea is in the last sentence. The other sentences support the main idea. In the third sentence, the author alerts us to a change of direction in his narrative by his use of the word *nevertheless*. By using signal words as clues, we can follow the author's ideas and discover his or her organizational patterns.

Recognizing Organizational Patterns

Understanding the author's organization in terms of main ideas and supporting details enables you to comprehend the logical pattern an author follows.

One common organizational pattern is cause–effect. Common signal words used in this pattern are *because, therefore, thus, consequently, due to,* and *hence.*

Another common pattern is a simple listing of events, ideas, or activities. Common signal words for this pattern are *and, also, first, 1, 2, 3,* and *finally.*

A third type is time order or sequence of events. This pattern is often used in historical descriptions or in directions. Common signal words are *next, then, after, once, at the same time, the second step,* and *finally.*

A fourth type of pattern is a summary of previous paragraphs or ideas. Signal words for this type include *to sum up, in summary,* and *in short.*

Some common relationships indicated by signal words include emphasis, addition, comparison, cause and effect, change of direction, example, time sequence, and conclusion. Here are examples of each kind of signal word:

Emphasis	Addition	Comparison
above all	also	again
actually	and	as much as
caution	another	both (and)
especially important	as well	in the same way
here again	besides	less than
indeed	first (second)	likewise
in fact	for one thing	more (than)
most important	furthermore	not only . . . but also
note that	in addition	similarly
notice	moreover	than
remember that	next	
the main idea	one (two . . .)	
	so too	
	then	
	1, 2, 3, . . .	

Cause and Effect	Change of Direction	Example
as a result	although	for example
because	but	for instance
consequently	(even) though	just as
for	however	like

Cause and Effect	Change of Direction	Example
for this reason	in contrast	such as
hence	instead	that is
since	ironically	to illustrate
so	nevertheless	
that is why	on the contrary	
therefore	on the other hand	
thus	or	
	otherwise	
	rather (than)	
	still	
	yet	

Time Sequence	Conclusion	
after	in closing	
at the same time	in conclusion	
before	in general	
first (second, . . .)	in short	
meanwhile	in summary	
next	so now	
now	to conclude	
soon	to summarize	
then	to sum up	
until		
when		
while		

EXERCISE 1: Signal Words

Look back at paragraphs D and E on pages 28–29 and locate the signal words they contain. Then list these words in the following blanks according to the relationship they indicate. Check your answers in the back of the book.

1. addition _____
2. comparison _____
3. cause and effect _____
4. change of direction _____
5. example _____
6. time sequence _____
7. conclusion _____

(There are no examples of "emphasis" in these two paragraphs.)

Summary

A key to effective reading is the ability to recognize subjects, main ideas, and supporting details. A paragraph usually contains one central idea. The other sentences in the paragraph support the main idea. Main ideas are usually found at the beginning of paragraphs, but they can also be in the middle or at the end. Important clues to main ideas and different kinds of support are provided by headings, different kinds of type and numbering, and signal words.

Comprehension Check

Circle the letter preceding the correct answer to the question. Then check your answers in the back of the book.

1. The main idea is
   a. the central idea of a paragraph.
   b. the same as the subject.
   c. one sentence.
   d. usually the longest sentence in the paragraph.
2. The subject of a paragraph can be found by asking
   a. who or what.
   b. where or when.
   c. why or how.
   d. all of the above.
3. The main idea is usually found
   a. in the first sentence.
   b. in the last sentence.
   c. in the middle of a paragraph.
   d. before the subject.
4. Recognizing the main idea will help you
   a. get better grades on tests.
   b. be a better reader.
   c. save time.
   d. do all of the above.
5. This chapter helps you understand
   a. how to study.
   b. how to take tests.
   c. how writers organize their ideas.
   d. how to concentrate on what you read.
6. Which is an example of a main idea?
   a. war
   b. victory at sea
   c. The war is over.
   d. (b) and (c)
7. Which of the following is the most likely to be a supporting detail for the main idea of a paragraph on roofing?
   a. There are many types of roofs.
   b. how to put on a new roof

    c. roofs

    d. An example is the red tile roof.

8. Which of the following might be the subject of a paragraph on insect-eating plants?

    a. Some plants eat insects.

    b. The Venus flytrap is an insect-eating plant.

    c. insect-eating plants

    d. all of the above

9. Name the four types of support discussed in this chapter.

    a.

    b.

    c.

    d.

10. What is the difference between a subject and a main idea?

_____

_____

EXERCISE 2: Main Idea and Support

Choose the main idea in each of the following paragraphs. Then check your answers in the back of the book.

1. Nature has given saltwater birds some amazing and unusual abilities. For example, the penguin has an organ above its eyes that lets it change salt water into fresh. The albatross can drink salt water since it has the ability to strain out and eliminate the excess salt.

    a. Some saltwater birds have unusual abilities.

    b. Birds can adapt to their environment in strange ways.

    c. The penguin and the albatross live in the same environment.

    d. Birds can drink salt water.

2. Many geographers now believe that 200 million years ago the east coast of South America fitted snugly into the west coast of Africa. The coasts of Norway, Scotland, and Ireland touched Greenland, and Greenland touched northern Canada. This means that the Earth once had a supercontinent. Geologists call it Pangea.

           Judson and Richardson, *Earth: An Introduction to Geological Change,* p. 276

    a. Continents can move around.

    b. Geography can tell us many interesting facts.

    c. Greenland was not always an island.

    d. The Earth once had a supercontinent now called Pangea.

3. Many people have found that reducing clubs, such as Weight Watchers and TOPS, provide needed group support. **Reputable** clubs teach you to prepare tasty, well-balanced, low-calorie meals. In addition, they provide a sense of belonging that helps dieters overcome feelings of guilt and shame. There is usually a fee involved in joining such groups (they are profit-making organizations), and they are not

    respectable

overweight

designed for the person who is only a few pounds overweight. But for **obese** people who have trouble staying on a diet, the reducing club may be an answer. These persons should be certain to check any weight-loss program with their physician beforehand, because most reducing group leaders are not qualified to judge a person's medical condition or nutritional requirements.

La Place, *Health,* p. 148

a. Reducing clubs can be helpful.
b. Reducing clubs usually suggest healthy diets.
c. The clubs provide a sense of belonging.
d. The clubs help dieters overcome feelings of guilt and shame.

4. Music is universal. It exists in some form in every part of the world inhabited by man. Its existence for thousands of years is proven by references in mankind's earliest writings, pictures, and **artifacts.** During all this time, and in all these places, music has developed in a **multitude** of different ways, each expressing the local culture and historical era of its creators. The seemingly endless **diversity** of human music is illustrated by a brief list of musical forms: symphony, **aboriginal** folk song, military march, rock and roll, **liturgical** mass, electronic music, and music of the Orient, to name only a few.

art objects

number
variety

native
worship-related

Ottman, *Elementary Harmony,* p. 19

a. Some music is more sophisticated than other music.
b. All human cultures have music.
c. Some parts of the world inhabited by humans have no music.
d. Music is not always written down.

5. The Amazon water lily is amazingly strong and can hold a person weighing over one hundred pounds. Natives of the Amazon sometimes place babies on these lily pads while looking for the plant's fruit underwater. They grind the seeds of the Amazon lily into flour.
a. The seeds of the Amazon water lilies are ground into flour.
b. The Amazon water lily is quite strong.
c. The fruit of the water lily is edible.
d. Water lilies come in a variety of sizes.

6. Each state has its own liquor advertising laws. In some states, you cannot show a drinking scene; in others, you can show a person holding a glass, but not bring it to his or her lips; in still others, you can picture only a bottle. In few industries does an advertising person need a lawyer more often than in liquor advertising.

Russell et al., *Otto Kleppner's Advertising Procedure,* p. 618

a. Some states have no laws concerning the advertising of liquor.
b. Liquor advertising is influenced by people who don't believe in drinking.
c. Liquor advertising laws vary from state to state.
d. You have to be careful not to violate the liquor advertising laws.

7. Accounts of slave musicians from the seventeenth century already describe instruments that are likely ancestors of the banjo. A variety of early names existed—banjar, bandore, banza—thus enabling historians to document a fairly consistent development of the banjo as an instrument accompanying African-American dance. In African-American slave society and in the South after the Civil War, the

banjo largely served rural forms of music. To the extent that it has survived in African-American communities into the twentieth century, it has **retained** its association with folk music.

kept

Nettl et al., *Excursion in World Music,* p. 299

    a. Banjos often accompany African-American dance.

    b. The banjo has been known by other names.

    c. Banjos were used by slaves.

    d. The North American banjo probably originated in West Africa.

8. Europe is indeed unified in several ways. Europe is, for example, a continent largely, though not completely, bounded by water. **Linguistically,** most people of Europe are related, closely in several ways and more remotely in others. Those languages not related to the larger Indo-European family, such as Hungarian and Finnish, may demonstrate European interrelations of their own. The cultural history of the continent, too, has sort of a unity, although sometimes that unity results only from attempts to **barricade** the continent from the cultures of Asia and Africa.

in language

block off

Scupin, *Cultural Anthropology: A Global Perspective,* p. 18

    a. Most Europeans speak related languages.

    b. Most Europeans are blood relatives.

    c. Europe is unified in several ways.

    d. Europe is a continent.

9. During its early history the average age of the United States population was kept down by high birth and immigration rates. In 1800 the median age was 16 years; in 1920 it was approximately 25 years; in 1986 it was 31.5, and the projected age for 2033 is about 41 years. The average life expectancy increased from 49.2 years in 1900 to 67.5 in 1950, to 75 in 1986, and should reach approximately 79 years in 2033. In 1900 there were only 3 million people in the United States over 65 years of age. The number had increased to 12 million in 1950 and to 28 million in 1986; the projected number for 2033 is 65.7 million. Between 1986 and 2033, the estimated percentage will increase from 12 to 21.5. The change will have extensive **repercussions** on the population at large.

effects

Horton et al., *The Sociology of Social Problems,* p. 167

    a. Immigrants are getting older.

    b. The U.S. population is getting older.

    c. Birth rates have dropped.

    d. The average life expectancy has increased.

10. Scientists have found that regular exercise helps to keep the heart healthy. Exercise aids the circulation of blood in the veins (where blood pressure is lower than in the arteries) and the flow of lymph in the lymph vessels. Exercise also benefits the heart itself. The heart becomes stronger, and the new and enlarged blood vessels that develop to feed the strengthening heart muscle lower the risk of heart attack. Another benefit of exercise is that it helps prevent being overweight. Finally, exercise reduces cholesterol levels in the blood.

La Place, *Health,* p. 380

    a. Exercise helps the heart.

    b. Poor circulation causes heart attacks.

    c. Exercise is good for you.

    d. Scientists have made new discoveries about preventing heart attacks.

EXERCISE 3: Main Idea and Support in Longer Selections

The following essay is comprised of three paragraphs rather than just one. Find the subject, main idea, and supporting details in the same way you did for a single paragraph. Remember to use the signal words as clues to the author's organization. Check your answers in the back of the book.

Posture and Stance

Posture, the way someone stands, sits, or walks, can send positive or negative nonverbal messages. Posture can convey self-confidence, status, and interest. Confident people generally have a relaxed posture, yet stand erect and walk with assurance. Walking with **stooped** shoulders and a slow, hesitating gait projects such negative messages as lack of assurance and confidence. The posture of persons of higher status is usually more relaxed than that of their **subordinates.** Interest is demonstrated by leaning forward toward the person you are conversing with, while leaning back communicates a lack of interest. The posture of people in the United States tends to be casual; they sit in a relaxed manner and may **slouch** when they stand. This behavior in Germany would be considered rude.

Posture when seated also varies with the culture. People in the United States often cross their legs while seated; women cross at the ankle and men cross with the ankle on the knee. Crossing the leg with the ankle on the knee would be considered inappropriate by most people in the Middle East. In the Arab world, correct posture while seated is important; avoid showing the sole of your shoe or pointing your foot at someone, as the lowest part of the body is considered unclean. When communicating with persons of another culture, follow their lead; assume the posture they assume. Remember that in most cultures, standing when an older person or one of higher rank enters or leaves a room is considered a sign of respect.

An awareness of cultural differences in facial expressions, gestures, and posture is important to successful intercultural encounters. Body language can **enhance** the spoken message or **detract** from it. Even though we usually believe that actions speak louder than words, in intercultural interactions what the person says may give a clearer picture of the intended message than accompanying body language. However, if a gesture is used in the wrong content, it may be difficult for a foreigner to understand the intended message. The best advice is probably to keep gestures to a minimum when communicating with persons in other cultures; learn the words for "good" or "yes" in the local language rather than relying on gestures.

Chaney and Martin, *Intercultural Business Communications*, p. 46

rounded

the people under them

slump

improve; take away from

1. What is the subject of the article?
2. Underline the sentence from the selection that best summarizes the main idea.
3. The following signal words were used in the essay. Identify the relationships they indicate (emphasis, addition, comparison, cause and effect, change of direction, example, time sequence, conclusion). If you have trouble, refer to the chart on pp. 32–33 for help.
   a. yet _____
   b. while _____
   c. also _____
   d. even though _____
   e. however _____
   f. remember that _____
   g. rather than _____

Reading Selection: Health

This reading is from a college textbook on health.

Health Foods and Food Fads

John La Place

Once a certain food is eaten, its original form is **irrelevant.** All proteins are reduced to amino acid molecules; all fats to fatty acid molecules; all carbohydrates to glucose molecules. Yet, some people believe that certain foods are transported directly to a special part of the body where they perform a service that the body cannot otherwise perform for itself. One superstition, for example, is that fish is a brain food. From what we know of digestion, it is obvious that the nutrients in fish could not possibly go directly to the brain. In a sense, all foods are brain foods, or none are.

    of no importance

Some also believe that certain combinations of food are harmful, or that the nutrients in certain foods are blocked if they are eaten in combination with other foods. Some of these food combinations are said to be fish and milk, milk and shellfish, and buttermilk and cabbage. Although we may **balk at** eating certain combinations of food, the stomach accepts all good food with impartiality. Fundamentally, people who subscribe to food fads are unusually concerned about their health, and this makes them easy victims of misinformation or fraudulent claims. At various times blackstrap molasses, wheat germ, honey, vinegar, and yeast have been touted as cure-alls or sources of

    refuse

all the nutrients necessary for health. In fact, the only ailments food may "cure" are those caused by specific vitamin deficiencies; and no one food, however nutritious, can supply all the necessary nutrients and vitamins.

Today, Americans are constantly subjected to a barrage of misleading advertising claims. We are told, for example, that we need vitamin and mineral supplements in our diets in order to remain healthy and vigorous. Just how susceptible to such advertising we have become is **attested** to by the flourishing health food industry. The mainstay for most health food stores is the sale of vitamins, which can account for as much as 90 percent of their business. They also carry products of such **dubious** worth as "natural potato chips" and bee pollen, which will supposedly add **vim** and **stamina** to our constitutions. They push claims for such questionable substances as lecithin (a soy product that supposedly unclogs the arteries), kelp, and rose hips. The arguments that many health food store supporters use are patently absurd, when not downright fraudulent. Some devotees claim that natural foods are better **assimilated** by the body than processed foods, because processors "pulverize the food"—a claim unsupported by any scientific research. Some "no salt" or "saltless" products have been laced with miso, soy sauce, or some other high-sodium additive.

The very term "health food" is misleading, for it implies that foods bought from common sources are not healthy. When confronted with claims of the superiority of health foods, wise consumers will maintain their **skepticism.** Any diet that includes proper amounts of foods from the four basic groups will contain more than enough of the nutrients and vitamins necessary for good health. The purchase of such foods is best made from a regular grocery store. Prices are lower than in stores specializing in "health foods," and the variety of foods available is much greater.

We will now examine contemporary nutritional beliefs concerning vegetarianism, organically grown foods, natural foods, macrobiotics, and megavitamins.

Vegetarianism

People become vegetarians for reasons as diverse as a religious conviction about the sacredness of life or the simple belief that animal products are unhealthy. Some studies have shown that pure vegetarian diets, being lower in fats than a normal diet, have produced a lower incidence of heart disease and cancer of the colon. There are degrees of vegetarianism, ranging from the strict *vegans,* who eat only fruits, vegetables, and grains, to the more permissive *lacto-ovo* vegetarians, who accept milk and eggs in their diets. Vegetarians must rely on a balanced combination of legumes, nuts, seeds, and grains for their protein (supplemented by dairy products, if their particular **regimen**

testified

doubtful
vigor
endurance

absorbed

doubt

system

allows them), and on dark green leafy vegetables (particularly if they are vegans) for their calcium. Otherwise, their diet does not differ all that much from the mainstream. Frequently, however, people who become vegetarian are extremely health-conscious and impose additional restrictions on themselves, such as eliminating sugar and salt from their diet.

Approximately 5 million Americans practice vegetarianism. If practiced knowledgeably and sensibly, it can provide a perfectly safe and healthful diet, but there is no evidence that a vegetarian diet is in any way superior to a well-balanced diet that includes animal products. It cannot be emphasized too strongly that vegetarians must carefully balance the amounts of essential amino acids in their meals in order to receive enough protein. In addition, a sufficient number of calories must be included to meet daily needs. If insufficient calories are consumed, protein is used as an energy source, thus depleting the supply that is essential for cell formation.

Even when exercising the utmost care, vegetarians cannot get Vitamin B12 from a diet lacking any animal protein, and must take vitamin supplements. Pregnant women should be especially cautious because a strict vegetarian diet can impose this and other vitamin deficiencies on their children, not only during pregnancy but afterwards through breast feeding.

Organically Grown Foods and Natural Foods

Organically grown foods have been grown in soil that has not been sprayed with pesticides, and have not had any artificial substances added to them. *Natural foods* are foods that contain no synthetic or artificial ingredients and have undergone no more processing than is generally done in a home kitchen. Certain jams, jellies, baked goods, and so on are called natural foods if they have been made from organically grown products, have received minimal processing, and contain no preservatives or additives other than salt and sugar. The organic and natural food fad started when people began to worry about what effect artificial chemicals might have on their health. However, even organically grown products have been shown to contain traces of artificial chemicals. Some **proponents** of organic foods claim that   **supporters** these foods are more nutritious than foods grown with chemical fertilizers. In fact, all fertilizers—natural or chemical—are broken down by food plants into the same inorganic elements. If anything, foods grown with chemical fertilizers may be somewhat more nutritious than "natural" foods, because chemical fertilizers are frequently designed to make up for deficiencies in the soil. Organically grown foods are usually more expensive than other commercially grown foods.

Some producers of organic foods may have higher costs because, for example, they lose part of their crop to insects—a direct result of not using pesticides. But organically grown foods are often more expensive simply because their distributors want to cash in on this food fad. Fraud is another possibility; investigators have discovered ordinary foods being sold as organic foods at a higher price.

Macrobiotics

A *macrobiotic* diet is one based mostly on grain, especially brown rice. It is less popular today than it was in the late 1960s and early 1970s. People who follow this diet drink little liquid and eat few dairy products. Meat, milk, and sugar are totally **banned.**   forbidden

The macrobiotic diet has some advantages: cheapness, an absence of cholesterol, and a low calorie count. But these advantages are far outweighed by the disadvantages. The diet lacks essential nutrients. People who follow it strictly may develop symptoms of severe malnutrition; in fact, there are documented cases of persons on a macrobiotic diet dying from scurvy.

Megavitamins

Can large, daily doses of Vitamin C prevent the common cold? Will Vitamin E supplements increase physical stamina and prevent heart attacks? Does extra Vitamin B increase energy and keep hair from turning gray?

Anyone familiar with popular health literature has come across all of these claims (or strong implications of them in advertising). Unfortunately, they are all unsupported by scientific evidence. As a 1978 Food and Drug Administration (FDA) report cautions, "Consumers should know that elaborate testimonials and miraculous claims result from mere guesswork, confusion, and often outright fraud." Most vitamin myths are based on the unfounded assumption that, if a little does good, a lot will do more good. For example, a Vitamin A deficiency is known to cause dry skin; an adequate amount of Vitamin A is therefore necessary to maintain healthy skin. This has been proven. But instead of a fantastic complexion, an excessive amount of Vitamin A can cause bone damage. Vitamin B deficiency caused the hair of experimental rats to turn gray. When they resumed their normal diet, their hair color was restored. Can we conclude that large doses of Vitamin B will prevent human hair from going gray? Alas, the evidence says no. In others studies, male rats deprived of Vitamin E became sterile but attempts to treat human sterility with massive doses of Vitamin E have proven **futile.** But what about Vitamin C? It has been widely promoted as a cure or preventative for the common cold. One study, in fact, showed evidence that massive doses may reduce the frequency and severity of colds by about 25 percent. In other studies, however, those who thought they were taking Vitamin C reported better results   useless than those who actually were taking it. The vitamin question is far from settled. Research continues, and many more fantastic claims will undoubtedly be made by **advocates** and marketers of vitamins. So far, however, tests indicate that *megavitamins*—vitamins in abnormally large doses that exceed the nutritional requirements of the body—have little or no value for normal individuals; on the contrary, they may have negative effects. Too much Vitamin D, for example, can lead to the deposit of calcium in soft tissue; and large doses of Vitamin C have been blamed for causing kidney stones. Vitamin poisoning is a very real danger for individuals who **overindulge** in the use of vitamins. Children are especially vulnerable. In reality, the **ingestion** of vast amounts of vitamins represents a form of drug abuse. These individuals are literally vitamin "junkies."

    In some conditions, pregnancy, for example, people do need vitamin supplements. But most people can get all the vitamins they need simply by eating a balanced diet.

supporters

**overdo
consumption**

Comprehension Check

Circle the letter preceding the correct answer. Then check your answers in the back of the book.

1. Which of the four fads is most concerned with the use of chemicals in growing food?
   a. vegetarianism
   b. organically grown foods
   c. macrobiotics
   d. megavitamins

2. Which type of diet is the least expensive?
   a. vegetarianism
   b. organically grown foods
   c. macrobiotic
   d. megavitamins

3. Which of the following statements is *not* true of organic foods?
   a. They are grown with organic fertilizer.
   b. They are grown without pesticides.
   c. They are more nutritious than ordinary food.
   d. They are more expensive than ordinary food.

4. Most people do *not* need vitamin supplements
   a. every day.
   b. when they have scurvy.
   c. during pregnancy.
   d. when they have a vitamin deficiency.

5. Which of the following practices is most healthful?
    a. Eat foods from the four basic groups.
    b. Eat only organic foods.
    c. Follow a macrobiotic diet.
    d. Supplement your diet with megavitamins.

6. A macrobiotic diet
    a. is high in protein.
    b. can cause health problems.
    c. is nutritionally sound.
    d. is based on dairy products.

7. Some distributors of organic foods engage in
    a. misleading advertising.
    b. misrepresentation of products.
    c. consumer fraud.
    d. all of the above.

8. A vegetarian diet that provides all needed nutritional elements is
    a. more difficult to prepare than a regular diet.
    b. more fattening than a regular diet.
    c. unsafe.
    d. more healthful than a regular diet.

9. Define macrobiotics _____
    _____

10. How does organically grown food differ from commercially grown
    food?_____

Questions for Discussion and Writing

1. La Place seems to feel that vitamin supplements are unnecessary or
    even dangerous. Do you agree or disagree with him? Give three rea-
    sons to support your opinion and examples to support each reason.

2. La Place says that "health foods" and organic foods cost more than the
    same food at the regular supermarket. Do you think these things
    should be more expensive? Support your idea with reasons and details.

3. Have you or anyone you know ever been on a diet or food program?
    Who? For how long? How did it differ from normal eating? Do you
    think it was successful? Why would you recommend or not recom-
    mend a similar plan to someone else?

EXERCISE 4: Reviewing Signal Words

The following signal words were used in the last reading selection. Identify the relationships they indicate (emphasis, addition, comparison, cause and effect, change
of direction, example, time sequence, conclusion). If you have trouble, refer to the
chart on pp. 32–33 for help. Then check your answers in the back of the book.

a. yet _____

b. for example _____

c. or _____

d. although _____

e. in fact _____

f. however _____

g. when _____

h. because _____

i. for _____

j. otherwise _____

k. but _____

l. in addition _____

m. thus _____

n. so far _____

o. on the contrary _____

EXERCISE 5: Skills Review—Scheduling

Go back to the evaluation of your study schedule in Chapter 1. Using your answers to the evaluation questions as a guide, write your schedule for next week on the form provided. First, write in the changes needed, based on the weaknesses in your first schedule. Then go back to the directions for preparing a schedule and rewrite. You may have to revise your schedule several times, since it usually takes a minimum of three weeks to break an old habit and substitute a new one. (Answers will vary.)

REVISED SCHEDULE

Long-Term Assignments				Top Priorities	
class	assignment	due			

	Mon.	Tues.	Wed.	Thurs.	Fri.	Sat.	Sun.	
								Totals per Week
Total Hours	in class							
	new assign.							
	review							

Reading Critically

3

Reading Critically

3

Thinking is the hardest work there is, which is the probable reason so few people engage in it.
Henry Ford

To be an effective reader, you must go beyond an understanding of the author's stated main ideas and details. You must be able to read critically and efficiently. Reading efficiency is the subject of Chapter 12, and critical reading will be discussed here. Three of the major critical reading skills are making inferences, understanding the author's purpose, and distinguishing fact from opinion.

Inference

For some purposes you must go beyond the literal meaning of the text and read between the lines to see the author's implications. For essay exams and term papers especially, you may have to analyze concepts, draw conclusions, or apply what you have read to new situations. Using inference in reading is similar to using inference in daily life. For example,

THE FROG PRINCE   Proctor & Lenier

If you look out the window and see clouds, you might infer that rain is likely. Your inference might lead you to carry an umbrella. Look at the cartoon and then try to answer the following inference questions:

1. Who was firing the bullets? _____
2. Were they firing at the Frog Prince? _____

3. What were they firing at? _____
4. Why was the moose in the water? _____
5. How does the Frog Prince end up on top of the moose? _____

You probably inferred from the cartoon that some hunters were shooting at the moose, who was in the water eating, and that the moose coincidentally surfaced where the Frog Prince was sitting.

Implied Main Idea

Sometimes main ideas are not directly stated; instead, they are implied by the author. For example:

The hot sun drained the workers within hours. The constant buzz of malaria-carrying mosquitoes made life miserable. Poisonous snakes were a constant danger. The jungle grew back almost as fast as the men could clear it. Many men died and had to be replaced.
Burner, Marcus, and Rosenberg, *America: A Portrait in History*, p. 463

Which is the main idea?

1. The sun was hot.
2. The conditions were difficult.
3. The men were working in the jungle.
4. People died of snakebite.

Sentence (2) is the correct answer. The other three sentences are examples of the difficult conditions.

Other Types of Inference

An implied main idea is only one type of inference. You may also need to draw conclusions, analyze concepts, or apply old knowledge to new situations.

The following statements are based on the sample paragraph we just read. Circle the letters preceding all sentences that are valid inferences. Do not circle the letters preceding statements that cannot be inferred from the paragraph or from your general knowledge.

1. The men were in a tropical climate.
2. The workers were afraid.
3. The work frustrated the men.
4. Jungle plants grow faster than regular plants.
5. There was a lot of rain.

All are valid inferences. You can infer sentence (1) from the mention of heat, malaria-carrying mosquitoes, and jungle. You can infer (2) from the mention of malaria and poisonous snakes. You can infer (3) because the jungle grew back quickly, making the work go very slowly. You can infer (4) based on your general knowledge that plants normally do not grow back as fast as you cut them down. Statement (5) can be inferred because it is general knowledge that all jungles are wet and that mosquitoes breed in water. Also, plants need water to grow quickly.

Here are two more paragraphs for practice.

Paragraph A

The wars of Napoleon, Bismarck's "lightning" wars from 1864 to 1870—even the Second World War—showed generals in control of the weapons at their disposal and competent to carry out the operations they had planned. The First World War was quite different. It demonstrated a failure of strategy and of military technique on a gigantic and **unprecedented** scale. In its bungling, infinitely wasteful character, it was more like the American Civil War than like its predecessors or successor among European conflicts. And, like the Civil War, it soon became a war of **attrition,** which, after four long years of slaughter and discouragement, finally came to an end only because one side gave out of men and material, overwhelmed by the numerical and industrial superiority of its **adversary.**

never before seen

wearing down

enemy

Hughes and Wilkinson, *Contemporary Europe: A History,* p. 33

A. Circle the letter preceding the implied main idea.
   1. The Second World War was run better than the First.
   2. World War II was like the American Civil War.
   3. World War I was poorly conducted and very costly.
   4. The generals in World War I were not as good as those in the Napoleonic wars.
   The answer is (3). Answers (1) and (4) are implied, but they are not broad enough to be the main idea. Answer (2) is not true.
B. In your own words, complete the following statements.
   1. The main idea is _____.
   2. The support is _____
   _____.

C. Circle the letter preceding all valid inferences.
   1. The generals in World War I were incompetent.
   2. Both sides were deficient in strategy and military technique.
   3. Both sides had equal numbers of men.
   4. The American Civil War also had incompetent generals.

Sentences (1), (2) and (4) are valid inferences. The generals in both World War I and the American Civil War are compared unfavorably with those in the wars of Napoleon and Bismarck. The author said that the war ended only because the loser was outnumbered and ran out of supplies.

Paragraph B

At Fort Loreto, located on a hill overlooking the city of Puebla, General Ignacio Zaragoza **exhorted** his men to heroically defend the city of Puebla. The inexperienced troops within the fort, in the center of a walled compound, fought **tenaciously.** By nightfall, over 1,000 crack French troops lay dead or dying outside of the walls. The fort

urged

stubbornly

held, and on May 5 General Latrille retreated to Orizaba in order to re-
group and **assess** his losses.

evaluate

Mayo, *A History of Mexico, From Pre-Columbia to Present*, p. 260

A. Circle the letter preceding the implied main idea.
1. The Mexican troops in the battle of Fort Loreto were inexperienced.
2. Because of their bravery in the battle of Fort Loreto, the Mexicans
were successful in defeating the French forces outside Puebla.
3. The battle of Fort Loreto was the turning point in the defeat of
French forces in Mexico.
4. Many Frenchmen died at Fort Loreto.

The correct answer is (2). Statement (1) is a detail. Statement (3) cannot be the main idea because the passage does not mention French forces
in all of Mexico, nor does it clearly imply a turning point. Statement (4) is
also a detail.

B. In your own words complete the following statements.
1. The implied main idea is _____.
2. The support is _____
_____.

C. Circle the letter preceding all the valid inferences.
1. The French were defeated at Fort Loreto.
2. The French surrendered to the Mexican general.
3. The Mexicans had only a few weapons and very little ammunition in the fort.
4. The victory at Fort Loreto is still celebrated by Mexicans.

Sentences (1) and (4) are valid inferences. The idea (1) that the French
were defeated can be inferred from the fact that they retreated to Orizaba.
The idea (4) that the victory is still celebrated can be inferred if you know
that May 5 (*Cinco de Mayo*) is a festive Mexican holiday. Neither (2) nor (3)
can be inferred. The author does not mention any French surrender (2).
The passage mentions only inexperience, not weapons and ammunition.

Author's Purpose

Authors write with three general purposes in mind: to inform; to en-
tertain; and to persuade. Critical reading is most necessary for persuasive
writing, just as critical thinking is most necessary when people are trying
to persuade us through other media, such as oral arguments, speeches,
TV ads, and political campaigns. When you can recognize the author's
purpose as a persuasive one, you should take a skeptical attitude and
read critically. Look for persuasive techniques, such as opinion presented
as fact, sources of doubtful credibility, and propaganda techniques (all
discussed in reading selections for this chapter). An author can also use
language to further his or her purpose. Material written for entertainment will often have a light, humorous, or tongue-in-cheek tone, whereas

informative material such as textbooks will usually have a direct, serious tone. An author of persuasive writing is especially likely to try to use language to influence the reader. For example, one party might describe its candidate as "flexible" or "open-minded" while the other party calls him a "wimp." Another candidate might be described as a "strong" or "decisive" while the opponent calls her "rigid" or "narrow-minded."

The author's purpose can often be recognized from the title. Write the numbers of the following titles under their purpose.

Inform	Entertain	Persuade
_____	_____	_____
_____	_____	_____
_____	_____	_____
_____	_____	_____
_____	_____	_____

1. Poland: 75,000 on Strike; 11 Mines Idled
2. The Ten Worst Jokes Ever Told
3. Health Care Denied Makes a Weak Nation
4. Public Art Can Make a Difference
5. California's Realtors Slate Convention

Titles 1 and 5 are informative, title 2 is entertaining, and titles 3 and 4 have a persuasive purpose. It is important to recognize that bias and persuasion can occur even in material with an informative purpose, such as a textbook. For example, until recently, U.S. history books minimized the contributions of women and minorities. Another example is that some high school biology textbooks are based on the theory of evolution while others are based on the theory of creation.

Fact Versus Opinion

Differentiating fact from opinion is a skill needed for recognizing bias. A fact is something that can be proved or disproved. An example of a fact is "The majority of voters supported Candidate X," where the number of votes can be counted. On the other hand, "French is a more beautiful language than Spanish" is an opinion, since beauty is in the eye of the beholder. Many writers disguise their opinions as fact, either as a persuasion technique or because they genuinely think their beliefs are true.

Using our definition of fact, write **F** before each factual statement and **O** before each statement of opinion.

Snowflakes are comprised of crystals.   1. _____

X-rated movies should not be seen by children.   2. _____

Smog alters the ozone layer.   3. _____

A person cannot be both honest and successful.

4. _____

To be healthy you should drink four glasses of milk a day.

5. _____

Statements 1 and 3 are factual. You can fairly easily prove or disprove them. Statements 2, 4, and 5 are opinions with which you may agree or disagree.

Summary

Critical reading means going beyond what is actually written and being able to draw conclusions, analyze ideas, evaluate what you read, and apply it in new situations. The skills of critical reading taught in this chapter are making inferences, recognizing the author's purpose, and distinguishing fact from opinion. These skills are particularly important in college, when the grading goes beyond objective tests of what you have memorized and involves essay exams and term papers.

Comprehension Check

Circle the letter preceding the correct answer. Then check your answers in the back of the book.

1. Which of the following does not require critical reading?
   a. analyzing concepts
   b. drawing conclusions
   c. applying what you read to new situations
   d. memorizing new definitions

2. Implied main ideas are
   a. found as frequently as stated main ideas.
   b. found in the middle of paragraphs rather than at the beginning.
   c. not stated by the author.
   d. all of the above.

3. An implication is made by
   a. the reader.
   b. both the author and the reader.
   c. someone who doesn't know the facts.
   d. the author.

4. To read critically you must
   a. first understand the literal meaning of a sentence or paragraph.
   b. go beyond the literal meaning by adding what you already know.
   c. look beyond the author's statements.
   d. do all of the above.

5. Which of the following fits our definition of a fact?
   a. Jennifer is more beautiful than Christina.
   b. Jeffrey is the smartest person in the class.
   c. Nicole gets better grades than Danielle.
   d. English is the hardest subject in college.

6. Which of the following test directions requires making an inference?
   a. List five types of support for the main idea.
   b. Define *testimony*.
   c. Underline the main idea in the following paragraph.
   d. Compare and contrast a dolphin and a chimpanzee.
7. If you saw a man wearing an overcoat in summer when the temperature was 100 degrees Fahrenheit, which of the following could you infer?
   a. He might be mentally ill.
   b. He could be hiding something under the coat.
   c. He reacts to heat differently than most people.
   d. All of these could be inferred.
8. Which of the following could you infer if someone were to tell you that all of his or her teachers gave unfair tests?
   a. The student doesn't know how to study.
   b. The student is not doing very well in school.
   c. The student, not the instructors, has the problem.
   d. All of these could be inferred.
9. An inference is _____.
10. The main idea of this chapter is _____
    _____.

EXERCISE 1: Critical Reading in Paragraphs

Here are some practice paragraphs. Answer the questions that follow them. Then check your answers in the back of the book.

Paragraph A

by their very nature   Human languages are **inherently** flexible and creative. Users of human languages, even small children, can create sentences never heard before by anyone. There are no limits to our capability to produce messages that refer to the past, present, or future. In contrast, animal communication systems in natural settings are rigid and fixed. The sounds of animals' communication do not vary and cannot be modified. The offspring of chimpanzees will always use the same pattern of vocalization as the parents. In contrast, the highly flexible nature of human languages allows for efficient and creative uses of symbolic communication.

Scupin, *Cultural Anthropology, A Global Perspective*, p. 79

Inference

A. Circle the letter preceding the implied main idea.
   1. Humans, even small children, can create sentences.
   2. Humans communicate more than animals.

3. Humans learn language the same way as animals.

4. Human languages are superior to animal languages.

B. List two examples of support:

_____

_____

C. If you can infer the statement from the paragraph, write *yes* in the blank. If you cannot infer the statement, write *no*.

Humans can communicate on more topics than can animals.	1. _____
Dolphins have a more complex system of communication than do chimpanzees.	2. _____
Deaf children can communicate complex thoughts.	3. _____
Children learn a second language more easily than adults do.	4. _____
Human speech often involves the use of symbols.	5. _____

Fact Versus Opinion

How could you prove that small children can create sentences never before heard by anyone?

_____

_____

Paragraph B

According to Dr. Lyman K. Steil, Sperry's listening consultant, if each worker in the country made only one $10 mistake a year because of poor listening—a secretary typing two letters incorrectly, for instance—the cost would be one billion dollars. Steil tells the story of a man whose company lost a $1.3 million sale because two salesmen either didn't hear or misinterpreted an important message from a prospective buyer. Another salesman nearly lost a $950,000 sale because he insisted on giving a 27-minute sales pitch, ignoring the client who had said four times that he was ready to buy.

Ross, *Speech Communication: Fundamentals and Practice,* p. 35

Inference

A. Circle the letter preceding the implied main idea.
 1. Secretaries frequently type letters incorrectly.
 2. People are usually guilty of poor listening.
 3. Good listening determines success in business.
 4. American businesses lose a lot of money because of poor listening.

B. List two examples of support.

_____

_____

C. If you can infer the statement from the paragraph, write *yes* in the blank. If you cannot infer the statement, write *no*.

Most companies have a listening consultant.	1. _____
Poor listening causes small mistakes rather than large ones.	2. _____
Most workers make at least 10 dollars' worth of mistakes a year.	3. _____
Listening can be improved.	4. _____
Good communication is vital to business.	5. _____

Fact Versus Opinion

How could you prove Dr. Steil's statement that it would cost one billion dollars if each worker made one $10 mistake a year?

_____

_____

Paragraph C

investors

The new government would be judged on how well it handled the crucial issue of unemployment, and here, almost immediately, it entered upon a desperate struggle with the **financiers.** Labor had been in power only four months when the Wall Street crash occurred. By the next spring, the effects of American withdrawals on the British economy were all too evident. Unemployment, which had stood at a million and a half at the beginning of 1930, reached two million by mid-summer, and at the year's end was two and a half million. Obviously a Labor government could not let these people starve: it must support them somehow, and the only method available seemed to be giving

welfare payments

the **"dole"** to larger and larger numbers of the unemployed.

Hughes and Wilkinson, *Contemporary Europe,* p. 207

Inference

A. Circle the letter preceding the implied main idea.
1. A new government was elected in Great Britain in 1930.
2. The Labor government in Great Britain faced a crisis in 1930.
3. Unemployment was worse in 1930 than at any other time in history.
4. The issue of unemployment is a problem for most governments.

B. List two examples of support:

_____

_____

C. If you can infer the statement from the paragraph, write *yes* in the blank. If you cannot infer the statement, write *no*.

Great Britain had high unemployment prior to the Wall Street crash.

1. _____

Economic problems in one country can cause a crisis in another.

2. _____

Great Britain had large amounts of money in banks in America.

3. _____

The unemployment in Great Britain was one factor in the Wall Street crash.

4. _____

The "dole" was a fact of British society prior to 1930.

5. _____

Fact Versus Opinion

How could the author prove that American withdrawals caused British unemployment?

_____

_____

Paragraph D

Thus far we have been speaking only of bright colors. But more often than not we shall be using colors of less than maximum brightness. A gray-blue is still blue, but it is far different from the blue on the color wheel. Although of the same hue, it is lower in intensity. This color would be shown as being nearer the center of the wheel—more gray, in other words. Colors on the **periphery** are of maximum brilliance. Colors nearer the center are less brilliant (of lower intensity) and are commonly referred to as tones.

edges

Corson, Stage Makeup, p. 11

Inference

A. Circle the letter preceding the implied main idea.
   1. Intensity and hue are the two major aspects of color.
   2. Colors of the same hue can vary in intensity.
   3. Makeup artists must learn to use colors of various intensity.
   4. The color wheel shows the various hues of colors.

B. List two examples of support:

_____

_____

C. If you can infer the statement from the paragraph, write *yes* in the blank. If you cannot infer the statement, write *no.*

The more gray a color has, the less intense it is.

1. _____

Brilliant colors are more intense.

2. _____

Hue and tone mean the same thing.

3. _____

Brilliant colors are used more often than dull ones in makeup.

4. _____

Blue is more intense than red.

5. _____

Fact Versus Opinion

Propose a scientific method (in other words, something other than people's subjective opinions) for judging the intensity of colors.

_____

_____

Paragraph E

Persistent frustration leads to tension. A frustrated person who cannot create a way or find a means to reduce frustration may become deeply troubled. Most of us sense this in ourselves and try to find satisfactory substitutes for unrealized goals. Rather than persist in the attempt to attain seemingly impossible goals, we find new ones that can be realized. In doing so, we learn to deal successfully with frustration.

Silverman, *Psychology,* p. 404

Inference

A. Circle the letter preceding the implied main idea.
   1. Tension if frustrating.
   2. Unrealized goals are frustrating.
   3. Most people learn to cope with frustration.
   4. People are naturally frustrated.
B. List two examples of support.

_____

_____

C. If you can infer the statement from the paragraph, write *yes* in the blank. If you cannot infer the statement, write *no.*

Frustration can increase.	1.	_____
Adults get more frustrated than children.	2.	_____
People have to reduce tension and frustration.	3.	_____
Most people can accomplish the goals they desire.	4.	_____
Most people can adjust their goals and still be happy.	5.	_____

Fact Versus Opinion

How could psychologists prove that frustrated people can become deeply troubled?

_____

_____

Paragraph F

The 35-millimeter camera is light in weight, easy to handle, and relatively inexpensive to use. It will produce either slides or prints. It can take excellent pictures under difficult light conditions. Thirty-five-millimeter cameras may have separate *viewfinders,* similar to those on pocket cameras, or through the lens viewing, generally called *reflex viewing,* with which you can see and compose the exact picture you are taking. On the latter type, you can interchange normal, *wide-angle, telephoto,* or *zoom lenses.*

Adams and Stratton, *Press Time,* p. 386.

Inference

A. Circle the letter preceding the implied main idea.
   1. A 35-millimeter camera is the best camera you can buy.
   2. A 35-millimeter camera is of limited use.
   3. Thirty-five-millimeter cameras are the easiest to use.
   4. A 35-millimeter camera has several good points.

B. List two examples of support.

   _____

   _____

C. If you can infer the statement from the paragraph, write *yes* in the blank. If you cannot infer the statement, write *no.*

   A 35-millimeter camera is a pocket camera.   1. _____

   If the camera has a separate viewfinder, you cannot use a zoom lens.   2. _____

   Thirty-five-millimeter cameras take pictures that develop in seconds.   3. _____

   Pocket cameras have reflex viewing.   4. _____

   If you have a separate viewfinder, you can take wide-angle photos without a separate lens.   5. _____

Fact Versus Opinion

How could the author prove or disprove that 35-millimeter cameras take "excellent" pictures under difficult lighting conditions?

_____

_____

Paragraph G

The city was on every tongue and in almost every book. Reform-minded Americans saw it as a political failure. Churchmen and women's groups considered it a moral disaster area. Social scientists and novelists viewed it as the home of emerging class distinctions, of extremes of wealth and poverty which they could not square with their ideals. Especially, they saw that normal commercial ethics met their **nemesis** in the city. Everywhere the supplying of urban services—   **powerful enemy** public or private—carried the stigma of corruption, much as railroad building had. Electric lights, trolleys, telephones, and subways did not lend themselves to various and competing efforts: they simply worked better as single enterprises. Monopolies, called franchises, became the standard means of providing for these services. This public sale of economic opportunity inevitably trailed bribery and theft in its wake. And

spending

outright public **expenditures** worked no better: a squat little County Court House cost the New York City taxpayers $13 million, about $9 million of it going into the pockets of city "boss" William Marcy Tweed and his friends.

Burner, Marcus, and Rosenberg, *America,* p. 384

Inference

A. Circle the letter preceding the implied main idea.
    1. New York City has always been the seat of corruption.
    2. Most people lived in cities by the turn of the century.
    3. There were many problems in New York City at the turn of the century.
    4. By the turn of the century, New York City was an unsafe place to live.

B. List two examples of support.

    _____

    _____

C. If you can infer the statement from the paragraph, write *yes* in the blank. If you cannot infer the statement, write *no.*

Few people thought that New York City was properly run.   1. _____

The building of the railroads had been characterized by corruption.   2. _____

Corruption is more likely when a monopoly supplies a service than when several different companies supply the service.   3. _____

Some politicians become very rich from cheating the public.   4. _____

There are advantages to monopolies.   5. _____

Fact Versus Opinion

Do you think the author can prove that the "public sale of economic opportunity inevitably trailed bribery and theft in its wake"? Why or why not?

_____

_____

EXERCISE 2: Practicing Critical Reading in Longer or Multi-Paragraph Selections

Here is a multi-paragraph reading selection. Read it and then answer the following questions. Then check your answers in the back of the book.

Normally, when we think of plants we think of things with roots and green leaves. In fact, of the 500,000 known species of plants, about 99 percent are just what we would expect. However, this description is too simple. We can see this if we examine the two main subkingdoms of plants.

The first subkingdom, Thallophyta, includes many unusual plants. Although most plants have little movement and are anchored to one spot by roots, several plants in this classification have no roots or have free floating roots. For example, algae can be found in this classification, as can seaweed.

The other subkingdom, Embryophyta, contains most of the ferns, grasses, vegetables, flowers, shrubs, and trees we think of as plants. But even here we can find unusual plants. For example, although moss is green, it has no real roots. And fungus is not green because it draws its nutrition from other trees or plants rather than producing its own food.

Hartmann et al., *Plant Science*, pp. 44–45

Inference

A. Circle the number preceding the implied main idea.
   1. Most plants do not have roots and leaves.
   2. All living things are divided into kingdoms.
   3. Plants live in the sea and on land.
   4. Some plants are very unusual.
B. If you can infer the statement from the selection, write *yes* in the blank. If you cannot infer the statement, write *no*. If you wrote *yes*, then on the line following the statement write the sentence(s) from which you made the inference.

The process of producing its own food is what makes a plant turn green.   1. _____

_____

There are more than two subkingdoms of plants.   2. _____

_____

You cannot define a plant as a green organism with roots.   3. _____

_____

Most plants produce their own food.   4. _____

_____

The Thallophyta subkingdom is larger than the Embryophyta subkingdom.

5. _____

_____

There are more species of plants than of animals.

6. _____

_____

Some plants in the Thallophyta subkingdom live in water.

7. _____

_____

Moss produces its own food.

8. _____

_____

Fact Versus Opinion

How could the author prove that what we normally think of as plants are "things with roots and green leaves"?

_____

_____

Reading Selection 1: Philosophy

Appealing to Reason: Deductive and Inductive Arguments

Lynn Z. Bloom

When you write persuasively you're trying to move your readers to either belief or action or both. You can do this through appealing to their reasons, their emotions, or their sense of **ethics,** as you know if you've every tried to prove a point on an exam or change an attitude in a letter to the editor. The next section discusses appeals to emotion and ethics; here we'll concentrate on argumentation.

fairness

An argument, as we're using the term here, does not mean a knockdown **confrontation** over an issue: "Philadelphia is the most wonderful place in the world to live!" "No, it's not. Social snobbery has ruined the City of Brotherly Love." Nor is an argument **hard-sell brainwashing** that admits of no alternative.

fight

forced changing of political or moral thinking argument

"America—love it or leave it!" When you write an argument, however, as a reasonable writer, you'll present a reasonable **proposition** that states what you believe. ("As we approach the twenty-first century, America remains the best country in the world for freedom, democracy, and the opportunity to succeed.") You'll need to offer logic, evidence, and perhaps emotional appeals to try to convince your readers of the **merits** of what you say. Sometimes, but not always,

good qualities

you'll also argue that they should adopt a particular course of action. ("Consequently, America should establish an 'open door' immigration policy to enable the less fortunate to enjoy these benefits, too." Or, "Consequently, America should **severely** restrict immigration, to prevent overcrowding and enable every citizen to enjoy these hard-won benefits.")

seriously

You'll probably want to identify the issue at hand and justify the significance early in the essay: "**Mandatory** drug-testing is essential for public officials with access to classified information." If it's a touchy subject, you may wish at this point to demonstrate goodwill toward readers likely to disagree with you by showing the basis for your common concern: "Most Americans would agree that it's important to protect children and **adolescents** from harmful influences." You could follow this by acknowledging the merits of their valid points: "and it's also true that drug abuse is currently a national crisis and deserves immediate remedy." You'll need to follow this with an explanation of why, nevertheless, your position is better than theirs: "But mandatory drug testing for everyone would be a violation of their **civil liberties,** incredibly costly, and subject to abuse through misuse of the data."

required

teenagers

freedoms

There are a number of suitable ways to organize the body of your argument. If your audience is inclined to agree with much of what you say, you might want to put your strongest point first and provide the most evidence for that, before proceeding to the lesser points, arranged in order of descending importance.

For an **antagonistic** audience you could do the reverse, beginning with the points easiest to accept or agree with and concluding with the most difficult. Or you could work from the most familiar to the least familiar parts.

unfriendly

No matter what organizational pattern you choose, you'll need to provide supporting evidence—through specific examples, facts and figures, the opinions of experts, case histories, narratives, **analogies,** and considerations of cause and effect. Any or all of these techniques can be employed in either *inductive* or *deductive* reasoning. Chances are that most of your arguments will proceed by induction, using a set of specific examples to prove a general **proposition.** Research scientists and detectives, among others, often work this way, gathering evidence, interpreting it, and formulating conclusions based on what they've found.

comparisons

proposal

An essay of deductive reasoning proceeds from a general proposition to a specific conclusion. The model for a deductive argument is the syllogism, a three-part sequence that begins with a major premise, is followed by a minor premise, and leads to a conclusion. Aristotle's classic example of this basic logical pattern is

Major premise: All men are mortal.
Minor premise: Socrates is a man.
Conclusion: Therefore, Socrates is mortal.

No matter what your argumentative strategy, you will want to avoid logical fallacies, errors of reasoning that can lead you to the wrong conclusion. The most common logical **fallacies** to be aware of are the following:

errors

- *Arguing from analogy:* comparing only similarities between things, concepts, or situations while overlooking significant differences that might weaken the argument. "Having a standing army is just like having a loaded gun in the house. If it's around, people will want to use it."
- *Argumentation ad hominem* (from the Latin, "argument to the man"): attacking a person's ideas or opinions by discrediting him or her as a person. "Napoleon was too short to be a distinguished general." "She was seen at the Kit Kat Lounge one night last week; she can't possibly be a good mother."
- *Argument from doubtful or unidentified authority:* treating an unqualified, unreliable, or unidentified source as an expert on the subject at hand. "They say you can't get pregnant the first time." "'History is bunk!' said Henry Ford."
- *Begging the question:* regarding as true from the start what you set out to prove; asserting that what is true is true. "Rapists and murderers awaiting trial shouldn't be let out on bail" assumes that the suspects have already been proven guilty, which is the point of the impending trial.
- *Arguing in a circle:* demonstrating a premise by a conclusion and a conclusion by a premise. "People should give 10 percent of their income to charity because that is the right thing to do. Giving 10 percent of one's income to charity is the right thing to do because it is expected."
- *Either/or reasoning:* restricting the complex aspects of a difficult problem or issue to only one of two possible solutions. "You're not getting any younger. Marry me or you'll end up single forever."
- *Hasty generalization:* **erroneously** applying information or knowledge of one or a limited number of representative instances to an entire, much larger category. "Poor people on welfare cheat. Why, just yesterday I saw a Cadillac parked in front of the **tenement** at 9th and Main."

mistakenly

slum housing

- *Non sequitur* (from the Latin, "it does not follow"): asserting as a conclusion something that doesn't follow from the first premise or premises. "The senator must be **in cahoots** with that shyster developer, Landphill. After all, they were college fraternity brothers."

in partnership with

- *Oversimplification:* providing simplistic answers to complex problems. "Ban handguns and stop organized crime."
- *Post hoc ergo propter hoc* (from the Latin, "after this, therefore because of this"): confusing a cause with an effect, and vice versa. "Bicyclists are terribly unsafe riders. They're always get-

ting into accidents with cars." Or confusing **causality** with **proximity:** just because two events occur in sequence doesn't necessarily mean that the first caused the second. Does war cause **famine,** or is famine sometimes the cause of war?

cause
physical closeness

widespread lack of food

Reading Selection 2: Journalism—Collateral Reading

Thinking as You Read

Julian Adams and Kenneth Stratton

Can you believe what you read? Is it the truth? And if true, is it the whole truth *or* merely part of the truth—a part that gives you a different impression from the one you would receive if you knew the whole story?

A free press may publish much that would not be printed if newspapers were controlled by the government. Most American editors and writers recognize a duty to their community and their readers. To the best of their ability, they report the news fairly, truthfully, and completely, yet there are ways in which they can fail. Editors must please their readers, who are not always interested in the absolute truth. Writers are human beings with human feelings, and they may allow their own ideas to creep into their reporting.

The responsibility, however, is not all on the side of the newspaper. If you, as a reader, do not think as you read, you may fail to understand what a newspaper is trying to tell you. Along with the privilege of receiving **uncensored** news, you must accept the responsibility of reading carefully. As you read the news or listen to someone speak—in person, on the radio, on television, or in motion pictures—you will need to consider certain points.

unaltered

Recognize and Understand Opinion

Opinion appears in every newspaper: editorials are opinions, as are daily columns, play and movie reviews, printed quotations, or speeches. In all of these, it is clear whose ideas you as a reader are receiving. Editorials state the opinion of the newspaper itself. Columns and reviews have **bylines** and contain writers' comments. A news analysis by an experienced reporter, containing that reporter's name in a by-line, will usually include personal comments. In addition, opinions may be expressed in news stories, if they are properly placed within quotes or follow a phrase like "Mr. Jones says that. . . ."

Most newspaper readers want and welcome opinion, when it is clearly identified, because it helps them weigh the news and form their own opin-

writers' names

ions. But their problem—and yours—is to keep the difference between fact and opinion clear.

Distinguishing Between Fact and Opinion

To a reporter, anything that really happens is a fact. If someone makes a statement concerning an event, the only positive fact is that that person talked. What was said must be considered personal opinion unless it is clearly established that the person was describing what actually had happened. The reporter notes what was said, being careful to name the source. If the reporter has reason to believe that the statement may be incorrect, the reporter may qualify it in some way, perhaps with words like **"assert"** or **"allege."** Contradictory statements may come from other sources. But the reporter reports them just the same!

state without proof

Here, responsibility for determining the truth shifts to you, the reader. To understand what actually happened, you must analyze the statements in the story. You must make a **distinction** between actual facts and personal opinions. Moreover, you must watch for conclusions which someone has reached. These are also opinions. Each time you find an opinion, first identify its source. Then consider it, accepting or rejecting it. Finally, use it to assist in forming your own judgment about the news event.

difference

Considering the Source of Information

Another distinction a newspaper reader must make is between facts and rumors; that is, statements made by a news source or by a reporter without sufficient authority. Most newspapers identify their news sources by name, or indicate the reporter's personal presence at a news event. But you must judge for yourself the authority of the person who is the source of a given news story. Is that person qualified to say this? Does he or she possess enough information to make such a judgment?

Perhaps even worse than the named news source who has no authority to make a statement is the unnamed source. This "individual" appears frequently in news of national or international politics. As an example, a government official who is making a decision may not, for some reason, wish to announce it yet, but an alert reporter may guess or be "tipped off" as to what will be said. The reporter may then report it as a rumor without naming the authority. There may be no reference to a source, or the reporter may state that the information comes from an "informed source" or a "usually reliable source."

Watching for Slanted News

A newspaper may present news in a biased or slanted way, either accidentally or intentionally. You, as a newspaper reader, are likely to misunderstand the true facts of a slanted news story. All the facts may not be there or may be presented so that their relative importance is not clear to you.

How might a slanted news story be written? In the limited time before a deadline, the reporter may not have time to gather all the facts and so may miss an important part of the story. An informant who furnishes the reporter with news may not know all the facts or may deliberately lie about some of them, but the reporter may not find this out. If the reporter has a strong personal opinion about the subject, the reporter may deliberately or unconsciously allow opinion to creep into the story. This may be done by what is written, by the choice of words suggesting favorable or unfavorable meanings, by emphasizing certain facts, or by omitting other facts.

Compare these paragraphs about the same news event. Would you say that either one, or both were slanted? If so, explain why.

The School Board today revealed plans for a $9,000,000 bond issue to enlarge and improve school facilities throughout the city. Of the $9,000,000, some $2,500,000 would be used to acquire land, while the remainder would rebuild two schools and provide for additions to 11 others.

The School Board revealed today that it plans to **condemn** private property and homes worth $2,500,000 including a square block in the downtown area, for expansion of school facilities. The condemnation would be part of a $9,000,000 school bond issue going before voters in the general **municipal** election.

tear down by government order

city

News may also be slanted by the way stories are arranged on a newspaper page or by the way a story is emphasized. A news item of major importance may be hidden on a back page, while **sensational** but unimportant stories fill the front page. Important stories may sometimes be left out entirely.

intentionally shocking

Slanted news is not always the fault of the reporter. The reporter might have received the information from a news source who believes that news should be "managed"; that is, that newspaper readers should be told only what the source's organization, company, or government agency wants them to know. Or the editor or publisher of the newspaper may have directed that a certain policy be promoted in the paper. Slanted news challenges your alertness and your ability to think clearly about what you read.

Looking Out for Propaganda

Propaganda is the name given to any organized attempt to influence your thinking or your actions. It may be good or bad, according to the purpose or intentions of its originator and the way it is used, as well as how its audience receives it.

Advertising, campaigning for political office, and promoting social or environmental concerns are examples of various activities in which propaganda is used. Nearly all advertising may be said to be a form of propaganda, for it is designed to persuade you to buy. Such advertising is honest and straightforward in its presentation of facts, although it may use some exaggeration and repetition to convince you. But the propaganda to watch for is the kind that tries to mislead you. Federal government agencies have recognized this recently and have taken action to ensure that advertisements for certain types of products are factual and truthful.

Propagandists appeal to you in many ways. Half-truths are common: "This deodorant proved best by extensive tests." Best for what? Who conducted the tests? What kind of tests? With what other brands of deodorant was it compared? Or promoters may present arguments on only one side of a question, making it impossible for you to reason intelligently unless you are willing to seek out the opposing arguments from other sources. Another device is to base a conclusion on too few examples: "These two teenagers were caught shoplifting, so every teenager who enters a store should be watched carefully."

Other propagandists want you to do something because "everybody's doing it." "Follow the crowd! Everyone's voting for this candidate!" Or you hear a **testimonial:** "Famous movie star Liz Smith chews this bubble gum." This implies that you should chew this brand because Liz is famous and wealthy, and in this way you will share something with her. At election time, candidates become "just plain folks" like you and me: they chat with voters, kiss babies, or share a meal in someone's home.

Use of "loaded" or misleading words, names, or phrases is another common means of spreading propaganda. Speakers or writers may use evil-sounding words to attack an idea or a person: "Nazi," "dictatorship," "agitator," "addict," "conspiracy," "antisocial." Or they may support their program with words that have a positive **connotation:** "crusader," "home," "love," "honorable," "truth," "American."

Most of these devices appeal to your emotions rather than to your common sense. It is easier to relax and be fooled than it is to consider carefully what you hear and read. This is why propaganda often succeeds. You don't bother to think statements through, and as a result you don't recognize propaganda when you see or hear it. Therein lies the greatest danger—as well as the greatest challenge—of today's high-speed methods of communication.

persons making organized attempt to influence your thinking

statement promoting a product

meaning beyond the dictionary definition

Comprehension Check

Circle the letter preceding the correct answer. Then check your answers in the back of the book.

1. Most newspaper people
    a. try to sensationalize to improve the circulation of their papers.
    b. use more opinion than facts when reporting stories.
    c. present slanted news.
    d. try to report news fairly and truthfully.

2. If a reporter writes, "Mr. Smith asserted that there was nothing wrong with the bridge that collapsed," the reporter is indicating that
    a. Mr. Smith has proof that the bridge was all right.
    b. Mr. Smith's statement may be incorrect.
    c. Mr. Smith is definitely covering up a scandal.
    d. Mr. Smith's statement is obviously true.

3. According to the authors of "Thinking as You Read," most newspaper readers
    a. are never fooled by propaganda.
    b. want opinions in their newspapers.
    c. always believe propaganda only.
    d. are only interested in the absolute truth.

4. In slanted news,
    a. some facts may be withheld.
    b. the reporter may not have had time to gather all the facts.
    c. the reporter may have allowed his or her opinions to enter the story.
    d. all of the above may be true.

5. Which of the following is the main idea of this reading?
    a. Don't trust newspaper editors.
    b. Many reporters distort the news.
    c. It's the reader's responsibility to think while reading, rather than the newspaper's responsibility to present factual news stories.
    d. Both newspapers and readers have a responsibility to attempt to separate fact from opinion.

6. Reading carefully means
    a. accepting news stories but not editorials as true.
    b. realizing that facts and opinions sometimes are intermixed in a news story.
    c. believing in propaganda because you cannot recognize it.
    d. trusting that newspaper reporters have sufficient information to report accurately.

7. The authors
    a. favor censoring opinions.
    b. believe that an uncensored press is valuable.
    c. believe there is no real difference between a free press and a government-controlled press.
    d. believe an uncensored press is dangerous to our freedom.

8. Which statement is intended to be factual?
   a. Brand X cleans your clothes like a tornado.
   b. The National Council on Highway Safety reports that highway deaths climbed 15 percent this year.
   c. "Star Wars" had the best special effects ever created for a movie.
   d. Blondes have more fun.

9. Slanted news is _____
   _____.

10. Propaganda is _____
    _____.

Questions for Discussion and Writing

1. Why is it important that we learn to recognize propaganda in a democratic society?

2. Television advertisements are famous for using propaganda and other faulty reasoning techniques. Do you think this is justified? Why or why not?

EXERCISE 3: Identifying Faulty Logic

Both of the longer articles you have just read concern faulty reasoning. Identify the following types of fallacies and propaganda by writing the appropriate symbol in the blank before each sentence. Then check your answers in the back of the book.

- OS   Oversimplification
- HG   Hasty generalization
- LL   Loaded language
- AD   Argument ad hominem
- NS   Non sequitur
- AA   Appeal to authority
- UID Argument from doubtful or unidentified source
- EO   Either/or reasoning

Buy a Flyrite umbrella. Mary Poppins never goes anywhere without hers.

1. _____

According to an executive at Apricot Computer, Inc., Micromush is proposing a secret buy-out of the computer giant.

2. _____

Hire Pied Piper Rodent Control, or you will never get rid of your rats.

3. _____

Don't let Santa Claus down your chimney. How can anyone trust a man in a furry red suit?

4. _____

Elect Mother Goose to the school board. She stand for love, family values, brotherhood, and animal rights.

5. _____

Avoid apples. Look what happened to Snow White!

6. _____

Pinocchio will make a perfect spokesperson for our new perfume. Just look at the size of his nose.

7. _____

When guns are outlawed, only outlaws will have guns.

8. _____

EXERCISE 4: Skills Review—Main Idea and Support

A. List four of the major ideas in the article "Appealing to Reason" and two pieces of support for each idea. Then check your answers in the back of the book for our sample answers.

1. _____
   a. _____
   b. _____
2. _____
   a. _____
   b. _____
3. _____
   a. _____
   b. _____
4. _____
   a. _____
   b. _____

B. List four of the major ideas in the article "Thinking as you Read" and two pieces of support for each idea. Answers will vary.

1. _____
   a. _____
   b. _____
2. _____
   a. _____
   b. _____
3. _____
   a. _____
   b. _____
4. _____
   a. _____
   b. _____

Reading Textbooks I: Preview, Question, Read

4

Reading Textbooks I: Preview, Question, Read

The important thing is to not stop questioning.
Albert Einstein

We often hear students complain, "I read the material three times and got only a D while one of my friends got an A by reading it once." Unfortunately, these students are probably telling the truth. Most students try to read textbooks and scholarly articles in the same way that they read novels and short stories: they start at the beginning and read straight through. Because the average textbook is more difficult and less exciting than most fiction, students often come to the end of a textbook chapter and suddenly realize that they don't remember much of what they've read.

PQ4R

PREVIEW   QUESTION   READ   WRITE   RECALL   REVIEW

PQ4R is a technique designed specifically for textbook reading. Using it will improve your concentration, reading speed, and memory of what you have read. PQ4R stands for Preview, Question, Read, Write, Recall, and Review. It takes advantage of the fact that most authors of textbooks write from an outline, attempting to emphasize those ideas that are most important. Usually, the ideas the author considers most important are the ones that will appear on tests. In this chapter we discuss the first three steps in PQ4R: Preview; Question; and Read. In the next chapter we will discuss the last three steps: Write; Recall; and Review.

Preview

You should preview both the entire book and each of the chapters. Preview the entire book at the beginning of the semester. Preview the individual chapters before you read them. Preview articles from journals or magazines the same way you do book chapters.

Previewing a book.   Previewing a book before you begin reading gives you a mental overview that helps you read more effectively. Reading a textbook without previewing is like going on a trip without looking at a map: you can easily become confused. These are the book parts you should preview:

Title page.   Read the title and any subtitles to learn the general subject of the book. The title of this book is *Keys to College Success.* The subtitle, *Reading and Study Improvement,* tells you which aspect of college success is the focus of the book. Check the name of a book's author or editor. If you know who the author is, you can take into account his or her biases as you read. For instance, a book about killer bees by a scientist would likely be different from one written by an author of popular novels. Editors are in charge of putting together books composed of writings by several people. Their beliefs influence which selections they choose. Check the copyright date to see how current the book is. In many fields, such as the sciences, information may become outdated very quickly. For example, the information about the planet Jupiter changed overnight when the Hubbell Space Telescope transmitted photographs showing formerly unknown moons. In 1991, as a result of the break-up of the Soviet Union, any discussion of countries in Europe and any map of the area became instantly outdated. Russia changed from being another name for the Soviet Union to being the name of only one country in the area. Suddenly there were new countries such as Kazakstan and Belarus. Today, because the world is changing so rapidly, it is not unusual for a geography textbook to have outdated maps even before it is sold. Sometimes the publisher and place of publication can be important. For example, an American history book written in the United States may have a different point of view about the American Revolution than a book written in England.

Introductory material.   Preliminary material can be called a preface, foreword, or introduction. Usually a preface is written by the author and a foreword is written by someone else. The introductory material is often the only place in the book in which the author's purposes in writing it are discussed. Reading the introductory material can give you a sense of the author as an individual. It should help you understand the point of view taken throughout the book. Sometimes instructions or suggestions are given about methods of reading the book.

Table of contents.   The table of contents lists in order all the major topics covered in the book. This outline of the book will help you put things into perspective as you read. It is wise to compare your course assignment sheet with the table of contents, because your instructor may differ from the author in what he or she considers important, or in the sequence in which he or she discusses the topics.

Appendix.   There may be one or more appendices at the end of a book to explain some part of the text or to give extra information.

Bibliography.   A bibliography, also found in the back of the book, is a list of materials the author has consulted in writing the book. These sources deal with the same or related topics and are useful if you are writing a paper. Be careful to determine whether the sources are recent if the subject that the book covers is one in which being up-to-date is important.

Glossary.   In the back of the book you may also find a glossary, which is a list of difficult, technical, or foreign terms in a particular field and their definitions. Even some familiar words have specialized meanings. For example, in this chapter *appendix* refers to part of a book rather than to part of a person. You are fortunate if your textbook has a glossary, because it will contain precise definitions of terms as they are used in that book. It will not contain all of the meanings of the word that you would find in a dictionary.

Index.   Some textbooks contain two indexes, a subject index and an author index. The subject index is an alphabetized list of topics included in the book along with the page numbers on which the topic is discussed. The author index has the same format, but it contains names of people (usually other researchers) to whom the author has referred in the book. In some books the subject and author indexes are combined. The index helps you quickly locate any information you need.

If you have not yet previewed this book, take a few minutes to do so. Then answer the following questions:

1. How many indexes does it have?
2. Is there a glossary?
3. What is the copyright date?
4. How many chapters are there?
    Answers: (1) one; (2) no; (3) 1998; (4) 12

Previewing a chapter or an article.   Previewing a chapter or an article before you read may seem time-consuming, but in fact it saves time. The preview should take no longer than a minute or two, depending on the length of the material and the number of visual aids you need to understand. There are two preview methods. The first works better when there are headings, subheadings, and a summary at the end. This method consists of reading (1) the title of the chapter or article, (2) all the major headings and subheadings in the chapter, (3) all the visual aids, and (4) the chapter or article summary. Use the second method when the chapter or article does not contain headings and/or a summary. First, read the first sentence of each paragraph and all of the visual aids. Then read the last paragraph or two.

What you are actually doing with either preview method is reading all the main ideas first. Previewing gives you a mental outline of the chapter and some advance information about the ideas you will encounter. This not only enables you to read with greater understanding; it also allows you to save time by skipping any material you already know.

If you were to preview the next chapter, you would see the following title, headings, and subheadings:

Reading Textbooks II: PQ4R—Write, Recall, Review

   I. Write
       A. Underlining
       B. Making marginal notes
       C. Applying the writing step
  II. Recall
       A. PQ4R method
       B. Supplemental review methods
           1. Outlining
           2. Flash Cards
           3. Study Maps
           4. Other self-generated graphics
 III. Review
  IV. Studying other assigned reading
   V. Summary

Using these headings and subheadings, answer the following questions:

   1. Do you underline first or make marginal notes first?
   2. Will outlining be discussed in this chapter?
   3. Under which heading do the authors introduce underlining and making marginal notes?
   4. In addition to the Recall Step in PQ4R, what are the four additional recall methods?
       Answers: (1) underline; (2) yes; (3) "Write"; (4) outlining, flash cards, study maps, other self-generated graphics

Previewing Visual Aids.   Textbooks often use visual aids to help the reader understand the material. Many textbook authors find it useful to refer the reader to these displays of the material being discussed. Visual aids include pictures, maps, diagrams, tables, and graphs. Using these aids effectively can help you mentally summarize a mass of material.

The first step is previewing visual aids is to read the caption (words immediately under or beside the visual aid, usually in smaller type than the rest of the text) to find the subject and sometimes the main idea. Second, if the caption does not explain the main idea of the visual aid, look at the visual aid and put the main idea in your own words. Third, look at the details. Last, see if there are any inferences (conclusions or generalizations) you can deduce from the material. Now let's look at the types of visual aids and the way to understand them.

Pictures.   These include drawings, photographs, and cartoons and are meant to give you a feel for the subject. Take a moment to orient yourself to the purpose of the picture and its relationship to the reading material. Read the caption and look at the picture. Here is a photograph from a health text. Look at it and then answer the questions.

"Killing time" with friends is actually an important health-promoting activity.
Donatelle et. al., *Access to Health,* p. 19

1.   What is the subject? _____

2.   What is the main idea? _____

3.   Find at least three details in the picture that indicate that the two women are friends.

   a.   _____

   b.   _____

   c.   _____

4.   Find at three details in the picture that indicate that the women might be "killing time" rather than working.

   a.   _____

   b.   _____

   c.   _____

Answers: (1) "Killing time;" (2) "Killing time" with friends is health promoting; (3) the closeness of the friends which includes their arms almost touching, their relaxed and comfortable look, and their posture of facing each other. (4) One woman has books on her lap but isn't studying; she also has her eyes closed; the other woman is looking at her friend and has no visible study material.

Diagrams.   Authors who are describing complex material often include diagrams to help you understand processes or concepts. This kind of visual aid must often be referred to as you read the text. However, before you read the text, you should be familiar with what the diagram illustrates, including the labels attached to the parts. Here is a diagram from a geology textbook. Use it to answer the following questions. Since diagrams are often complex or highly technical you may have to read the material more than once to understand them.

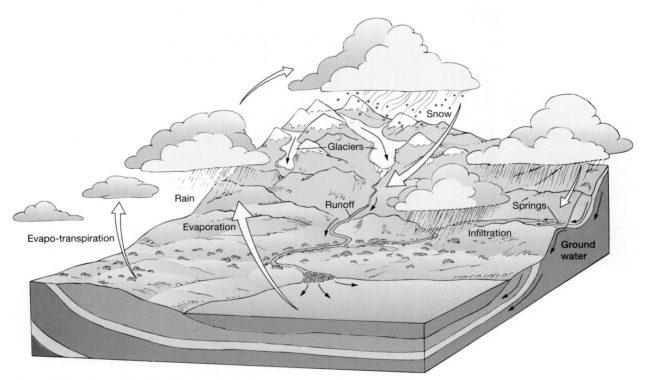

Figure 2–9: Diagram of the Water Cycle
Judson and Richardson, *Earth: An Introduction to Geological Change*, p. 7

1.   When glaciers melt, what is the term for the water after it melts?
2.   What is the step in the water cycle by which water leaves the ground and becomes airborne?
3.   What is water below the ground called?
     Answers: (1) runoff; (2) evaporation; (3) ground water.

Maps.   A map, or any other visual aid, often has more study value than the printed text surrounding it and therefore deserves your careful attention. Whether or not you're a visual learner, pay careful attention to any map or other visual aid.

Note that the information contained in the map below took many paragraphs to explain. While the text may add details to essential information, it is the map itself that consolidates the major ideas.

When reading a map, be sure you understand the legend (the little box usually found at the bottom or top) that tells you what the symbols mean. Also, notice if there is a scale at the bottom that shows you the relationship between the distances on the map and real distance. For example, the map may be on a scale of one inch for each mile of actual distance. Use the following map to answer the questions below it.

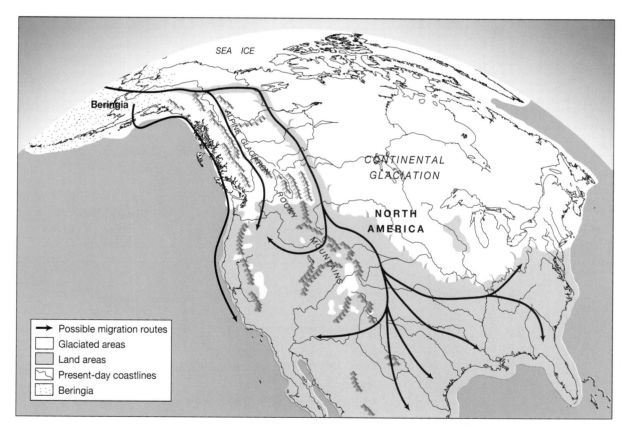

Faragher et. al. *Out of Many*, p. 5

1. What is the subject? _____
2. What is the main idea? _____
3. How many possible migration routes are shown on the map?_____
4. How many of the migration routes were through narrow glacial corridors? _____
5. What had happened to the water in the Bering Straits that allowed people to cross from Asia to North America? _____

Answers: (1) Beringia Migration Routes; (2) People migrated across the Bering Straits during the Ice Age; (3) 7; (4) 2; (5) The water was frozen where the Bering Straits are today.

Tables.   Authors can visually compare several pieces of information by using tables. Tables consist of columns of information. With any table, begin by looking at the title and at the caption to get an overview of the subject matter. Next, look for any labels along the top or side to see how the information has been subdivided. Finally, you can analyze the information vertically and horizontally to see the relationship between items.

Look at the table below from a chemistry text and answer the questions which follow.

Subfield	Subject	Example
Organic chemistry	Study of substances containing carbon	Preparing aspirin or acetaminophen
Inorganic chemistry	Study of all substances that do not contain carbon	Understanding how a car battery works
Analytical chemistry	Study of what is in a sample and how much of it is there	Measuring the amount of a particular pesticide in ground water
Physical chemistry	Study of the structures of substances, how fast substances change, and the role of heat in chemical changes *(thermodynamics)*	Understanding the changes that occur when ice melts to give liquid water
Biochemistry	Study of the chemical reactions in living systems	Understanding how saliva breaks down some of the foods we eat and chew

The Five Subfields of Chemistry

1. Name the 5 subfields of chemistry. _____ _____

2. Give an example of a biochemical process. _____ _____

3. Define analytical chemistry. _____ _____

4. What do you call the study of substances which contain carbon? ____ _____

5. To understand how a car battery works, which subfield of chemistry would you study? _____

Answers: (1) Organic chemistry, inorganic chemistry, analytical chemistry, physical chemistry, biochemistry; (2) Understanding how saliva breaks down some of the food we eat as we chew; (3) Study of what is in a sample and how much of it is there; (4) Organic chemistry; (5) Inorganic chemistry.

Graphs.   Like tables, graphs compare two or more things. A graph can clearly show trends or changes in information. The common types of graphs are the *bar graph,* the *line graph,* the *pie or circle graph* and the *pictograph.* When reading a graph, you should begin with the caption and then look at the graph to determine the information being compared and the units of measurement being used. Usually the line at the base of the graph indicates how it is being measured.

Here, adapted from a food sciences textbook, are two bar graphs with the same information. The first one is a *vertical bar graph* where information is displayed in vertical columns. The second shows the information displayed horizontally and is called a *horizontal bar graph.* Look at the vertical bar graph and answer the questions which follow it.

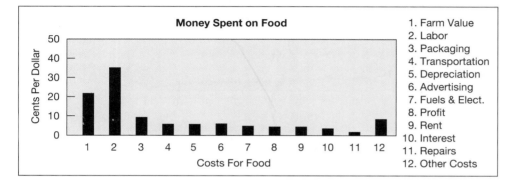

1. What is the largest component of "money spent on food"? _____
2. Approximately what fractional part of a dollar is consumed by farm value? _____
    Answers: (1) labor and (2) approximately 22%.

Now look at the horizontal bar graph and answer the questions which follow it.

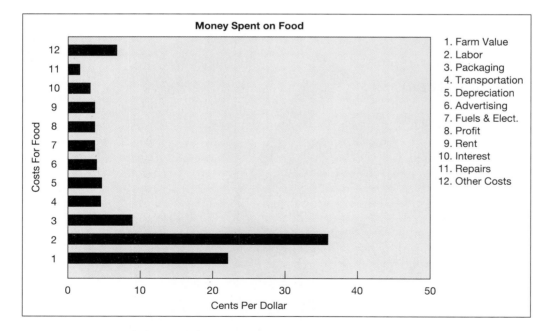

1. What is the third largest component of "money spent on food"? ____
2. What is the smallest component of "money spent on food"? _____
    Answers: (1) packaging and (2) repairs

Here is the same information presented on a line graph. Notice that the three lines show the same information as the different bars on the bar graphs. The same data can be presented in different graphic forms. The line graph connects the midpoints at the tops of the imaginary bars. Study this graph and then answer the questions that follow.

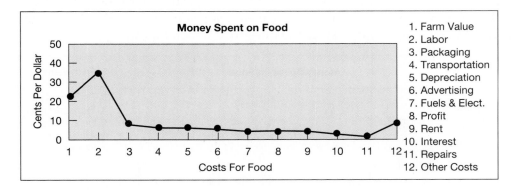

1. For each dollar Americans spend on food, how much of it goes for advertising costs? _____
2. For each dollar Americans spend on food, is more spent on rent or repairs?_____
   Answers: (1) approximately 4% and (2) rent

A third kind of graph is the circular or pie graph. On this type of graph, the information is divided into "slices" that total 100 percent. Here

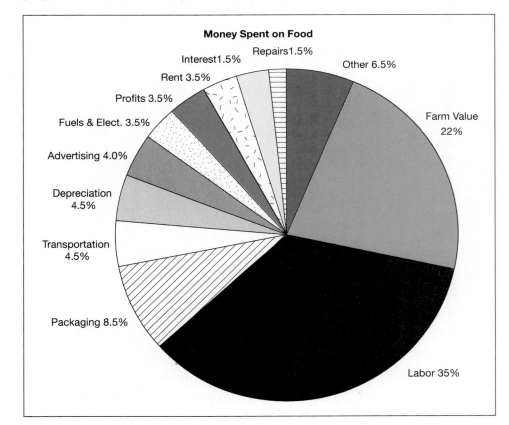

is a pie graph version of the data from the previous bar graph. Look at the pie graph and then answer the questions that follow.

1. For each food dollar Americans spend, is more spent on transportation or on advertising?_____
2. Every item except "farm value" is a part of the "marketing bill." How much of every dollar spent on food is spent on the "marketing bill"? _____
   Answers: (1) transportation and (2) 78%

Pictograph.   A *pictograph* is a graph using a pictured object or objects to display ideas or information. The following is a pictograph conveying the same information as the previous graph forms.

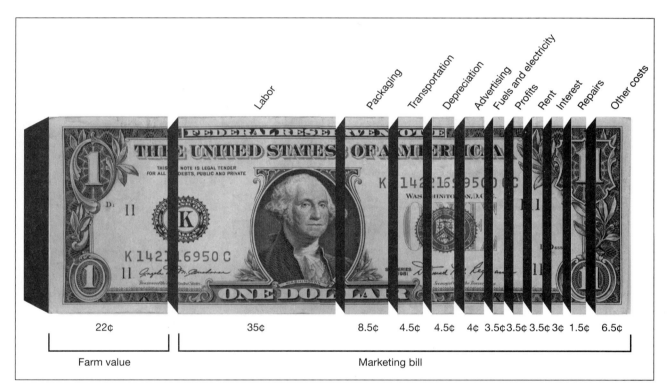

Bennion, *Introductory Foods,* p. 28

1. What component of the graph costs twice as much as the repair component? _____
2. Is labor part of "farm value" or "marketing bill"? _____
   Answers: (1) interest and (2) "marketing bill"

Now that you have studied several types of graphs, which did you find the easiest to use? _____
   Why? _____
_____
_____

Question

The second step in PQ4R is to create questions about the material you have just previewed. Make up some questions based on the first heading. For example, after reading the first major heading in Chapter 5, you might ask questions such as these:

1. What is included in the writing step?
2. What do you write?
3. Why do you write after you read rather than while you read?

Now look at the major headings in Chapter 5, pp. 106–134, and make up three questions you might ask about the review step.

1. _____
2. _____
3. _____

Some possible questions are:

- How much should you try to review at one session?
- What should you review?
- What is the difference between the recall step and the review step?
- Why are recall and review two separate steps in PQ4R?

Here are some questions that would fit most any topic: What is the author's main point? What is the author trying to say? Why is it important? What might I be asked about this on a test? What are the answers to the five W's (who, what, where, when, why) and how?

The questioning technique improves your studying because it makes you focus on looking for answers. Knowing what you're looking for arouses your curiosity and keeps you alert. For example, can you remember how many blue cars you have seen today? You probably can't. However, if you knew that tomorrow you would be asked how many blue cars you had seen, you would start paying attention to them. You would know what you were looking for. The questioning technique gives the same kind of purpose to your reading.

Here are the headings from a chapter in a biology textbook.

1. Living Things Are Both Complex and Organized
2. A Good Scientist Is Prepared to Take Advantage of Chance Events

Make up three questions about the first heading.

1. _____
2. _____
3. _____

Here are some questions you might have asked:

- How are living things organized?
- What are the complex features of living things?
- In what ways are living things different from nonliving things?

Now, make up three questions about the second heading.

1. _____
2. _____
3. _____

Here are some questions you might have asked:

- What is one characteristic of a good scientist?
- What is a chance event?
- How can a good scientist take advantage of a chance event?

The next heading in this chapter is "Read." Before you read the section, make up three questions based on the heading.

1. _____
2. _____
3. _____

Read

The next step is to read the same section of the material you have previewed and made questions for. Do not underline or make notes unless you suddenly have a thought that's too important to lose. Look for the answers to your questions and for any other important ideas. Always read for ideas; don't read sentence by sentence unless the material is so difficult that you can't understand it in any other way. When you finish reading, stop and try to answer the questions you asked yourself. Now, answer the questions you just asked during the question step.

1. _____
2. _____
3. _____

Summary

Techniques for reading textbooks and scholarly articles differ from those used for reading fiction. An efficient technique for reading textbooks and articles is PQ4R. PQ4R consists of *previewing* the material before reading, asking *questions* based on the preview, *reading* to answer the questions, *writing* in the textbook, testing for immediate *recall*, and *reviewing* to aid long-term memory. In this chapter we discussed the first three steps. You preview a whole book and then each chapter to get a general idea of what it contains. You formulate questions to help you focus on the important information and to arouse your curiosity. During the reading step, concentrate on understanding the ideas. Then try to answer the questions you asked during the question step. A chapter preview is done on the whole chapter, but the question and reading steps are done by section.

Comprehension Check

Circle the letter preceding the correct answer. Then check your answers in the back of the book.

1. When a book has an editor instead of an author, we know that
   a. the editor was one of many authors of the book.
   b. the authorship is anonymous.
   c. the editor has put together writings by several other people.
   d. the book is written like a newspaper.
2. The reason for a separate question step in PQ4R is that
   a. you need to look the material over twice before you read it.
   b. you need a reminder to look at the questions in the back of the chapter.
   c. very few textbooks have questions in the back of the chapter.
   d. questioning will help you focus on what is important.
3. Previewing helps to grasp
   a. examples.
   b. implications.
   c. facts.
   d. main ideas.
4. The main idea of this chapter is that
   a. PQ4R is the only method for reading textbooks.
   b. there is a specific method for reading textbooks.
   c. there are several items to preview in a textbook.
   d. textbooks are difficult to read.
5. PQ4R is effective because
   a. it breaks down textbook reading into an organized series of steps.
   b. it uses the textbook author's organization as a study device.
   c. it forces the reader to be actively involved at each stage.
   d. all of the above.
6. From this chapter you can infer that
   a. PQ4R is an efficient method for reading newspapers.
   b. PQ4R involves remembering as well as reading the material.

    c. the steps in PQ4R can be done in any order as long as you read before you review.

    d. PQ4R is very complex.

7. Another implication is that
      a. each step of PQ4R is a building block for the next step.
      b. previewing is the most important step in PQ4R.
      c. PQ4R is known to most textbook writers.
      d. all of the above.

8. Previewing a chapter gives you an idea of
      a. how long the chapter is.
      b. how unfamiliar you are with the material.
      c. the author's organization of ideas.
      d. all of the above.

9. Previewing a chapter means _____
   _____ .

10. In the Question Step of PQ4R, you _____
    _____ .

EXERCISE 1: Previewing Your Textbooks

This exercise will help you practice what you have learned in this chapter. Take a textbook that you are currently using in another class and answer the following questions about it.

Title Page
- Name of author _____
- Title _____
- Publisher and place of publication _____
- Copyright date _____
- Have you ever heard of the author? _____
- What does the title tell you about the topic of the book? _____
  _____
- Was the book published recently enough to be current in its field? __
  _____

Table of contents
- How many chapters are there? _____
- What topics seem the most interesting? _____
- What topics seem the most difficult? _____
- What topics might be boring? _____
- What is the longest chapter in the book? _____
- Do the topics seem to be presented in a logical order?_____
- Is this the same order your instructor is following in class? _____
  _____

Preface or introduction

- What is the purpose of the book? _____
- Is there anything in particular that the author wants you to know about this book? _____

Appendix

- How many appendices are there? _____
- What do the appendices contain? _____

Bibliography

- Does it seem up to date? _____

Glossary

- If there is a glossary, give an example of a word whose definition in the glossary differs from its definition in the dictionary. What is its special definition? _____

Index

- How many indexes are there? What are their titles? _____
  _____

Previewing a Chapter

- Does the book use graphs and illustrations? __ tables? __ diagrams? __ headings? __ subheadings? __ summaries? __ different typefaces? __ questions at the end of the chapter? __ outlines at the beginning? __

EXERCISE 2: Previewing a Preface

Here is the preface of a college textbook on speech communication. Read it and answer the questions that follow. Then check your answers in the back of the book.

PREFACE

TO THE PROFESSOR

This edition has undergone a major overhaul. You will find it more *course directed, streamlined,* and much *less cluttered.*

Each previous edition prided itself on adding new and vital theory, research, and explanation. After eight editions, in which little was eliminated while compressing the "good stuff" to keep the book in one volume, it clearly was time for some cutting and reorganization.

The new organization of chapters (now reduced to 13) is designed to meet the typical beginning public speaking course as I found it in your course descriptions and syllabi.

A sharper focus on student speechmaking made eliminating some of my favorite topics less painful and, of course, helped eliminate the clutter that had developed over the course of so many editions.

The ninth edition is still eclectically informed mostly by the behavioral sciences and communication theory, but I have not forgotten my rhetorical roots. The pragmatic chapters covering speech purpose, gathering materials, organizing ideas, opening and closing a speech, outlining, and so forth have been strengthened. My favorite content chapters are leaner but still attempt to teach students something more than skills alone. If you're among the blind reviewers who forced me to overhaul . . . thanks, I owe you one.

Raymond S. Ross

P.S. Please ask my publisher to provide you with the new *Instructor's Manual.* It has all the usual ancillaries plus extensive pedagogical notes.

TO THE STUDENT

If you've read what I said to your professor in the paragraphs above, you know that even experienced writers and speakers sometimes take the communication process, listening habits, and audience analysis for granted. All three of these matters are discussed in the first three chapters. Read them first since they, together with language, set the frame in which the other chapters fit. If your first assignment involves introducing a classmate, you may want to look at Chapter 12.

I hope you enjoy the book. I know you will enjoy the class. It's one of the few in which you get to really know your classmates.

Is the skill worth learning? Lee Iacocca, a fellow Michigander, thinks so—"The most important thing I learned in school was how to communicate."

Good luck,
Professor Ross
Ross, *Speech Communication,* p. xiii–xiv

1. Whom does the author address in the preface?_____
2. How is this edition different from previous editions? _____
   _____
3. How many editions of the book have been printed? _____
4. What chapters does the author think students should read first? Why? _____
   _____
5. How many chapters are there in the current edition? _____

EXERCISE 3: **Previewing a Table of Contents**

Preview the table of contents at the front of this text, *Keys to College Success.* Then refer to it if necessary to answer the questions that follow. Then check your answers in the back of the book.

1. In which chapter will you most likely find information on taking essay tests? _____
2. In what chapter are critical reading techniques discussed? _____
3. What are the parts of the library discussed in Chapter 10? _____
4. Does the book discuss ways to improve concentration? _____
5. Does the book have a glossary? _____
6. In what chapter would you probably find a discussion about using collateral materials? _____
7. Does the book contain answers to the exercises? _____
8. What types of additional materials are in the back of the book? _____
   _____

EXERCISE 4: **Previewing a Glossary**

Review the following partial glossary from a literature anthology and answer the questions that follow it. Then check your answers in the back of the book.

Epithalamion.   A song or poem in honor of a wedding or the bride or bride-groom.

Essay.   A relatively short work of personal or impersonal nonfiction prose that discusses subjects of self-revelation, individual tastes and opinions, and criticism; most essays are persuasive or informative.

Ethnicity.   Original nationality of a group that is part of a larger group.

Exact rhyme.   Rhymed words having the same vowels and end consonants.

Exodos.   The final episode in a Greek play.

Explication.   *(explication de texte)* An intensive, word-by-word examination and interpretation of a written work.

Exposition.   Presentation of information.

Eye rhyme.   Words that suggest rhyme based on similar spelling but do not actually rhyme when pronounced (example: drought, ought).

Fable.   A brief narrative with an obvious moral often having animals as the characters.

Fairy tale.   A fictional story having mysterious or supernatural characters (for example, giants, witches, and so forth) and events that may impart a moral or lesson.

Falling action.   The action that takes place after the climax, also called denouement and resolution.

Farce.   Comedy based on broad or low humor, filled with swift physical action and ridiculous situations.

Fiction.   Narrative writing based on an author's imagination as opposed to real history or actual fact in drama, stories, poems.

Figurative language (figures of speech).   Words used in such a way as to express meaning beyond the literal; use of figures of speech such as apostrophe, hyperbole, metaphor, simile, personification, or synecdoche.

Flashback.   A device by which a character looks back at or reenacts events, also exposition.

Flat character.   A one-dimensional character lacking complexity, a stereotype (example: the villain).

Foil.   A minor character whose purpose is to provide contrast with a major character, thereby setting the major character in relief.

Folktale.   A fictional story often passed on in the oral tradition with ordinary women and men as heroes, often having supernatural characters or events and a lesson or moral.

Foot.   A metrical unit of rhythm, having two or three syllables, where the stressed syllable or syllables are arranged in a particular order.

Foreshadowing.   Subtle indication of future events.

Framework.   The internal or external structure of a work of literature.

Free verse.   Poetry having only irregular rhyme or no rhyme at all.

1. List three of the words you know have definitions not presented in this glossary: _____, _____, and _____.

2. Which figure of speech is also the name of a punctuation mark? _____

3. Which word would also be found on the blueprint of a house?_____

4. What do you call two words that have the exact same vowels and ending consonants? _____

5. Why is a "flat character" called "flat"? _____00

Bloom, *The Essay Connection*, p. 786

EXERCISE 5: Using an Index

Below is a partial page from an index in a history book. Use this page to answer the questions that follow.

Index

Bymes, James F., 439–40
Byzantium, 2

C

Caetano, Marcelo, 565
Callaghan, James, 558

Calvino, Italo, 418, 420
Cambodia, 461
Cambrai, Battle of, 68
Cambridge, 171, 172
Cameroon, 114, 468
Camus, Albert, 413
Canada, 24, 164, 459
Canary Islands, 295

Caporetto, Battle of, 67, 68
Carnap, Rudolf, 181
Carol, King of Romania, 165
Cartel des Gauches, 157
Cassino, 346
Catholic Action, 225
Catholic Church, Roman (see also individual
    countries), 224–25, 234
  educational institutions, state aid to, 427
  (*Quadragesimo anno*) 276–77, 430, 431
  Rerum Novarum, 276, 430, 431
  and second Vatican council, 431–32
  and worker priests, 430
Catholicism, Roman, 276–78
Central Powers, 37–39, 47, 51, 53, 62, 68
Chadwick, Sir James, 174
Chamberlain, Austen, 165, 226
Chamberlain, Neville, 165, 208, 209, 302, 304–9,
    320
Champagne offensive (First World War), 47
Cocteau, Jean, 188
Cold War:
  Berlin crisis, 443–44
  colonial wars, 462–63
  diplomacy during, 439–41
  Korean War and, 449–50
  Marshall Plan and, 441–42, 448
  origins of, 437–39

reduction of tensions in, 475–76
  Truman doctrine, 441–42
Collaboration in Second World War, 335–36
Cologne, 394, 424
Colonial empires, liquidation of, 460–69
COMECON (Council for Mutual Economic Aid),
    512–13
Cominform, 442–43
Comintern (see Third International)
Common Market:
  British membership, 531, 568–69
  enlargement of, 535, 568–71, 570
  (map), 588
  origins, 529–31
Compagne, 70, 109, 319
Concentration camps, 232, 235
Concert of Europe, 8, 29
Confessional Church, 235, 429
Congo, 23, 24, 459, 468
Constantine, King of Greece, 52, 564
Constantinople, 53
Consumers, European, growing demands of,
    506–7, 527–29, 540
Contraception, 595–97
Corfu, 52
Corsica, 306
Coventry, 323
Craxi, Bettino, 526, 590

Hughes and Wilkinson, *Contemporary Europe,* p. 603

1. On what page would you find information on the Concert of Europe? _____
2. What are the names of the king of Greece and the king of Romania who are discussed in this book? _____
3. In what war did the Champagne offensive take place? _____
4. What is Chadwick's first name? _____
5. What do the initials COMECON stand for? _____
    _____

EXERCISE 6: Using PQ4R in Longer Selections

Preview

Using the techniques you have learned in this chapter, take one minute to preview the following short reading from a physics textbook. Since there are no headings or subheadings, use the first sentence of each paragraph to become familiar with the subject. Be sure to look at the photograph carefully because it demonstrates the main idea. Also, notice that the author uses signal words, which will help you preview more effectively. After you have finished the preview, answer the following questions. Then check your answers in the back of the book.

1. What is the subject of the selection? _____
2. What is the main idea? _____
3. When does an air bag inflate? _____
4. Will the article talk about how the air bag inflates? _____

Question

Now that you have a good idea of the content and organization of the selection, ask three questions you think will be answered when you read. Answers will vary.

1. _____
2. _____
3. _____

Read

Read to find the answers to your questions and to others you might think of while you read.

The Automobile Air Bag

Air bags are installed on many new cars. The bags, along with seatbelts, are safety devices designed to prevent injuries to passengers in the front seat in automobile collisions. (Back-seat air bags are also available.)

When a car collides with something immovable such as a bridge **abutment,** or has a head-on collision with another vehicle, it stops almost instantaneously. If the front-seat passengers have not "buckled up" (and there are no air bags), they keep moving until acted upon by an external force (Newton's first law). For the driver, force is supplied by the steering wheel and column; for the passenger, by the dashboard and/or the windshield.

support

Even when everyone has buckled up, there can be injuries. Seatbelts absorb energy by stretching, and they spread the force over a wide area to reduce the pressure. However, if a car is going fast enough and hits something truly immovable, there may be too much energy for the seatbelts to absorb. This is where the air bag comes in. The bag inflates automatically on hard impact (Fig. 1), cushioning the driver (and the front-seat passenger if both sides are equipped with air bags). In terms of impulse, the air bag increases the stopping contact time—the fraction of a second it takes your head to sink into the inflated bag is many times longer than the instant in which your head is stopped by the dashboard. A longer contact time means a reduced impact force, and thus much less likelihood of an injury. (The total impact force is also spread over a larger area of the body, so the force on any one part of the body is less.)

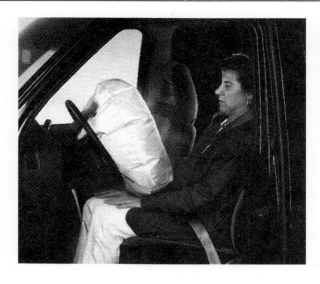

Figure 1 **Impulse** and **safety.** An automobile air bag increases the contact time, thereby decreasing the impulse force that could cause injury.

An interesting point is the inflating mechanism of an air bag. Think of how little time elapses between the front-end impact and the driver hitting the steering column in the collision of a fast-moving automobile. We say such a collision takes place instantaneously, yet during this time the air bag must be inflated! How is this done?

First, the air bag is equipped with sensors that detect the sharp **deceleration** associated with a head-on collision the instant it begins. If the deceleration exceeds the sensors' threshold settings, an electric current in an igniter in the air bag sets off a chemical explosion that **generates** gas to inflate the bag. The complete process from sensing to full inflation takes only on the order of 25 thousandths of a second (0.025 s).

The sensors' signals go first to a control unit, which determines whether a frontal collision is occurring rather than a system **malfunction.** (Accidental **deployment** could be dangerous as well as costly.) Typically, the control unit compares signals from two different sensors for collision verification. The unit is equipped with its own power source, since the car's battery and alternator are usually destroyed in a hard front-end collision. Sensing a collision, the control unit completes the circuit to the air bag igniter. It heats rapidly and initiates a chemical reaction in a sodium azide propellant. Gas (mostly nitrogen) is generated at an explosive rate, which inflates the air bag. The bag itself is made of thin nylon that is covered with cornstarch. The cornstarch acts as a lubricant to help the bag unfold smoothly on inflation.

Air bags offer protection only if the occupants in the front seat are thrown forward, since the bags are designed to **deploy** only in front-end collisions. They are of little use in side-impact crashes. It is therefore essential that, whether or not the car is equipped with air bags, *all* passengers wear their seatbelts at *all* times.

slowing down

creates

mistake
setting in motion

activate

Wilson, *College Physics*, p. 186

Now answer the three questions you asked before you read the article.

1. Answer: _____
2. Answer: _____
3. Answer: _____

EXERCISE 7: **Using PQ4R with a Textbook Selection**

Preview

Using the techniques you have learned in this chapter, take two minutes to preview the following selection from a psychology textbook. Read the headings and sub-headings. When you come to a visual aid, read the caption to find the subject and then look at the table, graph, or picture to discover the main idea. Then check your answers in the back of the book.

1. What is the subject of the selection? _____
    _____

2. What is the main idea of the selection? _____
    _____

3. What indication is there that this selection will discuss the different uses of personal space in different cultures? _____
    _____

4. How many types of interpersonal distance will be discussed? _____

5. According to the picture in the library, how do people protect themselves from having their personal space invaded? _____
    _____

Question

Now that you have a good idea of the content and organization of the selection, ask three questions you think will be answered when you read it. Answers will vary.

1. _____
2. _____
3. _____

Read

Read to find the answers to your questions and to others you might think of while you read. When you are done, answer the questions in the Comprehension Check.

Personal Space

Stephen Worchel and Wayne Shebilske

When we speak of territoriality, we refer to the use of fixed or **tangible** pieces of property that remain even when the person goes away. A number of years ago another type of territorial behavior was identified in humans (Hall, 1959, 1966). After observing people in many cultures, Hall reported that people act as if they "own" the space that directly surrounds them. Hall found that no matter where they are, people maneuver to keep others from trespassing on the area directly surrounding their bodies.

touchable

This area, or *personal space,* is like a bubble surrounding the person wherever he or she goes. Even though we are generally unaware of our spatial behavior, we tend to follow very regular and predictable rules concerning it. The term *proxemics* was coined to describe the study of this personal space.

Hall was most interested in our use of space when we are with other people. He watched people from a number of different cultures interacting in various situations, and concluded that humans use basically four different interaction distances. As can be seen from Table 17–1, the chosen distance is affected by the type of interaction and the relationship between the people involved.

Appropriate Relationships and Activities

Intimate distance (0 to $1\frac{1}{2}$ feet)	Intimate contacts (e.g., making love, comforting) and physical sports (e.g., wrestling)
Personal distance ($1\frac{1}{2}$ to 4 feet)	Contacts between close friends, as well as everyday interactions with acquaintances
Social distance (4 to 12 feet)	Impersonal and businesslike contacts
Public distance (more than 12 feet)	Formal contacts between an individual (e.g., actor, politician) and the public

Table 17–1
Types of Interpersonal Relationships and Activities and Interpersonal Space

The Functions of Interpersonal Distance

It's not hard to see why we claim fixed pieces of property. But why do we need to have a bubble of space around us?

The fact that most interaction distances (except for the intimate distance) are large enough to keep people out of one another's reach led Evans and Howard (1973) to suggest that personal space plays the important function of controlling aggression. Keeping a "neutral zone" between people may **inhibit** physical violence by keeping people apart. For example, Kinzel (1970) found that violent inmates had

limit

larger personal spaces than did nonviolent inmates. The violent prisoners did not trust others, and their large personal space zone served as a **buffer** of protection. It has also been reported that people keep greater distances when they are angry (O'Neal et al., 1980).

area that deadens a shock

The distance at which we interact determines the way we communicate. In order to see this, talk with a friend at the intimate distance (about 12 inches away). What do you see and hear at this distance? In addition to the person's voice, you can also hear his or her breathing. You can see facial details, such as wrinkles and muscle twitches, observe the focus of your friend's eyes, and even spot drops of sweat on his or her forehead. Each of these channels may be used to communicate a message. While you get greater **clarity** from some channels, at the intimate distance you cannot observe your friend's hands, feet, or body posture. Thus, while the intimate distance opens some channels, it closes others. Now try talking at the social distance (5 or 6 feet). At this distance hand and body movements are easily observed, but eye contact is more difficult and you cannot observe small changes in muscle tone.

clearness

Also, we often show the degree of intimacy we feel toward another person by how close we get to that person; we stand closer to people we like than to people we dislike (Argyl & Dean, 1965). You can verify this by putting a larger than normal interaction space between you and a very close friend. The friend's first response may be to "close the gap" between the two of you. However, if you continue to back off, he or she will probably ask, "What's the matter with you. Are you angry at me?"

What Affects Interaction Distances?

What determines how close you get to other people? In some cases, such as in a crowded subway, you have little choice about your distance. However, in most cases, you do determine the space that separates you from others. The nature of the relationship, mood, age, sex, culture, and physical surroundings influence the distance people keep between themselves and others. Let's look at how two variables, culture and sex, influence our personal space.

Culture Background. In his early research into personal space Hall studied people from many cultures. He found that Latin Americans, Arabs, Greeks, and French people interact at closer distances than Americans, Germans, and English people. This information may seem to be only a bit of **trivia,** but there is an amusing story, often called the "Latin Waltz," that shows why such cultural differences can be important. The story involves two men, one from Mexico and one from the United States, who met at a party. As their conversation progressed, the Mexican moved closer to his new acquaintance in order to establish a "comfortable" interaction distance. The American, however, quickly felt uneasy with this close distance, and moved back-

unimportant detail

ward to establish a spacing that was comfortable for him. This backward movement brought the Mexican charging in to close the gap between them. Like two dancers in perfect step, the conversationalists waltzed around the room. Neither was trying to be impolite and neither was even conscious of his behavior. Each was simply trying to establish a distance that was comfortable for him.

It's funny to imagine two men dancing around the room, but cultural differences in spatial behavior can have important consequences. In many large cities people from different cultural backgrounds interact on a daily basis. Differences in language and customs can sometimes make these meetings difficult or stressful (Worchel & Cooper, 1983). There is additional discomfort if people must silently battle for comfortable interaction distances. Further, since most people are unaware of their spatial behavior, they are likely to have a difficult time realizing the real source of stress in these cross-cultural encounters.

Sex.   It seems that somewhere in our early learning of how to be a boy or girl, there is a lesson on spatial behavior, and that lesson appears to be different for each sex. The most generally observed sex difference is that females have a smaller personal space than do males (Aiello & Aiello, 1974; Heckel & Hiers, 1977). Also, mixed-sex pairs interact at closer distances than do same-sex pairs (see Figure 17–2).

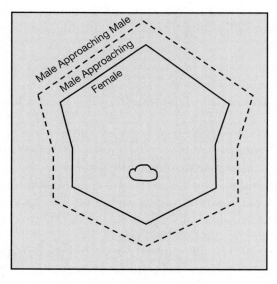

Figure 17–2. Personal space zones tend to be egg-shaped rather than neat round bubbles.

Horwitz et al., *Personal Space,* 1964

There is one interesting exception to this rule: When women start an interaction with a stranger, they keep a greater distance from a man than from a woman (Dosey & Meisels, 1969). As we have seen, intimacy can be communicated by spacing, and it is likely that women are especially careful not to communicate nonexistent feelings of attraction to a strange man. A similar line of reasoning has been used to explain why men have greater interaction distances in same-sex **dyads**   **pairs** than do women. Hall (1966) points out that in Western societies taboos against male homosexuality are strongly stressed, and as a result men are particularly sensitive about "keeping their distance" when interacting with other men.

In addition to distance, there seem to be another page in the lesson book on sex and spatial behavior. Imagine yourself seated at an uncrowded library table, minding your own business, when suddenly a stranger takes a seat too close to you. The stranger invades your personal space by taking either the seat next to you or the seat opposite you. Which type of invasion would make you more uncomfortable? Byrne and his colleagues (1971) found that men reacted more negatively to frontal invasions, while women were most upset by invasions from the side. In an interesting observation related to this finding, Fisher and Byrne (1975) found that when men sat down at a library table they most often placed their personal belongings on the table in front of them. This acted as a barrier against frontal invasions. Women, on the other hand, placed their belongings in adjacent chairs, thus ensuring against invasions from the side.

People go to great lengths to protect their personal space from intrusion. In libraries people may build a barricade of books and personal belongings to keep others at a distance. Men generally are most concerned with protecting the frontal space, while women guard the space to their sides.

Responses to Invasion of Personal Space

You may want to try the following experiment—it won't win friends, but it will show something about what it means to violate someone's personal space. During a conversation slowly move closer to your companion; if the other person retreats, continue your charge. How does the other person respond to this?

The most common response is likely to be stress. The other person will probably feel tense and uncomfortable and you may observe some fidgeting (Worchell & Teddlie, 1976). What you cannot observe is the "internal fidgeting" your attack is likely to set off. Your victim's heart rate and blood pressure will increase and muscles are likely to become **taut** (McBride et al., 1965).

tight

Another common response is flight: Your victim is likely to move away from you. This reaction was dramatically demonstrated by Sommer (1969) in a university library setting. When a female seated alone at a table was spotted, an experimenter approached and took a seat immediately next to the unsuspecting subject. In 70 percent of these cases the subject had left the table within a 30-minute period after the intruder arrived. In a control condition where there was no invasion of the area, only 10 percent of the subjects abandoned their table in the same time period.

If your own victim does not flee or if you're successful enough to maneuver him or her into a corner where flight is impossible, you should begin to see blocking movements. Earlier we discussed the fact that close distance communicates intimacy. Researchers reported that a number of other nonverbal behaviors also communicate intimacy (Argyle & Dean, 1965). For example, you can signal that you like other people by maintaining eye contact with them, leaning toward them, and facing them directly rather than placing your folded arms or shoulders between them and you. According to Argyle and Dean, all of these channels are used together to signal the degree of intimacy you wish to have. In fact, they form an **equilibrium** system so that too much intimacy in one channel can be compensated for by reducing intimacy in other channels. Thus, if you move into other people's personal space, which signals intimacy, their response might well be to reduce eye contact or turn their bodies away from you ("giving the cold shoulder"). In order to show this, Argyle and Dean had subjects converse with a confederate at distances of 2, 6, or 10 feet. As can be seen in Figure 17–3, the closer the subjects were to the confederate, the less eye contact they maintained (Argyle & Dean, 1965).

balance

Finally, you will probably find that your inappropriate closeness to another person is likely to cause him or her to dislike you. This reaction has ben found even in situations where the violation was not deliberate. One exception to this finding occurs when people interpret the violation as a sign of friendliness on the part of the invader (Schneider & Harsuick, 1979).

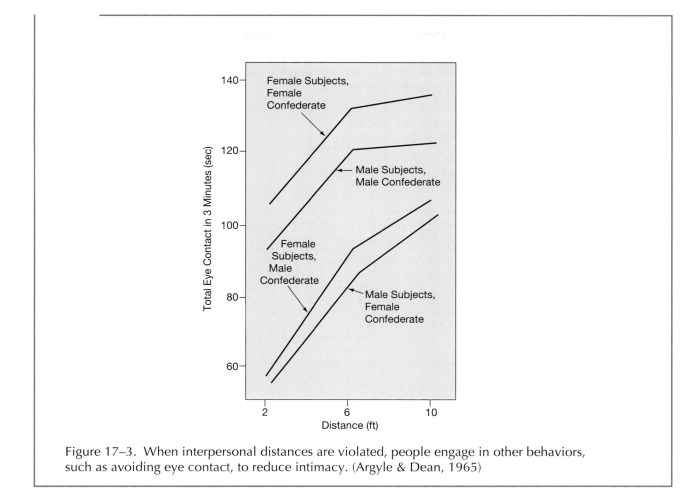

Figure 17–3. When interpersonal distances are violated, people engage in other behaviors, such as avoiding eye contact, to reduce intimacy. (Argyle & Dean, 1965)

Now answer the three questions you asked before you read the article.

1.   Answer _____

2.   Answer _____

3.   Answer _____

Review

Because this section is not a complete chapter, we will omit the Review Step. If you were studying the whole chapter, you would use the Review Step at the end of your study session to pull the sections together. Now take the following Comprehension Check.

Comprehension Check

Circle the letter preceding the correct answer. Then check your answers in the back of the book.

1. We tend to
   a. be aware of our spatial behavior.
   b. change our conception of our body bubble with age.
   c. follow regular and predictable rules concerning our personal space.
   d. understand proxemics.

2. The space that is $1\frac{1}{2}$ to 4 feet from a person is called
   a. public distance.
   b. personal distance.
   c. intimate distance.
   d. social distance.

3. The amount of personal space you feel comfortable with
   a. depends on where and with whom you are.
   b. is fairly consistent no matter where you are.
   c. is based on fixed or tangible pieces of property around you.
   d. is about five inches in front and back of you.

4. People from which culture tend to stand closest to one another?
   a. American
   b. English
   c. Latin American
   d. German

5. The main idea of the article is that
   a. personal space is a method of communication.
   b. we still act like other animals.
   c. we would be aggressive if we didn't maintain a body bubble around us.
   d. recognizing and understanding personal space is important to understanding human behavior.

6. Hall's studies
   a. are widely disbelieved by others.
   b. pioneered the area of personal space.
   c. dealt with animal and human behavior.
   d. were conducted only on Americans.

7. If you were studying in the library and someone you did not know sat next to you, according to Hall's research, you would probably
   a. begin a conversation.
   b. place your books in front of the person to make him or her move.
   c. get up and leave within a short time if you are a woman.
   d. begin a fight if you are a man.

8. A person moving to the United States from Greece would probably
   a. find Americans standing uncomfortably close during conversations.
   b. appear shy to Americans.
   c. adjust quickly to the differences in personal space.
   d. see Americans as standoffish.

9. Name the four areas of space that are like a bubble around a person, starting with the closest. _____   _____
   _____   _____

10. Define proxemics. _____

_____.

Questions For Discussion and Writing

1. Now that the United States is more multicultural in its population than ever, what problems could arise in business and social situations because of differing concepts of personal space? _____

_____

2. What specifically have you learned in this article that you can apply to your own life?_____

_____

3. How will our increasing population be affected by the impact of proxemics?_____

_____

4. What will be the effects of more immigrants and tourists coming to the United States? What possible adjustments in attitudes will likely occur and in which groups? _____

_____

EXERCISE 8: Skills Review—Main Idea and Support

Read the article and fill in the items below.

Health Watch

Flu—The Unbeatable Bug

Every winter, a wave of influenza sweeps across the world. Thousands of the elderly, the newborn, and those already suffering from illness **succumb,** while hundreds of millions more suffer the fever and muscle aches of milder cases. Occasionally, devastating flu varieties appear. In the great flu **pandemic** of 1918, the worldwide toll was 20 million dead in one winter. In 1968, Hong Kong flu infected 50 million Americans, causing 70,000 deaths in 6 weeks. As recently as the winter of 1984–85, the Centers of Disease Control estimated that about 57,000 Americans died from the flu.

give in

epidemic

The Flu Virus

Flu is caused by a virus that invades the cells of the respiratory tract, turning each one into a factory for manufacturing new viruses.

The outer surface of the virus is studded with proteins, several of which serve as **antigens** recognized by the immune system. People survive the flu because their immune systems inactivate the viruses or kill off virus-infected body cells before the viruses finish reproducing. This is the same mechanism by which other viruses, such as mumps or measles, are conquered. So why don't people become immune to the flu, as they do to measles?

substance stimulating antibodies

The answer lies in the flu virus' uncanny ability to change. The viral genes that code for the antigenic proteins **mutate** rapidly: there are 10 mutations in every million newly synthesized viruses. A single mutation usually doesn't change the properties of the antigen very much. Four or five, however, may change it enough so that the immune system doesn't fully recognize it as the same old flu that was beaten off last year. Some of the memory cells don't recognize it at all, and the immune response produced by the rest doesn't work as well as it should. The virus, although slowed down somewhat, gets a foothold in the body and multiplies until a new set of immune cells recognizes the mutated antigen and starts up a new immune response. And so you get the flu again this year.

change

Audersirk and Audersirk, *Biology: Life on Earth*, p. 738

I. (main idea) _____

   A. _____

      1. _____

      2. _____

      3. _____

   B. _____

      1. _____

      2. _____

      3. _____

      4. _____

Reading Textbooks II: Write, Recall, Review

5

Reading Textbooks II: Write, Recall, Review

  I. Write
      A. Underlining
      B. Making marginal notes
      C. Applying the Writing Step
  II. Recall
      A. PQ4R method
      B. Supplemental recall methods
          1. Outlining
          2. Flash cards
          3. Study maps
          4. Other self-generated graphics
 III. Review
 IV. Studying other assigned reading materials
  V. Summary

5

In Chapter 4 you learned the first three steps of PQ4R—Preview, Question, and Read. This chapter will teach you the last three steps—Write, Recall, and Review. The Preview and Review Steps are done on whole chapters; the Question, Read, Write, and Recall Steps are done on sections of chapters.

As an experiment, read the following paragraph. Then underline and make notes as you would in a textbook. Later in this chapter you will have an opportunity to analyze your technique.

Divorce

The ending of any intimate relationship is painful. *Divorce,* the legal termination of a marriage, is especially so, because marriage merges two lives on many levels of experience. For some individuals, divorce is an unbearable personal defeat; for others, the termination of an unsatisfactory marriage represents an opportunity for personal growth. Whatever its emotional impact, divorce inevitably presents a series of practical and social problems: the division of property, the establishment of new living quarters for at least one of the partners, the setting forth of financial obligations, the working through of emotional responsibilities toward any children, and the simultaneous adjustment to a single status.

La Place, *Health,* p. 235

Write

Underlining

The two ways of marking a textbook are underlining (or highlighting) and making marginal notes. Many students underline too much: they underline whole paragraphs or sometimes a full page. Some students go to the other extreme, marking only the words in boldface or italics. Neither method serves the purpose of underlining, which is to provide a quick way of reviewing so that you don't have to reread the whole book when studying for a test. If you underline 10 percent of your book, then you will save yourself from rereading 90 percent of the material. You shouldn't underline more than 20 percent of a book or article unless the material is highly technical.

After you've previewed the chapter, asked questions, read the section, and answered the questions, you are ready to mark the book. First, underline the main ideas. Second, underline key supporting details, such as statistics and examples, if you think they will appear on a test. If you don't think they will be on a test, don't underline them. Complete sentences shouldn't be underlined; underline key words only. When you have finished underlining, read what you've marked to see if it makes sense.

Making Marginal Notes

In addition to underlining, it is also useful to make notes in textbooks. Put question marks next to passages you don't understand. Put asterisks (*) next to the most important passages. Then write other notes to yourself. Note any disagreement you have with the author; refer to material you have read elsewhere; note examples from your experience and predictions of what might be on a test. Notes in a textbook should be brief. As with underlining, do not write any notes until you have thoroughly read and understood a section.

When you have finished marking your textbook, write down any specific questions you have about the material. If there is any specialized vocabulary that you want to remember, write the words and their definitions on flash cards.

Now, go back and in the margin write short notes to remind you of the main ideas you need to remember. You will use these notes as questions in the Recall Step for self-testing. Don't write the main idea; write only the subject you want to remember and use it to test your memory of the main ideas and related details.

Applying the Writing Step

We have underlined and noted the sample selection that follows. First, read the underlining only. Then read the selection and note how little material needs to be underlined to capture the main idea.

The Right to Profits

Profits may be defined as the excess of income over costs and other expenses. The **lure** of profits is the key to the effectiveness of a **capitalistic** society. Under a capitalistic economic system, prestige   **temptation** and comforts—in short, the good life—are keyed to earning power, because profits earned belong to the individual earning them. This **incentive,** coupled with the freedom to freely choose one's economic   **motivation**

critics

life, provides an individual with the incentive to improve efficiency and increase production as a means of increasing his earning capability. Thus, we have a society of individuals, each striving to improve his position in life. How interesting that the result of this individualized self-interest results in a national economy whose production of goods and services is second to none and whose citizens enjoy a standard of living far beyond that offered by any competitive system. Our **detractors** are many and much of their criticism is well-directed, but it is likely that the fault is not with the economic system, but with its political application.

Diamond and Pintel *Introduction to Contemporary Business,* p. 6

Each marginal note mentions a subject (profits, capitalistic system, national economy, problems) and specifies what information about the subject is needed (definition, function, effect, source). This two-part format makes it easy to use the notes for self-testing.

Now that you are familiar with this system of underlining and making marginal notes, turn to the beginning of this chapter and correct any of the underlining and note-taking that you did. When you finish, compare your sample with ours.

Divorce

Def. of divorce

Reactions to divorce

Ex. of problems

The ending of any intimate relationship is painful. *Divorce,* the legal termination of a marriage, is especially so, because marriage merges two lives on many levels of experience. For some individuals, divorce is an unbearable personal defeat; for others, the termination of an unsatisfactory marriage represents an opportunity for personal growth. Whatever its emotional impact, divorce inevitably presents a series of practical and social problems: the division of property, the establishment of new living quarters for at least one of the partners, the setting forth of financial obligations, the working through of emotional responsibilities toward any children, and the simultaneous adjustment to a single status.

La Place, *Health,* p. 235

There is no single perfect method of underlining and making marginal notes. However, if you underlined either a great deal more or a great deal less than we did, you may have underlined too much or too little to study effectively for a test. If, you did not have a marginal note where we put one, you may have missed an important major idea. If you had more marginal notes than we had, it may not be a problem here but in a textbook chapter it could decrease the amount of material you could recall during a test. Too many marginal notes could result in your remembering less because you had too many clues to the underlining. Remember, the purpose of underlining and making marginal notes is to find the most important information and organize it. You don't have to underline exactly what we underlined or use the same words in the marginal notes, but our samples reflect the thinking of many students and instructors who participated in field testing of all of the subjective answers in this text. Therefore, the answers provide a strong guide for efficient studying.

If someone asked us which was the most useful study skill we learned in college, we would answer **organizing.** Organization doesn't come naturally; people don't normally think in an organized manner. Ideas come haphazardly, seemingly without relation to anything else. And although our thoughts may be clear to us, they cannot easily be communicated to anyone else, either in speech or in writing, as long as they remain in a disorganized form. However, the PQ4R technique is only one way to find the author's organization pattern. You can arrange the raw material in several different ways using other forms of graphic organizers.

Recall

The Recall Step tests your understanding and strengthens your memory of what you have read. There are a number of techniques you can use during this step. These include visual aids using text only, such as covering a page and looking at self-test notes, making outlines, and making flash cards. Other visual aids use both text and graphics. These include study maps and self-generated graphs. (Chapter 4 discussed the various types of graphs you might choose to make.)

Taking Time Now Will Save Time Later

Testing yourself is much quicker than rereading the whole section two or three times and still not being sure you understand it. If you can't understand and/or remember what you read immediately after reading it, there is very little chance that you will remember it for a test. The more memorization of details the course requires, the more time you should spend on the Recall Step.

Covering a Page and Self-Testing (the Recall Step of PQ4R)

First, cover the page in your book and look only at your self-test notes. Use each note to test your memory of the main ideas and important details. Next, check what you remembered against the underlining in the book, jotting down any topics you missed. Continue testing yourself until you can recall all the important points.

EXERCISE 1: Underlining and Making Marginal Notes

In each of the following paragraphs, underline what you believe you would have to memorize for a test. Then write a marginal self-test note in the margin.

A. Astronomical evidence supports the theory, called the *Big Bang,* that the universe began perhaps as long as twenty billion years ago when a dense, hot, supermassive concentration of material exploded with **cataclysmic** force. Within about one second, the tem-   **disastrous**

basic

change

perature of the expanding universe cooled to approximately 10 billion degrees and **fundamental** atomic particles called protons and neutrons began to appear. After a few minutes, atoms of the least complex elements—hydrogen and helium—had formed and the initial **conversion** of energy to matter in the young universe was over.

Kenneth Pinzke in Tarbuck and Lutgens, *Earth Science*, p. 6

Check your answers for Paragraph A in Appendix A before going to Paragraph B. Analyze any differences.

government

absolute control

belief system

B. The year 1789 is one of the great milestones of modern history, for it marked the beginning of the revolution in the most powerful state on the Continent of Europe. The revolutionary motto—Liberté, Egalité, Fraternité ("Liberty, Equality, Fraternity")—seemed to promise a new democratic **regime.** What it actually provided was a republic dependent first on the Reign of Terror, then on the less terrible but less democratic Directory, and finally on the **autocracy** of Napoleon, who transformed the First Republic into the First Empire. His determination to dominate the whole of Europe led to his ultimate defeat and the restoration of the Bourbons. But by then the **ideology** of liberty, equality, fraternity had attracted so many supporters not only in France but also among victims of the French expansion that a full restoration of the Old Regime was impossible.

Brinton, Christopher, and Wolff, *Civilization in the West,* p. 350

Check your answers for Paragraph B in Appendix A before going to Paragraph C. Analyze any differences.

withdrawal

disorder

family

C. The 1920s and 1930s saw increasing numbers of women going to college and seeking gainful employment afterward. World War II brought a tremendous demand for labor, and women gained a major foothold in industry. By 1950, 34 percent of all adult women were in the labor force. After the war, however, there was a period of **retrenchment.** People sought relief from the **turmoil** of the depression of the 1930s and the war years of the early 1940s in a return to **familistic** values. While two children had been the norm before the war, couples now wanted three, four, or even five. The symbolic phrase of the day was "togetherness," and the suburban housewife became the model American woman.

Horton et. al. *The Sociology of Social Problems,* p. 251

Check your answers for Paragraph C in Appendix A. Analyze any differences.

Supplemental Recall Methods

There are times when you cannot remember the material you think is important by just reviewing your underlining and marginal notes. At these times you may need to supplement your recall techniques by using outlining, flash cards, study maps, or other types of graphics. Each of these methods will be discussed in this section. We will only discuss each technique as it relates to reading and remembering for tests. In other chapters, we will discuss these as aids to note-taking, taking essay tests and writing papers. Just as there is not one definite way of underlining or making a set of marginal notes, one type of supplemental review method is not superior to another. Which one you choose will depend on your learning style and the nature of the material you are trying to remember. Also, remember that there is no single correct way of outlining, making flash cards, designing studying maps or creating other types of graphics. Our samples are just that, samples. Yours may differ but be as helpful to you. The important thing is to capture all of the information you need to remember in a logical manner.

Outlining

Outlining is extremely valuable for understanding difficult material and recalling information for tests because it places ideas in a visual relationship to one another. Look at the outline that follows. It is a picture of an organizational pattern. It lets you see the relationships between ideas by putting all of the major ideas under one type of heading (Roman numerals) and supporting ideas under the other symbols (A, B, C). Any detailed support for those ideas appear under that idea but further indented and with other symbols (1, 2, 3). The outline of the paragraph makes obvious in a visual way the relationships between the ideas in the paragraph. Since it adds a visual image to the organization, some students find material in outline form easier to recall. It depends on your learning style.

The following is an outline of the paragraph on *Divorce* located on p. 106. Go back and look at the paragraph to see the underlining and marginal notes.

Divorce

  I. Definition of divorce
     A. Legal termination of marriage
     B. Ending of the merging of two lives on many different levels
 II. Reaction to divorce
     A. Personal defeat
     B. Opportunity for personal growth
III. Practical and social problems
     A. Division of property
     B. New living quarters
     C. Emotional responsibilities toward children
     D. Adjustment to single status

Notice the similarities between the marginal notes and the statements after the Roman numerals (I, II, III). Also you will see that most of the underlined ideas are on the outline under the capital letters (A, B, C, D). This is a typical two-level outline.

Look at the outline again to help answer the questions below. You will find the answers within the next section: "Rules of Outlining."

1. What do the Roman numerals represent? _____
   _____

2. How do you know that the ideas after the capital letters are less important than the ones after the Roman numerals? _____
   _____

3. If you have Roman numeral I what else must you have? _____
   If you have a capital A, what must you also have?_____
4. How many ideas should each point on an outline have? _____
5. What is the purpose of the title of an outline?_____
   _____

Rules of Outlining

1. The different levels in an outline are indicated by different symbols and by how close to the left-hand margin they are. The farther an idea is to the right, the less important it is. In a formal outline major ideas are indicated by Roman numerals (I, II, III). However, the symbols you choose for different levels are not as important as using the same type of symbol (I, A, or 1) for other equally important ideas. The same is true for how much you indent. In most cases, it doesn't matter if you indent two or five spaces, but it is important that equal ideas (shown by similar symbols) are equally indented.

2. Each heading in an outline should contain only one idea. For example, take the sentence from the paragraph on divorce: "For some individuals divorce is an unbearable personal defeat; others the termination of an unsatisfactory marriage represents an opportunity for personal growth." If we were to outline this sentence, we would give these two ideas separate headings *A. Unbearable defeat* and *B. Opportunity for personal growth.*

3. All subheadings must relate to the main heading of which they are a part. For instance, you wouldn't put a subheading on *Opportunity for personal growth* under the heading for *Problems.*

4. Whenever you make a heading or a subheading, you must make at least one more at the same level. For example, you can't have a I without a II, or an A without a B.

5. Each point in an outline should be written as a statement, not as a question. The statements in an outline can be phrases (just the subject) or full sentences. Most of the time, using the shortest phrase possible or even abbreviations makes an outline easier to remember. For example, you could write, "4 post-divorce problems or "There are 4 post-divorce problems." However, an outline would never have questions such as "What are the 4 post-divorce problems?" In addition, you should not mix phrases and sentences in the same outline.

6. Make sure that you indent correctly and put a period after each Roman numeral, letter, or number.
7. Capitalize the first letter of the first word in each heading and sub-heading.
8. Every outline should have a title which serves the same purpose as a title for a paragraph. It summarizes the information that follows.

Outlining Ideas

You already know a great deal about organizing ideas from the discussion of main ideas in Chapter 2. In identifying the subject of a paragraph, its main idea, and the support for the main idea, you use the same skills that are needed for outlining. Some ideas are more important than others. For instance, of the two categories *fruit* and *apple,* fruit is broader; apple is more specific since it's a type of fruit. Therefore, you can describe the relationship between fruit and apple as follows:

I. Fruit
   A. Apple

Apple is subordinate to fruit. In another type of relationship, both concepts are of equal importance. For example, you could outline the relationship between fruits and vegetables like this:

I. Fruits
II. Vegetables

The outline below has three levels.

I. North America (broad or general idea)
   A. United States (subpoint of 1)
      1. Texas (subpoint of A)

Texas is part of the United States, which is part of North America.

Now that you understand the principles of outlining, arrange the following words on the outline provided. Then look at the answers that follow.

History	I. _____
Business	A. _____
College subjects	1. _____
American history	2. _____
European history	B. _____
Accounting	1. _____
Typing	2. _____

Answers: The broadest category, I, should have been *College subjects.* *History* and *Business* could have been either A or B. Under *History* you should have written *American history* and *European history* (in either order), and under *Business* you should have written *Accounting* and *Typing* (in either order).

Now that you can organize a list on an outline we provided, fill in the missing parts of the following outlines that are partially completed. After you have finished all of the examples, check your answers with the ones which follow.

1.   I.   Parts of a computer system
        A.   Processor (also called the "computer")
        B.   _____
        C.   Monitor
        D.   Printer

2.   I.   Areas of mathematics
        A.   _____
        B.   Geometry
        C.   Trigonometry
        D.   _____

3.   I.   Types of pollution
        A.   _____
        B.   Land
        C.   _____

4.   I.   First four steps in PQ4R
        A.   _____
        B.   Question
        C.   _____
        D.   Write
           1.   _____
           2.   Marginal notes

Answers: In the first example, the missing part of the computer system is the *Keyboard,* in Example 2, *Algebra* and *Calculus* are the missing areas of mathematics; in Example 3, the broadest category is *Types of pollution* while the answers for the two blanks are *Air pollution* and *Water pollution;* in Example 4, the missing steps are *Preview* and *Read* and the blank under the Write Step should be *Underlining.*

Outlining Paragraphs

Just as some words are broader than others, there are also levels of generality among phrases and sentences. Within a paragraph, a sentence may state or imply the subject of the paragraph or the main idea of the paragraph (the author's statement about the subject), or it may give details that support the main idea. A sentence that contains all or part of a main idea is broader than one that contains supporting details. The most important sentences are usually at the beginning of a paragraph, but they may also be found in the middle or at the end. In the following examples, put I before the more important sentence; put A before the more specific one. (In some cases, both sentences are equally important; indicate this by writing I and II before the sentences.)

Following is a paragraph on magic and a partially filled-in outline for you to complete. After you have finished, compare your answers with ours which follow.

Magic for Entertainment

Magic for entertainment can be divided into several classes. Close-up magic involves tricks with small objects such as coins and cards, and can be performed right under the audience's nose. Because the objects are small, close-up magic is meant for groups of 25 or fewer people. Cabaret magic, which is traditionally done in nightclubs, involves tricks with slightly larger objects such as scarves, top hats, and small animals. Cabaret magic is usually performed for audiences of fewer than 100 people. Stage magic involves large tricks such as sawing a person in half, producing an elephant, or making a piano float. Stage magic can be performed before thousands of people at a time.

J. Lenier for *Keys to College Success*

Magic for Entertainment

I. Close-up magic
   A. Involves small objects
   B. _____
II. _____
   A. Done in nightclubs
   B. _____
   C. Audiences of fewer than 100 people
III. Stage magic
   A. _____
   B. Audiences up to thousands

Answers: After I.B. you should have written *25 people or fewer.* After II. you should have written *Cabaret magic.* After II.B. you should have written *Slightly larger objects.* After III. A. you should have written *Large tricks.*

Read the following paragraph on the American Revolution and fill in the outline that follows. Look for signal words to use as clues. Then check your answers in the back of the book.

Causes of the American Revolutionary War

One cause of the Revolutionary War was the ethical question of independence from England. A more important cause was the economic advantage of not having to ship colonial goods to and from England for distribution. For example, the Navigation Act of 1660 ensured England's **monopoly** over colonial exports by requiring that goods be transported on British ships and that certain products be shipped only to England. Also, the Staple Act of 1663 required that

total control

most non-English goods bound for America be shipped through England, where they were taxed and put on English ships.

Adapted from Bruner et. al. *America,* pp. 102–111

Causes of the American Revolutionary War

I. _____

II. Economic issue of shipping more

    A. _____

        1. Exports must go on British ships

        2. _____

    B. Staple Act of 1663

        1. Non-English imports shipped via England

        2. Non-English imports taxed

        3. _____

Answers: I. *Ethical question of independence.* II. A. *Navigation Act of 1660: England's monopoly.* II. A. 2. *Certain exports must go to England.* II. B. 3. *Non-English imports on English ships only.*

EXERCISE 2: Outlining Paragraphs

When a reading selection has a title, the title is usually the subject of the selection. The paragraphs in this exercise do not have titles. In these paragraphs there is only one major idea; therefore, it would be the same as the main idea. Write the main idea of the paragraph on the line after Roman numeral I. Then write the supporting details on the lines underneath. When you have finished outlining all of the paragraphs, check your answers in the back of the book.

strong

1. A recent study of Stanford University Medical School suggests that people who engage in **vigorous** exercise, such as jogging six miles a day, can eat about 600 calories more than people who don't exercise, and that they weigh about 20 percent less. This is partly because exercise uses up calories. But even more important, it seems that exercise causes the body to burn calories at a faster rate for up to fifteen hours afterward. In other words, your body "idles" faster after the exercise is over, even if you are sleeping.

    I. _____

        A. _____

        B. _____

2. Sea gulls have interesting courtship habits. When a female gull spots an attractive single male, she struts back and forth, fluttering her tail feathers. If he does not drive her away, she nuzzles him and pecks at his bill. At first he holds back, but she doesn't give up. Finally he signals his surrender. He throws up.

I. _____
   A. _____
   B. _____
   C. _____
   D. _____

3. Glaciers, rivers of slowly moving ice, can take several forms. Three of the most common types are valley glaciers, piedmont glaciers, and ice sheets. Valley glaciers, also called mountain glaciers or Alpine glaciers flow down the valleys between mountains. Piedmont glaciers form when two or more valley glaciers joint together at the bottom to form a sheet of moving ice on the plains below. Ice sheets are shaped like mounds and spread out because of the pressure of their own weight. Small ice sheets are called ice caps, and huge ones that cover large sections of a continent are called continental glaciers.

I. _____
   A. _____
   B. _____
   C. _____
      1. _____
      2. _____

EXERCISE 3: Outlining Longer Paragraphs

Read the selection and then complete the outline that follows. Then check your answers in the back of the book.

The Beginnings of Chemistry

The many areas under investigation by chemists today reflect the explosion of interest in and understanding of chemical processes. Some of these processes have been known for a long time. For example, the ancient Egyptians and Chinese were well acquainted with the process of fermentation in the production of alcoholic beverages. Some of the foundations of modern chemistry trace back to the early Greeks and Arabs. Democritus (about 460–370 B.C.), a Greek, proposed a theory on the atomic structure of substances that **preceded** — came before — John Dalton's atomic theory by 2200 years. Al-Khowarizmi, an Arab mathematician, devised the number zero in about A.D. 825, providing the mathematical expression so essential to modern science. In the Medieval period, European alchemists experimented endlessly in a **fruitless** — useless — attempt to turn lead and other common metals into gold. Only recently, in the twentieth century, have scientists been able to **transform** — change — platinum to gold (at great cost).

supported

Two of the most important names in the founding of chemistry as a science are Robert Boyle (1627–1691) and Antoine Laurent Lavoisier (1743–1794). Boyle strongly **advocated** experimentation in the search for knowledge. Boyle's study of the effect of pressure on the volume of a gas is an example of the scientific method. Lavoisier is often considered the father of the science of chemistry. He demonstrated that combustion is the result of the combination of a fuel with oxygen from the air. Lavoisier used the scientific method to reveal that the popular theory of combustion was wrong and opened the door to a new way of looking at substances.

Seese and Daub, *Basic Chemistry*, p. 6

The Beginnings of Chemistry

I. Pre-chemists
   A. Egyptians and Chinese—Process of fermentation in making alcohol
   B. _____
      1. Democritus (about 460–370 B.C.)—a theory of atomic structure
      2. Al-Khowarizmi (A.D. 825)—the number zero
   C. _____
II. Early chemistry
   A. _____
      1. Advocated experimentation in search of knowledge
      2. Used scientific method—the effect of pressure on the volume of gas
   B. _____
      1. Father of chemistry
      2. _____
      3. Used scientific method to prove old theory of combustion wrong
      4. Opened door to new way of looking at substances

Flash Cards

If you find that you cannot recall all that you need to remember using the PQ4R Recall Step, you may find it useful to make flash cards. They are especially good to use for detailed information that demands almost word for word recall such as definitions of terms, formulas, and dates. Flash cards can be used for extra review on information you have difficulty remembering from your marginal notes and underlining. For instance, if you need to memorize the capitals of the United States, you could write each state on the front and the capital on the back. Then, you could eliminate the ones you know and study only those that you need to learn.

They could even be used for a small outline or as cue cards on marginal notes. They have some unique advantages. First, they provide a method whereby you can do multiple reviews of small amounts of information. They are light and easy to carry so that you can review their information whenever and wherever you have time. Third, flash cards help you focus your review periods on what you still do not remember. You can easily remove information that you no longer need to review by removing the appropriate flash card. Finally, you can mix the cards so that you are not always reviewing the information in the same order.

You can use flash cards when you find there are certain marginal notes that don't remind you of the underlining. Here is an example from the paragraph on the *Beginnings of Chemistry.*

Front   Back

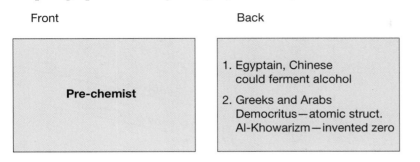

Pre-chemist

1. Egyptain, Chinese could ferment alcohol

2. Greeks and Arabs Democritus—atomic struct. Al-Khowarizm—invented zero

It is a good idea to put two types of self-test items on flash cards. As you review your notes and your textbook, pay attention to any terms or concepts in your self-test column that you think you will not remember, such as *the definition of invertebrates* or *names of the instruments in a symphonic orchestra.* Put the self-test on the front of a flash card and the answer on the back, noting the page of the textbook or the date of the lecture from which it came, as in the following sample:

Front   Back

def. of invertebrate

A living creature lacking a backbone or spine ex. insects/mollusk

In addition to self-test items, test yourself on broader ideas that you think might appear on a test. These ideas might combine several pages of self-test columns into a few major topics, such as the *similarities* and *differences between two stories by O. Henry* or *causes of the Industrial Revolution.* Here is an example:

Front   Back

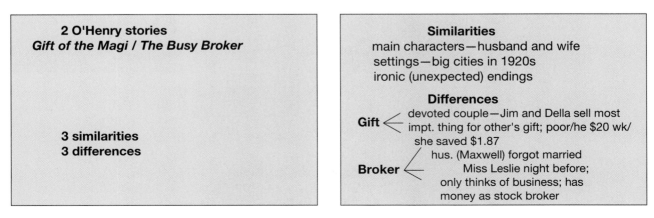

2 O'Henry stories
Gift of the Magi / The Busy Broker

3 similarities
3 differences

Similarities
main characters—husband and wife
settings—big cities in 1920s
ironic (unexpected) endings

Differences
Gift ⟨ devoted couple—Jim and Della sell most impt. thing for other's gift; poor/he $20 wk/ she saved $1.87
hus. (Maxwell) forgot married Miss Leslie night before;
Broker ⟨ only thinks of business; has money as stock broker

Study Maps

Another method of presenting ideas visually so that they are easy to remember is creating a study map. You begin a study map by drawing a circle ○ in the middle of a blank piece of paper. Then you draw a line outward for each major idea. Minor ideas are put on lines from each major idea. A simple study map might look like this. As an example we have mapped a paragraph you have already read (See page 115).

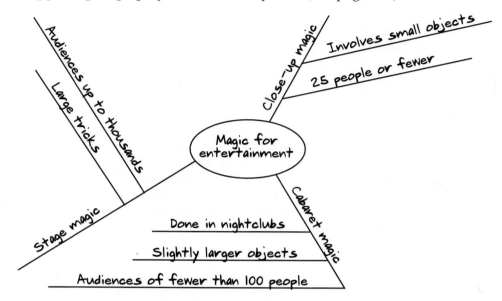

The more complex a subject is, the more you will find different symbols helpful. An outline uses I, II, III to show the major ideas. We suggest rectangles ☐ on your study map. An outline uses A, B, C for the next level of ideas. We suggest using a triangle △ on a study map. You can make these even more memorable by making the circle the biggest symbol, the rectangles a little smaller, etc.

Another way to make a study map more memorable is to make each set of symbols in a different color. See how different the study map below looks from the one in black and white.

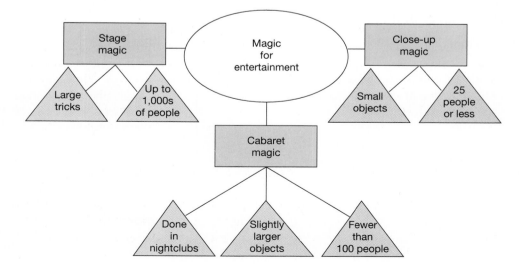

Next, you will complete a study map based on the following paragraph on which you have already done underlining, made marginal notes, and created an outline. This will give you the opportunity to compare the three review techniques.

Causes of the American Revolutionary War

One cause of the Revolutionary War was the ethical question of independence from England. A more important cause was the economic advantage of not having to ship colonial goods to and from England for distribution. For example, the Navigation Act of 1660 ensured England's monopoly over colonial exports by requiring that goods be transported on British ships and that certain products be shipped only to England. Also, the Staple Act of 1663 required that most non-English goods bound for America be shipped through England, where they were taxed and put on English ships.

Adapted from Bruner et. al. *America,* p. 102–111

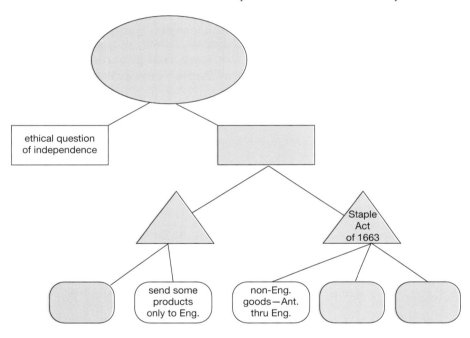

Answers: In the circle should be the title "Causes of the American Revolutionary War." The subject has two major subdivisions; in the blank rectangle should be "Economic issue of shipping more important." This subtopic is further divided into two subtitles. The blank triangle should be *Navigation Act of 1660*. This last area is again subdivided. The missing one is *Certain exports must go to England.* The second subdivision of *Economic issues more important, Staple Act of 1663,* has three subdivisions; the missing ones are *"Non-English imports taxed",* and *"Non-English imports on English ships only."*

Now compare the completed map with the outline you completed on page 116. The relationships between the ideas are the same.

Organizing ideas is a crucial skill for reading, memorizing, taking tests, making notes, and making oral or written reports. Outlining and mapping are efficient ways of organizing ideas because they give visible form to the relationships between the ideas.

Some words, phrases, and paragraphs are broader or more important than others. Understanding the relationships between ideas in an outline or a study map requires the same skill as understanding the relationships between main ideas and supporting details.

Other Self-Generated Graphics

Not only can you interpret graphics found in textbooks, you can also create them. By doing so, it will be easier for you to see the interrelationship of various bits of information. For example, if you need to learn the percentages of various ethnic groups in a state or country you can create a bar or pie graph such as those shown in Chapter 4. When studying drama, you may find that charting the emotional ups and downs of a character on a line graph may help you understand the character's development. By becoming aware of the power of graphics, you may find creating them an additional tool in your study toolbox.

You have now completed the first five steps of the six-step PQ4R— Preview, Question, Read, Write, and Recall. Before going on to the final step (Review), use Steps 2, 3, 4, and 5 on each section of material you plan to study today. If you plan to read a chapter of sociology during your study session, study each two or three page section of the chapter using these four steps.

Review

When you have finished your study session, combine all the Recall Steps into one major review. Use your marginal notes to test yourself on all the material you covered in the session. Keep reviewing until you remember all the important ideas.

Because memory constantly needs to be refreshed, you should review the material periodically until the final exam. How often you need to review depends on the subject, the type of exam, and how familiar you are with the material. If the course requires a great deal of memorization, you may need a thorough review about once a week.

Studying Other Assigned Reading Materials

The PQ4R method works only with factual material presented in an organized manner. Other methods are more appropriate for poems, novels, stories, plays, and some types of essays. For example, a special type of prereading should be used on these materials; it will be discussed in Chapter 11 under "Scanning and Skimming."

If your additionally assigned reading materials are non-fiction, they are probably suited to PQ4R. However, you may have to adapt the method to your purpose. If you are going to be tested on the outside reading in the same way that you are examined on the textbook, then you could use the standard PQ4R method. If, however, you are reading the material for a book report or for participation in class discussion rather than for a test, then the Recall and Review Steps would probably not be necessary since you wouldn't have to retain the material over time. On the other hand, if the instructor has indicated that the material was assigned for a particular purpose, such as to give an example of a viewpoint that contrasts with that of the author of your textbook, then you would not have to give equal attention to all the ideas in the selection. In this case, you would only pay attention to ideas which contrasted with those in your textbook. When doing a comparison or contrast of two readings or a lecture and a reading, underlining and making marginal notes on the two pieces of material would probably not be as helpful as a supplementary graphic such as a chart. In short, when reading supplementary materials be sure of the purpose and then choose the appropriate write, recall and review methods.

Summary

The last three steps in PQ4R are Write, Recall, and Review. The Write Step consists of underlining and making marginal notes in a section of a textbook chapter after you have read it. The Recall Step involves utilizing one or more of the following techniques: using the marginal notes for self-testing, outlining, making flash-cards and study maps, and other self-generated graphics. When you compose self-test items in advance, you help yourself in four ways: (1) you direct your studying; (2) you limit the number of surprises that await you on the test; (3) you reduce the chance that you will "blank out," and (4) you increase the number of questions that will look familiar to you. The Question, Read, Write, and Recall Steps are repeated for each major section of the chapter. The final step, Review, is a self-testing session that pulls all the sections of the chapter together. The Review Step should be repeated periodically. For studying other assigned reading materials, PQ4R should be adapted to the purpose of the assignment.

Comprehension Check

Circle the letter preceding the correct answer. Then check your answers in the back of the book.

1. The proper time to underline is
   a. while you are reading.
   b. before you read.
   c. after you read.
   d. never.
2. Unless material is highly technical, it is unwise to underline more than
   a. 5 percent.
   b. 20 percent.
   c. 50 percent.
   d. 75 percent.

3.   PQ4R is a technique to
   a.   increase your reading speed.
   b.   increase pleasure obtained from reading.
   c.   improve your vocabulary.
   d.   help you read textbooks.

4.   PQ4R requires you to
   a.   guess what the instructor will ask on a test.
   b.   read the chapter several times.
   c.   cram the night before the test.
   d.   memorize word for word.

5.   Headings at the same level in an outline
   a.   are indicated by the same notation.
   b.   have the same indentation.
   c.   have similar importance.
   d.   do all of the above.

6.   An outline aids memory because
   a.   it requires reading the material several times.
   b.   it organizes ideas.
   c.   it's necessary for writing essays.
   d.   it makes small details important.

7.   Outlining a reading selection can be difficult because
   a.   it's hard to remember the notation.
   b.   in the selection the most important ideas may not appear first.
   c.   the important ideas may be implied rather than stated.
   d.   (b) and (c) are both correct.

8.   Which of the following is not an advantage of using flash cards?
   a.   You can arrange them in different order for different study sessions
   b.   You can pinpoint specific material to review.
   c.   They are harder to lose than PQ4R notes.
   d.   You can remove them from the pile when you understand the concept.

9.   In addition to the Recall Step in PQ4R, what other techniques could you use to supplement your studying of difficult material? _____
   _____
   _____

10.   What are the three steps in creating a complex study map? _____
   _____
   _____
   _____

Questions for Discussion and Writing

1.   Why do you think it is helpful to learn several types of recall techniques?

2.   Do you like using one recall technique more than the others? Which one? Use the following questions to assist you in analyzing why you prefer one type over another.

A. Do you find it easier to make outlines or create other types of graphic materials?

B. Do you find it easier to remember outlines or other types of graphic materials?

C. How do you think this reflects what you discovered about your learning style in Chapter 1?

EXERCISE 4: Using PQ4R with a Textbook Selection

Preview

Using the techniques you learned in Chapter 4, take one minute to preview the following selection on the origins of American democracy. Then answer the following questions. Check your answers in the back of the book.

1. What will the selection talk about? _____

2. What three aspects of American democracy will be discussed?

    a. _____

    b. _____

    c. _____

Question

Now that you have a good idea of the content and organization of the selection, ask three questions you think you will answer by reading it.

1. _____

2. _____

3. _____

Read

Read to find the answers to your questions and others you might think of while you read. Remember not to underline or make marginal notes until after you have read the entire selection.

Reading Selection: Political Science

American Democracy

James MacGregor Burns, J. W. Peltason,
Thomas E. Cronin, and David B. Magleby

It is the week before an American election, the **culmination** of an intense, year-long campaigning. During this last week, television and the newspapers are full of political ads: "A vote for Gabrillino is a vote for the people" one says under a picture of Frank Gabrillino, the Dem-

end

ocratic candidate for governor. He is shown with Mrs. Gabrillino, a successful real-estate broker. There are pictures of the Gabrillinos' three children. Gabrillino's campaign themes have stressed that he is not a politician, just a man of the people. He accuses his opponent, Sarah Wong, who has been in office for two terms, of being soft on criminals and blames her for the state's economic downturn. Gabrillino insists that if Wong is reelected, the state is doomed. Wong—behind in the polls, although recently catching up, emphasizes her experience, her concern for all the people, and her willingness to **defy** the special interests. She is a Republican, but she plays down her party **affiliation** since in this state a majority of the voters have been Democrats in the past.

challenge
membership

The two candidates have accused each other of all kinds of misdeeds. As the campaign progresses, their ads become more negative, more focused on personalities than on political issues and positions. Gabrillino makes much of the fact that 20 years ago Wong indicated she had doubts about the majority and **efficacy** of the death penalty, even though as governor she has not **commuted** any death sentences and has allowed two people to be executed. Wong's supporters charge that Gabrillino is fuzzy-hearted, soft-headed, and a tool of left-wing professors. There are **endorsements** in the newspapers: Professors for Wong, Teachers for Gabrillino, Students for Wong, Chicanos for Gabrillino, Asians for Gabrillino. Each candidate carefully plants letters to the editor in all the newspapers. Local radio and television talk shows feature the candidates, and the candidates' organizations supply callers to attack their opponents.

effectiveness
changed

recommendations

Election day: Only half the eligible voters bother to vote, and exit interviews indicate that the race is too close to call. That night, projections based on 5 percent of the vote make it clear that Gabrillino will get 48 percent of the vote, Wong 46 percent, and minor parties the rest. At 11:00 p.m., Wong calls Gabrillino, congratulates him on his victory, makes a **concession** speech before her disappointed workers, and thanks them for their support. Gabrillino speaks to his cheering supporters at another hotel ballroom, stating that his election was a great victory for the people.

giving up

Elections are a familiar process that Americans take for granted. Many people look upon elections with **disdain,** saying, "it's all politics." But in fact, American elections are remarkable. They conclude with what in the course of human history is a rare event: the peaceful transfer of political power. What is unusual is what is not happening. Even though the day before the election Wong and her followers were insisting that if Gabrillino became governor there would be chaos and corruption, once the vote was counted there was no thought by anybody in any political party that Gabrillino should not become governor. When her term was up, Wong did not resist turning power over to the man she had called corrupt. It never crossed her mind to try to stay in office by calling on the state police to keep Gabrillino from taking power. None of Wong's supporters considered taking up arms or

scorn

going underground or leaving the country. (Actually, they concentrated on how they could win the next election.) Nor did Gabrillino or his followers ever give any thought to punishing Sarah Wong and her supporters once they gained power. The Democrats wanted to throw the Republicans out of office, not in jail.

It was just a routine election—democracy at work. Most of the time in most nations, those in power got there either because they were born to the right family or because they killed or jailed their opponents. During most of human history, no one, and most especially not an opposition political party, could openly criticize their government. During most of human history, a political opponent was an enemy.

Defining Democracy

The word "democracy" is nowhere to be found in the Declaration of Independence or in the U.S. Constitution, nor was it a term used by the founders of the Republic. Democracy is hard to define. It is both a very old term and a new one. It was used in a loose sense to refer to various undesirable things: "the masses," mobs, lack of standards, and a system that encourages *demagogues* (leaders who gain power by appealing to the emotions and prejudices of the **rabble**).   **common masses**

Because we are using the term democracy in its political sense, we will be more precise. The distinguishing feature of democracy is that government **derives** its authority from its citizens. In fact, the word   **gets** comes from two Greek words: *demos* (the people) and *kratos* (authority or power). Thus democracy means government by the people, not government by one person (the monarch, the dictators, the priests) or government by the few (an oligarchy or aristocracy).

Ancient Athens and a few other Greek cities had a *direct democracy,* in which citizens came together to discuss and pass the laws and select the rulers by lot. These Greek city-states did not last, and most turned to mob rule and then resorted to dictators. When the word "democracy" came into English usage in the seventeenth century, it **denoted** this kind of direct democracy and was a term of **derision,** a   **defined** negative word, usually used to refer to mob rule.   **contempt**

James Madison, writing in *The Federalists,* No. 10, reflected the view of many of the framers of the U.S. Constitution when he wrote "such democracies [as the Greek and Roman] . . . have ever been found incompatible with personal security, or the rights of property, and have in general been as short in their lives, as they have been violent in their deaths." Democracy has taken on a positive meaning only in the last one hundred years.

These days it is no longer possible, even if desirable, to assemble the citizens of any but the smallest towns to make their laws or to select their officials directly from among the citizenry. Rather, we have invented a *system of representation.* Democracy today means *repre-*

sentative democracy or, in Plato's term, a *republic* in which those who have governmental authority get and retain authority directly or indirectly as the result of winning free elections in which all adult citizens are allowed to participate.

The framers preferred to use the term "republic" to avoid any confusion between direct democracy, which they disliked, and representative democracy, which they liked and thought secured all the advantages of a direct democracy while curing its weaknesses. Today, and in this book, democracy and republic are often used interchangeably.

Like most political concepts, democracy **encompasses** many ideas and has many meanings. Democracy is a way of life, a form of government, a way of governing, a type of nation, a state of mind, and a variety of processes.

includes

Democracy as a System of Interacting Values

As we approach the twenty-first century, the democratic faith may be as near a universal faith as the world has. A belief in human dignity, freedom, liberty, individual rights, and other democratic values is widely shared in most corners of the world. The **essence** of democratic values is contained in the ideas of popular consent, respect for the individual, equality of opportunity, and personal liberty.

core

Popular Consent. The **animating** principle of the American Revolution, the Declaration of Independence, and the resulting new nation was *popular consent,* the idea that a just government must derive its powers from the consent of the people it governs. A commitment to democracy thus entails a community's willingness to participate and make decisions in government. Intellectually these principles sound unobjectionable, but in practice they mean that certain individuals or groups may not get their way. The commitment to popular consent must involve a *willingness to lose* if most people vote the other way.

life-giving

Respect for the Individual. Popular rule in a democracy flows from a belief that every individual has the potential for common sense, rationality, and a notion of fairness. Individuals, democrats insist, have important rights; collectively, those rights are the source of all legitimate governmental authority and power. These notions pervade all democratic thought. They are woven into the writings of Thomas Jefferson, especially in the Declaration of Independence: "All men . . . are endowed by their Creator with certain **unalienable rights.**" Constitutional democracies make the person—rich or poor, black or white, male or female—the *central* measure of value. The state, the union, and the corporation are measured in terms of their usefulness to individuals.

rights that cannot be taken away

Equality of Opportunity. The importance of the individual is enhanced by the democratic value of *equality*. "All men are created equal and from that equal creation they derive rights inherent and unalienable, among which are the preservation of liberty and the pursuit of happiness." So reads Jefferson's first draft of the Declaration of Independence, and the words indicate the **primacy** of the concept.

> importance

But what does equality mean? What kind of equality? Economic, political, legal, social, or some other kind of equality? Equality for whom? For blacks as well as whites? For women as well as men? For Native Americans, descendants of the Pilgrims, and recent immigrants? And what kind of equality? *Equality of opportunity* (almost all Americans say they want that), but also *equality of conditions?* This last question is the toughest. Does equality of opportunity simply mean that everyone should have the *same place at the starting line?* Or does it mean that an effort be made to equalize most or all of the factors that during the course of a person's life might determine how well he or she fares economically or socially?

President Herbert Hoover posed the issue this way: "We, through free and universal education, provide the training of the runners: we give to them an equal start; we provide in government the umpire of fairness in the race." Franklin D. Roosevelt also sought to answer the question by proclaiming a "second Bill of Rights" that announced *Four Freedoms*—freedom of speech and expression, freedom of worship, freedom from want, and freedom from fear. Roosevelt's New Deal and its successor programs had tried to advance the **egalitarian notions** and basic security that he asserted were the rights of human beings everywhere.

> ideas of equality

Personal Liberty. Liberty has been the single most powerful value in American history. It was for "life, liberty, and the pursuit of happiness" that independence was declared; it was to "secure the Blessings of Liberty" that the Constitution was drawn up and adopted. Even our patriotic songs **extol** the "sweet land of liberty."

> praise

Liberty or *freedom* (used interchangeably here) means that all individuals must have the opportunity to realize their own goals. The essence of liberty is self-determination. Liberty is not simply the absence of external **restraint** on a person (freedom from); it is the individual's *freedom to act* positively to reach his or her goals. Moreover, both history and reason suggest that individual liberty is the key to social progress. The greater the people's freedom, the greater the chance of discovering better ways of life.

> barriers

Basic values of democracy do not always coexist happily. Individualism may conflict with the public good. Self-determination may conflict with equal opportunity. The right of General Motors to run its automobile factories to maximize profit, as compared to the right of automobile workers in those factories to join unions or share in the running of the plants, illustrates this type of conflict in everyday life.

Over the years the American political system has clearly moved toward greater freedom and more democracy. A commitment to democracy is in many ways a twentieth-century idea. People throughout the world are more attracted to democracy today than ever before. Recent events in China, Germany, Poland, the Czech Republic, Slovakia, Russia, and South Africa are evidence that the dream of freedom and democratic government is universal.

Far more people dream about democracy than ever experience it, and many new democracies fail. To be successful, democratic government requires a political process as well as a governmental structure. In both areas, the American experiment is instructive.

Democracy as a System of Interrelated Political Processes

To become reality, democratic values must be **incorporated into** a *political process,* a set of arrangements for making decisions and managing the public's business. The essence of the democratic process is respect for the rules of fair play, which can be seen in the tradition of free and fair elections, majority rule, freedom of expression, and the right to assemble and protest.

included in

Fair and Free Elections.   Democratic government is based on free and fair elections held at intervals frequent enough to make them relevant to policy choices. Elections are one of the most important devices for keeping officials and representatives accountable. **Crucial** to modern-day definitions of democracy is the idea that *opposition political parties* can exist, can run candidates in elections, and can at least have a chance to replace those who are currently holding public office. Thus political competition and choice are crucial to the existence of democracy.

essential

While all citizens should have equal voting power, free and fair elections do not imply everyone must or will have equal political influence. Some people, because of wealth, talent, or position, have more influence than others. How much extra influence key figures should be allowed to exercise in a democracy is a question for democrats. But at the polls a president or a pick-and-shovel laborer, a newspaper publisher or a lettuce picker, casts only one vote.

Majority (Plurality) Rule.   The basic rule of a democracy is that those with the most votes take charge of the government, at least until the next election, when a new majority may be voted in to take charge. In practice, *majority rules* is often *plurality rule,* in which the largest bloc takes charge, even though it may not constitute a true majority, with more than half the votes. While in charge, those elected have no right to **curtail** the attempts of political minorities to use all peaceful means to become a majority. So even as the winners take power, the losers can go to work to try to get it back at the next election.

limit

The American system of constitutional democracy allows people a say in who will decide important issues. Through the system of representation, people can participate indirectly in the great debates and decisions about laws and public policies.

Should the will of the majority prevail in all cases? Americans answer this question in a variety of ways. Some insist majority views should be enacted into laws and regulations. But perhaps the more widely held view is that an effective representative democracy involves far more than simply **ascertaining** and applying the statistical will of the people. It is a more complicated and often untidy process by which the people and their agents inform themselves, debate, compromise, and arrive at a decision, and do so only after thoughtful deliberation.

determining

Freedom of Expression.   Free and fair elections depend on access to information relevant to voting choices. Voters must have access to facts, competing ideas, and the views of candidates. Free and fair elections require a climate in which competing, nongovernment-owned newspapers, radio stations, and television stations can flourish. Expression by such media should be protected from government censorship.

The Right to Assemble and Protest.   Citizens must be free to organize for political purposes. Obviously individuals can be more effective if they join with others in a party, a pressure group, a protest movement, or a demonstration. The right to oppose the government, to form opposition parties, and to have a chance of defeating **incumbents** is not only vital; it is a defining characteristic of a democracy.

office holder

Now, answer the three questions you asked before you read the article.

1. Answer_____
   _____
2. Answer_____
   _____
3. Answer_____
   _____

Write

Go back and underline or highlight important ideas that might appear on a test. Make marginal notes for self-testing. Check Appendix B for sample underlining and marginal notes.

Recall

Go back to the selection, cover the text, and use the self-test statements in the margin to help you recall the main ideas and important details. Check each section to see whether you remembered your underlining. Did you forget anything important? If you left out any important ideas, repeat this Recall Step until you can recall everything correctly.

EXERCISE 5: Using Graphic Organizers

The study map below is an aid to the reading selection on "American Democracy." Fill it in and then compare your answer to ours in Appendix C.

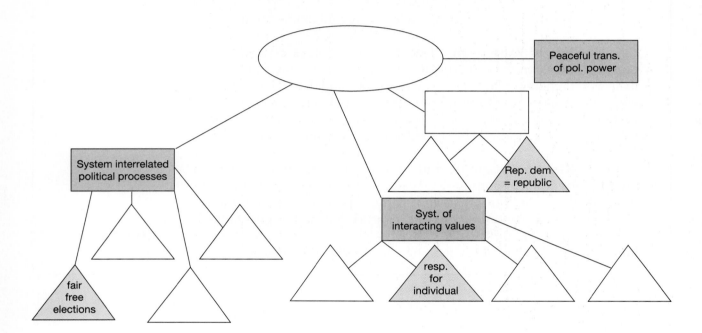

Review

Because this section is not a complete chapter, we will omit the Review Step. If you were studying the whole chapter, you would use the review step at the end of your study session to pull the sections together. Now take the following comprehension check.

Comprehension Check

Circle the correct answer to each question below. Then check your answers in the back of the book.

1. Which of the following was *not* true during most of human history?
   a. Most citizens could criticize their governments.
   b. One's political opponents were the enemy.
   c. Those in power often killed or jailed their opponents.
   d. Many in power got there by being born into the right family.

2. The single most important value in American history has been
   a. honesty.
   b. liberty.
   c. justice.
   d. mercy.

3. Which is *not* one of Roosevelt's "four freedoms"?
   a. freedom from fear
   b. freedom of speech and expression
   c. freedom of worship
   d. freedom from income tax

4. Democracy was defined in
   a. the Declaration of Independence.
   b. the Bible.
   c. the Constitution.
   d. none of the above.

5. A commitment to "popular consent" must involve
   a. a drive to win at any cost.
   b. a dedication to your favorite candidate in an election.
   c. a willingness to lose if most people vote the other way.
   d. a commitment to a political party.

6. The "freedom from want" means
   a. you should have everything you want.
   b. people in the United States want too much.
   c. everyone should have food, clothing, and housing.
   d. the government wants the people to pay too much in taxes.

7. The interrelated political processes of a democracy include *all but* which of the following?
   a. majority rule
   b. freedom of expression
   c. annual elections
   d. the right to assemble and protest

8. American government today is
   a. a direct democracy.
   b. a republic.
   c. a dictatorship.
   d. a monarcy.

9. The word "democracy" comes from two Greek words: *demos*, meaning _____; *kratos*, meaning _____.

10. Name one of the presidents mentioned in the article. _____

Questions for Discussion and Writing

1. What kinds of social programs (such as Medicare or food stamps) should the federal government provide?

2. In the fake election at the beginning of the article, only 50% of the eligible voters bothered to vote. In fact, this is a large amount for a typical American city, state, or even federal election. Why do you think so few people vote? How could the number of people voting be increased?

EXERCISE 6: Skills Review—Signal Words

The following signal words were used in the reading selection. Identify the relationships they indicate (emphasis, addition, comparison, cause and effect, change of direction, example, time sequence, conclusion). If you have trouble refer to the chart on pp. 32–33 for help. Check your answers in the back of the book.

a. but _____

b. in fact _____

c. when _____

d. even though _____

e. because _____

f. moreover _____

g. rather _____

h. since _____

i. actually _____

j. thus _____

Reading Textbooks III: Working with Technical Material

Reading Textbooks III: Working with Technical Material

6

To err is human, but to really foul things up requires a computer.
Anonymous

When you are reading technical textbook material, you may feel that you are reading information in a foreign language. **FACE IT, YOU ARE.** Technical material is a horse of a different color, or should we say "an equine of a variant hue"?

This type of reading is one of the reasons students often "dread the sciences." You may find observing insects in nature fascinating, but the thought of spending a semester reading about entomology (let alone carrying around that thick textbook) can reduce even the best student to a nervous wreck. Nursing candidates often say that "'micro' is the flunk-out course" for pre-nursing students. Students seeking AAs or BAs look at the general education requirements for the degree and find their eyes riveted anxiously to choices like "Introduction to Chemical Properties," "Human Biology," and "Introduction to the Physical Sciences."

For many students, courses with a lot of technical reading appear to be barriers to their career goals. Why do classes with this type of reading seem so intimidating? We suspect that it is a combination of the following: (1) the difficulty of the subject matter; (2) a difficult reading style; (3) the requirement to understand and remember large amounts of complex information; (4) the need to analyze this information; and (5) the necessity of applying this information in various technical formats, such as experiments, lab reports, and problem-solving tests.

Although you may feel that technical writing is not "user friendly," there are ways of coping with the special problems that this type of reading presents, of getting past the difficulties of the reading and enjoying the interesting and important information offered through these courses. Fortunately, you will find that the study techniques in this chapter and in Chapter 9, on test taking, will give you the keys you need to succeed. Here are some suggestions that will help you "slay the technical beast."

Know Your Foe

One of our nontechnically oriented colleagues defines technical material as "any reading that makes you feel knots in your stomach or puts you to sleep." Unfortunately, although this definition may be physiologically accurate for some students, it has little practical application. The first problem is that not all the reading in subjects that we think of as technical, like math, science, computer science, engineering, or even auto mechanics, is in fact technical in presentation. Books on these subjects often have sections (especially passages on the history of the field, an overview of the subject, or even a biography of a famous person in the field) that are of the same type of nontechnical reading you have been doing in the last two chapters. If you do not recognize this, you may spend needless time and energy painstakingly picking apart material that is more appropriately read in a totally different way. While the first article below, "Honda," is from a textbook entitled *Auto Mechanics,* it is not written in a technical style.

Honda

Honda is a young automotive company. Unlike most other companies, Honda has its origins only after the end of World War II. Motorcycles were the company's first products, with automobiles added in 1962. The company came into being when Soichiro Honda, the son of a village blacksmith, rounded up 500 war surplus generator engines and put together motorized bicycles at his tiny Honda Technical Research Institute. By 1947, the company was building its own 50-cc two-stroke engines for bicycles. They were the engines that laid the foundation for all the motorcycles, automobiles, and power units that have since been produced by Honda.

Mitchell, *Mitchell Auto Mechanics,* p. 1

Likewise, textbooks in fields generally thought of as nontechnical, such as history, English, fashion design, music, and business administration, will frequently have portions that contain paragraphs or whole chapters of technical information. The following article is an example of technical material from a textbook in a field generally considered nontechnical: fashion design. In fact, a textbook in any field can have material written in a technical or nontechnical manner. Therefore, you must be able to adapt your textbook reading style to the reading material at hand.

Consumer Spending

The amount of money consumers spend on fashion and other goods depends on their income. Income as it affects spending is measured in three ways: personal income, disposable income, and discretionary income. Personal income is the gross amount of income from all sources, such as wages, salaries, interest, and dividends. Disposable income is personal income minus taxes. This amount determines a person's purchasing power. Discretionary income is income left after food, lodging, and other necessities have been paid for. This is the money available to be spent or saved at will.

If the total personal income, disposable income, or discretionary income for an entire country is divided by its total population, the result is the average per capita income in each category. Income is related to the economic situation. Although incomes in the Western world have risen in recent years, so have prices. Thus, income is meaningful only in relation to the amount of goods and services it can buy—its purchasing power. Inflation, recession, the international value of currency, and productivity affect purchasing power.

Frings, *Fashion: From Concept to Consumer*, p. 37

It is a fact of modern existence that you will find the reading of technical material a regular part of your nonacademic experience. Every time you read the manual of a new electronic device, follow a recipe, or study a booklet from the Department of Motor Vehicles, you are reading technical material. The reality is that as you speed along the technological highway, you will be faced with more and more technical information to decode and digest.

Keep in mind that technical writing in any field has certain common characteristics.

The Subject Matter Is	The Textbook Usually Has
Information-dense	A specialized vocabulary with very precise definitions
Extremely cram-resistant	Complex diagrams loaded with information
Very specialized	Many examples of problems to solve
Reading the Textbooks Requires	
Prerequisite knowledge (from previous chapters or earlier courses)	
Slower reading of material	
Multiple readings of material	
Chunking material into smaller, more understandable reading segments	

Regarding technical material, **don't even consider skipping the painful parts.** Definitions, formulas, diagrams, and graphs are often the focal point of test questions. Furthermore, since technical material depends heavily on cumulative knowledge (remembering definitions or formulas from previous chapters), trying to skip material rather than taking the time to read and understand it can have disastrous long-range effects on your success in the class. Your understanding of this material requires that you change your reading approach from the beginning.

Make It Friendlier

To deal with technical information, you will need to modify the reading method, PQ4R. As a first step, get acquainted with the textbook. Begin with an expanded **Preview Step.** In this type of previewing, you have two purposes: (1) familiarizing yourself with the material by overviewing what you are about to read; and (2) beginning to make the reading less difficult by being sure you understand all of the technical vocabulary and graphics before you actually begin to read. With pencil and paper in hand, as you skim the material in one chapter, locate the specialized vocabulary and write the terms down. Next, see if they are defined in a glossary in the back of the book. If there is no glossary, see if they are defined in the chapter. If you think they have been defined in a previous chapter, use the index to see if there are pages on which to look. Then write down the terms and form your own minidictionary to make it easier to find the information later.

Technical words have a specific definition that may be totally different from what you believe. For example, the word "work" when used in technical material means "the result of a force acting through a distance" (Wilson, *College Physics*, p. 102; also Ellinger and Halderman, *Automotive Engines*, p. 17). Although you may think that answering the questions in this book is "work," your efforts would not fit the technical definition above! One good thing about technical words is that they frequently have a standard technical definition. In other words, their definitions are usually the same from one subject to another (the same definition in math, chemistry, physics, auto mechanics, etc.). Also, they are usually defined the same way from one country or language to another. Therefore, whether you study physics in China, France, or the United States, the technical definition of a word, such as "force," will likely be "something capable of changing an object's state of motion" (Wilson, p. 102). Once you have become acquainted with the vocabulary, another important thing to do during the Preview Step of technical material is to take the time to look at any graphics (drawings, tables, diagrams, pictures, or graphs) in the chapter you are studying. Read their titles, labels, and captions to get a feel for the contents of the chapter. Understanding these often unlocks the meaning of the chapter before you read the text.

Look at the following diagram of the tongue. Preview the diagram by reading the title, labels, and captions. Notice how much you can learn just by studying these on the graphic below.

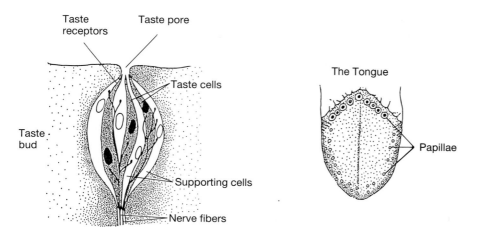

Figure 1.3 Drawing of the tongue, showing papillae on the surface. Taste buds are located on the sides and at the base of many of the papillae. Taste buds near the tip are more sensitive to sweet and salt, those on the sides are more sensitive to sour, and those near the back are more sensitive to bitter. Diagram of an individual taste bud containing tiny taste receptors that come in contact with the substance being tasted, taste cells, and nerve fibers that carry the message from the taste bud to the brain for interpretation.

Bennion, *Introductory Foods*, p. 10

Without looking back to the diagram, see how many facts you can remember.

1. The title is _____.
2. Papillae are located _____.
3. Do all papillae have taste buds?_____.
4. Where are the taste buds for bitterness concentrated on the tongue?
    _____.
5. What are the two tastes detected toward the front of the tongue?
    _____ and _____.
6. The label for the first diagram reads _____.
7. The second diagram shows the parts of _____.
8. Write any two of the six labels on the second diagram:_____
    _____.

Now look back at the diagram to see how much you actually remembered just from previewing it.

Question Everything

The **Question Step** may be easier with technical material than with other types of reading. This type of material usually has many headings, subheadings, and signal words. Turn these into questions. Next, use the title, labels, and captions on the graphics to create other questions. These aids usually give a fairly complete overview of the contents of the chapter. As you can see, careful previewing and questioning before you begin to read technical material will make it much "friendlier" because your comprehension while reading will not be slowed by your failure to understand the words or general ideas. Now you are ready for the **Read Step.**

Take Your Time

Frequently it is necessary to read technical material more than once. Your first reading may yield only a general idea of what the author is trying to explain. You may also find it important to read smaller sections than a whole chapter. Stop reading each time you feel the need to do so.

Write Right

Try a variety of techniques for the **Write Step.** First, go back to the section you have just read and underline. Then make marginal notes. Try covering the section and see if you can remember the underlined information by looking at the marginal notes. To practice this step, go back to the article on fashion, underline, and make marginal notes. If you can remember most of the underlining by just looking at the marginal notes, this may be the only technique you need in this step. However, if you find that you cannot recall 80 percent of the material soon after reading it, you will have to do more. As was discussed in the last chapter you can try outlining, creating study maps or other self-generated graphics or making flash cards. You might also try duplicating the graphics, eliminating the headings, and then seeing if you can recall the various parts.

Try this method on the following diagram of the tongue.

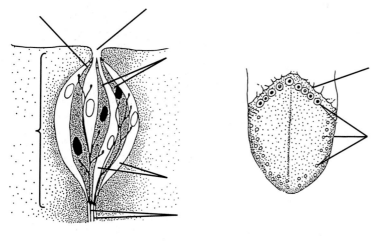

Bennion, *Introductory Foods,* p. 10

Can you remember the parts? If so, this method will be useful for you. If you don't remember enough, you may have to draw each diagram in your spiral notebook without looking at the graphic and then return to the book to see how accurate your drawing is. By actually redrawing the picture instead of just filling in blanks, you are forced to recall more material. If you are still having problems, put the graphic, or portions of it, on the front of flash cards and the labeled graphics on the back.

Practice/Practice/Practice

With technical material, the **Recall Step** is also modified. To learn technical material, not only do you need to read it, you almost always need to use it. Try doing each exercise in the book yourself because the right answer is already there for you to check. Answer every question. These are often the key to unlocking the theoretical material in the textbook because they are its application. Know how to do each step of a problem, not just the answer. If there is a **study guide,** great! The author has taken the time to give you some personal instruction on how to study the material. Spend at least half of your allotted study time doing the work in it. Remember, the author has probably put in materials developed over years of working with students in your type of class. No one wants you to fail this class. The author wants the book to work, and the instructor wants every student to do well. Have a positive attitude, and remember, if this were easy material, the author wouldn't have written a study guide. If the teacher gives you handouts, study them carefully and do any extra work given. If the instructor has gone to the trouble of making additional handouts, it is because he or she knows you need extra work to understand the material. If all of the regular classroom materials don't help you remember the text, use your flash cards. By doing this, you are able to divide your study and review time to concentrate on the parts that are hardest for you to recall. By analyzing your learning style and recall capacity, you will maximize your learning strengths and compensate for your weaknesses.

Look at the following diagram. You can quickly see that it is much more complex than the first two you studied; therefore, you should first organize a plan of attack. Perhaps you will decide to study it level by level, from top to bottom, or to study each half separately. You can use a combination of these plans of attack or work diagonally. Now that you have decided on an approach to studying the diagram, utilize that approach for five minutes.

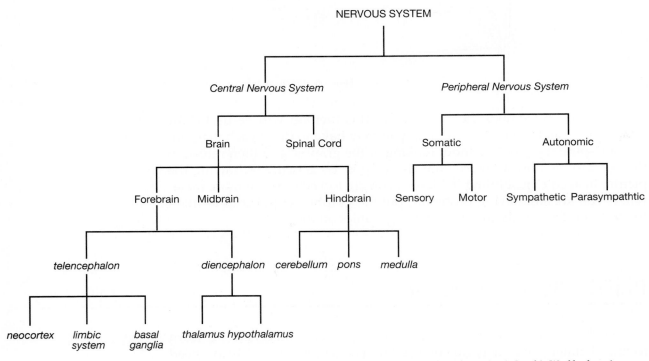

Kristal, *A Guide to the Brain: A Graphic Workbook*, p. 1

Now look on the next page, covering this page and fill in as many of the blanks as you can on the study guide for the diagram.

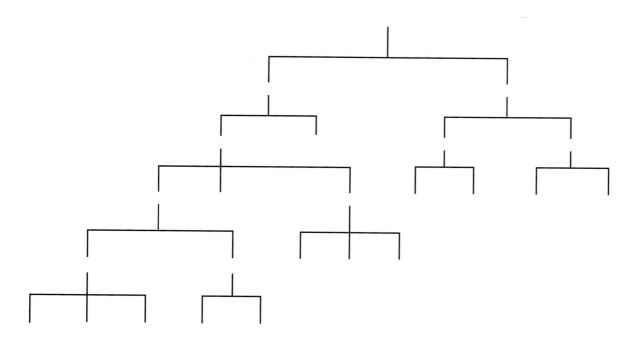

How much did you recall?

1. You should have been able to fill in at least 10 of the 24 blanks if you had a successful study plan. How many did you remember? _____

2. Were the labels you remembered put on the proper line?_____

3. Analyze your recall pattern. Did you remember sections of information? _____

   Did you remember more on one side of the diagram than on the other? _____

   Are you satisfied with how much you remembered for the amount of effort you exerted? _____

4. How would you go about a second review to try and recall more information? _____

   _____

   Would you study the diagram for a longer period? _____

   Would you study in several shorter study session? _____

   Would you benefit from studying only one half of the diagram at a time?_____

   Would it be better for you to divide the diagram and study all the major headings first, or do you think it would be better to study the whole left side until you remembered it and then do the same with the right side? _____

5. Would you benefit from transferring parts of the diagram to flash cards to study in between your regular study session? _____

Answering these questions is one way to begin to better understand your personal learning style. This method works for visual aids in the same way that marginal notes help with underlining. If all you do is try to look at the graphics until you remember them, your mind will be limited to rote memory (see Chapter 8). Your mind is just rereading information, not processing it into meaningful units. On the other hand, if you try and reconstruct the graphic by adding all of the important information, you are forced to group the information into meaningful units for recall. You know what you have learned.

Use any type of writing or combination of underlining, writing, and drawing that helps change the complex language into understandable material that you can remember. Taking time now can save hours later. After you have underlined the key ideas, reread the section to see if it is easier to understand. You may find it necessary to underline more than you would in predominantly nontechnical textbooks; however, you still need to limit the amount you underline. Be sure and reevaluate your underlining after you have studied the graphic material. Often you will find that the graphic material duplicates what you have underlined. You may find that studying the graphic material helps you recall the underlining more than marginal notes do. If this is the case, center your studying around the visuals and return to the text to see if you have forgotten any essential information. You already know that highlighting isn't magically going to help you understand the material. If you find that you are underlining or highlighting more than 40 percent of a chapter, try paraphrasing the information (writing the information in your own words). No matter how you decide to simplify the reading, you won't be able to memorize that much writing. You may find it useful to outline the material. Some students find this is the only way they can absorb and remember this kind of material.

Of course, it takes longer than underlining and making marginal notes and usually takes more time than paraphrasing. However, if it matches your learning style, it is well worth the time because you will remember more later. If you do decide to outline the material, be sure to use a spiral notebook that has been labeled with the name of the course. In this way, all of your outlining will be in one place and you can use it to study for the midterm and final exam. If you have also drawn your own diagrams, these should be done in the same spiral notebook so that they won't be lost or misplaced for future review.

If there is no official study guide, create your **own** study guide. It is very important that all of your study techniques be related. Therefore, as soon as you finish doing the exercises in the book or working with the study guide, return to the text and reread your study material. Add any extra thoughts you have, now that you have had a chance to work the problems. This will help unify the writing in the book, the graphics, and your notes into a personal study guide. Try covering your material as you did in the last chapter and see what you can remember. What you can't remember now, you won't remember later.

Overlearn

The **Review Step** with technical materials can take longer than with nontechnical material because the quantity of material you must retain requires that you *overlearn.* This means that you may have to review the text and graphics many times. It may also require additional learning experiences such as study groups or having a tutor, if your personal Review Step does not yield sufficient learning for you to do well on the tests. Give yourself more review time than you think you will need. Space your study times so that you don't become overloaded with information before you can digest it. Review your earlier materials often to maintain an overview of what you have already learned. With technical material this is even more important than with other kinds of reading material. A chapter in history or English usually doesn't require you to remember specific information from the previous chapter, but a chapter in chemistry will often use terms, formulas, and information from prior material.

We suggest that you use flash cards for definitions, theories, formulas, parts of diagrams, and sample problems to make these easier to review. On each card, put a major idea on the front and the answer on the back.

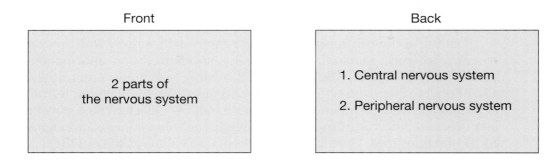

Review your flash cards often. Take them with you to use in between classes or during other free moments.

Try Another Source

If you still don't understand what you are trying to learn, try one of the suggestions below.

1. Use **collateral readings.** If you don't understand or remember what the author of your textbook is saying, try another textbook or a reference source in your college library. Sometimes, by reading a second explanation, you get a better overall picture. It's like finding the missing piece to a puzzle. You are no longer trapped in the details.
2. Form a **study group.** You have probably heard the expressions "misery loves company" and "two heads are better than one." Both say-

ings are probably true when it comes to trying to understand and remember technical data. In other words, study groups can be especially useful when it comes to reviewing technical information. Sometimes working together, comparing notes, and seeing and hearing others' ideas helps each member of a group understand what no one individual had quite put together alone.

3. Get a **tutor.** There are usually tutors available in your Learning Center who have been recommended by your professor. If there isn't free tutoring and you can't learn the material in the course, ask your instructor if he or she knows of a former student who tutors. This might be expensive but so is having to take the course again. If you know you need help, don't wait until it's too late. No one can work miracles for you during finals if you are not already passing the course. You should know if your study techniques are working by the second test. If the class only has a midterm and a final, evaluate how much you know the fourth week of the semester or the third week of the quarter. By then you will know if you're having serious problems. Be realistic. Your fate in the course will usually get worse if you keep using ineffective methods.

Summary

Reading technical information successfully will require you first to recognize technical material, which is often specialized and information-dense, and then to alter your usual PQ4R reading techniques accordingly. In the Preview Step, you will need to spend more time previewing technical vocabulary and graphics. On the other hand, the Question Step may be easier because you can turn the many headings, subheadings, and signal words into questions. During the Read Step, you will need to read the material slowly and more than once. For the Write Step, use the familiar techniques of underlining, developing marginal notes, and creating flash cards. In addition, to handle the complex information, you may find it useful to photocopy graphics, "white out" the headings, and then write them in or draw the graphics from memory. As with the Preview Step, expect the Recall Step to take more time. Do all exercises, solve all problems, and carefully evaluate your understanding of the material and your ability to apply it. If you find that you are not understanding 80 percent of the material, form a study group or get a tutor. If you apply these steps, technical material should not be a barrier to achieving your academic goals.

Comprehension Check

Circle the letter preceding the correct answer. Then check your answers in the back of the book.

1. One way in which technical reading matter differs from regular reading material is that it is more
   a. persuasive.
   b. humorous.

   c. information-dense.
   d. poetic.
2. Technical material
   a. is found only in scientific and mathematical texts.
   b. can be found in any subject area.
   c. is easy to skim.
   d. has changed very little since the Renaissance.
3. The precise definitions of most technical words
   a. will be less necessary as computer software replaces textbooks.
   b. make international communication difficult.
   c. aid scientists in their communications.
   d. are identical to their most common definitions.
4. The step of PQ4R that may be easier with technical material is the
   a. Recall Step.
   b. Write Step.
   c. Review Step.
   d. Question Step.
5. Applying PQ4R to technical material requires you to
   a. skip the graphics.
   b. ignore the vocabulary.
   c. follow the same procedures as with regular reading.
   d. adapt each step somewhat.
6. Which of the following is not characteristic of technical material?
   a. cram-resistant
   b. information-dense
   c. easy to comprehend
   d. builds on prior knowledge
7. The best way to approach technical vocabulary is to
   a. immediately look up each term in a dictionary.
   b. guess the meaning from its context.
   c. as with the reading of non-technical material, write down each word new to you.
   d. make flash cards.
8. Your grade in a course based on reading technical material will likely depend on your ability to
   a. write essays.
   b. memorize material.
   c. write term papers.
   d. apply what you have learned in problem-solving situations.
9. Technical vocabulary is _____.
10. To "overlearn" technical material, you can _____
   _____.

Questions For Discussion and Writing

1. How do the techniques for reading regular textbook material and technical textbook material differ?
2. What are some of the clues that you can use to identify technical portions of textbook materials?

EXERCISE 1: Identifying Technical and Nontechnical Material

Look at each paragraph below. Based on the density of information, technical vocabulary, and previous knowledge required for understanding, put **T** for technical and **NT** for nontechnical on blue lines below. Check your answers in the back of the book.

Plate Tectonics

1. _____

active

hollows

**doubt
assumption**

Within the last few decades, a great deal has been learned about the workings of our **dynamic** planet. In fact, many have called this period a revolution in our knowledge about the earth which has been unequaled at any other time. This revolution began in the early part of the twentieth century with the radical proposal that the continents had drifted about the face of the earth. This idea contradicted the established view that the continents and ocean **basins** are permanent and stationary features on the face of the earth. For that reason, it was received with great **skepticism.** More than 50 years passed before enough data was gathered to transform this relatively simple **hypothesis** into a working theory which weaved together the basic processes known to operate on the earth. The theory that finally emerged, called *plate tectonics,* provided geologists with a comprehensive model of the earth's internal workings.

Lutgens and Tarbuck, *Essentials of Geology,* p. 16

Using a Microscope

2. _____

unsteady

**3-sided blocks of
glass which splits
white light into
colors, thin metal
plate which
controls opening
for light**

When picking up the microscope always use two hands, one grasping the arm and the other supporting the base. Always rest the microscope directly on the laboratory table, not on a notebook or other less reliable support. Keep the microscope squarely in front of you when it is in use. Avoid leaving it in a **precarious** position near the edge of the desk. When you have completed your work return the microscope to the cabinet.

Identify the parts of your microscope and learn the function of each. The base and arm were mentioned previously. The object to be examined is mounted on a slide that is placed upon the stage. Light passes from the illuminator through the slide and into the objective lens (mounted on a revolving nosepiece). The light is focused by the objective lens to form an image by mean of **prisms** in the barrel. The top lens of the microscope, called the ocular (ocular lens), magnifies the image as the light passes on to the eye. The **diaphragm** (iris diaphragm) mounted beneath the stage is used to control the amount of light passing through the lens. Two focusing adjustments raise and lower the stage; these are a coarse adjustment knob, the large knob, and a fine adjustment knob, the small knurled knob.

The revolving nosepiece supports a low- and a high-power **objective.** These may be marked in several ways. The low-power objective may have 10X, 16mm, N.A. .25, or all three engraved on it and may also have green banding. The 10X means that the lens's contribution to the microscope's magnifying power is tenfold; that is, it forms an image inside the barrel that is 10 times as large in any dimension as the specimen on the slide. The 16mm is not in itself a measure of magnification, but instead indicates the distance between the specimen and the focal point of the objective lens. The N.A. is an abbreviation for numerical **aperture.** The high-power objective is marked 43X, 4mm, N.A. .55, or all three and has yellow banding.

lens nearest object observed

opening

Underhill et al., *General Zoology: Laboratory Guide,* p. 1

The Characteristics of Living Things

On your way to class tomorrow morning, notice the **astonishing array** of creatures that live even in a place as domesticated as a city or a college campus. Of course there are grass, bushes, trees, dogs, cats, sparrows, and lots of people. But if you look more closely, you may also encounter insects and earthworms, a spider spinning its web, and mushrooms in the shade beneath a bush. And in your mind's eye, picture the creatures too small to see: yeast making bread rise at the bake shop, **protozoa** squirming around in a pond, even the bacteria on your teeth that give you "morning mouth" when you wake up.

3. _____
remarkable variety

single-celled animals

Why is there such as astounding diversity of living things? How do they interact with one another? In what ways are bacteria, plants, and people alike, and what makes them so different? What processes must occur in the body of each organism for it to live? These are a few of the questions biologists ask in their quest to understand life on Earth, and that we invite you to ask too, as we explore biology together. For although we are part of the web of life, we humans are more than just another strand; only we can contribute that particular brand of **exuberance** that comes from understanding the nature of the Earth and its inhabitants, and appreciating the beauty of it all. We are life's way of understanding itself.

liveliness

Audersirk and Audersirk, *Biology: Life on Earth,* p. 37

EXERCISE 2: Review of PQ4R Techniques

Return to the three sections above and use the appropriate PQ4R technique to prepare them for study. Don't forget to mark technical vocabulary that you would have to define before reading the paragraph.

EXERCISE 3: Understanding Graphic Aids

Study the following diagram of a microscope using the technical PQ4R technique.

The Compound Microscope

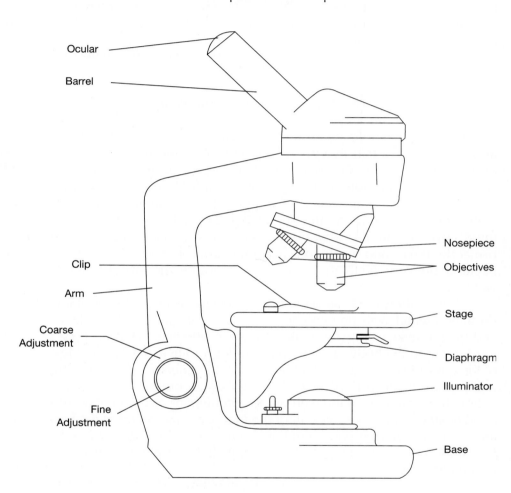

Ocular

Barrel

Clip

Arm

Coarse
Adjustment

Fine
Adjustment

Nosepiece

Objectives

Stage

Diaphragm

Illuminator

Base

Underhill, et al. *General Zoological Laboratory Guide,* p. 2

To see how much you remembered cover this page and fill in the diagram on the next page.

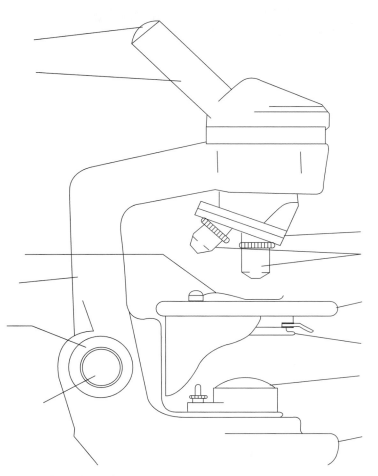

Look back at the paragraph describing how to use a microscope (pp. 148–149). Now that you have studied the diagram of a microscope, reevaluate your underlining and marginal notes. Answer the following questions:

1. What underlining could have been left out? _____
   _____

2. What is explained better by the diagram than by text? _____
   _____

3. What information does the paragraph contain that you didn't know from studying the diagram of the microscope?_____
   _____

4. Now that you have seen how important graphics are in technical reading, will you need to change your study methods? If so, how? __
   _____

EXERCISE 4: Using PQ4R with a Textbook Selection

The following two readings are from a nursing text and a health text. Do a modified PQ4R technique on both selections. Then answer the questions on page 158. The first article is from the nursing text.

Preview

Using the techniques you have learned in this chapter, take two minutes to preview the following selection from a nursing textbook. Read the headings and subheadings. When you come to a bullet • read the key terms. When you are finished you should be able to answer the following questions.

1. What is the subject of the selection?
2. What is the main idea of the selection?
3. What indication is there that this selection will discuss more than how to do CPR?
4. What does ABC stand for in this article?
5. What should you do to see if the air way is blocked?

Question

Now that you have a good idea of the content and organization of the selection, ask three questions you think will be answered when you read it.

1. _____
2. _____
3. _____

Read

Read to find the answers to your questions and to others you might think of while you read. When you are done, answer the questions in the comprehension check.

Reading Selection 1: Nursing

Cardiopulmonary Resuscitation

Rose Schniederman, Susan Lambert and Barbara Wander

Cardiopulmonary resuscitation is a basic, life-saving procedure for sudden **cardiac** or **respiratory arrest.** The technique of CPR provides basic emergency life support until emergency medical help arrives. CPR keeps oxygenated blood flowing to the brain and other vital body organs until medical treatment can be given to restore normal heart function.

heart/breathing stoppage

Schniederman, Lambert, and Wander, *Being a Nursing Assistant,* pp. 74–76

Note!

The following material is not intended to be a CPR course. An authorized CPR course includes practice on **manikins** supervised by a certified trained instructor to direct you in CPR with written and performance examinations. The American Heart Association and the American Red Cross, as well as other community service organizations, offer classes in CPR. Most health care institutions require all employees to be certified in CPR and to complete **periodic recertification.** *Remember,* only a person who has been trained in CPR can perform the rescue techniques. The only way of learning CPR is to enroll in an approved, supervised program.

dummies

repeated relicensing

There are three basic rescue skills to CPR. These are referred to as the ABC's of CPR:

- A, airway
- B, breathing
- C, circulation

Airway

The most important factor in successful resuscitation is the opening of the airway. There are many possible causes of an **obstructed** airway. The most common cause in an unconscious person is the back of the tongue.

blocked

There are several recommended methods for opening the airway that help to correct the position of the tongue. (a) The head-tilt **maneuver** is a simple repositioning of the head. This procedure is not recommended for use on any patient with possible injuries to the head, neck or spine. The **trauma** patient should be conscious. This procedure can be used on unconscious nontrauma patients. (b) The head-tilt, chin lift maneuver provides for the maximum opening of the airway. It is useful on conscious and unconscious patients and is one of the best methods for correcting obstruction caused by the tongue. This procedure is not recommended for use on any patient with possible neck or spinal injuries. (c) The jaw-thrust maneuver is the only widely recommended procedure for use on unconscious patients with possible neck or spinal injuries.

technique

severely injured

Breathing

Mouth-to-mouth rescue breathing is the most effective way of getting oxygen into the lungs of the victim. Pinch the **nostrils** shut using the hand that is on the victim's forehead. Open your mouth wide and place it tightly over the victim's mouth. Blow two breaths lasting 1 to 1½ seconds on **inspiration,** then remove your mouth. Turn your head to the side with your ear close to the victim's mouth and listen

nose openings

breathing in

for a return of air. If there is no return of air, recheck the head and neck position. If the airway is obstructed, no air can flow to the lungs.

After you have given the victim two breaths, check to see if the heart is beating. To feel the **carotid** pulse, use your hand that has been lifting the chin. With the tips of your fingers find the groove next to the adam's apple and feel for a pulse. If the heart is beating you must breathe for the victim at a rate of 12 breaths per minute (one breath every 5 seconds) for an adult while maintaining the open airway. If the heart is not beating (no pulse) you will have to pump the heart and circulate the victim's blood using external chest **compressions.**

    neck

    pushes

Note: To protect both the victim and yourself when performing CPR a protective device must be used as a barrier. The barrier will protect the victim and yourself from transferring any communicable diseases either individual may be carrying. There are many types of protective barrier devices; your instructor and the facility where you are working will determine which device you will use.

Circulation

External chest compression with mouth-to-mouth resuscitation will allow oxygenated blood to circulate to the brain and other organs. To perform external chest compression, kneel next to the victim's chest. Place the heel of one hand on the lower half of the **sternum,** place your other hand on top, and knit the fingers of the top hand through the fingers of your bottom hand to keep your fingers off the chest wall. As you compress downward your shoulders should be directly over the victim's midline and your arms straight. For an adult victim depress 1½–2 inches. When you release this pressure, do not remove your hands from the sternum. These compressions should be rhythmic so that compression and release are of equal **duration.** Deliver 15 compressions for every 2 breaths when you are providing mouth-to-mouth rescue breathing. Deliver a rate of 80–100 compressions per minute.

    breast bone

    length of time

1. Answer_____
2. Answer_____
3. Answer_____
4. Other information _____

Write

Go back and underline or highlight important ideas that might appear on a test. Make marginal notes for self-testing.

Recall

Go back to the selection, cover the text, and use the self-test statements in the margin to help you recall the main ideas and important details. Check each section to see whether you remembered your underlining. Did you forget anything important? If you left out any important ideas, repeat this recall step until you can recall everything correctly.

Create a map that includes the major ideas on a separate sheet of paper.

Review

Because this section is not a complete chapter, we will omit the review step. If you were studying the whole chapter, you would use the review step at the end of your study session to pull the sections together.

EXERCISE 5: Using PQ4R with a Textbook Selection

Preview

Using the techniques you have learned in this chapter, take two minutes to preview the following selection from a health textbook. Read the headings and subheadings.

1. What is the subject of the selection? _____

2. What is the main idea of the selection?_____

Question

Now that you have a good idea of the content and organization of the selection, ask three questions you think will be answered when you read it.

1. _____

2. _____

3. _____

Read

Read to find the answers to your questions and to others you might think of while you read.

This reading from a health text is an example of using a second source to help understand your textbook.

Reading Selection 2: Health—Using Collateral Reading

Artifical Respiration

John La Place

A person who ceases to breathe will become unconscious and may die within a very few minutes. To reestablish breathing, artificial respiration must be given immediately. The mouth-to-mouth technique is the most efficient. Fears of contracting AIDS through administering artificial respiration to a stranger do not appear to be well-founded; the Centers for Disease Control have not reported a single case of AIDS attributable to exposure to infected saliva.

1. Place the victim on his or her back.
2. Open the victim's mouth and pull the tongue forward.
3. Clear the mouth of any obstructions.
4. Pinch the nostrils together.
5. Place your mouth over the victim's to form a tight seal and breathe into it quickly until the victim's chest rises.
6. Remove your mouth and listen for air leaving the victim's chest. If no air leaves, try again.
7. If there is still no air exchange, turn the victim on his side and slap his back between the shoulder blades. Again check the mouth for obstructions and start over. Continue this process until an air exchange is felt.
8. Now breathe into the victim's mouth (with the nostrils held shut) until the chest rises, at a rate of 12 times a minute, removing your mouth each time to let air escape. (For infants, breathe shallowly into both the mouth and the open nostrils at a rate of 20 times a minute.)
9. Continue until the victim is breathing normally or until help arrives.

Choking

For the purpose of our discussion, choking may be defined as a stoppage of normal breathing due to an obstruction of the windpipe, or esophagus. A large number of deaths occur each year as a result of this form of choking, and it is only recently that something has been done about it.

The Heimlich Maneuver, developed in 1973 by a Cincinnati throat surgeon, is an emergency first-aid technique that causes a sudden burst of air through the esophagus to expel an obstruction (see Figure A–1). Pressure is exerted upon the victim's breastplate, just below

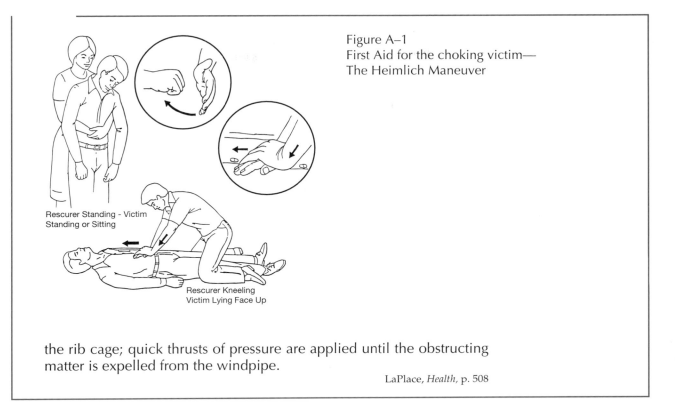

Figure A–1
First Aid for the choking victim—
The Heimlich Maneuver

Rescurer Standing - Victim
Standing or Sitting

Rescurer Kneeling
Victim Lying Face Up

the rib cage; quick thrusts of pressure are applied until the obstructing
matter is expelled from the windpipe.

LaPlace, *Health,* p. 508

Now, answer the three questions you asked before you read the
article.

1. Answer_____
2. Answer_____
3. Answer_____
4. Other information _____

Write

Go back and underline or highlight important ideas that might appear on a test. Make marginal notes for self-testing.

Recall

Go back to the selection, cover the text, and use the self-test statements in the margin to help you recall the main ideas and important details. Check each section to see whether you remembered your underlining. Did you forget anything important? If you left out any important
ideas, repeat this recall step until you can recall everything correctly.

On your own paper create a map that includes the major ideas.

Review

Because this section is not a complete chapter, we will omit the Review Step. If you were studying the whole chapter, you would use the Review Step at the end of your study session to pull the sections together. Now take the comprehension check that follows.

EXERCISE 6: Using Collateral Reading

Answer the following questions. Then check your answers in the back of the book.

1. Did you understand all the information in the first article?
    _____

2. What information in the first selection, if any, did you understand better after reading the excerpt from the health book?
    _____
    _____
    _____

3. What information in the first article did not appear in the second?
    _____
    _____
    _____

4. The first article was meant to represent textbook reading; the second, collateral reading. What did you learn from the second reading that you hadn't learned from the first?
    _____
    _____
    _____

Comprehension Check

Circle the letter preceding the correct answer. Then check your answers in the back of the book.

1. The main idea of the first article is that
    a. it is difficult to do the mouth-to-mouth breathing technique.
    b. there are certain steps to follow in saving someone with the mouth-to-mouth breathing technique.

    c. when someone stops breathing, you must give that person mouth-to-mouth breathing or he or she will die.

    d. anyone can do mouth-to-mouth breathing techniques.

2. The main idea of the second article is that
   a. mouth-to-mouth breathing and the Heimlich Maneuver each has specific steps that must be done in a specific order.
   b. anyone can learn mouth-to-mouth breathing.
   c. mouth-to-mouth breathing is more important to learn than the Heimlich Maneuver.
   d. the major reason people stop breathing is choking.

3. Which is the most efficient way to reestablish breathing according to both articles?
   a. Call an ambulance.
   b. Call 911.
   c. Administer the Heimlich Maneuver.
   d. Administer mouth-to-mouth breathing.

4. If a victim's heart is **not** beating,
   a. you should **not** begin mouth-to-mouth breathing.
   b. you should double the number of breaths per minute.
   c. you must begin by pressing on the area over the victim's heart before you begin mouth-to-mouth breathing.
   d. you will have to pump the heart and do mouth-to-mouth breathing.

5. The most important factor in successful resuscitation is
   a. using a protective device.
   b. the age of the victim.
   c. counting the number of breaths per minute.
   d. opening the airway.

6. CPR
   a. is successful for reviving most victims.
   b. is only successful in half the cases.
   c. only works 20 percent to 30 percent of the time.
   d. is very dangerous for both the victim and the person giving it.

7. According to the Centers for Disease Control, exposure to AIDS-infected saliva
   a. will cause you to be infected 50 percent of the time.
   b. will not cause you to be infected with HIV.
   c. is extremely dangerous.
   d. has caused only a few people to get AIDS.

8. The first step in the mouth-to-mouth breathing technique is
   a. to clear the mouth of any obstructions.
   b. to place the victim on his or her back.
   c. to breathe into the victim's mouth at a rate of 12 times a minute.
   d. is not the same in the two articles.

9. What are the first three steps in giving mouth-to-mouth breathing?__

_____

_____

10. Describe the steps in the Heimlich Maneuver. _____

_____

_____

Questions For Discussion and Writing

1. Since CPR doesn't work in 70 percent to 80 percent of the cases, is there any reason to be taught how to do it? _____

2. How does CPR differ when used on adults and on young children? _____

3. Why do you think a person has to take a class in CPR before being considered qualified to do it? _____

EXERCISE 7: Understanding Tables

Compare the information on the following tables and then read the paragraph. After you have done both, answer the questions that follow. Then check your answers in the back of the book.

Table 2–1
Some Metric Units
of Mass, Volume,
and Length

Prefix	Number of Basic Units	Mass	Volume	Length
kilo =	1000	kilogram (kg)	kiloliter (kl)	kilometer (km)
(basic unit)	1	gram (g)	liter (L)	meter (m)
deci =	0.1	decigram (dg)	deciliter (dL)	decimeter (dm)
centi =	0.01	centigram (cg)	centiliter (cL)	centimeter (cm)
milli =	0.001	milligram (mg)	milliliter (mL)[a]	millimeter (mm)
micro =	0.000001	microgram (μg) or gamma (γ)	microliter(μL)	micrometer (μm) or micron (μ)
nano =	0.000000001 0.0000000001			nanometer (nm) angstrom (Å)

[a]The millimeter (mL) and the cubic centimeter (cm^3 or cc) are exactly equivalent, because L = 1 dm^3 by definition. Hence, 1 cubic meter = 1000 liters.

Type of Measurement	English System		Metric System
Mass	1.00 pound	⇔	454 grams
Length	1.00 inch	⇔	2.54 centimeters
	1.00 mile	⇔	1.61 kilometers
	1.09 yard	⇔	1.00 meter
Volume	1.06 quart	⇔	1.0 liter
	1.00 pint	⇔	473 milliliters
	1.00 gallon	⇔	3.78 liters

Table 2–2
Some English–
Metric Equivalents

Mass, weight, length, volume, and density can be measured using two methods: (1) English-based units and (2) the metric system. In addition, scientists sometimes employ a system of units called the International System of Units, abbreviated SI from the French *Système International,* which is based on the metric system and described in Appendix I. English-based units (see Appendix I), such as the foot and the pound, are used primarily in the nonscientific community in the United States. The *metric system,* developed in nineteenth-century France, is used throughout the rest of the world (even in Great Britain) and in the world scientific community. Civilian and business interests in the United States are gradually adopting the metric system, as shown in Figure 2–3. For example, the chemical industry is now in the process of converting to the metric system in the shipping and billing of industrial chemicals.

The metric system has as its basic units the gram (g), a measure of mass; the liter (or litre, L), a measure of volume; and the meter (or metre, m), a measure of length. The units for mass, volume, and length in the metric system are expressed in multiples of 10, 100, 1000, and so on, similar to some parts of our monetary system. For example, the prefix "centi-" represents 1/100 of a basic metric unit, just as a cent represents 1/100 of our basic monetary unit, the dollar.

Table 2–1 shows the prefixes used to define multiples or fractions of the basic units, as well as specific multiple metric units of mass (gram), volume (liter), and length (meter). You must learn these units and their equivalents in order to work problems. For example, you should know that 10 dg = 1 g, 100 cm = 1m, and 1000 mL = 1 L. To give you a better sense of how much—or how little—these units represent, Table 2–2 shows the English-based equivalents of some common metric measurements.

Two special units are used to measure very small lengths, the nanometer and the angstrom. A *nanometer* (nm) is 1/1000 micron and an *angstrom* (Å) is 1/10 of a nanometer (or 1/10,000 of a micron). This means that 1000 nm = 1μ, 10Å = 1nm, and 10,000 Å = 1 μ.

In the metric system, the units of density generally used for solids and liquids are g/mL (g/cm^3), and the units generally used for gases are g/L. Density has units of mass/volume, and whenever the density of a substance is expressed, the particular units of mass and volume must be given. For example, the density of water is 1.00 g/mL in the metric system and 1000 kg/m^3 in the SI. It is not enough to express the density of a substance as a pure number without units.

Daub and Seese, *Basic Chemistry,* pp. 15–18

1. How many grams equal a pound? _____
2. Where did you find this information? _____
3. In the metric system, what is the basic unit of measurement for volume?_____
4. What units are the "English-based equivalents?" _____
   _____
5. On what information did you base your answers to Questions 3 and 4? _____
6. What are the two units that must be given for density? _____
   _____ and _____
7. Where did you find the answer for Question 6? _____
8. Do you think you remember more material by seeing the information on a table or discussed in a paragraph? _____

(Answers will vary. This is another clue to your style of learning.)

EXERCISE 8: Skills Review—PQ4R, The Question Step

A. Here are five textbook headings. Make up three questions based on each one. Answers will vary.

1. White-Collar Crime: An Upper-Class Specialty _____
    a. _____
    b. _____
    c. _____

2. Magnetism _____
    a. _____
    b. _____
    c. _____

3. Food Safety _____
    a. _____
    b. _____
    c. _____

4. The Roles of Congress _____
    a. _____
    b. _____
    c. _____

5. Bankruptcy _____
    a. _____
    b. _____
    c. _____

B. Take three headings from a textbook in one of your other classes and make up three questions based on each one. Answers will vary.

1. Title of textbook _____

    Course _____

    Heading _____
    a. _____
    b. _____
    c. _____

    Heading _____
    a. _____
    b. _____
    c. _____

    Heading _____
    a. _____
    b. _____
    c. _____

Learning
from Lectures

7

Learning from Lectures

7 | The palest ink is better than the most retentive memory.
Chinese Proverb

In the preceding chapters of this book, we discussed learning from written material. This chapter focuses on learning from lectures. There are many inborn similarities between learning from reading and learning from listening, such as looking for main ideas and supporting details, but there are also differences. The main difference is that when you are studying your textbook, you can reread as often as you need to. When you are listening to a lecture, however, what you miss is gone forever. Taking notes is absolutely essential to remembering what was said.

At the beginning of teaching a course in note-taking, one of the authors of this book was casually talking about the subjects the course would cover, the assignments, and the basic principles of good note-taking. Noticing that none of the students was taking notes, she decided to demonstrate how information that does not seem important, or that students are sure they'll remember, can be turned into test questions. After a 25-minute presentation, she asked the students to write the answers to 15 simple short-answer questions such as "When will your first assignment be due?" The highest score was four correct. The students quickly realized that they had made a mistake by not taking notes from the very beginning of class. Although the quiz was not graded, everyone learned a great deal from it. They learned first that notes are important even on the first day; second, that you forget most of what you hear if you don't write it down; third, that even seemingly unimportant information can be important to answering test questions; and fourth, that a casual, conversational presentation of ideas doesn't mean that what is said isn't important. Needless to say, everyone in the class took notes after that.

Listening and Observing

The first step in taking good notes is to ensure that you will be able to listen closely to and get the most out of a lecture. You can accomplish this by doing the following things.

1. *Come to class prepared.* Do the reading assignment. By doing so you will become familiar with key terms and important concepts. This makes it easier for you to recognize what is significant in the instructor's lecture and helps you to avoid feeling that you must write down everything he or she says. If you don't understand part of the reading assignment, you can ask questions during the lecture. Additionally, being prepared will help you avoid the embarrassment of asking questions that reveal that you haven't done the reading.

   Review your notes from the previous class meeting. This not only gives you additional preparation for exams; it also gives you perspective on the topic to be covered at this class meeting.

2. *Sit as close as possible* to the instructor. This helps you concentrate because your line of vision is clear and you can hear well. You may also make a good impression on the instructor—unless you plan to use the time to write letters or take a nap (don't).

3. *Come to class early* enough to get a good seat and have your notebook and pen ready when the instructor begins a lecture. Many instructors use the first few minutes of class to give a brief overview of the topics to be covered in the lecture. Listening carefully to this introduction will prepare you mentally for taking notes.

4. *Listen for verbal cues.* When the instructor uses signal phrases, such as "The most important difference is . . . ," prepare to write. If the instructor uses numbers, such as "The three major theories are . . . ," number the items in your notes.

5. *Watch for nonverbal cues.* If the instructor slows down and stresses a point, or writes something on the board, write it down. Your instructor may also unconsciously signal important points by leaning forward, increasing eye contact, or changing the number or type of hand gestures.

How Not to Take Notes

When Steve was a freshman, he made a useless attempt to write down everything his psychology instructor said. By the time he had finished writing one sentence, the instructor was two sentences ahead of him. Steve was so busy writing that he missed more than half of the lecture. After a week he was so disgusted that he bought a tape recorder. He ended up with 20 one-hour tapes by midterm, for just *one* of his classes. When he tried to take notes from the tapes, he had to stop the recorder every five minutes to finish writing down what had been said. It took him 3 hours to transcribe the first tape, and then another 20 minutes to read what he had written. Steve realized that at this rate it would take him weeks to prepare for his midterm exam, which was now only four days away. In desperation he borrowed Sandra's notes and photocopied them. However, they made no sense to him at all; he even wondered if he and Sandra had really been at the same lectures. Steve gave up and withdrew from the class.

Steve's story illustrates several mistakes that students make when taking notes:

1. Trying to write down everything the instructor says is a mistake. People talk much faster than you can possibly write (the average person speaks at about 125 words per minute, while the average person writes no more than 60 words per minute). It's a poor use of limited time to write what you already know, or to write complete sentences, or to write more explanation than you need.

2. Using a tape recorder is a mistake. It only postpones the time when you have to organize the lecture so that you can recall it for an exam. The whole reason for taking notes is to have the instructor's key points in brief form so that you can recall them for tests.

3. Using shorthand is a mistake because this technique encourages you to try and write words or symbols for everything the instructor says. First, as stated in number 1, you don't want or need to record everything the instructor says. Second, unless you are unusually fast, you will still have problems keeping up with the instructor. Third, you are concentrating on recording every word, rather than choosing to listen to the important ideas. As with tape recording, this only postpones trying to organize the lecture into study notes. Finally, while you are trying to take shorthand, you rarely have time to look at the instructor, so you miss many of the nonverbal cues the instructor uses to emphasize important ideas.

4. Photocopying someone else's notes is a mistake. Since a good note-taker keeps up with the instructor by writing what he or she thinks is important to remember and doesn't already know, the notes are not the original lecture. In addition, your classmate has probably used symbols and abbreviations that you may not recognize. These factors, not to mention the difficulty of reading someone else's handwriting, make it difficult to understand and almost impossible to learn from someone else's notes. When you miss a class, instead of borrowing and copying notes, try to get another student to use his or her notes to talk to you about the lecture while you take your own notes. The other student will make the connections between ideas so that they will make sense to you. Also, you will have a chance to ask questions. Both of you will learn more by actually discussing the notes.

How to Take Notes

1. *Buy a notebook that you can easily organize,* such as a loose-leaf or spiral-bound notebook. You should make divisions for separate courses and have a way to file handouts with your notes. Wide-ruled paper is easy to read. Write in pen or use a pencil dark enough that you don't get eyestrain trying to read what you have written.

2. *Leave a margin at the top of the page.* Use it to write down assignments and other important information that you don't want to forget.

3. *Leave a two-inch margin at the left side of the page.* (Notebook margins aren't wide enough.) You will use this column for self-testing, which is discussed later in this chapter.

4. *Always put the date of the lecture at the top of each page and number the*

pages, especially if you are using a loose-leaf notebook. Pages have a way of getting out of order.

5. *Use speed writing.* Speed writing consists of using a minimal number of words, eliminating unnecessary strokes, and using abbreviations and symbols. Forget the rules of penmanship and try for speed. Here is a sample:

Speed writing should not look like this.

Speed writing should look like this.

Make up a system of symbols and abbreviations that is comfortable for you. In each field, some words are used often. Abbreviate them. Here are some common speed-writing abbreviations to get you started.

w/	with	=	equals
w/o	without	≠	does not equal
vs	versus, against	t/f or ∴	therefore
comp or *cf*	compare with	*bec* or *cuz*	because
ie	that is	+	also, plus, and
eg	for example	≈	equals approximately
NYC	New York City	<	greater than
subj	subject	>	less than
soc	sociology	↑	increased
#	number	↓	decreased
cont'd	continued	**imp't**	important
def	definition	**yr**	year
♂	male	**mt**	month
♀	female	+	and
pos	possibly	**wt**	weight
prob	probably	**ans**	answer

Now add words that you would like to abbreviate and create a symbol you can use.

Word	Abbreviation	Word	Abbreviation
_____	_____	_____	_____
_____	_____	_____	_____
_____	_____	_____	_____
_____	_____	_____	_____
_____	_____	_____	_____

Remember that the most important thing in speed writing is that you can read it later. Don't abbreviate your notes to the point that you forget what the instructor said. It is wise to review your notes immediately after class so that you can fill in words you might need.

Another principle of speed writing is that it's faster to cross out words or make insertions than it is to erase and rewrite.

Your speed writing will improve automatically if you practice these principles as you take notes:

6. *Listen actively instead of passively.* Write down only the main ideas and just enough examples or other details so that the ideas make sense to you. Although your instructor may be speaking at 125 or even 160 words per minute, and you can write about half as fast, you can understand at least 500 words per minute. Therefore, you have plenty of time to listen actively and make decisions while the instructor is talking, so long as you aren't trying to take down every word. Copy word for word only when necessary—for example, an important definition, date, or name. If you miss something, don't ask the person next to you what was said, because you will both miss the next idea. Just leave a blank and ask your neighbor when the class is over. If you both have what was said before and after what you missed, it won't take very long to fill in the missing material.

7. *Use visual organization.* Write key ideas toward the left and indent details underneath. A formal outline style is unnecessary, but it helps to have the most important ideas stand out visually. Leave plenty of space. Crowding your notes together saves paper but makes them harder to read, and it is impossible to add to them, which you will want to do if another, related point is made during the lecture or if you remember something later that you want to add.

8. *You should never have more notes than absolutely necessary.* Of course, no one can tell you how much to write. If you are familiar with the material, either from past experience or because it's in the textbook, and you're sure you won't forget it, just a word or two will remind you that the topic was discussed.

9. *Review your notes immediately after the lecture.* Fill in any blanks; if necessary, compare your notes with those of another student. Write in the left margin any unfamiliar words and any questions you may have. Don't bother to recopy your notes.

EXERCISE 1: Speed Writing

Now try taking some notes. Don't read the sentences in the selections that follow. Instead, ask your instructor or a friend to read them one at a time in a normal speaking voice while you take notes on your own paper. When you finish, compare your notes with our notes. Remember that no two people take notes exactly alike; our samples in Appendix D are just a guide.

1a. Basically, the gas turbine engine consists of two sections: a gasifier section and a power section.

1b. When we refer to distribution, we are normally talking about wholesale and retail trade.

1c. Nepal, located in the Himalaya Mountains, is one of the least developed and most isolated countries in the world.

Now practice taking notes on longer selections. You will have to listen to the second sentence while you are still writing notes on the first one.

2a. The main emphasis of community mental health centers is on prevention. Consultation, education, and crisis intervention are used to alleviate problems before they become serious.

If you think you missed something important, don't ask the person
next to you what the teacher just said. It is not only rude to the professor
and disturbs other people, the most important reason not to talk during a
lecture is that both you and your neighbor will miss the next part of the
lecture. You will just get farther behind. Write what you think was said
and leave a space in your notes so that you can check after the lecture is
over. Even if you did not hear the instructor's exact words, your at-
tempted notes and the blank space will help you locate where you missed
something so that you can ask the instructor or a classmate later.

2b. Osteoporosis is a disease that affects many older people, especially
small, thin Caucasian and Asian women. To prevent it, those at risk
should eat foods rich in calcium, engage in weight-bearing exercise,
and perhaps take calcium supplements.

2c. On September 14, 1901, Theodore Roosevelt became the youngest
President of the United States. He succeeded William McKinley, who
had been assassinated by an anarchist in Buffalo, New York.

The next selections are even longer.

3a. The first mechanical calculator was the abacus. It was probably used
by the Babylonians as early as 2200 B.C. In the Far East it began to be
used in the thirteenth century. It is still used today in the same way it
was centuries ago.

3b. Because your clock radio has its antenna inside, turning the radio
around can sometimes improve reception. Your radio might sound
better in another room, farther from the source of static. Sometimes
grounding is the problem, which may be solved by turning the plug
around in the outlet.

3c. Most people falsely believe that diamonds are the most valuable stones
in the world. Contrary to popular belief, it is rubies that, carat for carat,
sell for more. Since 1955 the supply of rubies has decreased, and their
value has increased dramatically until now they are worth more than
emeralds, sapphires, and diamonds.

Studying Your Notes

The process of studying your notes involves adapting the last four
steps of PQ4R (Read, Write, Recall and Review).

Read

If possible, reread your notes right after class to be sure that they
make sense to you. The longer you wait to reread them, the more likely
you will forget what the teacher said.

As soon as you can, you need to go back and do the Write Step. Before you start this step, you must be sure that your notes are complete. If it
has been an hour or more since you took notes, be sure to read them again

to refresh your memory. If a part of the notes no longer make sense, call a classmate and ask that person to look at his or her notes to try to make sense of that part of the lecture. Remember, as we said at the beginning of the chapter, it is a mistake to ask your classmate what he or she wrote or to make a copy of the notes. All you will have is the minimum recall of what your friend thought was said by the instructor. Taking a moment to talk with a fellow student about what was said will help both of you to recall more of the lecture. Be sure to call a student who takes good notes.

Write

Use the left-hand column on the notebook page for marginal notes—specific questions, comments, or references to pages in the textbook. Write any unfamiliar vocabulary on flash cards. Next, write brief self-test items in the left-hand column for all the major points you want to remember. For example, if the lecture covered three types of reading—study reading, regular reading, and partial reading—you might write in the margin "3 types of reading" so that you could test your memory on the three types. Since you will use the items for self-testing later in the Recall Step just as you did in Chapters 5 and 6, don't write the answers. Write just enough information for self-testing.

Recall

Now, one page at a time, cover your notes so that only the left-hand column is visible. Test your knowledge of the main ideas and important details with the same method you use for studying textbooks. Keep self-testing until you have good recall of the entire lecture.

Review

About once a week, depending on the difficulty of the course, review your notes for the entire week by using the Recall Step just described. Periodically review your notes for the entire term. It is wise, when reviewing, to compare the self-test column in your notes with the self-test column in your textbook. How often you review should be determined by how fast you forget material. The review will refresh your memory.

EXERCISE 2: Using the PQ4R Write Step with Lecture Notes

Here is a page of notes you will recognize because the lecture is about the topic of this chapter, note-taking. Read the sample and then make marginal notes from our notes. Check your answers with our sample answers in Appendix E.

Assign. due Sept. 12   Sept. 10
   take notes in another class
   read Chap. 2 of back
                              Note - taking

Listen + observe better
   1. Prepare - read bk + notes
   2. Sit close
   3. Come early + have paper + pen out
   4. Listen for verbal cues signal
        words - e.g. "most imp." "3 maj. theories"
   5. Look for nonverbal cues
         inst'r ⎰ slows down
                 ⎱ uses board

Don't
   1. Write it all
   2. Use tape rec. or shorthand
   3. Xerox other's notes

Do
   1. Buy notebook ÷ subj. - large lines
   2. Write, NOT PRINT - use pen
   3. Leave 2" margin on lft
   4. Date top of pg + # pgs
   5. Speed write
        no extra strokes
        don't erase / cross out
        abbrev. + use symbols
          e.g. w/ = with
               ≠ = not equal
               ∴ = therefore
        write only what's necessary

After class
   1. Review notes
   2. Don't recopy
   3. Write ? in lft. margin

EXERCISE 3: Taking Speed Notes in Lectures

Ask a friend to read the following short lecture to you as if he or she were lecturing. Take notes on your own paper.

Financial Aid

Financial aid is available to students who attend either two-year or four-year colleges. Financial aid can take the form of a grant, a scholarship, on campus work, or a loan. A grant doesn't have to be paid back. A scholarship, like a grant, doesn't have to be paid back, but it is given to a student who has a high grade-point average as well as financial need. Working on campus provides the student with money while allowing him to adjust his working hours around his school schedule. A student loan must be paid back, but many colleges offer loans that have low interest payments and don't require repayment until after a student finishes his education. If you need money to stay in school, you should apply to the financial aid officer at your school. He or she can determine your needs and make available one or more of the above financial programs to assist you.

Evaluating Your Notes

Now turn the page and compare your notes with ours to see if you included all of the topics which we covered in our notes. If you added notes which we didn't have, reevaluate whether you would really need that information to recall this paragraph for a test. Remember, your goal is to take only needed notes because people talk much faster than you can write. Now look at your writing style. Did you follow our suggestions for "speed writing" or did you lose time by writing words out that could have been abbreviated, by adding fancy loops, by printing and/or being compulsively neat?

Read

Since you have just taken notes on this short selection, you won't have to reread them before moving to the Write Step.

Our notes on financial Aid

	Financial Aid
	Avail. at 2yr. or 4 yr. schools
	grant - not pd. back
	scholarship - not pd. back
	on campus work - Adj. hrs. to you
	loan - low interest - pd. back
	See financial Aid office if you need $

Write

Return to your notes on the financial aid practice "lecture" and add marginal notes. Because the selection is so short, underlining isn't necessary. Check your recall column against ours in Appendix E.

Recall

This paragraph is obviously a very short example of taking lecture notes but if your marginal notes are weak, you might find you cannot even recall this limited amount of information. It is a good idea to cover up the paragraph and check yourself.

Review

Since this paragraph only has a few marginal notes and no underlining, you would not have to review it by itself. In this case you would wait until you had several days of lecture notes to review.

Summary

Learning from lectures is similar to learning from reading materials. A major difference is that taking lecture notes requires improved listening and observation habits. Taking good notes depends primarily upon being able to recognize main ideas and supporting details. Note-taking is also helped by techniques such as speed writing and informal outlining. Study your notes by applying the last four steps of PQ4R: Read, Write, Recall, and Review.

Comprehension Check

Circle the letter preceding the correct answer. Then check your answers in the back of the book.

1. In note-taking it is
   a. wise to write down every word because anything you miss may be gone forever.
   b. impossible to write down every word.
   c. necessary to write down every word you can.
   d. never necessary to write down exactly what a teacher says.
2. Listening and observing are improved by
   a. using a tape recorder.
   b. making your notes easier to understand.
   c. making your notes easier to study later.
   d. accomplishing (b) and (c).
3. Speed writing
   a. is an organized system like shorthand that uses symbols to represent most words.
   b. is useful in only a few classes, such as math and science.

   c. depends on memorizing as many symbols as possible.

   d. uses symbols and abbreviations that vary from person to person.

4. Which phrase belongs in a self-test column?

   a. 6 causes of Civil War

   b. gas turbine engine—2 sections: gasifier + power

   c. TR Pres. in 1901

   d. ∴ = therefore

5. Using a tape recorder

   a. saves you from having to rewrite the notes later.

   b. saves you time and energy.

   c. doesn't help you organize the lecture.

   d. saved John from having to drop the psychology course.

6. Taking lecture notes

   a. indicates that you have a weak memory.

   b. usually improves your grades.

   c. interferes with listening.

   d. comes naturally to most students.

7. When you miss a class you should

   a. go to the instructor and ask what was covered.

   b. have a classmate talk to you about the lecture so that you can take notes.

   c. photocopy someone else's notes.

   d. wait until the next class and copy someone else's notes.

8. When taking notes in class, you should leave plenty of space between your notes because

   a. you may want to add to them if a related topic is mentioned later in the lecture.

   b. crowding makes the notes hard to read.

   c. you may remember something later that you want to add.

   d. all of the above are true.

9. Name two ways in which speed writing differs from regular writing.

   a. _____

   b. _____

10. List three of the nine suggestions in this chapter for successful note-taking.

   a. _____

   b. _____

   c. _____

Questions for Discussion and Writing

1. This section has given many suggestions on how to improve your note-taking skills. Which three will you try immediately? In what classes will they be most helpful?

2. After doing the practice lessons in speed writing, which techniques do you think you will be able to do immediately and which do you think you will have to practice before you can add them to your

note-taking skills? How do you plan to practice these more difficult skills?

EXERCISE 4: Note-Taking

Have someone read the following selection to you while you take notes on your own paper. Then compare your notes to our sample notes in Appendix F.

Reading Selection 1: Speech Communication/Note-Taking

Nonverbal Communication and Note-Taking

Minnette Lenier and Janet Maker

Nonverbal communication includes gestures, facial expressions, tone of voice—everything except actual words. Nonverbal communication is the reason that we understand and remember more from a live lecture than we do from a tape-recorded lecture.

Since note-taking requires the student to make instant decisions about which ideas are important, nonverbal clues can be valuable to the student who knows how to read them.

Although the science of nonverbal communication has not advanced enough to enable us to translate correctly the meaning of every gesture, there are some general principles that will help the observant student recognize when the instructor is making an important point.

One obvious clue that an idea is important is that the instructor writes it on the chalkboard. But it is also helpful to observe how much time the instructor spends explaining what is on the board and how many times he refers to it during the rest of the lecture. Physical closeness and verbal attention indicate that the subject under discussion is important to the speaker.

Another clue to important ideas is whether the instructor takes time to prepare lecture notes and to bring books to class. An instructor generally uses notes when she wants to make sure that certain ideas are not forgotten. When the instructor reads from notes, it is a good idea to write down what she says.

If the instructor brings books or handouts to class, one can conclude that she would not have made the extra effort unless she considered the material important.

There are several less obvious clues to important ideas. First, when a person is talking about ideas that she considers important, she will move closer to the listener, either by walking or by leaning forward, and eye contact will increase. Second, when a speaker slows down and makes more frequent pauses, or raises his voice, one can usually assume that the ideas are important. (An exception to this rule is the instructor who is not prepared and is stumbling over his words.) Finally, watch for nonverbal signals. One instructor signals important ideas by taking off his glasses. Another walks around to the front of her desk. A third clears his throat before every major idea.

In conclusion, learning from lectures is **facilitated** by being observant. Students who watch for nonverbal clues during the lecture will likely be more successful than students who look only at their notebook.

helped

After you check your notes against ours, go back to your notes, underline important ideas and fill in the recall column.

The following article was chosen for this chapter to emphasize the importance of careful listening. After reading it, see if you retained the important parts by taking the Comprehension Check.

Reading Selection 2: Speech Communication

You Can Overhear, but You Can't Overlisten

Albert J. Vasile and Harold K. Mintz

How to Be a Better Listener

Diogenes, a Greek philosopher 2300 years ago, put it very wisely when he said, "We have two ears and only one tongue in order that we may hear more and speak less."

To be a better listener you must first want to be one. You must realize the many benefits of improved listening, and you must be prepared to exert the required effort. When you come to class you know that you'll hear people talk, so prepare yourself to listen. Develop a positive attitude toward the speakers. Tell yourself that you'll hear some **exhilarating** topics and that in all probability you'll learn something new. Motivation can spell the difference between just hearing something and listening and understanding it.

exciting

If you're planning to attend a lecture or listen to a speech outside class, you can get ready for it by learning what you can about the speaker. Who is she? What's her background? Is she an authority on the subject? What's her motive for speaking? By increasing your interest in the speaker and her subject before the event, you can't help but listen more effectively.

The following are some suggestions for **honing** your ability to listen:

sharpening

- Develop your vocabulary.
- Concentrate on the message.
- Keep an open and objective mind.
- "Read" the speaker.
- Put yourself in the speaker's shoes.
- Take notes.
- Compensate for a speaker's flawed delivery.
- Get ready for the wrap-up.

Develop Your Vocabulary

Once you commit yourself to improving your listening efficiency, the best step you can take is to expand your vocabulary.

Fully understanding the meanings and inferences of words is **crucial** to your total comprehension of a speaker's intended message. Being able to put the speaker's language in proper **perspective** is a significant first step in developing your listening efficiency.

critical

context

Concentrate on the Message

Interpersonal communication should be on a constant beam from the speaker to the listener and back to the speaker. Don't interrupt this beam by daydreaming or **succumbing** to distractions. Try not to think about last night, this morning, or tonight. If your thoughts begin to wander, take charge and direct them back to the speaker and her message. If the speaker is boring, challenge yourself to make the effort.

giving in

Another obstacle to total concentration is the fact that we think much faster than we speak. A comfortable speaking rate lies between 130 and 160 words per minute. The brain, however, can deal with approximately 500 words per minute. So you can see that while we're listening, we have quite a bit of spare time. We must guard against becoming distracted during this spare time.

From the moment the speaker approaches the stand, **rivet** your eyes onto her. Remember that eye contact is as important to the speaker as it is to the listener. Look interested and you will be interested. Watch her facial expressions and gestures while she's speaking. You can receive many clues to her meanings by observing her mannerisms. Gestures can be **eloquent,** indeed.

fix

expressive

Beware of distractions. Little things can throw you off: books dropping, people talking and coughing, fire sirens wailing. The speaker himself can be distracting. His outfit may be as loud as the fire engine, his gestures may be uncontrolled, or he may be constantly swaying. If these or other distractions occur, then you must intensify your concentration on the message because nothing inspires a speaker more than an interested audience.

Keep an Open Mind

Don't have the attitude, "I know what she's going to say and she's all wet." **Preconceived** opinions narrowly limit your ability to benefit from a true communicative experience. Be objective. Hear the speaker out. Then, if you disagree, ask her to clarify certain points. Give the speaker every courtesy that you would want if you were speaking.

previously held

Keeping an open mind is one of the more difficult techniques to master for effective listening because many people may be opinionated and make hasty judgments. They establish personal views even before the speaker opens her mouth. A person's grooming, posture, walk, and eye contact can nonverbally transmit positive or negative messages.

"Read" the Speaker

If the speaker gives his speech a title, grasp it. Closely follow the introduction and the main points. In the introduction he should state what will be covered. Take note and anticipate the main points. How do they relate to the other points mentioned? Is he accomplishing what he set out to do? What about the soundness of his ideas? Are they valid? Is he logical? Does he have supporting material and how does he use it? These are just some thoughts to consider while you're listening.

Put Yourself in the Speaker's Place

You may be better able to understand and absorb a talk if you try to put yourself in the speaker's place (emphatic listening). This means you must strive to feel, think, act, and react like the speaker. What motivated her to select this topic? What is her educational and professional background? What are her qualifications to speak on this subject? What action or reaction is she seeking from the audience and why?

If you can successfully place yourself in the speaker's shoes, not only will you understand her message better, but you will take a giant step toward becoming a more effective listener.

Take Notes

Taking notes can enhance your listening ability because it engages you in two activities—listening and writing. The secret to taking notes is to jot down only the main points. Whatever format of note-taking works for you is the one you should use—complete sentences, phrases, or key words. Writing down key points as you hear them helps you grasp and remember them.

Compensate for a Speaker's Flawed Delivery

Not all speakers have read this book (what a shame!), thereby denying themselves some of our practical principles that might help **alleviate** bad delivery habits. Poor speech habits can **detract** from the message the speaker is trying to convey. He may talk in a **monotone** or pause often with *uh's, er's,* and *you know's.* Playing with notecards, eyeglasses, or a watch may discourage the audience from listening efficiently.

solve
take away
single tone

In this case, what you must do—and it isn't easy—is to separate the speaker from the speech. Just remember, many speakers have significant things to say but, unfortunately, erect obstacles that **impede** listeners. If you can discipline yourself to ignore the speaker's **deficiencies,** you may be rewarded with some valuable viewpoints and insights.

block
shortcomings

Get Ready for the Wrap-Up

Be ready for the conclusion of the talk. It will be the speaker's final chance to imprint her message in the minds of the listeners. At this time she may repeat some important points that you may have missed during the talk. Listen for them and ask yourself the following crucial questions: Did I get her message? Do I agree, or do certain points need **clarification?** What were her strongest and weakest arguments?

clearing up

Since some students—especially those whose first language is not English—may hesitate to ask questions, I would like to emphasize its importance for two reasons. First, asking questions will enable you to better understand the subject, and second, it will give you valuable experience in speaking. And if you're a beginner in our language, the more you speak it, the sooner you will master it.

So, for all concerned, never be too embarrassed to ask questions. There is no more important process in education than asking questions.

Comprehension Check

Circle the letter preceding the correct answer. Then check your answers in the back of the book.

1. What is the first step in becoming a better listener?
   a. practicing listening to many speeches
   b. wanting to be a better listener

    c. learning to listen faster

    d. finding out about the speaker's background

2. Which of the following will sharpen your ability to listen?

    a. concentrating on the way something is said as well as on what is said

    b. keeping an open mind

    c. identifying with the speaker

    d. all of the above

3. According to the selection, most people speak

    a. about 130 to 160 words per minute.

    b. about 200 to 300 words per minute.

    c. approximately 500 words per minute.

    d. fewer than 100 words per minute.

4. Which of the following do the authors mention as an obstacle to concentration?

    a. daydreaming

    b. thinking faster than others speak

    c. becoming bored with a speaker

    d. all of the above

5. The main idea of the selection is that

    a. concentration can be improved.

    b. listening is a skill that can be improved.

    c. most people are poor listeners.

    d. people should talk faster than they do.

6. Keeping an open mind

    a. increases our concentration.

    b. enables us to benefit by hearing a variety of points of view.

    c. makes us better speakers.

    d. enables us to challenge ideas with which we do not agree.

7. We can infer that

    a. good listeners are good speakers.

    b. most speakers are good listeners.

    c. there are several barriers to good listening.

    d. a good speaker can make anyone agree with his or her ideas.

8. The authors seem to believe that

    a. speakers don't communicate very well.

    b. most speakers bore their listeners.

    c. you can force yourself to listen to uninteresting people.

    d. learning a foreign language makes people better listeners.

9. List three of the suggestions the author gives for improving your listening ability.

    a. _____

    b. _____

    c. _____

10. According to a study by Rudolph Verbeber and Ann Elder, "An Analysis of Student Communication Habits," the average college student spends approximately 20 percent of the day reading, 20 percent speaking, 10 percent writing and as much as 50%, listening.

a. Research studies including a series of studies by Ralph Nichols concluded that most people listen with less than 50% efficiency.

After observing yourself for the next three school days, what do you think is your listening efficiency (how much you pay attention): in most of your classes _____, in this class _____, on your job _____, with your friends _____?

b. After 15 minutes how much do you think you can remember (repeat with accuracy) of "what you heard": in most of your classes _____, in this class _____, on your job _____, what your friends said _____?

c. Over the next three school days evaluate yourself. How much of your day do you think you spend writing (including taking lecture notes)? _____ reading? _____ speaking? _____ listening? _____

d. What does this information tell you about the importance of improving listening for you? _____

e. What does this information tell you about the importance of improving your note-taking ability? _____

Questions for Discussion and Writing

1. What is the difference between listening and hearing?
2. After working in this chapter and reading this article, how will you change your listening and note-taking techniques?
3. How can improving your vocabulary increase your listening efficiency?

EXERCISE 5: Review of Main Idea, Support, and Signal Words

In the following reading selection, circle the main ideas and underline the key supporting ideas.

Reading Selection 3: International Business

Gestures in International Business

Lillian H. Chaney and Jeanette S. Martin

Gestures are another important aspect of body language. Gestures can be emblems or symbols ("V" for victory), illustrators (police officer's hand held up to stop traffic), regulators (glancing at your watch to signal that you are in a hurry), or affect displays (someone's face turning red with embarrassment). Gestures are used to add emphasis or clarity to an oral message. Although the meaning of gestures depends upon the context, here are some general guides to interpreting the meaning of gestures in the United States (Axtell, 1991):

- Interest is expressed by maintaining eye contact with the speaker, smiling, and nodding the head.
- Open-mindedness is expressed by open hands and palms turned upward.
- Nervousness is sometimes shown by fidgeting, failing to give the speaker eye contact, or jingling keys or money in your pocket.
- Suspiciousness is indicated by glancing away or touching your nose, eyes, or ears.
- Defensiveness is indicated by crossing your arms over your chest, making fisted gestures, or crossing your legs.
- Lack of interest or boredom is indicated by glancing repeatedly at your watch or staring at the ceiling or floor or out the window when the person is speaking.

Although regional differences exist, people in the United States typically use moderate gesturing. They rarely use gestures in which elbows go above shoulder level as this is interpreted as being too emotional or even angry; one exception is waving hello or good-bye. Italians, Greeks, and some Latin Americans use vigorous gestures when speaking while Chinese and Japanese people tend to keep their hands and arms close to their bodies when speaking. Most cultures have standard gestures for such daily situations as greeting someone and saying good-bye; learn and respect such gestures when conversing with persons of another culture.

Here are some additional guidelines for gesturing in various cultures (Axtell, 1991):

Figure 4.2 "V" for Victory Gesture

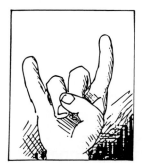
Figure 4.3 Vertical Horns Gesture

- The 'V' for victory gesture (Figure 4.2), holding two fingers upright with palm and fingers faced outward, is widely used in the United States and many other countries. In England, however, it has a crude **connotation** when used with the palm in.

  implied meaning

- The vertical horns gesture (raised fist, index finger and little finger extended, Figure 4.3) has a positive connotation associated with the

University of Texas Longhorn football team. This gesture has an insulting connotation in Italy, but in Brazil and Venezuela it is a sign for good luck. In other cultures, such as Italy and Malta, the horns are a symbol to ward off evil spirits. This symbol has various meanings in U.S. subcultures, such as Satanic **cults** (cult recognition sign signifying the Devil's horns). Therefore, it should be used only when you are sure the other person understands its intended meaning.

devoted groups

- The thumbs-up gesture (Figure 4.4) is widely recognized as a positive signal meaning "everything is OK" or "good going." Although well known in North America and most of Europe, in Australia and West Africa it is seen as a rude gesture.
- The "OK" sign (Figure 4.5), with the thumb and forefinger joined to form a circle, is a positive gesture in the United States, while in Brazil it is considered obscene. The gesture has still another meaning in Japan; it is a symbol for money.
- The beckoning gesture (Figure 4.6, fingers upturned, palm facing the body) used by people in the United States for summoning a waiter, for example, is offensive to Filipinos, as it is used to beckon animals and prostitutes. Vietnamese and Mexicans also find it offensive.
- The head nod in most countries means "yes," but in Bulgaria it means "no."

Figure 4.4 Thumbs-Up Gesture

Figure 4.5 "OK" Gesture

Since one culture's gestures may be misinterpreted by people in another culture, avoid using gestures when communicating in international business settings until you become knowledgeable about the meaning of such gestures.

Figure 4.6 Beckoning Gesture

Questions for Discussion and Writing

1. Now that you realize how easy it is to misunderstand the meaning of gestures, in what situations will you have to be more aware? What do you think you will do differently?

2. Misinterpreting gestures can lead to serious problems. Picture yourself working in another country or being a politician, and describe the kinds of problems you could experience.

EXERCISE 6: Review of Using Graphic Organizers

In Exercise 5, you began to graphically organize the material by indicating different types of information with different types of visual cues. Now, take the information you marked and use it to create a stronger visual image. First, decide whether the information could best be remembered in an outline, on a map, or on a chart, and then create it, using your own paper.

Bring your graphic organizer to class so that you can compare it with others' work to see how different people have organized the same information. Decide whether your graphic organizer suits your individual learning style or whether someone else's might have been more helpful.

Improving Memory

Improving Memory

It is notorious that the memory strengthens as you lay burdens upon it, and becomes trustworthy as you trust it.
Thomas De Quincey

Five Keys to Memory Improvement

One thing all students wish for is a better memory. You may be surprised to learn that everyone's ability to store items in short-term memory is about equal. However, not everyone has learned the techniques for using memory equally well. This chapter presents five steps to improve your memory: attention, selection, organization, review, and application.

Attention

Look at the illustration. What do you see?

PARIS
IN THE
THE SPRING

Did you read "Paris in the the spring"? Probably not, because we see what we expect to see. Not paying attention to what was actually written caused you to make the error. Paying attention is the first step in improving your memory: if you are not paying attention to something, you will not learn it. Have you ever been reading a book when you suddenly realized that you hadn't understood the last three pages? If something is not thoroughly learned, it cannot be remembered. One way to ensure that you pay attention is to become interested in what you are learning. If you use the PQ4R technique explained in Chapters 4, 5, and 6, studying will become more interesting. The first two steps in PQ4R, previewing and questioning, will give you a logical framework so that what you read will become more meaningful. For example, a psychology book chapter that deals with Freudian, behaviorist, and humanist theories will be more meaningful if you know that these are the three major theories of personality, and if you have asked yourself questions about them: What are their similarities and dissimilarities? What research supports each of them? How thoroughly does each explain human behavior? How well does each explain what you know about yourself?

Selection

You cannot memorize an entire textbook. You must, therefore, use *selective* attention: concentrate on what is important and ignore what is not. If you are reading a textbook chapter, you must understand the main ideas before you can determine which details to memorize. Attempting to memorize indiscriminately because you don't really grasp what you are reading will inevitably lead to failure. If you have previewed a chapter or a book and are aware of its key points, you will have a better chance of distinguishing the trees from the forest. What your instructor says in class is another important clue. If he or she stresses a particular concept, it is likely to appear on a test.

Organization

Take one minute to look carefully at the following words:

cow, horse, trout, sparrow, eagle, shark, whale, tuna, albatross, sheep, salmon, elephant, canary, blackbird, sardine

Now take a piece of paper and write as many of the words as you can remember without looking back at the list. Write the number you remembered here: _____. Here is the list again, but rearranged to make the words easier to remember:

Mammals	Fish	Birds
cow	trout	sparrow
horse	shark	eagle
whale	tuna	albatross
sheep	salmon	canary
elephant	sardine	blackbird

Take one minute and try again to memorize the words. Then write them on a separate piece of paper, and put the number you remembered here: _____. You probably did better this time.

Now suppose that you need to memorize the names of all 50 states of the United States. Trying to remember them in random order is extremely difficult, but there are several ways you could group them:

1. visually, by picturing in your mind a map of the United States;
2. chronologically, by date of admission to the Union;
3. in alphabetical order;
4. by categorizing them geographically—North, South, Midwest, etc.

Any of these organizational schemes will make memorizing easier. Choose the one that works best for you.

When we see or hear something in isolation, we remember very little of it. We might hear Chinese being spoken, but unless we can organize the sounds into words and the words into sentences, we won't remember what we heard. Similarly, we can remember vocabulary words better if we can organize words into families based on their prefixes, roots, and suffixes.

The Preview Step in PQ4R helps you remember what you read because it gives you an overview into which you can fit the parts. We classify ideas in memory in much the same way that information is stored in a filing system. If you want to remember a fact, you must have a category in which to file it. For example, we classified the 15 items in the list of animals into three categories—mammals, fish, and birds. Abstract concepts can be classified, too. If you know that William Wordsworth was a Romantic poet and that Alfred, Lord Tennyson, was a Victorian poet, and if you know the general characteristics of the Romantic period and the Victorian age, you can compare the writing of those periods more easily. You can classify composers, artists, and historical events using the same scheme. Making meaningful associations between related facts helps you classify and remember them. The material presented in textbooks is organized, but you will better understand that material if you attempt to associate it with everything else you know.

Recall and Review

The major problems in recall are 1) failure to learn the material thoroughly in the first place; 2) failure to recall the cluster of information from a cue. However, even if the first factors are not the reason, we forget at a frighteningly rapid rate including material that we have learned.

Recent research indicates that memories don't just fade away. Instead, new learning interferes with recall of old learning. In your mental filing system, new learning covers up old memories, making them harder to retrieve. If you learn American history and then English history, it will be harder for you to remember American history than if you had learned nothing else. If you study and then sleep for eight hours, you will remember most of what you learned. But if you remain awake for the same eight hours, you will forget up to twice as much. Prior learning can also interfere with retrieval of later learning. If you take Spanish your freshman year and French your sophomore year, you will find Spanish words interspersed in your French conversation.

If you can't reduce interference by sleeping after each study session, it's a good idea to include breaks between subjects.

To retain information for an extended period, such as from the beginning of a course to the final exam, you must review the material periodically. The frequency of review will depend upon the number of unfamiliar concepts you must memorize. Research indicates that cramming the night before an exam is much less effective than reviewing previously learned material once a week or so.

The best way to review is by **self-testing,** as in the Recall Step of PQ4R that was taught in Chapter 6. By self-testing you may discover any misunderstood or incorrectly learned material before it's too late.

Overlearning also helps. Overlearning means continuing to study something that you have already learned well enough for one perfect recall. Overlearning facilitates retention. You can use overlearning by continuing to test yourself even after you are scoring 100 percent correct. If you overlearn your material and regularly review it, recalling should not be a problem.

Application

If possible, apply what you have learned. If you are learning French, speak French whenever you can. Form the habit of translating into French the names of objects you encounter. If you are learning theories, try to find people with whom you can discuss them. If you encounter new words, use them in your conversation.

Forgetting

Forgetting is normal. In fact, if we didn't forget, we would be bombarded with information. Short-term memory which only holds information for a few seconds also holds a very limited amount of information. That material either must be processed into long-term memory, or written down for later learning. Otherwise, it will be lost.

We even forget things we are sure are in our long-term memory. Take a moment to write down the names of the seven dwarfs from "Snow White." Then, look at the following explanation.

_____   _____   _____   _____

_____   _____   _____

Most people can only name five but forget the names of the other two. The ones most frequently forgotten are "Doc" and "Bashful." If you didn't name all seven, were we right in predicting which you would forget? It's not mind-reading. Those are the two that don't end in "y." They would need special review just as some parts of your textbook would be harder to remember than others.

The Keys to Memory Improvement

You can reduce forgetting and improve memory by practicing certain skills.

1. **Be motivated.** You can actually work at being alert and stimulated by what's happening in class. A large part of learning is really wanting to learn and paying attention to *what's happening right now.*
2. **Practice.** Memory, just like any other skill, improves with practice.
3. **Gain confidence** in your ability to remember and in your ability to use aids to increase memory. Doubting your abilities leads to anxiety. That decreases your ability to process information. Relaxed, alert listening improves your ability to transfer ideas to long-term memory and retrieve ideas later. Negative thinking usually leads to negative results.
4. **Stay turned-in.** You can't pay attention to two things at once. If you are distracted in class, you will never even hear what a teacher is saying. While studying if you are listening to the radio or watching television, you cannot be studying effectively.
5. **Focus.** Remember not all data presented to you will be equally important. In lectures, listen for both ideas and details. When reading textbooks, look for what you think will be on a test.
6. **Associate.** Anything that you can join with something you already know (no matter how crazy the connection) will help you organize your thoughts. Don't think of yourself as a sponge soaking up isolated facts. You are a thinker, a processor and an analyzer of information.
7. **Don't overload the circuits.** Listen to lectures and read textbook chapters in chunks. Don't think of an hour lecture as an hour. Break it into segments that you can deal with. Concentrate on what is going on at the time. When reading textbooks, look for headings and subheadings to help you break chapters into 2 to 3 page readable segments. Always break tasks into parts. Just like food, learning is easier to digest in bites.
8. **Garbage in, garbage out.** If you don't group material in units, with cues to remember each chunk, you probably won't find the information in your memory bank later. A marginal note, for example, is an excellent cue to the information in a section of a book or lecture.
9. **Memories may face, ink doesn't** (or at least not as quickly). Human memory is not perfect. Don't try to remember what you can write down. Whether it's to remember needed groceries, a dentist appointment, your friend's birthday, or a class lecture, notes help tremendously.

Understanding versus Rote Memory

There are two major ways to remember—by rote and by understanding. The rote method involves using a mechanical aid; understanding involves classifying ideas and making meaningful associations. Difficult concepts are best remembered by understanding them. Specific facts, such as phone and social security numbers, are easier to remember by using a mechanical technique. A poem, a speech, and lines in a play are best remembered by a combination of understanding and mechanical devices.

Material learned by understanding is retained longer than material learned mechanically. In addition, learning by understanding can be helpful in some situations. For instance, you can remember mechanically how to start a car, but if your car won't start, understanding the starting process could be useful. However, because mechanical learning is a necessary part of every college student's life here are some basic techniques.

Learning by Rote

Learning by rote memory is done by repeating material over and over. For example, you may have learned "The Pledge of Allegiance to the Flag" or the "Preamble to the Constitution" by rote memory. You have no memory of the parts. You probably cannot start in the middle and remember the rest. You learned to recite these from beginning to end with no or little understanding of what you were saying. The keys to learning something by rote memory are 1) repetition 2) breaking the material into smaller units if you cannot remember all of it at one time. If you must remember something word for word, it is often useful to add another dimension to your practice. For parts you find difficult to remember, use a mnemonic.

Using Mnemonic Techniques

Mnemonic techniques are devices to aid memory. A general rule is that any type of memory device must be simple, clear, and vivid. You don't remember the ordinary or the everyday event, but you do remember the unusual, the funny, or the personal. For example, to remember that the root *fer* means to carry, picture yourself on a ferry being carried across a river.

Now let's consider several mnemonic techniques.

Visual Association.   The following is an example of *visualization.* In ancient Greece, senators spoke in an organized manner without notes for hours. Their trick? They kept the parts of their speeches organized by picturing a house. Each section of a speech was placed in a different room of the house. Then, they imagined themselves walking from room to room as a way of keeping track of where they were in a speech. This technique can help you keep anything from a list of errands to the chapters in your textbook in mental order.

Grouping.   Grouping means classifying on the basis of some common characteristic. That is what we did when we rearranged the list of animals earlier in this chapter.

Rhyming.   This method uses rhyming words to help you remember.

- "In fourteen hundred and ninety-two, Columbus sailed the ocean blue."
- "**I** before **e** except after **c,** or when **e** sounds like **a** as in *neighbor* and *weigh.*"
- "Thirty days hath September, April, June, and November. . . ."

Be careful not to mix up your rhymes, or you could end up with this:

- In fourteen hundred and ninety-three, Columbus sailed the deep blue sea.

Sound system.   You can break words into the sounds they make in order to remember them. Use this method for scientific words, formulas, names, and foreign words. An example is the formula for the area of a circle: $A = \pi r^2$. You can remember the phrase "pies are square"; think of a square pie.

This method doesn't help with spelling, only with sound. Be careful that you don't confuse what the key sounds stand for. One memory expert tells of a man who visualized a woman with a large stomach to help him remember that her name was Mrs. Hummock. Unfortunately, when he met her several weeks later he said, "Good day, Mrs. Kelly!" falsely remembering his key word as *belly* (Lorayne, *Super Power Memory*, p. 102).

Acronyms.   Use acronyms to help you remember lists of words. The first letters from each word in a list form a key word, name, or sentence.

In music, "every good boy does fine" are the lines on the treble clef. FACE stands for the spaces on the treble clef.

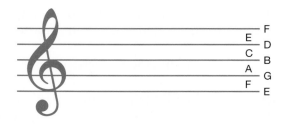

In science, MVEMJSUNP are the first letters of the names of the nine planets: Mercury, Venus, Earth, Mars, Jupiter, Saturn, Uranus, Neptune, Pluto. You might remember them by the phrase, "Mercury's very eager mother just served us nine potatoes."

In art, ROY G. BIV stands for the colors of the spectrum: red, orange, yellow, green, blue, indigo, and violet.

In history, "Washington and Jefferson made money at jacks; Van

Buren had to put Taylor's flower pot back" stands for the names of the first 15 presidents in order—Washington, John Adams, Jefferson, Madison, Monroe, John Quincy Adams, Jackson, Van Buren, Harrison, Tyler, Polk, Taylor, Fillmore, Pierce, and Buchanan.

In geography, HOMES stands for the Great Lakes—Huron, Ontario, Michigan, Erie, and Superior.

Remember our original list of animals? You might use the sentence "Call him tonight; speak to every short white tuna" to stand for cow, horse, trout, sparrow, eagle, shark, whale, tuna. Note that we used the first two letters of *sparrow* and *shark* to avoid confusion, and the whole word *tuna* to distinguish it from *trout*.

Using Mnemonics: Relating Word Parts and Meanings

One way to remember word parts is to associate them with words you already know. For example, you might think of *tractor* to remember *tract*, meaning "to draw or pull." Another memory technique is to visualize scenes that include the word parts and their meanings.

Here are examples of ways you can associate word parts and meanings through mental pictures.

Word	Meaning	Mental picture
spec, spic, spis	see, look	an *inspector* looking at *spec* words
press, prim, prin	squeeze, press	a woman *pressing* *press* words
mob, mot, mov	move	a *mob* riding on a loco*mot*ive going to a *mov*ie
log, logy	word, speech, reason, study of	you sitting on a *log* studying a *log*ic book
vid, view, vis	see	your mother seeing you on tele*vis*ion inter*view*ing your favorite film star

Mnemonic systems are useful and easy once you take the time to learn them. They are handy when you are studying for tests, but they should not be used as a substitute for remembering things by understanding them.

Concentration

We frequently hear our students complain, "My mind wanders. I have trouble concentrating when I study. When I get to the bottom of a page, I can't remember anything I've read." They often blame themselves for their lack of willpower. However, we believe that inability to concentrate and study effectively is *not* caused by lack of willpower alone. The major cause is poor study habits. In this book we present efficient techniques for study and concentration, but it will be up to you to practice those techniques until they become habitual.

The main enemies of concentration are distractions. Distractions can come to you either from outside or inside. To study effectively, you will have to cope with distractions from both sources.

External Distractions

You are probably aware of the need for a proper study environment: a well-lit desk in a room relatively free from noise and interruptions. If you have three toddlers, or a roommate who cannot live without the sound of loud rock music, you may have to study in the college library. However, eventually you can learn not to be distracted. In one experiment, certain students took a test in a room with a 500-watt spotlight, five buzzers, seven bells, a 90,000-volt rotary spark gap, two organ pipes, a 55-pound circular saw, a phonograph, three metal whistles, acrobats, and a photographer taking pictures. These students performed as well on the test as another group of students who were tested in a quiet room. They had learned to ignore distractions. They had started practicing concentration in a noisy room by reading material that was easy and very interesting. When they were able to block out the external noise, they shifted to more difficult and less interesting material. Using the same techniques, you should be able to learn to concentrate even when your roommate is giving a party in the next room.

Internal Distractions

You may find that even in a quiet room you have trouble concentrating. Mental conflict, irrelevant thoughts, daydreaming, boredom, and fatigue can be more distracting than noise.

Mental conflict.   The conflict caused by studying when you really want to be doing something else, such as going to a movie, will drain your energy and make your study time much less effective. You can reduce mental conflict by taking a realistic course load so that you have time for rest and recreation. In addition, become involved in what you are studying. Read actively. When you finish a major section, try to underline the main ideas. Jot down questions and comments that come to mind about the material you are reading.

Irrelevant thoughts.   You may find thoughts intruding while you study: "Return that overdue library book!" "Don't forget to buy a Mother's Day card!" Keep a pad and pencil next to you while you work. Once you have made a note of the irrelevant thought, you can forget about it and concentrate on studying.

Daydreaming.   If your thoughts drift to things like last Saturday's date or an upcoming party, it won't help to write them down. Instead, make a checkmark on a pad whenever you catch yourself drifting off. You will find that the number of checkmarks per hour will decrease dramatically once you start keeping a record.

Boredom and fatigue.   One way to fight off boredom is to alternate one subject with another when you study. There is no rule that you have to spend a four-hour block of time on one subject. Another way to reduce boredom is to take study breaks every hour or so. Try to do something different for 5 or 10 minutes. When you are in the middle of writing a paper, a break to write a letter may not be as relaxing as a break to walk the dog. Taking a break is always better than staring at a book without absorbing anything. Not only does the staring stop you from resting, but it also establishes the habit of nonconcentration while studying.

If you find that you are fatigued after two or three hours of studying, you may need to have your vision checked. One way to avoid eyestrain while reading is to close your eyes or look away from your books for a few seconds every half-hour or so.

Summary

Everyone can improve his or her memory through five steps: paying attention, selecting the important facts and ideas, organizing the material to be memorized, periodically recalling and reviewing, and applying what has been learned. Forgetting is caused by inadequate initial learning and by interference of old learning with new learning, and vice versa. To minimize such interference, students should take a break if possible before switching from one subject to another.

There are specific techniques that can improve memory: 1) be motivated, 2) practice, 3) gain confidence, 4) stay turned-in, 5) focus, 6) associate, 7) don't overload the circuits, 8) garbage in, garbage out, 9) memories may fade, ink doesn't, 10) memory aids aid memory.

Information can be memorized by understanding or by rote. Understanding is generally better, but for mechanical learning, mnemonic techniques, or devices to aid memory, may be useful.

Many students find it difficult to concentrate. Concentration is improved by (1) having a good study environment to minimize external distractions and (2) developing effective study techniques to minimize internal distractions such as daydreaming, mental conflict, and boredom.

Comprehension Check

Circle the letter preceding the correct answer. Then, check your answers in the back of the book.

1. The best way to memorize a speech is
   a. to use a mnemonic system.
   b. to understand what it means.
   c. to write it out.
   d. to do both (a) and (b).
2. The best way to remember material for a test is
   a. to read it carefully several times.
   b. to cram the night before.
   c. to test yourself on the significant ideas.
   d. to underline as much of the material as possible.
3. The purpose of this chapter is
   a. to tell you about mnemonic devices.
   b. to show you how you can improve your memory and concentration.
   c. to show you how to organize your ideas.
   d. to teach you the steps in memorization.
4. The main purpose of mnemonic systems is
   a. to make studying more interesting.
   b. to improve your understanding of facts.
   c. to shorten your study time.
   d. to improve retention.
5. The ability to concentrate
   a. depends on the absence of external distractions.
   b. depends on the time you spend in the library.
   c. can be increased.
   d. is reduced for a busy person.
6. What step in the memory process is Henry employing when he uses the concepts he learned in his psychology class to analyze his girlfriend?
   a. selection
   b. organization
   c. recall and review
   d. application
7. From your knowledge of mnemonic principles, which image do you think would be easiest to recall?
   a. you studying in the library
   b. you reading a chapter on memory
   c. you sitting on a bird's nest with a beehive in your hand
   d. you taking notes in class

8. You could conclude from this chapter that it is easiest to remember
   a. main ideas.
   b. isolated details.
   c. names and faces.
   d. dates.
9. List the five steps to improving your memory.
   a. _____ d. _____
   b. _____ e. _____
   c. _____
10. List three internal and three external distractions.

   Internal   **External**

   a. _____ a. _____
   b. _____ b. _____
   c. _____ c. _____

Questions for Discussion and Writing

1. What can you do to reduce or eliminate the internal and external distractions you listed in question 10?
2. Which of the mnemonic devices seems the most useful for you, and why would it help more than the others?

EXERCISE 1: Selectivity

Read the following paragraph. In the blanks below it, write five or six key words or phrases that would help you remember the content of the paragraph. Then check your key words against our sample key words in the back of the book.

Virtual Reality

Ever since Jules Verne published his great science fiction yarn, *Twenty Thousand Leagues Under the Sea,* about a boat that could actually submerge and travel for months without surfacing, the real world has been imitating the literary imagination. When I was a boy, many decades ago, the comic book detective Dick Tracy spoke into a wrist telephone. Today, as I drive down the highway, I see people carrying on telephone conversations while steering with one hand. Even that most impossible of all science fiction dreams, walking on the moon, is now a reality. Indeed, it happened so long ago that my students these days have heard about it from their parents. . . . The latest wrinkle is a pair of virtual reality helmets that allow two people to enter the same imaginary space or virtual reality, and even to play ball in it. The makers promise that before too long, you will be able to climb into a body suit and make virtual love to an imaginary, but quite visible, partner. It sounds too much like the Holodeck on the Enterprise for comfort.

Wolff, *About Philosophy*, p. 220

1. _____   4. _____

2. _____   5. _____

3. _____   6. _____

Now, close your eyes and see if you can picture the six words. If you wrote down a good key word, you should be able to remember the word and the example from the paragraph.

EXERCISE 2: Organization

Rearrange the following terms in four categories of six items each. Label each of the four categories. Then check your answers in the back of the book.

sculpture	metaphor	parliament	Congress
dissection	opera	punctuation	geology
literature	president	organism	harp
constitution	etymology	tempera	microscope
election	vocabulary	easel	chemistry
keyboard	prime minister	biology	grammar

1. _____ **2.** _____   **3.** _____   **4.** _____

a. _____ _____ _____ _____

b. _____ _____ _____ _____

c. _____ _____ _____ _____

d. _____ _____ _____ _____

e. _____ _____ _____ _____

f. _____ _____ _____ _____

EXERCISE 3: Retention

Without looking back at Exercise 1, visualize the key words you wrote. Then take a piece of paper and try to write as much of the paragraph as you can. Now, return to the paragraph and see how much of the actual paragraph you were able to call up from long-term memory. Answers will vary.

EXERCISE 4: Mnemonics

List 10 words you must remember for a class, for work, or for your outside activities, such as daily chores or items for a shopping list.

1. _____   6. _____
2. _____   7. _____
3. _____   8. _____
4. _____   9. _____
5. _____   10. _____

Using the first letter of each word, make up a mnemonic word or phrase to help you remember the list. Answers will vary.

_____

_____

_____

Reading Selection 1: Psychology

Improving Memory

Gordon H. Bower

Years ago psychologists often studied the accuracy of eyewitness reports, such as occur in courtroom testimony, by playing out some kind of **scenario** before a class of unsuspecting students. What became immediately apparent in such studies was the tremendous **variability** of the details the witnesses reported seeing. They would, of course, forget details regarding the appearances of the actors as well as any names or dates mentioned; and they would forget exactly what was said or who said what. They were likely to misjudge the **duration** of events and fail to remember the order of specific events. There were often gross distortions.

These studies also found a difference between letting the witness freely narrate his recall of the **episode** and having him answer cross-examination questions. As time passes, a person's free account typically becomes shorter as he forgets details, although it does not necessarily become more inaccurate. However, in a cross-examination the witness is forced to make definite statements about items that hover on the dim margins of his memory. Suggestions and leading questions that probe these gray areas can induce the witness to believe in distorted versions of the episode and produce wide errors.

Lawyers are, of course, familiar with techniques that lead witnesses to desired conclusions. Consider the slight difference between

short drama
change

length

occurrence

the questions "*Did you* see the professor hit the student?" and "Didn't you see the professor hit him?" The second strongly suggests that the questioner knows the action happened, just as does the phrase "*Don't* you remember seeing the professor hit the student?"

Even subtler are questions that use definite articles to **insinuate** a **presupposition.** "Did you see the pistol in the student's pocket?" results in more yeasaying than the question phrased with the indefinite article, "Did you see a pistol in his pocket?" And, once the witness is committed to one false presupposition—for example, that the student had a pistol—he can be led by suggestion along a road of vague agreements as to what must have been so, given that presupposition.

Subtle wording of questions can also influence the estimates a witness makes. For example, police officers and lawyers find that estimates are increased by suggestion when they ask "How tall was your **assailant**?" rather than "How short was he?" and "How old was he?" instead of "How young was he?"

After watching a film showing two cars colliding in a traffic accident, witnesses were asked "About how fast were the cars going when they smashed into one another?" Their estimates averaged around 40 mph. Other witnesses were asked "About how fast were the cars going when they *bumped* into one another?" and their estimates averaged around 30 mph. The influence of such subtle suggestions as these can be quite **substantial.**

One of the subtle and **insidious** influences of leading questions is that they can alter a person's memory of an event. A witness tends to **integrate** into his memory any presuppositions hidden in questions he was asked soon after the event. For example, suppose after showing you a film of a car accident I ask you "About how fast was the sports car going as it ran the stop sign and turned into the intersection?" and you give me some estimate. A week later, if I test your memory, you are likely to say that you saw a stop sign when in fact there was none in the film.

The same integration can be seen with the "smashed" versus "bumped" question. Several days after they were originally at the scene of the car accident, witnesses who earlier had been asked the "smashed" question were more likely to say they had seen broken glass than those who had had the "bumped" question. The witnesses in these experiments were unaware that they had swallowed the presuppositions in the leading questions. They did not realize their memories were **hodgepodges** of the original events plus later inputs from leading questions or remarks from other witnesses.

The distortions found in eyewitness reports can be **compounded** by passing the report from one subject to another. This is, of course, what happens when rumors are spread through a community. As the story circulates from one link in the chain to the next, there is a simplification of the story, a suppression of the unfamiliar or strange, and a sort of collective effort to understand. There is also a tendency to attribute motives to the characters, and to invent causes that connect

> slyly introduce
> assumption

> attacker

> important
> sly

> blend

> a jumble

> increased

otherwise unrelated parts of the rumor. Such distortions are the basis for **atrocity** rumors that circulate during wartime.

brutality

Memory is apparently unreliable, given to invention, and even dangerous—but it is still the source of continuity in our culture and richness and meaning in our lives.

Reading Selection 2: Psychology—Using Collateral Reading

Eyewitness Testimony

Charles G. Morris

Jurors in court cases are generally willing to believe eyewitnesses. Faced with conflicting or **ambiguous** testimony, they are tempted to put their faith in someone who actually "saw" an event with his or her own eyes. However, this faith in eyewitnesses may be unjustified (McCloskey & Egeth, 1983). Although eyewitness accounts are a unique and essential form of courtroom testimony, studies clearly show that people who say "I know what I saw" often mean "I know what I *think* I saw." And these people can be wrong.

unclear

Consider this **scenario.** Two women enter a bus station and leave their belongings unattended on a bench while they check the bus schedule. A man enters, reaches into their baggage, stuffs something under his coat, and leaves. One of the women returns to her baggage and, after checking its contents, exclaims, "My tape recorder has been stolen!" Eyewitnesses sitting nearby confirm her story when contacted by insurance investigators; many eyewitnesses are able to provide a description of the missing tape recorder, including its color, size, and shape. In fact, there never was a tape recorder! The man and women were assisting psychologist Elizabeth Loftus in a study of the **fallibility** of eyewitness testimony (Loftus, 1983).

scene

chance to make mistakes

Increasingly, the courts are recognizing the eyewitness problem. For example, judges instruct juries to be skeptical of eyewitness testimony and to evaluate it critically. How serious are these reservations about traditional courtroom procedures? Take the case of Father Bernard Pagano, a Roman Catholic priest who found himself accused of a series of armed robberies in Wilmington, Delaware. After one witness contacted the police to say that Father Pagano looked a great deal like the man in a sketch being circulated by the local media, no less than seven eyewitnesses positively identified the priest as the **perpetrator.** In the middle of the trial, however, another man—whose resemblance to Father Pagano was not even close—confessed to the crime (see the accompanying photographs). How did the court become involved in such a potential **miscarriage** of justice? Well, it seems that the notion of a **larcenous** priest became **plausible** because the media had highlighted the fact that the **culprit** was unusually "gentlemanly": polite, articulate, well dressed, and so on. Furthermore, in

doer

**failure
thieving, believable, guilty person**

presenting pictures of suspects to eyewitnesses, the police had apparently mentioned that the culprit could be a priest. Naturally, Father Pagano was the only suspect in **clerical** garb, and it would seem that the witnesses' memories adjusted to accommodate the fact that they were presented with the picture of a priest. Needless to say, Father Pagano was more fortunate than many falsely accused people. Commenting on over 1,000 cases in which innocent people were convicted, Wells (1993) concludes that errors made by eyewitnesses were the single most important cause of false conviction.

churchly

Father Bernard Pagano (right) was identified as an armed robber by seven eyewitnesses and was nearly convicted for crimes actually committed by the man on the left.

The structure of police lineups is part of the problem. In one study, hundreds of college students saw videotapes of staged robberies. Some of the students saw videotapes of traditional police lineups of suspects appearing **simultaneously.** Thirty-nine percent of these students identified an innocent person as the robber under these conditions. Other students saw videotapes of suspects who appeared one at a time. The error rate under these conditions fell to 19 percent (Cutler & Penrod, 1988). Clearly, eyewitness testimony is fallible, but there are some ways that its reliability can be improved.

at the same time

For over 20 years, Elizabeth Loftus (1993b; Loftus & Hoffman, 1989) has been the most influential researcher into eyewitness memory. In a classic study, Loftus and Palmer (1974) showed subjects a film **depicting** a traffic accident. Some subjects were asked, "About how fast were the cars going when they hit each other?" Other subjects were asked the same question, but with the words, *smashed, collided, bumped,* and *contacted* in place of *hit.* The researchers discovered that people's reports of the cars' speed depended on which word was used in the question. When they were asked about cars that "smashed into each other," they reported that the cars were going faster than if they were asked simply about cars that "contacted" each other. In another experiment, subjects were also shown a film of a collision, and then asked either "How fast were the cars going when they hit each other?" or "How fast were the cars going when they smashed into each other?" One week later, subjects were asked some questions

showing

about the accident they had seen on film the week before. One of the questions was "Did you see any broken glass?" More of the subjects who had earlier been asked if the cars had smashed into each other reported that they had seen broken glass than did the subjects who had been asked simply if the cars had hit each other. Obviously, then, the strategies according to which questions are posed to witnesses by police, lawyers, and other investigators can make a difference in subsequent eyewitness accounts. Based on studies such as these, Loftus and Palmer concluded that eyewitness memory is unreliable because wit-

The issue of recovered memories has legal as well as psychological implications. In 1990, a woman named Eileen Franklin testified that she had recovered memories of her father killing her friend 20 years earlier. Her father was eventually convicted of murder.

nesses cannot **disentangle** their memory of the original event from information and suggestions they received after the event.

separate

There is considerable controversy about whether memory for the original event is actually destroyed and replaced with a new memory that is a **fusion** of the original event and new information received after the event. M.K. Johnson and Raye (1981) and D.S. Lindsay and Johnson (1989) suggest that the original memory is not actually destroyed; instead, people are sometimes unable to tell the difference between memory for things that actually happened and memory for things that they merely heard about or imagined. If you imagine an event in a particularly vivid way, you may later have difficulty remembering whether the event actually happened or you imagined it. Similarly, if you hear information about an event after it has occurred, when you try to recall that event, you might confuse your memory of that information with your memory for the original event. D.S. Lindsay (1993) suggests that if people paid more attention to the source of their memories, eyewitness accounts and memories in general would be less **biased** by information and suggestions received after the actual event.

combination

prejudiced

Eyewitness research may have implications for the study of recovered memories of **traumatic** events, such as childhood sexual abuse.

shocking

Nobody denies the **enormity** of the problem of sexual abuse or the intensity of the suffering of incest survivors. Sometimes memories of such events do not surface until many years later. This phenomenon has legal as well as psychological consequences, because individuals who recover memories sometimes accuse other people of abuse or other criminal behavior that allegedly occurred many years in the past. Some observers (e.g., Loftus, 1993a) are concerned about the accuracy of memories recovered so many years after the original event. Although Loftus does not doubt that many such memories accurately reflect actual incidents, she also notes that in at least some cases other sources (such as the media and even psychotherapists) may have shaped people's recollections of early childhood experiences. For example, in some cases, wellmeaning psychotherapists might **unwittingly** create false memories by asking questions that lead the client to imagine vividly something that never actually happened.

    Other researchers (e.g., Bird, 1994; Olio, 1994) have criticized Loftus for appearing not to take the stories of incest survivors seriously enough. They have argued that false accusations are rare and that it is destructive to make incest survivors doubt the reality of their memories.

    Given the **volatile** nature of this issue, it is likely to remain highly controversial for the foreseeable future. Its resolution will depend on our increasing understanding of the nature of long-term memory and of the extent to which it changes over time.

hugeness

unknowingly

changeable

EXERCISE 5: Comparing Collateral Reading

You probably will have to look back at the two readings before answering these questions. Answering these questions will help you compare and evaluate each reading as well as help you see how reading both articles gave you a better understanding of how the memory works.

1.   Did you understand all the information in the first article? _____ If not, what confused you? Answers will vary.

    _____

    _____

    _____

2.   What information in the first selection, if any, did you understand better after reading the excerpt from the second reading? Answers will vary.

    _____

    _____

    _____

3. What information in the first article did not appear in the second?

_____

_____

_____

_____

_____

_____

4. What information in the second did not appear in the first?

_____

_____

_____

_____

_____

5. How do the two selections differ in their description of how our memory can be distorted?

_____

_____

_____

_____

_____

_____

6. Are there other areas in which the two authors seem to disagree?

_____

_____

_____

_____

_____

_____

7. How do the two articles overlap in their information?

_____

_____

_____

_____

_____

_____

Comprehension Check

Circle the letter preceding the correct answer. Then check your answers in the back of the book.

1. Students who saw staged incidents in their classes
    a. couldn't remember anything.
    b. could remember anything except who said what.

    c. remembered completely what happened.

    d. made different reports of the same event.

2. The students forgot
   a. how long an incident took.
   b. the order of events.
   c. what the people looked like and wore.
   d. all of the above.

3. As time goes on, a person's account of a real event typically
   a. becomes shorter.
   b. becomes longer.
   c. becomes more accurate.
   d. (b) and (c).

4. As a story is circulated, people
   a. make it more complex.
   b. make it longer.
   c. make it stranger.
   d. give motives to the characters.

5. The main idea of the first selection is that
   a. one should watch out for lawyers.
   b. one should observe more carefully.
   c. memory is undependable.
   d. memory is not very useful.

6. The main idea of the second selection is that eyewitness testimony
   a. is usually very accurate.
   b. needs to be considered carefully by a jury.
   c. should not be allowed in court.
   d. is usually the best evidence a lawyer can have.

7. Why was Father Pagano declared not guilty of armed robbery?
   a. His lawyers proved he was in church giving mass.
   b. The seven eyewitnesses admitted during the trial that they were wrong.
   c. Someone else confessed to the crime.
   d. His lawyers proved the eyewitnesses were lying because they didn't like the priest.

8. According to the first article, the most accurate eyewitness testimony occurred when a witness
   a. was reminded of what the people had done.
   b. was cross-examined.
   c. was allowed to freely narrate what he saw.
   d. was asked about the event again after several weeks.

9. What are two of the reasons errors in eyewitness testimony occur?
   a. _____
   b. _____

10. According to the first article, what are two things that happen to eyewitness reports when several eyewitnesses talk about an event they saw?
   a. _____
   b. _____

Questions for Discussion and Writing

1. In the second article, Morris says that witnesses who say "I know what I saw" really mean "I know what I think I saw." Do you believe that eyewitness testimony should be used in court? If so, what could be done to help make it more accurate?

2. After reading this chapter, what can you do differently to help improve your memory?

EXERCISE 6: Review of Supplementary Recall Techniques

Read the following article on the problems with IQ tests, and create a graphic organizer that would help you study for a test. Use any of the supplementary recall techniques that you learned in Chapter 5. Answers will vary.

Test Content and Scores

One major criticism of IQ tests is directed at their content. Many critics believe that intelligence tests are concerned with only a very narrow set of skills: passive verbal understanding; the ability to follow instructions; common sense; and, at best, scholastic aptitude (Ginsberg, 1972; Sattler, 1975). For example, one critic observes "intelligence tests measure how quickly people can solve relatively unimportant problems making as few errors as possible, rather than measuring how people grapple with relatively important problems, making as many productive errors as necessary with no time factor" (J.M. Blum, 1979, p. 83).

These critics suggest that if there is one thing that all intelligence tests measure, it is the ability to take tests. This would explain why people who do well on one IQ test also tend to do well on others. And it would also explain why intelligence test scores correlate so closely with school performance: Academic grades also depend heavily on test scores. Notice that this criticism of intelligence tests challenges the assumption that academic achievement depends on intelligence. Rather, it proposes, neither academic achievement nor intelligence tests measure abilities that are necessary for real-life situations that require successful intellectual activity. Thus it should not be surprising that there is a tendency to "abandon the term IQ and replace it with a more accurate descriptor, such as school ability or academic aptitude" (Reschly, 1981, p. 1097). However, recent reviews of the evidence have reasserted the claim that both school grades and intelligence tests are good predictors of occupational success (Barret & Depinet, 1991). Thus, this particular criticism of intelligence tests may have to be reconsidered.

Still other critics suggest that the content and administration of IQ tests discriminate against minorities. It has been pointed out that high scores on most IQ tests require considerable mastery of standard English, which biases the tests in favor of middle- and upper-class white people (J.M. Blum, 1979). Moreover, white middle-class examiners may not be familiar with the speech patterns of lower-income black children or children from homes where English is not the primary language, a complication that obviously does not encourage good test performance (Sattler, 1975). In addition, certain questions may have very different meanings for children of different social classes. The Stanford-Binet, for instance, asks, "What's the thing for you to do if another boy hits you without meaning to do it?" The "correct" answer is, "Walk away." But for a child who lives in an environment where survival depends on being tough, the "correct" answer might be, "Hit him back." This answer, however, receives zero credit on the Stanford-Binet.

Morris, *Psychology,* p. 328

Taking Tests

9

Taking Tests

9 | What you don't know doesn't hurt you, except during an examination.
Anonymous

Mark the following statements as true or false.

T F   1. Good students aren't nervous before a test.
T F   2. On an exam it's safest not to guess when you don't know an answer.
T F   3. Once you've marked an answer on a test, you should never change it.
T F   4. When you are taking a test, it's wise to answer the easy questions first.
T F   5. On an essay test it's important to outline your answers before you begin writing.

The first three statements are usually false, and the last two are true. This chapter will teach you techniques that will help you be less nervous when preparing for and taking tests. By using these techniques you can get better test grades with less effort.

Coping with Test Anxiety

If you become anxious about preparing for and taking exams, you're normal. In fact, the few people who aren't worried about tests don't do as well as those who are. A little anxiety is a motivation; without any fear, many people would watch television rather than study. The question, then, isn't how to avoid feeling anxious but rather how to make your anxiety work *for* you instead of against you. Students who use anxiety destructively procrastinate until just before the exam, so that they have to read twelve chapters in five courses and write two reports three days before final exams begin. These students know none of the tricks of taking tests, and so when the exams are passed out, they panic and cannot even remember what they *do* know.

Most people are more comfortable taking tests after they learn the techniques that lead to success in preparing for and taking exams and after they have had a lot of practice taking tests successfully.

Preparing for Tests

Review Continually

Your preparation for tests should start at the beginning of each course. The PQ4R method forces you to review your textbook reading, and the self-testing technique described in Chapter 8 forces you to review your notes after class. These types of immediate review are very important aids to memory.

Intermittent review during the term also helps you remember. The more you have reviewed the material, the less you will have to memorize at the last minute. If your text has a study guide or if your instructor has prepared course objectives, it is wise to make them an integral part of your study program. If the course requires you to solve problems, as in math or some of the sciences, make sure that you understand the operations and procedures described in your textbook and class notes. You can best check your understanding by working sample problems that require using the necessary principles.

Make a Schedule

Making a schedule is especially important before final exams, particularly if your exams cover the entire course content. Plan your time prudently so that you finish your major reading and any reports or other assignments at least three weeks before the final exam and about two weeks before midterms. Make up a special exam schedule, using the daily schedule illustrated in Chapter 1. During the three weeks before finals, plan at least six review sessions for each course.

Find Out As Much About the Test As You Can

Don't miss the class meeting before the exam, because that is when your instructor is likely to give information pertinent to the test. Ask the following questions:

- What kind of test will be? Objective tests (true–false, multiple choice, matching, and fill-in) usually require more attention to specific details, whereas essay exams tend to require an overall understanding of the main ideas.

- How many questions will there be, how many points is each question worth, and how much time will be allowed? The answers to these questions will give you an idea of how to budget your time in studying for and taking the test and will indicate how much material is to be covered.

- What material will the test cover, and which topics from the reading and lectures will be emphasized? Be sure that you know exactly which chapters will be covered. If you can find out which topics will be stressed, so much the better. If the test was written by the members of the department as a whole, it is likely to cover the textbook only, since not all lecturers stress the same points. If your instructor wrote the test, any material discussed in his or her lectures could appear, even if it's not in the book.

- How will the test be scored? Will there be a penalty for guessing, and if so, what is the penalty? For example, on the Scholastic Aptitude Test (SAT), the penalty is ¼ the number wrong subtracted from the number right. So, if you have 80 questions right and 20 questions wrong, your score is 75. Since there are five multiple choice and answers for each SAT question, your chance of being right on a wild guess is ⅕, or 20 percent. Because this is less than the ¼, or 25 percent, that will be subtracted if you are wrong, you shouldn't guess. However, if you can eliminate one of the choices (you don't know the answer, but you know choice "b" is definitely wrong), your chances of being right will equal the penalty. If you can eliminate two or more answers, you should always guess, because the odds will be in your favor. Therefore, you must figure out in advance of the test your guessing strategy and follow it.

Make Flash Cards

When you compose self-test items in advance, you help yourself in four ways: (1) you direct your studying; (2) you limit the number of surprises that await you on the test; (3) you reduce the chance that you will "blank out;" and (4) you increase the number of questions that will look familiar to you.

Put two types of self-test items on flash cards. As you review your notes and your textbook, pay attention to any terms or concepts in your self-test column that you think you will not remember, such as "definition of invertebrate" or "six causes of air pollution." Put the self-test item on the front of a flash card and the answer on the back, noting the page of the textbook or the date of the lecture from which it came, as in the following sample:

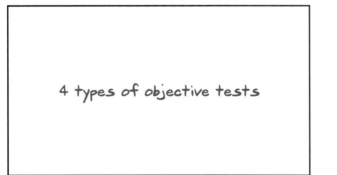

Front

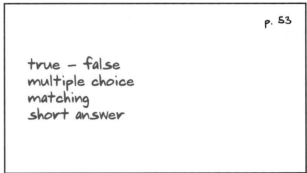

Back

In addition to self-test items, test yourself on broader ideas that you think might appear on the test. These ideas might combine several pages of self-test columns into a few major topics, such as "similarities and differences between two major theories" or "causes of the industrial Revolution." Here is an example:

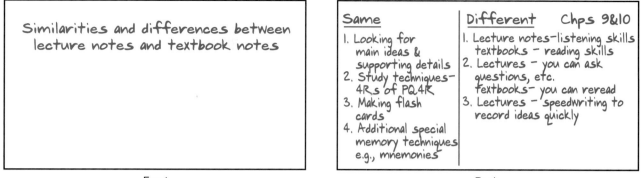

Front   Back

Try to anticipate what your instructor might ask on the test, concentrating on main ideas rather than on details. The wording of the question on the test isn't important as long as you know the content. For example, the following questions all cover the same topic:

Fill in: PQ4R stands for

P _____

Q _____

R _____

R _____

R _____

R _____

Fill in: A technique for reading and studying textbooks is _____.

True or False: The P in PQ4R means "preview."_____

PQ4R is a method of memorization. _____

There is a recommended method for reading a textbook.
_____

Multiple choice: Which step is not an R in PQ4R?_____
a. Read
b. Remember
c. Review
d. Recall

Essay: Discuss how to read a textbook.
Explain how to read a textbook.
List the steps in PQ4R.

Again, put the test item on the front of a flash card and a brief summary of the answer on the back. If necessary, use the mnemonic techniques discussed in Chapter 8.

Carry both sets of flash cards with you for quick review every time you have a few free minutes. In Chapter 8 we discussed the importance of overlearning; keep testing yourself a few times after you are sure you can remember the answer, then retire the card. By exam time your pile of flash cards should be very small.

Get Enough Sleep

The night before the exam, study for a few hours, and then get a good night's sleep. *Don't* go to a movie or watch television, because the new stimuli may cause you to forget what you studied. If you have time for another review immediately before the exam, it may help.

Come to the Exam Prepared

Make sure that you have everything you need—pen, paper or blue book for essay exams, watch, calculator (make sure the batteries are new!), machine-scorable test form (commonly known as Scantrons) if needed, and so on. Equally important is being psychologically prepared. Get to the exam on time. Not only does this ensure that you will hear the directions, it also gives you time to calm down and organize your thoughts. Try to relax; you've done the best you could to prepare and that's all you can expect of yourself. Even if you haven't done the best you could, feeling anxious and guilty won't help you now. Stop thinking about what you need to remember and concentrate instead on test-taking techniques.

Cramming

Cramming, or trying to learn new material quickly for an exam, is not as effective as regular reviewing. However, if you *must* cram, be selective. Since you won't be able to memorize everything, select the vital points. Read your class notes and preview the textbook; then decide which main ideas and details are the most important. Change the items you have selected to self-test questions, put them on flash cards with the answers on the back, and review as much as you can. Forget about that good night's sleep the night before the exam: it's better to be tired and know something than to be well rested and know nothing.

Taking Tests

Exams can be divided into three categories: objective, essay, and problem solving. Some exams include more than one type of question. Objective exams require you to recognize the correct answer; essay exams require you to recall information with no clues. Problem solving is often required in courses such as math and chemistry.

Objective exams contain true–false, multiple-choice, and/or matching questions. Short-answer questions are like essays in that there are no clues, but they are like objective tests in that there is usually one correct answer to be filled in.

A primary general rule in taking any type of test is to follow directions carefully.

Here is a sample test. Have your instructor or someone else time you. You have only five minutes to complete this test. Work quickly and carefully. Read over the entire test before you begin.

1. Circle all words in this sentence that contain the letter **r**.
2. Write your age in months here: _____
3. Write all the even numbers from 0 to 25 here: _____
4. Write in the right-hand margin the names of the four most recent presidents of the United States.
5. Cross out the word **the** every time it occurs in the first five instructions.
6. Underline all the five-letter words in the first four instructions.
7. If you can buy three pencils for 5 cents, how many can you buy for 25 cents? _____
8. Ignore the first seven instructions. _____

This trick test shows how not reading instructions can cause you to waste time. Skipping the instructions can also lower your grade on a test or even cause you to fail.

A second general rule for test taking is to budget your time carefully. Suppose you were taking a two-hour final exam. How much time would you spend on each of the following tasks?

1. skimming the test to find out the types of questions and the points allotted to each type _____
2. answering 25 multiple-choice questions worth 25 points total

   _____
3. answering 5 short-answer questions worth 25 points total

   _____
4. answering 1 essay question worth 50 points

   _____
5. checking your answers after completing the test

   _____

Although you should need to spend less time on the questions you know best, a rough general division is one or two minutes for skimming the test, about 10 minutes for checking answers, about half the remaining time on the essay question, and about one-fourth of the time on each of the 25-point sections. This division of time will probably earn you the most points.

Answering Objective Questions

1. *Read the directions* carefully to be sure that you mark the answers in the right way. If the exam is machine-scored, be sure to use the right type of pencil, make no extra marks on the paper, and erase completely any answers that you change.
2. *Find out if there is a penalty for guessing.* Most of the time, guessing will increase you score. If there is no penalty, you should always guess. For example, on a true–false test, you have a 50 percent chance of being right even if the test is written in a language you can't read. However, if you can make an educated guess, the odds in your favor are even higher. If there is a penalty, you must calculate at what point guessing will raise your score.
3. *Skim the exam* to find out how quickly you will have to work, and budget your time accordingly.
4. *Answer the easy questions first.* Read each question carefully and take only a few seconds to decide on an answer. If you don't understand the question, ask the instructor. Answer the questions you know and those about which you can make an educated guess. Put a check mark beside those you are not sure of and return to them later. (Make sure you erase the check marks if the test is machine-scored.) Skip the questions you can't answer, check-marking them also in the hope that later questions will provide clues. For example, if one question asks you to name the father of psychoanalysis and you can't remember the answer, a later question might jog your memory by mentioning Sigmund Freud.

    After you have gone through the whole test, reread and answer the questions you checked. Don't take a lot of time over the answers; assume that the instructor is not trying to trick you unless he or she has a habit of writing tricky questions. The most obvious answer is probably the right one.
5. *Check your answers.* When you have completed the test, take the 10 minutes you allotted to reread it completely, checking every answer. Contrary to superstition, you *should* change an answer that seems wrong when you reread the question. If you are using a separate answer sheet, periodically make sure that the numbers on the test match those on the sheet. When you are answering the 50 multiple-choice questions, Question 37 is not the place to discover that you are marking the space for Question 38 on your answer sheet.

True–false questions.   Circle the correct answer.

Sample question

Example: *Illegal* means "a sick bird."   T   F

1. Watch out for absolute words such as *always, never,* and *entirely.*   T   F
   Since few things in life are always true, questions using those words
   are often false.

2. If any part of the statement is wrong, the whole thing is false. For ex-   T   F
   ample, "The Volkswagen is a small foreign car made in France" is
   false.

3. If you have to write in the answer rather than circling it, write out the   T   F
   whole word. Most teachers will mark ambiguous answers such as *F*
   and *T* wrong.

Multiple-choice questions.   Circle the letter preceding the correct
answer.

Sample question

A housefly is

a. a home with wings.
b. a common insect that buzzes and often annoys.
c. a zipper used as a door.
d. a new type of airplane.

1. Read *all* the alternatives before answering, because sometimes there
   are answers such as *(a) and (c)* or *all of the above.* Also, many multiple-
   choice tests ask you to mark the best answer, in which case more
   than one may be correct but one is better than the others.
2. Watch for grammatical structure, as in "The largest body of water is
   an (a) ocean, (b) river, and (c) lake." The word **an** is a clue.
3. If all else fails, the longest answer is often the correct one.

Matching questions.   Fill in the blanks.

Sample question

Write the letter of the correct spelling in the blank before its definition. You may use
each choice more than once.

_____ 1. the end you don't want to   a. but
                turn to a billy goat   b. butt
_____ 2. what the goat might do to (1)   c. Butte
_____ 3. the end of a cigarette   d. none of the above
_____ 4. a city in Montana
_____ 5. a politician's favorite word

1. Find out whether each answer is used only once. If you are allowed
   to write on the test, cross out each letter after you've used it so that
   you can better see what's left.
2. Read all the items on both columns before answering any question,
   and answer those you know first.

Short-answer questions. Fill in the blank.

Sample question

Taking tests makes me _____.

1. If you have only a minute or two per question, treat the items as you would objective questions. Write as quickly as possible, doing the easy ones first, then going back to fill in the others. If the answers are more like essays in length, follow the directions for essay tests.
2. If you don't know the answer and there is no penalty for guessing, write anything reasonable that you can think of.

Answering Essay Questions

Essay questions may require anything from short answers to long essays. Instructors usually score them by comparing each student's answer with a list of all the points that should have been covered. Therefore, simply trying to write everything you know will usually earn a low grade. Here are some things to remember when answering essay questions.

1. *Read the directions* carefully and do exactly what is asked. If the question requires you to *list* or *enumerate,* as in "List the six major types of transportation," just write the numbers 1 through 6 with a type of transportation after each. If you are asked to *outline,* you must indicate in outline form which ideas are more important than others, exactly as you did in Chapter 5. Your opinion is generally not wanted unless you are asked to *criticize* or *evaluate,* and even then it's a good idea to cite authorities before you give your ideas. When you are asked to *discuss,* decide which points are the most relevant and provide a rationale for your choices.

   Here are some instructions (1 to 9) of the type frequently found on essay tests. Match the instructions with the types of answers (a to i) you might give.

_____ 1. Criticize the statement, "What you don't know won't hurt you except during examinations."

_____ 2. Outline the major ways to expand vocabulary.

_____ 3. Contrast speed writing and regular writing.

_____ 4. List the words that PQ4R stands for.

_____ 5. Compare lecture notes and textbook notes.

_____ 6. Discuss how to improve your ability to take notes.

_____ 7. Trace the events leading to the Civil War.

_____ 8. Summarize the reasons some people do poorly on tests.

_____ 9. Diagram the major parts of the internal combustion engine.

a. Describe the events in order.
b. Stress differences.
c. Show similarities.
d. Give your opinion with some supporting data.
e. Examine in detail.
f. Give one point at a time.
g. Describe with sketches or charts.
h. Visually structure important ideas, indenting subpoints and using appropriate symbols.
i. Put things in a nutshell: state the major points.

Answers: 1d, 2h, 3b, 4f, 5c, 6e, 7a, 8i, 9g

2. *Read all the questions* and the directions. Pay attention to the number of questions, how many points each is worth, and which are the easiest. If you are allowed to choose which questions to answer, make up your mind quickly and stick to your decision. If the instructor says you may choose three out of five, do not answer more than three since the instructor probably won't read more than three answers.

3. *Make a schedule.* Decide how much time you can allot to each question. Give more time to those that are worth more points and that are harder for you. Schedule enough time to make an outline of each answer.

4. *Answer first the questions that are worth more points and are easiest for you.*

5. Before you begin to write, *make a sketchy outline* on scratch paper of your answers to *all the questions* you plan to answer. The reason for this is that by the time you are outlining Question 3, you may suddenly remember something important that you omitted in Question 1. It is easier to add a point to an outline than to try to squeeze it into an essay you have already written. Also, when you've finished your outline, you will no longer have to recall and write at the same time. You will then be more relaxed, and you can concentrate on writing grammatical sentences in legible handwriting. (There is research evidence that well-organized and neatly written answers get higher grades. But don't recopy your answers; it takes too much time.)

6. *Write a brief introduction* to each answer, using signal words. One sentence using the key words in the question is usually sufficient; for example, "There are three similarities between X and Y."

7. Make your main points stand out by using *signal words* such as *first* and *next.*

8. At the end of the essay, *write a very brief closing statement* signaled by words such as *in conclusion* or *in summary.*

9. If there are any questions to which you don't know the answers, *write something* anyway; you might pick up a few points. If you write nothing, you will score zero. Leave space between answers in case you remember something later, and don't crowd your answers. This is no time to save paper.

Here is an example of a correctly written essay. The instruction was: "Compare and contrast skimming and scanning." As a first step, the student made an outline:

	Skimming & Scanning	
	I. Compare	
	A. Don't read every word	
	B. fast	
	C. partial comprehension	
	II. Contrast	
	A. purposes	
	B. techniques	

Now the complete essay, written from the outline:

Skimming & Scanning

Skimming and scanning are forms of partial, rapid reading. They differ in purpose and techniques.

Both skimming and scanning can be done at rates up to thousands of words per minute. They involve skipping unnecessary material; therefore, the reader will not remember everything the author presented. One cannot remember what one hasn't read.

In skimming, the reader looks for main ideas, skipping unimportant details. Skimming can be used to preview, review, and overview material. An example of skimming might be looking quickly through a newspaper. Scanning, on the other hand is used to locate specific details. Main ideas will be overlooked. Examples of scanning might vary from finding a particular date in a textbook to finding a name in a phone book.

Since the purposes in skimming and scanning differ, techniques also differ. When skimming, the reader looks for main ideas, usually contained in the first sentence of each paragraph. He will pay attention to signal words and typographical clues such as italics, boldface, and underlined phrases. In scanning, the reader looks for key words or numbers that are contained in the question he is trying to answer. He will stop to read only after he has located the key word.

In conclusion, skimming and scanning are both necessary techniques for reading efficiency. Good readers will be skilled at both.

Answering Problem-Solving Questions

Handle a problem-solving test, for instance in math or chemistry, as you would an essay or a short-answer test. If there are only a few problems, handle them as in an essay test: read the directions; find out which are worth the most points; and do the easy ones first. If you receive partial credit for doing part of the problem, do it, even if you know the final answer is wrong. If you have no idea how to begin solving the problem, you can't follow the suggestion for essay exams, which was to write something anyway. You will have to leave it blank. If the test includes many problems, then follow the suggestions for short-answer tests.

Reviewing Tests

When your test is returned to you, read it over and make sure you understand all of your mistakes. If your instructor does not comment on why your answer was wrong, either in a note written on your exam or during class discussion, ask during his or her office hours. It's important to know the correct answer, because the same idea may appear on a final exam. Or, if this *is* the final exam, you may need the information for a higher-level class in the same subject area.

Another reason to review your tests is to examine your test-taking techniques—whether you tend to change answers from right to wrong or from wrong to right, whether you pick up clues within the test, whether you misread questions, and whether you allot your time properly. You may also want to analyze the types of questions the instructor writes: Are the questions based more on the book than on the lectures? Are the questions tricky? Do they focus more on main ideas or on details?

Summary

Students normally worry about tests. However, anxiety can be controlled and higher grades can be earned by using good test-taking techniques.

Preparing for tests begins early in the term and includes reviewing continually, making an exam schedule, making up exam questions to use in self-testing, and finding out as much about the exam as possible. Get enough sleep the night before and come to the exam prepared, both physically and psychologically.

Cramming should be avoided, but if it is necessary, the key is to be selective: try to memorize only the points most likely to appear on the test.

Exam questions can be divided into **objective, essay,** and **problem-solving** questions. For all three types it's essential to follow instructions carefully and to budget time appropriately. Objective exams include true–false, multiple-choice, matching, and short-answer tests. For each type there are special test-taking techniques. Essay exams vary in length and are usually scored against a list of points to be covered, determined in advance by the instructor. Read directions carefully, outline answers before writing, and answer only what is asked. Problem-solving tests can be handled like essay exams if there are a few major questions or like short-answer tests if there are many short problems.

Students should review returned tests to make sure they understand their mistakes, to evaluate their test-taking techniques, and to analyze the kinds of questions the instructor asks.

EXERCISE 1: Structuring Your Studying for Tests

An objective test on this chapter follows. To begin studying for it, refer to your self-test columns for the chapter and in the space following, write 5 key terms or ideas you think might appear on the test. Then check your answers against our sample answers in the back of the book.

1. _____
2. _____
3. _____
4. _____
5. _____

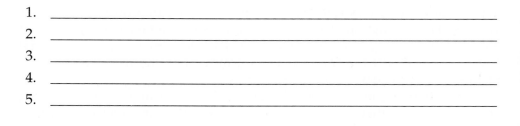

EXERCISE 2: Beginning to Study for Tests

Make flash cards either from the items in Exercise 1 or from broader questions that might include several items. Choose topics that you could not recall in your self-testing. Put one item on the front and a brief answer on the back. Review these cards until you know the information. The subject area and content of flash cards will vary.

EXERCISE 3: Taking Objective Tests

The following exercise, which serves as a substitute for this chapter's Comprehension Check, is meant to determine how well you study for tests and how well you take them. Take 45 minutes to finish the exercise. Then check your answers in the back of the book.

Multiple-choice questions (10 points)

Circle the correct letter preceding the correct answer.

1. Being moderately anxious about taking tests
   a. results in poor grades.
   b. hurts your test-taking skills.
   c. can help you.
   d. should be avoided, because it causes mental blocks.
2. When taking a test,
   a. begin with the first question and answer each in order.
   b. don't waste time guessing.
   c. answer the easy questions first.
   d. divide your time equally between objective and essay questions.
3. You should make a final exam schedule
   a. the week of the exam.
   b. that allows at least six reviews for each class.
   c. as soon as the class begins.
   d. all of the above.

4. The first rule of test-taking is
   a. answer the most difficult questions first.
   b. to follow the directions.
   c. write the answers to essay questions first.
   d. never guess on true-false questions.

5. In preparing for tests you should
   a. postpone studying until the last week so that you won't forget much.
   b. not be concerned about what type of test it will be.
   c. not worry about studying the details, since you're unlikely to remember them.
   d. review continually throughout the course.

6. You should outline an essay exam because outlining will
   a. make the essay easier to write.
   b. impress your teacher.
   c. always raise your grade.
   d. save you from having to write out the material.

7. Objective tests
   a. offer better opportunities for guessing than essay tests do.
   b. require less studying than essay or problem-solving tests.
   c. require you to study only details.
   d. do all of the above.

8. The primary reason for preparing flash cards is to
   a. reduce anxiety.
   b. increase attention to details.
   c. help you remember possible test items.
   d. show you how much you don't know.

9. Answering essay questions is usually more difficult than answering objective questions because
   a. you must organize your information before writing.
   b. you don't have favorable odds of getting the correct answer by chance.
   c. you must depend on your memory of ideas and details.
   d. all of the above are true.

10. Which of the following essay questions asks for your opinion?
    a. Compare learning from lectures and learning from textbooks.
    b. Enumerate the steps in preparing a weekly schedule.
    c. Discuss the importance of finding main ideas and supporting details in reading.
    d. Evaluate cramming before examinations.

Short-answer questions (20 points)

Fill in the blanks.

11. Leaving all your studying until the night before the test is called
    _____.

12. _____ exams require recall rather than recognition.

13. _____ exams include questions such as multiple-choice and matching.

14. Self-test cards used for continual review are called _____.

15. Before answering an essay question you should _____ it.

16. You should allow about _____ minutes at the end of the test period to check your answers.

17. Studying information you can already remember is called _____ _____.

18. _____ are like objective questions because you usually have only one answer to fill in, but they are like essay questions because there is a minimum of clues.

19. The purpose of preparing self-test questions is _____.

20. _____ questions are difficult to answer because they contain no clues.

True–false questions (10 points)

Circle the correct letter.

T F 21. The only way to reduce test anxiety is to obtain qualified professional help.

T F 22. Objective tests include true–false, multiple-choice, matching, and essay questions.

T F 23. The night before a final exam you should go to a movie or watch television to relax.

T F 24. Departmental tests usually cover textbooks and lectures.

T F 25. When studying, it is usually best to concentrate on main ideas rather than on details.

T F 26. Cramming the night before an exam increases retention more than regular periodic reviewing does.

T F 27. Overlearning is one of the steps in PQ4R.

T F 28. Essay exams require more recall than objective exams do.

T F 29. You should answer the difficult questions first to get them out of the way.

T F 30. Both objective and essay tests require budgeting your time appropriately.

EXERCISE 4: Evaluating Test-Taking Skills

Evaluate your skills as revealed by the objective test you just took. Answers will vary.

1. How many questions did you change answers from right to wrong?

_____

2. Did you pick up clues to answers by reading other questions? _____
   Give an example. _____

3. Did you misread any questions? _____
   If so, list the numbers: _____

4. Did you answer the easy questions first? _____

5. Did you review your answers after you finished the test? _____

6. Did you skim the test before you began? _____
   If so, how did it help you? _____

7. I found the _____ questions (fill in the type) most
   difficult because _____
   _____ .

EXERCISE 5: Evaluating and Rewriting a Bad Essay

The following essay was written by a student who has problems writing essays. He wrote only what you see. The assignment was: "Explain why students should review a test after they get it back." Take a piece of paper and (1) evaluate the essay; (2) outline your answer to the assignment question; (3) rewrite the essay, being careful that you don't make similar mistakes; and (4) compare your essay with the essay that follows.

The Bad Essay

Review means go over it. That means you should go over tests when you got them back because it is ~~important~~ important. It is important to review them so you'll know what you missed. Also what the teacher asked you on the test. Picking up clues is important too. I'm not sure how much reviewing a test can help because I haven't ~~tried~~ tried it yet. You *This should be earlier* should review what you missed so you won't miss it again if the teacher ~~asks~~ asks it on the next or on the final. I never thought about doing it because I'm usually thinking about the grade I got. Oh I almost forgot you you should review tests to see if you spent your time right. That's as important to your getting a good grade as anything else. As I was saying I haven't tried it yet but I am sure it will help me.

In the "good" essay, note the use of signal words to indicate main points and support. Note also that each major idea is clearly indicated so that the instructor will have no trouble following what is written. Finally, note that the essay has a clear introduction and conclusion that include the main idea of the essay.

The Good Essay

I. Know corrections
    A. final exam
    B. other courses
II. Test-taking technique
    A. changing answers
    B. reading directions
    C. clues in text
    D. time
III. Types of questions
    A. book vs lecture
    B. tricky
    C. main ideas vs. details

There are three major reasons for reviewing a test after it is returned.

One reason is that reviewing teaches the student the correct answer to any question she missed. This is particularly important if there is a chance that she wil need the imformation for the final exam or for a higher-level class in the same field.

A second reason for reviewing a test is that the student can examine her test-taking techniques. For example, she would want to check whether she changes answers appropriately, whether she reads directions correctly, whether she makes good use of available time.

Finally, reviewing a test enables the student to analyze the instructor's questions. She could find out whether the instructor bases her questions more on the baOk or on the lectures, whether the questions are tricky, and whether the questions focus on main ideas or on details.

In conclusion, it is to student's advantage to review tests after they are returned.

EXERCISE 6: Answering a Question on an Essay Test

Now that you have written and evaluated an essay test question, take a separate sheet of paper to answer the following essay test question. First, briefly outline your answer to help you organize your thoughts. Then write your answer in paragraph form. Answers will vary.

Topic: Discuss the similarities between taking essay tests and taking objective tests.

Questions for Discussion and Writing

1. Which of the test-taking techniques discussed in this chapter are you going to use immediately?
2. Which of the test-taking techniques will take practice before you can use them on a test? How do you intend to practice them?
3. Which of the test-taking techniques do you find too difficult to use at this time? How can you modify these techniques to your learning style?

Reading Selection 1: Psychology

Coping with Exam Stress

Charles G. Morris

Until recently students coping with the stress of final-exams week have usually been on their own resorting to such staples as gallons of coffee and Coca-Cola or Pepsi to keep themselves going while cramming. Some complain of difficulty studying. Others are afraid that at the critical moment they will forget the titles of Shakespeare's tragedies. Still others stay up late at night feverishly memorizing the series of events that led to the breakup of the Communist bloc in Eastern Europe. But increasingly colleges and universities have been rushing to the rescue, providing undergraduates and graduate students with aerobics programs, counseling, stress-reduction workshops, and other services. At the University of California at Los Angeles, stress-reduction workshops teach students to picture themselves calmly answering tough test items. At New York University students can choose from among over 50 programs to help them reduce prefinal tension. One group, "Peers Ears," boasts walk-in office hours and a student-trained counseling staff. At Pennsylvania's Swarthmore College students participate in a campus-wide "Howl" the night before exam week. And at the University of Washington in Seattle the Hall Health Center Mental Health Clinic opens its doors to an **influx** of students during exam week. At this time the clinic, its director reports, sees more graduate and professional students than undergraduates, more seniors than juniors, and more first-year students than sophomores.

rush

Such new programs have not entirely replaced the old standbys. During exam week at the University of California at Berkeley for example, the manager of a popular off-campus cafe still increases his order of coffee from the usual 400 pounds to 550.6.

Dead Grandmothers

Exam stress can even be lethal. Its victims are not students, but surprisingly, grandmothers. Professor John J. Chiodo of Clarion University describes:

I entered the ranks of academe as well prepared as the next fellow, but I was still unaware of the threat that midterm exams posed to the health and welfare of students and their relatives. It didn't take long, however, for me to realize that a real problem existed. The onset of midterms seems to **provoke** not only a marked increase in the family problems, illnesses, and accidents experienced by my students, but also above-normal death rates among their grandmothers.

stir up

I tried to figure out the connection. Was it because grandmothers are hypersensitive to a grandchild's problems? When they see their grandchildren suffering from exam anxiety do they become anxious too? Does the increased stress then cause stroke or heart failure? It seemed possible; so it followed that if grandmothers' anxiety levels could be lowered, a good number of their lives might be prolonged. I didn't have much direct contact with grandmothers, but I reasoned that by moderating the anxiety of my students, I could help reduce stress on their grandmothers.

To make a long story short, the results of my plan to reduce student anxiety were spectacular. At the end of the quarter there had not been one test-related death of a grandmother. In addition, the amount of sickness and family **strife** had decreased dramatically. The next two quarters proved to be even better. Since then, I have refined my anxiety-

tension

reduction system and in the interest of grandmotherly longevity would like to share it with my colleagues. Here are the basic rules:

- Review the scope of the exam.
- Use practice tests.
- Be clear about time limits.
- Announce what materials will be needed and what aids will be permitted.
- Review the grading procedure.
- Review the policies on makeup tests and retakes.
- Provide study help.
- Make provision for last-minutes questions.
- Allow for breaks during long exams.
- Coach students on test-taking techniques.

I have been following these rules for 13 years now, and during that time have heard of only an occasional midterm-related death of a grandmother.

Reading Selection 2: Psychology—Collateral Reading

Test Anxiety

Human Behavior Magazine

University of Michigan students have just as many quizzes, midterms and finals as their counterparts throughout the country, but they have an advantage over their **brethren** from Florida, Nebraska and the like. It's a 10-week Test Anxiety Program that combines biofeedback, counseling and "self-coaching strategies," in the words of its founder, James D. Papsdorf, Ph.D., a psychology professor on the Ann Arbor campus. The program, now in its third year, is the first of its kind in the nation. It began as relaxation therapy geared to help students stop smoking. That proved so successful that Papsdorf was urged to apply the biofeedback and counseling approach to test anxiety.

brothers

Success Rate

With the results in, Papsdorf says 85 to 90 percent of the students who complete his program report decreased anxiety. Equally impressive are the results with the university's medical school students, often referred to Papsdorf when they are placed on academic probation.

"The medical students have always been number one wherever they've been," he says. "They've been very competitive, and they've always come out on top. They have a temptation to think I've got to know everything and, of course, they can't. When they study for a test, some med students try to review everything they've ever learned." A full three-quarters of the medical students referred to Papsdorf have raised their grades sufficiently to be taken off academic probation since completing his program.

Participants are seated next to a biofeedback machine, which is connected painlessly to their fingertips. By looking at the machine's readout, they are able to observe such bodily processes as skin temperature, pulse and muscle tension. The students actually learn to control their ability to relax by practicing a series of exercises, according to Papsdorf. Subjects are instructed to tighten and release their muscles, practice deep breathing and focus their thoughts on a relaxing situation. Through their responses, they learn which thoughts will help them relax.

Flip-Flop Strategies

Of the 150 persons who have completed the program, the students benefiting the most have a few characteristics in common. "Those who have good basic study skills seem to derive the greatest help," the professor believes, "those who already know how to schedule their study time, how to concentrate on study goals." Predictably, students with poor skills are less successful. "Even after we've calmed them down, and taught them not to fear testing, they still don't know how to study," Papsdorf observes.

He theorizes that anxiety may trigger "a flip-flop strategy," a physiological switchover from the use of one brain hemisphere to another. "The student begins a test and looks at the problems rationally," he explains. "He's in what I call a 'left hemisphere' strategy. Then something happens. A retrieval block occurs, and he goes into a 'right hemisphere' situation. He just can't get back to the other side, and that's where the data is."

Anxious students are more prone to "flip-flop," Papsdorf says, offering a metaphor to support his case: "They start with the task of chopping down a single tree. It works all right, but then they look up and see the whole forest, and it overwhelms them. They don't know what to do."

Self-Coaching

Along with the weekly hour-long biofeedback sessions, subjects also spend an hour a week in counseling with a graduate assistant. "Really, all we're trying to do is keep them from flopping," Papsdorf says, "to keep them in the same hemisphere. Anxious students have a tendency to think in 'musts' and 'shoulds.' 'I must learn everything. I should do well.' The biofeedback opens them up, teaching them to relax. The counseling makes them receptive to self-coaching, a confrontation of irrational thinking."

As might be expected, the program may have applications in areas other than teaching students how to choose between answers A and B. "We're looking into speech-related anxieties such as stuttering," Papsdorf says, "and we're working with the athletic department to research a 'competition anxiety,' a situation in which an athlete in individual competition, such as swimming, becomes tense and fails to perform up to potential." Working with him on that project is Canadian John Jamison, Ph.D., a professor on sabbatical from Lakehead University in Thunder Bay, Ontario.

Additional applications might be found in treating mathematics anxiety, in which students have a tendency to freeze when facing difficult math tasks, and in what Papsdorf calls "management of management stress." In that condition, researched in a dissertation by Peter Vagg, a colleague of Papsdorf, executives fall prey to such work-related stresses as deadlines, competition and dealings with **abrasive**　　**annoying**
colleagues. "Some anxiety in a business situation is expected and probably not harmful," Papsdorf believes. "Too much is bad."

Other Uses

Papsdorf has started holding day-long seminars for business executives to help them **ward** off that abrasive fellow worker. Those of us　　**block**
who don't have access to a biofeedback machine, according to Jess Ghannam, who works with Papsdorf, can learn to ease our tension by concentrating on warming skin temperature. "One sign of general anxiety is cold hands," he claims. "If you concentrate on warming your hands, you can raise the skin temperature and reduce anxiety. And never say to yourself, 'I must accomplish this,' or that something 'has to happen.' Many people **generate** their own high anxiety level by　　**create**
putting unreasonable pressures on themselves."

Comprehension Check

Circle the letter preceding the correct answer. Then check your answers in the back of the book.

1. Which is a technique that colleges are *not* using to help students during finals?
    a. pep rallies
    b. aerobics
    c. stress-reduction workshops
    d. workshops on how to stay up all night to cram for exams

2. Which is not a technique that Morris suggests a teacher use to reduce test anxiety?
   a. Use practice tests.
   b. Make the test as short as possible.
   c. Review the scope of the exam.
   d. Be clear about time limits.

3. When biofeedback machines are not available, students
   a. can't do anything about test anxiety.
   b. can help themselves by concentrating on raising skin temperature.
   c. can help themselves by determining to do better on tests.
   d. can convince themselves that the anxiety isn't real.

4. When this article was written, the Test Anxiety Program was
   a. a new program.
   b. being proposed.
   c. in its first year.
   d. in its third year.

5. Dr. Papsdorf believes that learning for tests occurs
   a. in the right hemisphere of the brain.
   b. in both hemispheres of the brain.
   c. in the left hemisphere of the brain.
   d. in the frontal lobe of the brain.

6. Students in the program are more successful
   a. if they have good study skills beforehand.
   b. if they take a study skills course at the same time.
   c. whether or not they have other skills.
   d. if they totally lack study skills and have everything to learn.

7. The kind of test anxiety discussed in this selection
   a. can cause students to fail tests.
   b. is best treated without the aid of a counselor.
   c. is traced to poor study habits.
   d. is suffered by every student.

8. Anxieties similar to test anxiety
   a. do not occur outside school.
   b. are not serious outside school.
   c. do occur outside of school.
   d. are impossible to treat because they are so complex.

9. The main reason to use biofeedback is _____
   _____.

10. Most students experience test anxiety because _____
    _____.

Questions for Discussion and Writing

1. Based on what you learned in the two articles, what can you do to reduce test anxiety?

2. What are some of the things a teacher can do to help you reduce test anxiety?

EXERCISE 7: Using Collateral Reading

Answer the following questions. Then check your answers in the back of the book. (Answers to questions 1 and 2 will vary.)

1. Did you understand all the information in the first article? Answers will vary.

2. What information in the first selection, if any, did you understand better after reading the excerpt from the human behavior magazine? Answers will vary.

3. What information in the first article did not appear in the second?

4. What information in the second did not appear in the first?

5. How do the two selections differ in their description of test anxiety and its causes?

EXERCISE 8: Skills Review—Note-Taking

Here are some sample lecture notes on test taking. Underline and make marginal self-test notes as if you were going to learn the information for a test. Check your answers in Appendix I.

Diff. below rdg. & listening — can't relisten

Good listening
    1. Come to class prepared
      read text
      review notes
    2. Sit close
    3. Come early
    4. Listen for clues
    5. Watch for nonverbal clues

How Not to Take Notes
    1. Don't try to write everything
    2. No tape recorders
    3. Don't copy someone else's notes

How to Take Notes
    1. Ger a notebook. you can organize
    2. Leave a margin at top
    3. 2" margin at left
    5. Date each pg & # pgs
    5. Use speed writing
      symbols & abbr.
      cross out
    6. Listen actively
      main ideas — few details
      speech 110–160 wpm
      understand 650 – 700wpm
    7 Use visula org.
      outline
    8. Review notes after lecture
      fill in, compare, questions, etc.
      don't recopy
    9. Write as little as possible

Studying notes
    Last 4 steps of PQ4R
      read
    write — underline & marginal notes
        flash cards
    recall — 1 pg. at a time
    review — about once a wk. depending on how hard

Using
the Library

Using the Library

I. The modern college library
II. Library catalogs of books
    A. Computerized catalogs
    B. Card catalog
    C. Cross-References
    D. Call Numbers
III. The stacks
IV. The reference section
    A. Computerized reference collections
    B. Dictionaries
    C. Encyclopedias
    D. Almanacs
    E. Yearbooks
    H. Atlases
    I. Manuals
    J. Handbooks
    K. Biographical information
V. The periodicals section
    A. General periodical indexes
    B. Computerized periodical indexes
    C. Choosing to use a computerized index or the Readers' Guide
    D. Special periodical indexes
    E. Current-events indexes
    F. File of periodical holdings
    G. Other computerized databases
VI. Other library services
    A. Librarians
    B. Reserve materials
    C. Audio-visual department
    D. Microforms
    E. Photocopiers
    F. Computers/typewriters

10 | Knowledge is of two kinds. We know a subject ourselves, or we know where to find it.
Samuel Johnson

Many students feel apprehensive when using the library, because they're unfamiliar with the different sources of information and their locations. However, students who can use the library effectively get better grades; in fact, it's impossible to write a good research paper without having a working knowledge of the library. This chapter will help you locate and use the main sources of information available in libraries. Begin by taking the library tour offered at your college. The tour will show you the locations of different materials, including the separate sections for stacks, for reference materials, for periodicals and for audio-visual material if it is not housed in a separate media center. The library catalog is the key to all of them.

The Modern College Library

The college library is one of the areas on campus that has been most affected by technological change. First came photocopy machines and electric typewriters. Next, old newspapers and magazines were put on microfilm and microfiche to save valuable library space. Today, almost everything in most libraries has been modernized with computers. The catalog to locate books once took a wall of file cabinets filled with cards. Now, most campus libraries have computerized their holdings. Any student can walk to a computer station, punch in a subject, author, or title, and, presto, the computer does the work. A student can quickly print out a list of books on practically any subject. Instead of lifting heavy volumes of the *Readers' Guide to Periodical Literature* that line the tables of the Periodicals room (the place where you would go to find magazines and newspapers), or flipping through rows are cards from the card catalog, you can now find one or two computer programs that offer complete lists of publications on key subjects. In addition, these lists break down subjects into smaller areas so that you can easily find the different topics you might choose for a paper. Sometimes these entries have abstracts (brief summaries) of what will be found in the books, magazines or newspapers, which lets you do even more research before leaving the computer. Finally, these programs can usually be printed so that you can leave with a printout of the most important information and even a summary of all the materials you want to read. You no longer have to write the information down. It is there at the push of a button.

There is no question: you must learn how your library operates. Doing so can save you hours of time when you are assigned a research paper. Don't be misled by the convenience of information found in encyclopedias and dictionaries on CD-roms or materials found while "surfing" the Internet. These sources can be a good place to begin a paper, but as a college student, you will be expected to use books, magazines, and newspaper articles as support when you write a term paper. For the bulk of material you will need for your paper, you will need to browse the library, not the Internet. These days, if you have access to a computer, you may have more information at your fingertips, but you can only let "your fingers do the walking" for a limited time before you walk to the library. In one recent television ad for a computer network, a man talks about how he can't go to the baseball game because he has to take his son to the library to research a report on dinosaurs. His friend replies that his computer can get all the necessary information in a flash plus handle a slew of other tasks virtually at the same time. A few minutes later the man leaves with the material on dinosaurs for his son (from an encyclopedia), plus a printout of the airline reservations he has just made and a receipt for the flowers he has just sent to his mother for her birthday. His mother may or may not appreciate the flowers, but a college professor is not going to appreciate research limited to material found in an encyclopedia as support for your term paper.

Library Catalogs of Books

Most college libraries have both a computerized card catalog and the traditional card catalog. Either one will have three kinds of entries: by author, by title and by subject. All three kinds of entries rather on a computer or on a card will contain the following information: author's complete name (and, if applicable, coauthor's name), full title (ignoring the words *a, an,* and *the*), publisher, place of publication, and date of publication.

Computerized Catalogs

Technology has had a major effect on the ways you find material in the library. You no longer have to look through rows of filing drawers to find the tray that contains the alphabetical section you wish to search. You no longer have to sort through a long tray of cards to find the one you seek. Now you can go to a computer and enter the information. It is fast and easy as long as you know what you want.

The sample following is typical of a computer entry. It contains the same information as the old card catalog system. The file is updated at least once a month so that it reflects what the library contains. Although each cataloging program differs most are similar to Figure 10–1. It is especially helpful if the entry tells you whether the book is available or has been checked out.

Figure 10–1 Shows a
Typical Computerized
Card Catalog Entry

AUTHOR(s): Ordovensky, Pat
TITLE: USA today financial aid to college: a quick guide
to everything you need to know

PUBLICATION DATA: Princeton University, N.J.:
Peterson's c 1994 154p

SUBJECT(s): Student aid--United States. College
costs--United States. Parents--United
States--Finance

LOCN: REF   **STATUS:** Not checked out
CALL #: LB 2337.4 073
ISBN: 94-26614

A few words of caution about using a computerized catalog to locate books, magazines, and newspaper material. First, a simple spelling error or not putting an "s" on a word could mislead you into believing that there is nothing on your subject in the library. Therefore, if you are using the computerized catalog, double-check your information if you don't find entries. Second, when using a computer catalog for either books or magazines, you may find an incredible amount of entries if you don't properly limit your search. For example, if you were to search for *nuclear* and *accident,* you might have a hundred or more references. The subject was too broad. You would have better luck using the two words together, *nuclear accident,* to search for the material. If too many entries still appeared, you could further limit it by adding two or more concepts such as a place (the United States), a date (1995–1999), or focus on one aspect such as *causes,* or *effects.* Your search would then be *causes of nuclear accidents and 1995–1999 and the United States.* (The working of the search varies from program to program so check how to write a limited entry). This same concept of using key words to locate material would be just as important when using networks of material such as found on the Internet. The larger the database you are exploring, the more you have to isolate exactly what type of information you want or need.

Card Catalog

Although many libraries now have their card catalogs on computer, it is still important for you to know how to use the traditional system. The regular card catalog lists all the books in the library. It is always in working order and its use is not limited by the availability of a computer.

To use the card catalog, you must understand two things. First, how you can find information and how to read the information on a card. Whether you are trying to find a book on the computerized system or in the catalog tray, the information is listed in three ways. You can find a source by the **author's name,** the first word in the **title** (ignore the words *a, an,* and *the*), or the **subject.** Figure 10–2 is a sample of a card catalog tray.

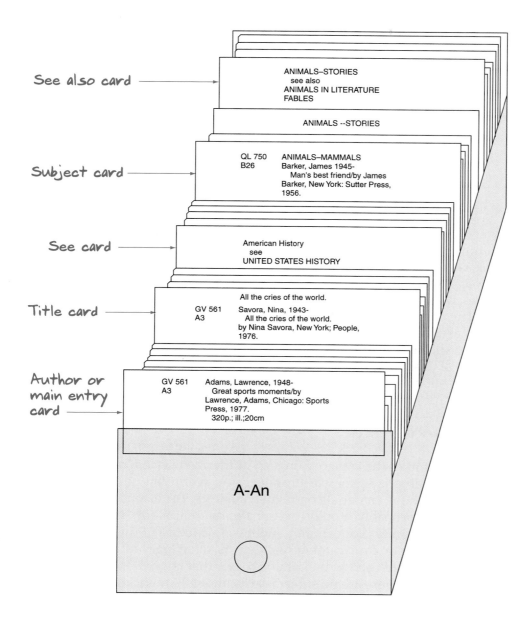

See also card

ANIMALS–STORIES
see also
ANIMALS IN LITERATURE
FABLES

ANIMALS --STORIES

Subject card

QL 750   ANIMALS–MAMMALS
B26   Barker, James 1945-
            Man's best friend/by James
         Barker, New York: Sutter Press,
         1956.

See card

American History
see
UNITED STATES HISTORY

Title card

All the cries of the world.
GV 561   Savora, Nina, 1943-
A3   All the cries of the world.
         by Nina Savora, New York; People,
         1976.

Author or main entry card

GV 561   Adams, Lawrence, 1948-
A3   Great sports moments/by
         Lawrence, Adams, Chicago: Sports
         Press, 1977.
            320p.; ill.;20cm

A-An

Below is a sample author entry (also called the main entry card). Title cards look just like author cards except that the title is on the first line, above the author's name. The title card for this book has *USA today financial aid for college* on the first line. Subject cards also look exactly the same except that the subject is on the first line, above the author's name. The subject card for this book has *STUDENT AID—UNITED STATES* on the top line of one card.

Figure 10–3 An annotated sample author (or main entry card).

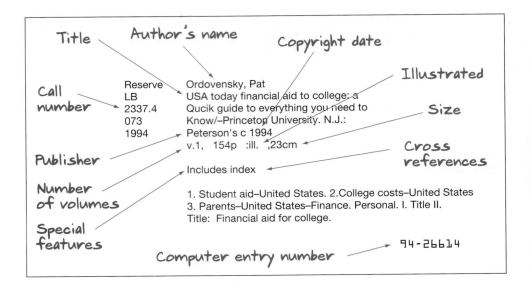

Figure 10–3 An annotated sample author (or main entry card).

The computer might offer additional information such as an abstract (summary) of the book and since it is kept current, it can tell you if the book is available. The card catalog will always note any special features such as illustrations or an index. In addition, it will always offer a physical description of the book including its size.

The computer might offer additional information such as an abstract (summary) of the book, but the card catalog will always note any special features such as illustrations and an index. In addition, it will always offer a physical description of the book including its size. However, as you can see, both sources offer the same basic information about a book.

Cross-References

At the top of the category on a computerized system or at the end of a group of subjects in the card catalog, you will often find *see also*. This entry refers you to materials on related subjects. For example, under "Education" you probably would find *see also* references for "College Education," "Community Education," and even "Medical Education." If the computer entry or card catalog has *see* it is referring you from a subject heading that is not used in the catalog to one that is used. In our sample of the card catalog there are no subject cards under "American History." The card tell you to *see* "UNITED STATES HISTORY."

Call Numbers

Each book in the library has a unique number that determines its place on the shelf. The numbers are based on the Dewey Decimal System or on the Library of Congress classification system. The computerized catalog and the older manual catalogs contain the same call numbers on the spines of the book. If the call number begins with a letter (for example,

M485.3), the Library of Congress System is being used. If it begins with a number (628.3), the Dewey Decimal System is being used. Other symbols in call numbers have special meanings:

R or *Ref.* indicates that the book is in the Reference section.

Fic., or just the author's last name, indicates that the book is fiction. Fiction is often filed separately from nonfiction and is not assigned a number.

Z means that the book is oversized and will not fit on the shelf. It is filed in a separate section.

B or *Bio.* indicates that the book is a biography. It may be shelved in a separate biography section.

The Stacks

After you have found a book's call number in the library catalog, the next step is to locate the book. The library stacks contain the majority of the materials that can be checked out. Some libraries have a *closed-stack system* in which you write the call number on a special slip and a library employee brings you the book. In an *open-stack system* you find the book on the shelves yourself. The open-stack system is much better for research. Since books on the same subject are shelved in the same area, you can very likely find additional useful materials on the same shelf. However, if an additional book is checked out or misfiled, you won't know that it exists unless you have come across it in the card catalog. This is why it is important to check both the card catalog and the shelf.

The Reference Section

Materials in the Reference section of the library contain well-indexed and usually up-to-date information. Use this section of the library to find quick answers to specific questions, such as "Who invented the fountain pen?" or "What is the zip code for Big Spring, Texas?" You can look up specific facts in reference books without reading the entire book. Reference books include dictionaries, encyclopedias, almanacs, yearbooks, atlases, manuals, handbooks, and biographical material. (Because most reference materials are not updated more than once a year, for extremely current information you will need to consult a magazine or newspaper in the Periodical section.) Reference books use the same call number system as the books in the stacks and are also shelved according to their numbers. However, reference materials do not circulate. Most libraries have a special librarian in the Reference section who can help you locate the information you need. There may also be computers in the Reference section that contain various computerized reference sources. You often can find the same reference materials for home computers. Here is a sample of reference materials available in computerized editions:

Computerized Reference Collections

Each day more sources can be found on computerized materials. These are the most popular collections that can be found in libraries and are available for home computers. They are updated yearly.

Microsoft Bookself
- *The American Heritage Dictionary*
- *The Original Roget's Thesaurus*
- *The World Almanac and Book of Facts*
- *The Concise Columbia Encyclopedia*
- *The Columbia Dictionary of Quotations*
- *The People's Chronology*
- *The Hammond World Atlas*
- *National Five-Digit Zip Code and Post Office Dictionary*

Compton's Reference Collection
- *Compton's Concise Encyclopedia*
- *The New York Public Library Desk Reference*
- *The MacMillan Dictionary of Quotations*
- *Webster's New World Dictionary*
- *Webster's New World Thesaurus*
- *Compton's World Atlas*
- *The Elements of Style*
- *The Elements of Business Writing*
- *J.K. Lasser's Legal and Corporation Forms for the Smaller Business*
- *The Office Guide to Business Letters, Memos, and Reports*
- *Resumes for Better Jobs*

Dictionaries

General dictionaries will be discussed in Chapter 11. The library Reference section includes general dictionaries such as *Webster's*, foreign-language dictionaries, and special subject dictionaries such as the following:

- *Chamber's Dictionary of Science and Technology*
- *Dictionary of American History*
- *Black's Law Dictionary*
- *American Political Dictionary*
- *Dorland's Illustrated Medical Dictionary*

Encyclopedias

Encyclopedias can be either general or specialized. In either case, they provide a broad overview of the subjects they include. Most multi-volume encyclopedias are updated annually by a yearbook.

General Encyclopedias. The *Encyclopaedia Britannica* is perhaps the most scholarly of the general encyclopedias. Since the fifteenth edition (1981) the *Britannica* has consisted of three parts: the 10-volume *Micropaedia* presents numerous concise articles and an index to articles in the *Macropaedia;* the 19-volume *Macropaedia* contains longer and more scholarly articles written on the major subjects; and the final section, *Propaedia,* outlines human knowledge to help place the individual articles in a larger context. Other encyclopedias, such as the *World Book Encyclopedia* and the *Encyclopedia Americana,* are less scholarly than *Britannica.*

Computerized Multimedia Encyclopedias
- Grolier's Encyclopedia
- Compton's Encyclopedia
- Encarta
- The World Book Encyclopedia for Multimedia

Special encyclopedias. Some encyclopedias, such as the following, cover specialized topics.

- *Encyclopedia of Sports*
- *Larousse Encyclopedia of Mythology*
- *The New Century Cyclopedia of Names*
- *International Encyclopedia of the Social Sciences*
- *Encyclopedia of World Art*

Almanacs

Some almanacs are general and others are specialized. General almanacs contain facts about almost everything. The almanac is a good place to look to find, say, the highest temperature ever recorded in the United States or the population of Anchorage, Alaska. Examples of almanacs follow.

- *The World Almanac and Book of Facts*
- *Information Please Almanac*
- *Almanac of American Politics*
- *Congressional Quarterly Almanac*
- *International Motion Picture Almanac*

Some of these almanacs such as *The World Almanac and Book of Facts,* can be found in computer reference collections.

Yearbooks

A yearbook is a compilation of developments that occurred during one year. Publishers of encyclopedias use yearbooks to bring their encyclopedias up to date. Some government agencies also publish yearbooks for example:

- *Statistical Abstract of the United States.* Published since 1878 by the U.S. Bureau of the Census, this volume is indispensable for finding figures on social, political, economic, and cultural activities.
- *Statistical Yearbook.* Published by the United Nations Department of Economic and Social Affairs since 1949, this yearbook is intended as a convenient summary of international statistics.

Atlases

An atlas is a book of maps, charts, and other geographical information. Atlases also can be either general or specialized. Examples include

- *Goode's World Atlas*
- *National Geographic Atlas of the World*
- *Rand McMally Road Atlas*
- *Oxford Bible Atlas*
- *The West Point Atlas of American Wars*

Some atlases such as The Hammond World Atlas and Compton's World Atlas can be found on computerized reference materials.

Manuals

A manual is a guide; it usually provides instruction or describes how something works. A few examples are

- *L.T.S. Government Organization Manual*
- *Manual for Writers of Term Papers, Theses, and Dissertations*
- *Manual of Cultivated Plants*

Handbooks

A handbook is a brief, handy reference that provides general information on a particular subject. Examples are

- *Occupational Outlook Handbook*
- *American Electricians' Handbook*
- *Handbook of Chemistry & Physics*

Biographical Information

To find reference material concerning people, look first in a biographical index such as the *Biographical Dictionaries Master Index* or the *Biography Index;* it will tell you the proper reference sources to consult.

There are a great many sources for biographical reference material, including biographical dictionaries, encyclopedias, and directories. Here are a few examples:

- *Webster's Biographical Dictionary* includes short biographies of men and women from every country and all historical periods.
- *Who's Who* is an annual biographical dictionary that includes prominent living persons (principally British) in many fields.
- *Who Was Who* includes biographies of those who died during a specific period, mostly reprinted from *Who's Who,* sometimes with the addition of new information.
- *Who's Who in America* includes living Americans.
- *Who's Who of American Women* lists outstanding American women.
- *Current Biography* covers world personalities; it is illustrated.
- *World Authors* lists authors from all countries of the world.
- *Dictionary of American Scholars* lists distinguished American scholars.

The Periodicals Section

A periodical is a magazine, newspaper, or scholarly journal published at regular intervals (weekly, monthly, quarterly). Since periodicals are issued more often than books are revised, they contain more up-to-date information. Some information in periodicals is so new that no books have yet been published on the subject. Periodicals are filed in the card catalog under their titles. Both general and special periodical indexes have been compiled to facilitate locating information in periodicals.

General Periodical Indexes

These indexes perform the same function with articles that the card catalog does with books. Entries are listed by author, title, and subject. The *see* and *see also* cross-references work just as they do in the card catalog.

Computerized Periodical Indexes

Two types of computerized periodical indexes are available. One has information similar to the *Readers' Guide;* the other indexes articles in technical journals. The formats to different computerized indexes may vary in order of information and abbreviations, but each gives information similar to the one following.

Figure 10–4 shows an entry.

Figure 10–4 A sample from a computerized Periodicals Index

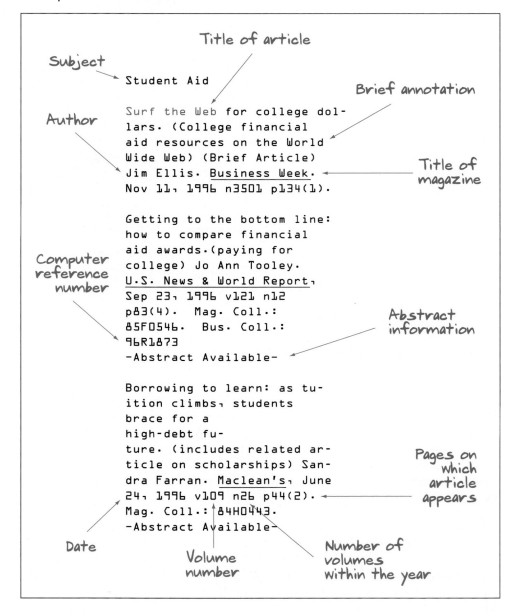

Readers' Guide to Periodical Literature. The *Readers' Guide,* published regularly since 1900, is a comprehensive index to more than 160 popular American nontechnical magazines. Each volume of the *Readers' Guide,* includes articles published between the dates printed on its cover.

Figure 10–5 A sample from the *Readers' Guide to Periodical Literature.*

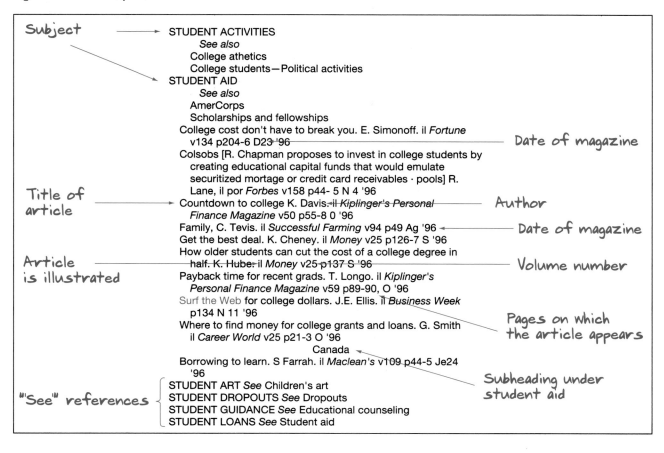

In general, it's a good idea to start with the most recent volume and go backward. However, if you are looking for information on a historical subject, such as something that happened in World War II, then you should start with the volumes most likely to contain the information you need. Hardback volumes cover a year or more; paperback volumes usually come out twice a month and contain the most recent information.

Choosing to Use a Computerized Index or the Readers' Guide

Many students prefer to use the computerized indexes thinking they are more valuable. They do save some time and work. For example, you can print out the information you wish instead of copying it by hand or machine. However, notice that the two entries above on financial aid contain a lot of the same information. Both sources are updated every month but the computer material is added to the existing data base while the *Readers' Guide* publishes monthly updates which are bound into a large volume once a year. The computer indexes sometimes have abstracts (summaries) of the articles such as the one on "Borrowing to learn." Notice that that entry is on both sources but the *Readers' Guide* identifies it as coming from Canada while the computer might or might not say this in the abstract. Look at the entry for "Surf the Web for College Dollars." It would not matter which source you used. So knowing how to use both indexes as well as the other indexes below can be very helpful. We have both seen students wait up to an hour for the use of a computer index while standing next to the *Readers' Guide* which would be as helpful.

Access: The Supplementary Index to Periodicals. *Access*, published since 1975, indexes 130 magazines not found in the *Readers' Guide* or other indexes, such as *Playboy, TV Guide*, and *Glamour*.

Special Periodical Indexes

Special periodical indexes such as the following cover particular fields:

- *Applied Science and Technology Index (1958–)*
- *Business Periodicals Index (1958–)*
- *Education Index (1929–)*
- *Humanities Index (1974–)*
- *Child Development Abstracts and Bibliography (1927–)*
- *Consumers' Index to Product Evaluations and Information Sources (1973–)*
- *Psychological Abstracts (1927–)*

Current-Events Indexes

The *New York Times Index* lists all *New York Times* articles since 1913 by subject. Entries provide synopses of the articles.

The *Public Affairs Information Service Bulletin* (PAIS), published weekly and bound annually since 1915, includes government publications, books, and pamphlets in the social sciences. PAIS is international in scope but includes only works written in English.

Facts on File, published since 1940, is a weekly digest of world news with a cumulative index for easy access.

Keesing's Contemporary Archives, published since 1931, is a loose-leaf weekly reference to world events with an up-to-date index. It excerpts information from various news media without attempting to analyze or comment.

File of Periodical Holdings

After you have obtained the name, date, and volume number of the periodical, and the page numbers of the article you need, you must locate the actual magazine. A special section of the library is usually set aside for current issues of periodicals; back issues are bound and are located in the stacks or may be available only on microfilm or microfiche. Most libraries have a separate list of the periodicals to which they subscribe, which includes their call numbers. If there is no separate file, you can find the call number in the general library catalog.

Other Computerized Databases

Some libraries at colleges and universities offer other computerized databases such as the E.R.I.C. system (which lists conferences presentations, research updates, research reports, theses, and dissertations), and the search might even include book reviews. Libraries may also have access through computers to other libraries. These will help you locate the most up-to-date materials on the topic. In many cases, the extra speed and thoroughness of such searches are worth the time and cost.

If your college has limited computerized materials, call the public library and other colleges in the area, because using computerized materials can save hours of time in researching for term papers and class reports.

Other Library Services

Librarians

In spite of all the technological advance, remember that the librarian is an invaluable resource. Fortunately, the computerization of the library hasn't resulted in any lessening of the excellent help provided by librarians. There never seem to be enough of these valuable people available, and anything that helps free their time to help with the really difficult searches only benefits everyone who uses the library.

Reserve Materials

Instructors put on reserve books and periodicals that will be used by many students. Books on reserve can be checked out only for short periods.

Audio-Visual Department

The library's collection of materials is frequently augmented by audio-visual materials such as films, filmstrips, audio cassettes, videotapes, records, Cds, laser discs, and in some colleges sophisticated multimedia packages. This department also frequently houses and maintains the hardware for audio-visual materials.

Microforms

Because it's not feasible to provide unlimited space for their materials, most libraries keep part of their collections on microfilm or microfiche. These microforms must be read on special machines.

Photocopiers

Library research has become much easier since photocopies were invented. Now students can copy their material at the library and read it at their convenience at home.

Computers/Typewriters

Most college libraries offer either computers for word processing or pay typewriters available for student use. You should check with the library and learning center sources to learn the location of these machines.

Comprehension Check

Circle the correct letter for each answer. Then check your answers in the back of the book.

1. Which of the following is *not* a reference book?
    a. *New York Times*
    b. *Encyclopaedia Britannica*
    c. *Occupational Outlook Handbook*
    d. *Who's Who*
2. Which of the following is *not* a periodical index?
    a. *Facts on File*
    b. *PAIS*
    c. *Readers' Guide*
    d. *Statistical Abstract of the United States*
3. The reason to begin your research with the major library catalog is that
    a. it's centrally located.
    b. it indexes magazine articles.
    c. it catalogs circulating material, reference material, and periodicals.
    d. all of the above.

4. What kind of book would you use to find the names of last year's members of Congress?
   a. an encyclopedia
   b. a handbook
   c. a yearbook
   d. a biographical index

5. You would ask a reference librarian
   a. to suggest possible sources for the information you need.
   b. to help you locate a book in the stacks.
   c. to help you check out a book.
   d. to do all of the above.

6. A book that can be checked out for one hour would be located in
   a. the Reserve section.
   b. the stacks.
   c. the Reference section.
   d. the Periodicals section.

7. A biography of a famous living American would be found in
   a. *Readers' Guide to Periodical Literature.*
   b. *Who Was Who.*
   c. *Current Biography.*
   d. *The Statesman's Year-Book.*

8. What features does a computerized periodical guide provide that is not found in the *Readers' Guide to Periodical Literature?*
   a. author's full name
   b. "see also" references
   c. an abstract of most articles
   d. the volume in which the articles appear

9. What are some of the advantages of using a computerized library catalog and/or periodical system?

   _____

   _____

10. What are some of the advantages of using a traditional card catalog and/or periodical system?

    _____

    _____

Questions for Discussion and Writing

1. Converting a library to a computerized system can cost thousands of dollars. Who do you think should pay for this expense and why?

2. Why do you or don't you think there will be a need for libraries in the year 2050?

3. With the advent of the Internet and the World Wide Web, will students still need to learn the steps in library research? Why or why not?

EXERCISE 1: Using a Computerized Card Catalog

Read the entry below and answer the following questions. Then check your answers in the back of the sample computerized book.

Figure 10–6 Entry from a computerized card catalogue

```
AUTHOR(s):      Young, Barry
TITLE(s):       Free stuff for science buffs/Barry Young.
Also called:    Subtitle on cover: Amazing Mr. Science's
                Guide to the Universe.

                Scottsdale, AZ: Coriolis Group Books,
                c1996. xvi, 302 p. : ill. ; 24 cm. The
                letter S in stuff in title is printed as a
                dollar sign.

                Barry Young hosts a radio talk show as
                Amazing Mr. Science.

                Includes index
SUBJECT(s):     Free material Directories.
                Science Miscellanea Popular works.
                Internet (Computer Network) Directories.
```

1. What key words might have led you to this book? _____
    _____

2. What is the author's name? _____
3. What is the book's copyright date? _____
4. What is the title of the book? _____

EXERCISE 2: Using a Computerized Periodical Entry

See the computerized periodical entry entitled "College Papers in Cyberspace." Use this entry to answer the following questions. Then check your answers in the back of this book.

Figure 10–7 Entry from a computerized periodical index

```
College papers in cyberspace, by Thomas Wanat;
   il v41 The Chronicle of Higher Education Nov.
   30, '94 pA22 (3)
```

1. Name three words or phrases that might have led you to this article.

    _____

2. What is the author's name? _____

3. What is the magazine's name? _____

4. What are the volume number and date of issue? _____

EXERCISE 3: Comparing a Computerized Periodicals Index Entry and a *Readers' Guide* Entry

Read the entries below and answer the questions that follow. Then check your answers in the back of the book.

Excerpt from
The Readers' Guide

STRESS
> *See also*
> Anxiety
> Crisis management (Psychology)
> Job stress
> Oxidative stress

Post-traumatic stress disorder

Time pressure

  Heart attacks: high hopes vs. high anxiety [research by Debra
    Moser] D. Vergano. *Science News* v150 p277 N 2 '96

  How do you prevent burnout? B. Sherman. il *Parents* v71
    p128-30 N '96

  The price of propriety [increased stress hormone levels in peo-
    ple with repressive personalities] R.M. Sapolsky. il *The
    Sciences* v36 p14-16 JUAg '96

  Smarter stress test? [effect of mental stress on heart; research
    by James A. Blumenthal] M. Munson and Y.L. Wolfe, il
    Prevention (Emmaus, Pa.) v48 p36+ O '96

  Stop stress with a deep breath. il *Health (San Francisco,
    Calif., 1992)* v10 p52-3 O '96

  Take two schnauzers and call me in the morning [dog owner-
    ship alleviates stress; research by Karen Allen] il *Psychology
    Today* v29 p16 JUAg '96

  The talking cure for stress [cognitive therapy; research by
    James Blumenthal] B. Carey. il Health *(San Francisco,
    Calif.; 1992)* v10 p68-74 N/D '96

  Why stress is bad for your brain [excessive exposure to
    glucocorticoids affects hippocampus] R.M. Sapolsky. bibl f
    il *Science* v273 p749-50 Ag 9 '96
                    Nutritional aspects
  Eat smart, beat stress. D. Brodey. il *Mademoiselle* v102 p56
    Jl '96

STRESS REDUCING EXERCISES

  Get ready . . . get set . . . relax! Sharp. il *Current Health
    2* v23 p21-3 D '96

December, 1996

STRESS

Ready . . . get set . . . relax! (stress management techniques) Katie Sharp. Current Health 2, Dec 1996 v23 n4 p21(3).
—Abstract Available—

The talking cure for stress. (includes related information on self-help cliches) (Cover Story) Benedict Carey. Health, Nov-Dec 1996 v10 n7 p68(7). Mag. Coll.: 86C1185.
—Abstract Available—

Something to wish for: time to relax. (survey identifies regions of the U.S. where stress-reduction is desired) (Brief Article) (Illustration) U.S. News & World Report, Nov 11, 1996 v121 n19 p17(1). Mag. Coll.: 86C1538. Bus. Coll.: 97T1489.

Stress busters! (strategies for dealing with stress) Lucinda Chriss. Woman's Day, Nov 1, 1996 v59 n17 p46(3). Mag. Coll.: 86C4215.
—Abstract Available—

Stressed out? 25 ways to cope. Ronald Klatz and Robert Goldman. Muscle & Fitness, Nov 1996 v57 n11 p136(4).
—Abstract Available—

Stressed out: are we having any fun yet? (unusual office stress relievers include playing with silly putty, blowing a trumpet and ripping memos into tiny pieces) (Brief Article) Anne Fisher. Fortune, Oct 14, 1996 v134 n7 p214(1).

Can you laugh your stress away? (laughing as therapy) (includes related article on how to laugh more) (Cover Story) Mary Roach. Health, Sept 1996 v10 n5 p92(5).
—Abstract Available—

Infotrac December, 1997

1. What are the titles of the two articles that appear in both sample entries?

   _____

   _____

2. Which index has an article on the value of having a pet as a way of reducing stress? _____

3. What are two samples of articles on the computer index which have summaries as well as the basic information?

   _____

   _____

4. How does the description for "The talking cure for stress" differ between the two types of indexes? _____

5. On what two entries would you likely find information in the effects of stress on the heart?

   _____

   _____

   _____

6. What is one possible reason that the article titled "Stressed out? 25 ways to cope" is not listed in the *Readers' Guide* but is found on the computer? _____

EXERCISE 4: Beginning a Research Project

Answer the following questions. Be sure to indicate the sources you used and the page numbers.

1. From an encyclopedia on CD Rom or a regular encyclopedia answer the following questions. Be sure to indicate the sources you used and the page numbers.

   What is the source? _____

2. On the basis of the information you read in this article, break your general topic into three subtopics. (Note: The computerized periodical system will break a general topic into subtopics from which you can choose.)

   a. _____

   b. _____

   c. _____

3. A person mentioned in my research is _____.

   In a biographical work, find out (a) for what the person is famous, (b) the person's date of birth, and (c) if dead, the date of death.

   What is the source? _____ pages? _____

   The person is famous because _____

   _____.

   Date of birth _____   Date of death _____

4. In the computerized periodicals program (or in the *Readers' Guide*), find an article on your topic.

   Author _____

   Title_____

   Magazine _____

Volume _____   Pages _____

Summarize the magazine article in a few sentences.

_____

_____

_____

_____

5. On the computerized card catalog (or in the card catalog), find two books on the topic.

   Author _____

   Title_____

   Author _____

   Title_____

Reading Selection 1: Library Research

Writing a Research Paper

John Lolley

For many students a term or research paper is an agonizing burden. Some will avoid an otherwise interesting course with a good teacher simply because they have heard that he assigns research papers. This is unfortunate because, like anything else, once you learn the proper way to write a paper it becomes routine and no longer a great bugaboo. There is a trick to writing papers and that is to do it systematically. Don't panic and do begin early. First, you should . . .

Choose Your Subject Carefully

The correct choice in most situations can be rewarding and the wrong choice can often be disastrous. This also applies in choosing your subject for a paper. If you choose a subject that is too broad or too general, you may find that there is too much material on it and you cannot possibly cover the subject adequately in one paper. For instance, a subject that would be too broad is "The Novels of Ernest Hemingway." There are literally hundreds of books about Hemingway's novels and it would be very hard for you to discuss all of them in a single paper.

If you find too much material on a broad subject, you may find too little on a narrow subject. An example might be a report on one of the minor characters in a lesser known novel by Hemingway. You could search until you were blue in the face and still not find enough for a paper if there isn't very much written on the subject.

Try not to select a subject that is over your head. There are few things more frustrating than trying to read a book or article that you cannot understand and then trying to write about it.

So choose your subject carefully, making it not too broad and not too narrow. Finally, try to select a subject that you are interested in. It's a lot easier to report on something you feel strongly about than on a subject that bores you to tears. Then . . .

Make a Preliminary Search for Material

First check the library catalog to see if the subject is listed. If it isn't, and if there are no related subjects, then you are in trouble. The subject is too narrow, too specialized, or too recent to be entered in the catalog. If you find the subject but there are many subtopics under it, the subject is too broad.

Now make a brief search through the periodical index that covers your subject. Again, if there are no entries or only a few articles under the entry, you may have to change the subject as you will probably need periodical articles for your paper. If the subject entry has many subtopics under it, you are out of the ball park. Use these subtopics to get you back in. They show how the main subject is broken down into more narrow areas within this subject.

Suppose you want to write on the subject of ecology. There is a subject entry in the *Readers' Guide* under "Ecology" with several general articles discussing it. One of the clues that tells you this subject is too broad is the many "see also" references:

Birds—Ecology	Mountain ecology
Environment	Paleoecology
Food chain (ecology)	Religion and ecology
Forest ecology	Seashore ecology
Freshwater ecology	Snow ecology
Human ecology	Zoology—Ecology
Marine ecology	

All of these entries relate to the main subject entry "Ecology." Many of them may have "see also" references further narrowing the subject.

Another clue that you may have too broad a subject is the number of subtopics within the subject. For instance, in the *Readers' Guide* these are some important subtopics under the subject entry "Environment":

Conferences	Poetry
Economic aspects	Study and teaching
Laws and legislation	Terminology

Any of these subtopics could be a subject for a paper.

Next, read an encyclopedia article. This will give you an overview. Likewise, if there is little or nothing in the encyclopedia, there may be little or nothing available in the library. A lengthy article divided into various subtopics will mean a subject is too broad or general.

Let's assume that, based on your preliminary search, you have selected a subject that is adequately covered in the library catalog and periodical indexes, a subject that is within your range of knowledge and ability, and a subject that you would enjoy reporting on. You are now ready to start your . . .

Introductory Reading

Read a chapter in a textbook on your subject. Skim through one of the books that comrpehensively covers the subject. Read one of the periodical articles. These preliminary readings will introduce you to the subject, help you further narrow it, and lead you to the next step . . .

Make an Outline for Your Paper

By now you should have a handle on your subject. You have an overview from the encyclopedia and the introductory reading has given you the dimensions that you wish for limiting your paper. You should prepare a tentative outline. The outline is one of the most important elements of a paper. Can you imagine building a house without first constructing the frame? The outline is the frame of the paper and to complete the paper you need only fill in the frame. First jot down the major topics or ideas that you are going to cover.

Let's say you want to write a paper on how to construct a house. Your major topics might be:

   I. Foundation
  II. Plumbing
 III. Frame
  IV. Outside walls
   V. Inside walls
  VI. Roof
 VII. Wiring
VIII. Insulation
  IX. Finishing

From these topics you can arrive at a *thesis statement,* a statement telling the main idea of the paper. The thesis statement for this example might be, "The proper way to construct a house is to proceed in a systematic step-by-step program." This statement tells what your paper will discuss.

The outline then breaks down or divides the thesis into the topics that discuss and support it. An outline for our paper might look like this:

Thesis Statement: The proper way to construct a house is to proceed in a systematic step-by-step program.

I. Foundation (the major topic that supports the thesis)
   A. Foundation forms (a subtopic discussing the major topic, foundation)
   B. Concrete (another subtopic under the major topic, foundation)
     1. Cement
     2. Sand
     3. Water
II. Plumbing
   A. Pipes
   B. Connecting joints
III. Frame
IV. Outside walls
V. Inside walls
VI. Roof
VII. Wiring
VIII. Insulation
IX. Finishing

After you have completed the outline you should begin . . .

Gathering Your Source Material

Teachers like you to use the full range of information available at the library for term or research papers—the regular circulating books, periodical articles, and reference books. You already know how to locate these sources: books through the library catalog, articles through the periodical indexes, and reference books in the reference collection.

You also know that the books on the same subject will be shelved together. Use the library catalog to find the call number of one book and you have them all. Don't indiscriminately pull them off the shelf though and check them out simply because your subject is mentioned in the title. Look through the table of contents in the front of the book and the index at the back of the book to be sure the book touches exactly what you are writing about. Check the writing style to make sure the book is at the level that you need—neither so elementary that it will not be a satisfactory reference nor so scholarly that you will not understand it. With each book or periodical that you finally select as source material, you should . . .

Prepare a Bibliography Card

A bibliography is a list of sources that you use for writing your paper. For each book that you use, prepare a bibliography card (usually a 3″ × 5″ card) listing the call number, the author, title, publisher, and place and date of publication. List the page numbers that you consulted. For periodicals you should also list the identifying information. Make a bibliography card for each source you consult so that later when you prepare the bibliography you will have the information available on the cards and you won't have to go back and hunt for it.

A bibliography card might look like this:

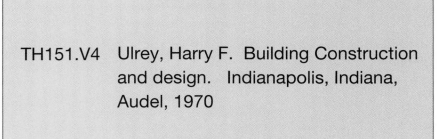

You are now ready to

Read the Source Material and Prepare Note Cards

As you read the source material, take notes on the facts and ideas that seem important enough for you to use in the paper. The note cards can be 3″ × 5″ cards or larger. It is better to go lightly over the material first before taking any notes. This enables you to get the whole picture of the chapter or article. You can then go back and take notes on the parts that directly relate to your subject.

The notes you are taking are the building blocks you use to complete the outline. The note cards will generally contain the following items:

1. The author and title of the book or article.
2. The topic heading from your outline to which this information applies.
3. The notes or thoughts that pertain to the topic.
4. The exact pages where the notes came from.

The outline topic heading serves to label all of the note cards that cover a particular topic. When you write the paper you can then easily assemble all the note cards under each topic.

"As I take the notes from the source material, can I use the author's exact words?"

Yes, it is permissible to use the exact wording that the author uses provided you give him credit. The way that you quote an author is to place quotation marks around the word, sentence, or phrase that he uses.

Normally when you write a term or research paper, you consult other authors' writings. It is perfectly all right to use their ideas and facts, but you must express them in your own words. This does not mean simply inserting or substituing words. You must take the central idea and write it as if you were the original author, with your language and your interpretation.

When you intend to use a direct quotation, record it on the note card, making sure that you have written exactly what the original author said. Be sure to note the page where the quotation was found. Often teachers will go back and check over your sources to be sure that you have given credit to the authors and have not used their words as your own.

The usual method for crediting an author is through the use of . . .

Footnotes

Footnotes are notes telling the source of a quotation. They are usually placed at the "foot" or bottom of the page on which you have written the quotation. They can also be listed on a separate page at the end of the paper.

"When should I use footnotes?" You should use footnotes for:

1. Direct quotations, the author's exact words.
2. Figures or statistics taken from another work.
3. An original concept or opinion of an author.

"What does a footnote look like?"

The following is a footnote for this quotation: "For ventilation of attics under gabled roofs, one square foot of clear opening should be provided for each 300 square feet of ceiling area."[1]

1. Harry F. Ulrey, *Building Construction and Design* (Indianapolis: Audel, 1970), p. 185.

Notice the number "1" after the last quotation mark at the end of the quotation. Each footnote is numbered, as you may have several for each page. This example is only one way to write footnotes; there are other ways. Ask your teacher immediately after he makes an assignment how and where he wants the footnotes. This footnote has the author's name (first name first), title of the book (underlined), the place of publication, publisher and date (in parentheses), and the page number that the quotation came from.

You may find at any time during your reading and notetaking that the outline has to be altered. You may decide to take a different course in writing the paper. Perhaps there wasn't enough material on all of the major topics.

You are moving right along though. In fact you should be ready for the . . .

First Draft of the Paper

It is always better to write a rough draft or first edition of your paper before the final product. With the outline as a guide fill in the text of the paper using your note cards for each topic as building blocks. Discuss each topic as it relates to and supports the thesis statement. Insert the footnotes where there is a need. You already know how and when to use reference books for supportive material.

Writing a rough draft accomplishes several things. You can tell approximately how long the paper is going to be.

Will you have to add or delete material, or will you have to . . .

Revise the Rough Draft

If you have examined the paper carefully, more than likely it will need some revision. Be sure that you have told the full story. Do the topics relate to the thesis? Have you given credit to other authors' works in the paper by using footnotes? Are grammar and spelling correct? Are sentence and paragraph structure developed into a cohesive unit? These are but a few of the things you should check for. Finally be sure that you are fully and completely satisfied with the paper. A lot of time and effort has probably gone into writing it and a polished paper can often mean the difference between a good or a poor grade.

Believe it or not, you are ready for the . . .

Final Copy

If possible you should hand in a typed copy of the paper. Make it neat. Keep the margins and spacing consistent throughout the paper. Prepare a cover sheet telling the title of the paper, the author (you), the date, the course number, and the teacher.

Normally, the last page of the final copy will be the . . .

Bibliography

As we previously mentioned, the bibliography is a list of the sources you have used to write your paper. It is an alphabetical listing by the author's last name. When the author is not given, the first word of the title is used in the alphabetical sequence. One way to write bibliographic entries is illustrated below. Notice the entries in a bibliography are not numbered.

Bibliography

Halperin, Don A. *Building with Steel.* Chicago: American Technical Society, 1966.

Merritt, Frederick S. *Building Construction Handbook.* New York: McGraw-Hill, 1965.

"Shelter in the Woods," *Architectural Forum,* March 1970, pp. 36–9.

Ulrey, Harry F. *Building Construction and Design.* Indianapolis: Audel and Co., 1970.

Wright, J. R. "Performance Criteria in Building," *Scientific American,* March 1971, pp. 16–25.

Notice the third and fifth entries. They are periodical articles. The first is unsigned and is entered in the alphabetical listing by the first letter in the first word of the article. The second is signed and is entered alphabetically by the author's last name.

Authors' Note

The style described in the reading for documenting sources is called the *footnote system* because the citation is at the foot or bottom of the page; there is a bibliography at the end of the paper. The style in which the citations are at the end of the paper is called the *endnote system.* There are three other common documentation styles that you will see in books and articles. When you are assigned to write a research paper, you must ask your instructor which style he or she wishes you to use. You can then buy the appropriate style manual in the bookstore, or borrow it in the library. Here are brief descriptions of the three other styles:

1. The *name-and-page system* is described in the *MLA* (Modern Language Association) *Handbook for Writers of Research Papers.* It uses citations in the text rather than footnotes, and instead of a bibliography there is a section at the end called "Works Cited."

2. The *name-and-year system* is described in the *Publication Manual of the American Psychological Association.* It uses a slightly different form of in-text citation, and the section at the end is called "References."

3. The *number system* is often used in the natural sciences and mathematics. It places numbers in parentheses in the text after a quote or paraphrase. The documentation at the end corresponds to these numbers, rather than being in alphabetical order.

   In this book we have used the footnote system because it is quicker for researchers to glance at the bottom of the page than to look for the notes at the end of the chapter or in the back of a book.

Comprehension Check

Circle the letter preceding the correct answer. Then check your answers in the back of the book.

1. After your introductory reading, you should
   a. make an outline.
   b. begin writing the paper.
   c. prepare a bibliography.
   d. begin reading additional material.

2. A footnote or endnote is needed
   a. when you paraphrase what the author says.
   b. when you quote the author directly.
   c. when you use statistics from another book.
   d. in each of these cases.

3. To get an overview of your topic,
   a. read a textbook chapter on it.
   b. read an encyclopedia article on it.
   c. make an outline.
   d. (a) and (b).

4. The author's main point in this article is that
   a. if your subject is too broad you can't write a good paper.
   b. writing a research paper is hard work.
   c. you should learn how to use the library.
   d. there is a systematic way to go about writing a paper.

5. Which of the following is not an acceptable form of citing a source?
   a. banknote
   b. endnote
   c. footnote
   d. in-text

6. The author implies that the best way to write a research paper is to
   a. break the work into subgoals.
   b. write many rough drafts of the paper.
   c. take as many book notes as possible.
   d. write your outline only after you have everything you want to include.

7. A bibliography
   a. should always include page numbers.
   b. is a list of quotations.
   c. is alphabetized by the titles of books, magazines and newspapers.
   d. is a list of sources that you have used to write your paper.

8. An outline of a paper should contain
   a. all the details in the paper.
   b. just the major topics.
   c. major and minor topics.
   d. all of the quotations in the paper.

9. The purpose of the preliminary search is to_____

   _____.

10. The reason to use note cards is that_____

   _____.

Questions for Discussion and Writing

1. What information did the article provide that you will find useful the next time you have to research a paper?

2. What is the most difficult part for you when writing a research paper? Did the chapter suggest anything that might help you break down this step into subgoals you can more easily accomplish?

3. What was the last research paper you had to write? In what subject? What grade did you get in the class? What grade did you get on the paper? Now that you have studied some basic strategies for writing a paper, what would you do differently if you had the chance to write that paper again?

EXERCISE 5: Skills Review—Memory/Graphic Organizers

Skim the following article on the limits of short-term memory (STM). Then, based on your evaluation of the article's organization, type of information, and your learning style, decide whether creating an outline, study map or other graphic organizer would best help you grasp and retain the information if you were studying for a test. Read the article.

Reading Selection 2: Memory

Capacity of STM (Short-term Memory)

The arcade fanatic absorbed in a game is **oblivious** to the outside world. Chess masters at tournaments demand complete silence while they **ponder** their next move. You shut yourself in a quiet room to study for final exams. All these examples illustrate the fact that there is a definite limit to how much information STM can handle at any given moment. Some years ago it was suggested that STM can hold at most 5 to 10 bits of information at the same time (G.A. Miller, 1956; Sperling, 1960). More recently, researchers have proposed that it may be more accurate to say that STM can hold as much information as can be repeated or rehearsed in 1.5 to 2 seconds (Baddeley, 1986; Schweickert & Boruff, 1986).

To get a better idea of the limits of STM, read the first row of letters in the following list just once. Then close your eyes and try to remember the letters in the correct sequence before going on to the next row:

1. CXW
2. MNKTY
3. RPJHBZS
4. GBMPVQFJD
5. EGQWJPBRHKA

unaware of

think about

Like most people, you probably found rows 1 and 2 fairly easy, row 3 a bit harder, row 4 very hard, and row 5 impossible to remember after just one reading. This gives you an idea of the relatively limited capacity of STM.

Now try reading through the following set of 12 letters just once and see if you can repeat them: TJYFAVMCFKIB. How many letters were you able to recall? In all likelihood, not all 12. But what if you had been asked to remember the following 12 letters instead: TV FBI JFK YMCA. Could you do it? Almost certainly the answer is yes. These are the same 12 letters as before but here grouped into four separate "words." This way of grouping and organizing information so that it fits into meaningful units is called chunking. The 12 letters have been chunked into four meaningful items that can readily be handled by STM—they are well below the 5-to-10-item limit of STM, and they can be repeated in less than 2 seconds. Here's another example of chunking. Try to remember this list of numbers:

106619451812

Remembering 12 separate **digits** is usually very difficult, but try chunking the list into three groups of four:

numbers

1066 1945 1812

Particularly if you are interested in military history, these three chunks will be much easier to remember than 12 unrelated digits.

By chunking words into sentences or sentence fragments, we can process an even greater amount of information in STM (D. Aaronson & Scarborough, 1976, 1977; Tulving & Patkau, 1962). For example, suppose you want to remember the following list of words: tree, song, hat, sparrow, box, lilac, cat. One strategy would be to cluster as many of them as possible into phrases or sentences: "The sparrow in the tree sings a song"; a "a lilac hat in the box"; "the cat in the hat." But isn't there a limit to this strategy? Would five sentences be as easy to remember for a short time as five single words? Simon (1974) found that as the size of any individual chunk increases, the number of chunks that can be held in STM declines. Thus, STM can easily handle five unrelated letters or words simultaneously, but five unrelated sentences are much harder to remember.

Data such as these lend support to the idea that the limit of STM might better be conceived as a 2-second limit rather than a 5-to-10-item limit: In both cases, there are only five items of information to be remembered, but it takes longer to repeat five sentences than it does to repeat five words. If there is a 5-to-10-item limit on STM, the sentences should be just as easy to remember as the individual words. But if there is a 2-second limit on information in STM, the sentences should be more difficult to remember than the individual words—and this is what research finds.

A dramatic example of the power of chunking was reported by Chase and Ericsson (1981). The subject in this case, known as SF, was a young man who had spent more than 250 hours in the laboratory over 2 years, purposefully using chunking to increase his short-term memory for strings of digits. At the time of the report, SF could accurately recall strings of more than 80 digits. He accomplished this **feat**   **achievement** by associating groups of digits with his already vast knowledge of common and record times for running races of particular lengths. The digit string 3492 might be broken out, for instance, as a chunk associated with a near-record time for the mile, 3 minutes, 49.2 seconds. SF, by the way, was no better than average at remembering strings that he could not relate to running, such as strings of letters.

Keep in mind that STM usually has more than one task to perform at once. During the brief time you spent memorizing the rows of letters on the previous page, you probably gave them your full attention. But normally, you have to attend to new incoming information while you work on whatever is already present in short-term memory. Competition between these two tasks for the limited work space in STM means that neither task will be done as well as it could be. In one experiment, subjects were given 6 random numbers to remember and repeat while performing a simple reasoning task. As a result, they performed their reasoning task more slowly than subjects who had simply been asked to repeat the numbers 1 through 6 throughout the task (Baddeley & Hitch, 1974). Similarly, if you had been asked to count backward from 100 while trying to learn the rows of letters in our earlier example, you would have been much less successful in remembering them. Try it and see.

Morris, *Psychology*, 233–234

Now that you have read the article, follow these 12 steps to evaluate your study techniques.

1. Plan your graphic organizer. This includes organizing the information and deciding if the use of color and shapes should be used to emphasize key material.
2. Take a piece of paper and create your study aid.
3. Evaluate the visual layout to be sure everything is clear and accurate.
4. Turn the paper over and see if you can recall the information.
5. If not, take another piece of paper and write or draw the parts you can remember.
6. Analyze what you remembered and what you forgot.
7. Decide whether the missing information requires that you supplement the study material by adding information or by using additional study aids such as flash cards or mnemonics to reinforce your memory. Supplement your study material and review it.
8. Repeat steps 4 and 5 until you are satisfied that you can recall the information in the reading article.

9. Take a piece of paper and draw your graphic (if you are outlining put the numbers and letters of the outline). Do not fill in any of the information.

10. Do something else for 1–2 hours.

11. Take the paper you created in step 8 and fill in the missing information.

12. Evaluate your study technique by answering the questions below.
    A. Was your graphic organizer complete? If not, what was wrong?
    B. Was the organizer you chose a good technique for you? If not, what other method do you think would have helped more?
    C. What types of information couldn't you remember? (facts, examples, major concepts)
    D. Did you forget a cluster of information or material from various parts of the reading?
    E. Did you need more detail on the graphic organizer to help remember what you had forgotten? Did you need to create additional study aids such as flash cards or mnemonics? Did you add color?
    F. Can you still recall everything on your organizer? (Answers will vary.)

EXERCISE 6: Skills Review—Taking Tests

Before taking the following 20-item objective test on using the library, go back and practice the test-taking skills you learned in Chapter 9. You might use the PQ4R method, or you could try to anticipate the items that would appear on such a test. You might also place 20 such items on flash cards and review them. Then take the test; and finally, check your answers in the back of the book.

Multiple-Choice Questions

Circle the correct letter.

1. The place to begin your research is
   a. the periodical index.
   b. the stacks.
   c. the traditional or computerized card catalog.
   d. an encyclopedia.

2. Which of the following types of cards will not be in the card catalog?
   a. author
   b. title
   c. subject
   d. index

3. A cross-reference card is a type of
   a. author card.
   b. title card.

   c.   subject card.

   d.   index card.

4. The call numbers of the Library of Congress classification system begin with

   a.   numbers.

   b.   the author's last name.

   c.   the subject.

   d.   letters.

5. Which book would probably not be in the Reference section of the library?

   a.   an encyclopedia

   b.   an anthology

   c.   an almanac

   d.   a dictionary

True–False Questions

Write T or F in the blanks.

_____ 6. *Who's Who* contains information only on famous Americans, living and dead.

_____ 7. An author card contains the author's year of birth.

_____ 8. There are two major library classification systems.

_____ 9. A closed-stack system differs from an open-stack system in that only students who attend the college can check out materials.

_____10. An atlas contains facts about almost everything.

_____11. A book on reserve must be used in the Reference section of the library.

_____12. The audio-visual department of the library contains current newspapers.

_____13. Most college libraries have word processing computers for use without charge.

_____14. Microfilm, microfiche and on-line databases are being used in more and more libraries.

_____15. The card catalog facilitates access to the stacks.

Fill-in Questions

Fill in the blanks.

16. Information on most of the materials that circulate in the library can be found in the _____.

17. The _____ section contains dictionaries, encyclopedias, and almanacs.

18. The book that indexes popular magazine titles is called the _____

_____.

19. _____ contains biographies mostly of famous living Britons.

20. The cataloging system based on numbers is called the _____ _____.

After you have checked your answers, go back to the questions you missed and try to analyze why you did not answer them correctly. Did you study the wrong material? Did you misread or misinterpret the question?

Improving Vocabulary

11

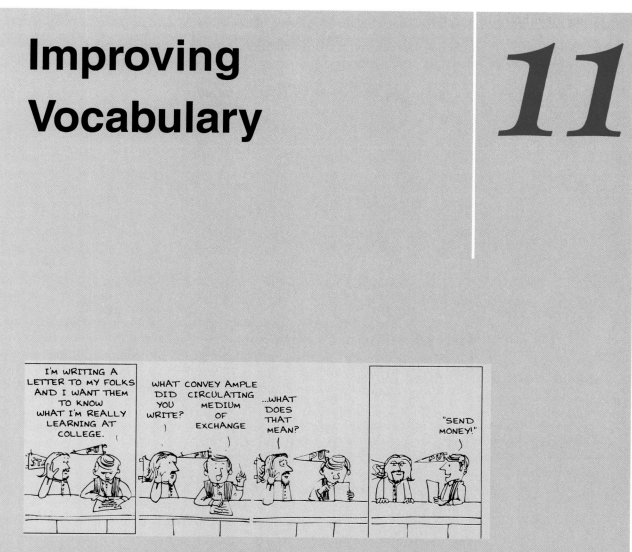

Improving Vocabulary

I. Five ways to enlarge your vocabulary
    A. Use the context
    B. Break words into smaller parts
    C. Become an etymology buff
    D. Write words down
    E. Use reference books
        1. Dictionary
        2. Thesaurus
II. Summary

Man does not live by words alone despite the fact that he often has to eat them.
Adlai Stevenson

What is vocabulary? Vocabulary is simply all the words in a particular language. The more words you know, the more you can express your ideas in speech and writing and understand the ideas of other people. You are no stranger to vocabulary. If you are an average American adult, you already know between 30,000 and 40,000 words.

Five Ways to Enlarge Your Vocabulary

Use the Context

The easiest and most common way to learn a new word is to figure out its meaning from the words surrounding it. Look at this sentence:

Most of the children in the room were well behaved; only Bill was obstreperous.

If you didn't know what *obstreperous* meant before you read this sentence, you now have an idea that it means noisy or unruly. This is called a **contrast** clue. You can figure out the meaning of the word obstreperous by contrasting it with *well behaved.*

A second type of context clue is **definition,** in which the sentence or paragraph gives you either a one-word synonym or a definition in several words. Here is an example:

Mentally ill people can have *hallucinations,* in which they hear or see things that aren't there.

In this sentence, hearing or seeing things that aren't there defines having hallucinations.

A third type of context clue is **example.** The context gives an example of the meaning of the word, as in this sentence:

Some people's conversation rarely strays from *pedestrian* topics such as the weather.

Here the weather is given as an example of a dull, and unimaginative, or pedestrian topic.

A fourth common type of context is **experience.**

Salary is one of the most important *determinants* of career choice.

In this case, anyone who has thought about careers knows that many people make decisions based on how much they hope to earn.

If you are skilled at using the context, you won't have to look up very many unfamiliar words in the dictionary. Each chapter in this book contains exercises in context vocabulary. But the best way to develop skill at context reading is simply to read a lot. Your vocabulary will improve from reading almost anything. Don't feel guilty if you don't read scientific books for pleasure; reading articles in the weekly television listings or the newspaper will improve your vocabulary, too.

Break Words into Smaller Parts

You can often conquer even a very long word by dividing it into its root and *affixes* (prefixes or suffixes). For example, the root *tract* comes from the Latin *trahere* or *tractus,* which means "to pull or draw." Using some common prefixes and suffixes, we have made 16 English words from this single root:

Prefix	Root	Suffix	Meaning
	trace		to draw over; to go over
	tract		expanse of land
	tract	or	machine for pulling other machines
	tract	ion	drawing something along a surface
re	tract		to draw back or in
ab(s)	tract		theoretical; drawn from the concrete
dis	tract		to divert; to draw away from
de	tract		to take or draw from
ex	tract		to pull out or draw out
con	tract		to draw or squeeze together
pro	tract		to draw out
sub	tract	ion	pulling or drawing from the whole
at	tract	ive	capable of drawing to oneself
con	tract	or	one who enters into a drawn-up agreement
in	tract	able	hard to manage; stubborn (hard to pull along)
pro	tract	or	an instrument used for geometric drawing

Unfortunately, using word parts to figure out the meaning of unfamiliar words is not always reliable. The familiar prefix *in* usually means "not" (invisible) or "into" (inside). However, it has another, less common meaning, "very" (as in inflammable). It could be dangerous if you thought that "inflammable" meant "not flammable." Many words no longer carry the literal meaning of their parts. The word *suppose* comes from the Latin prefix *sub* (under) and the root *pose* (put). *Suppose* no longer means "to put under."

Become an Etymology Buff

Etymology is the study of the origins of words. Finding the origins of words is fun, and it helps you enlarge your vocabulary. Did you know that the word *fornication* comes from the Latin word *fornicatus,* which means "arched" or "vaulted"? Prostitutes in ancient Rome used to stand in archways to solicit business.

Words come into English from many different languages. Latin and Greek are probably the largest sources. We still use Latin and Greek roots to make new words. For example, the word *astronaut* comes from the Greek roots *astro,* meaning "star," and *nautes,* meaning "sailor." An astronaut sails among the stars. A *cosmonaut* is one who sails the universe (from the Greek *kosmos,* meaning "universe").

Other languages give us new words, too. *Goulash* and *hula* are Hungarian and Hawaiian, respectively. Sometimes meanings are confused when words are imported. One story has it that we got the word *kangaroo* when an explorer pointed to a kangaroo and asked "What's that?" and his Aborigine guide replied, "Kangaroo," which in Aborigine means "I don't know." Knowing a foreign language can sometimes help you recognize unfamiliar English words. Knowing that the Spanish word *facil* means "easy" can help you understand that the English word *facilitate* means "to make easy."

Names of people and places can also become words. It is said that *tuxedo* derived from the formal dress men wore at the Tuxedo Club in New York. (Incidentally, the word originally came from the Algonquin Indian language, where it means "he has a round foot").

Words such as *scuba* and *tip* are acronyms ("scuba" stands for "self-contained underwater breathing apparatus"). "Tip" came from the sign placed on a box near the doors of English inns, suggesting that patrons contribute "to insure promptness."

A few words are simply made up out of thin air. It is said that when George Eastman, founder of Eastman Kodak, was looking for a name for his camera, he coined the work *Kodak* just because he like the letter *k.* Others combine two words into a new word. Recently *downsizing* has become familiar to the business world. No one in business now needs a definition of what was once called *consolidation* or "pulling in the purse strings." You still may not be able to find "downsizing" in a dictionary.

Write Words Down

If you are too busy to look up an unfamiliar word in the dictionary, or if you have looked it up and keep forgetting its meaning, write the word down. One very efficient way to study new words is to put each word on a flash card and review the cards every time you have a few minutes between classes. As soon as you think you have mastered a word, put its card in a reserve pile that you review much less often. As you add new words, you can keep retiring words you have mastered, so that your stack won't keep getting taller.

Use Reference Books

Dictionary. If you cannot figure out a word's meaning from its context and if you can't break it into recognizable parts, you have no choice but to use the dictionary. Look at the following page from *Webster's New World Dictionary* as you read on.

Two *guide words* appear at the top of each page, one above each column. The one on the left is the first word on the page, and the one on the right is the last word on the page. Using the guide words helps you quickly locate the word you want. For example, if the guide words at the top of the page are *toddy* and *toluene,* you know that *toilet* will be on that page because alphabetically *toilet* comes between *toddy* and *toluene.*

The **main entry** is in boldface type. If a raised number appears to the right of the main entry, as it does after *toll* in the sample, it is a **multiple entry.** That means that the same word will appear in two or more entries, each with a different definition. Dots separate the syllables of the main entry.

The **pronunciation key** for *toga* tells you that the *o* can be pronounced like the *o* in *toe.* In some dictionaries, the pronunciation key is not at the bottom of the page but at the front of the dictionary. Using the pronunciation guide below, choose the correct pronunciation for the word *together.*

fat, āpe, cär; ten, ēven; is, bīte; gō, hôrn, to͞ol, look; oil, out; up, fur; get; joy; yet; chin; she; thin; *then;* zh, leisure; ŋ, ring; ∂ for *a* in *ago, e* comply, *u* in *focus;* ' as in *able* (ā'b'l)

a.   to geth'∂r   b. to͞o get'or   c. to͞o geth'∂r   d. t∂ get'h∂r

The correct answer is **c.**

The dictionary also tells you which syllables to accent when you pronounce a word. The word *token* (to'k∂n) is accented on the first syllable.

The **part of speech** can sometimes affect the definition. The *n.* after *toilet* means the word is a noun. The *adj.* after *tolerable* means that the word is an adjective. But some words can be used as several parts of speech. For example, look at *token.* As a noun, *token* means 1. "a sign, indication, symbol" 2. "a keepsake" 3. "a metal disk to be used in place of currency". As an adjective, it can mean either "symbolic" or "merely simulated; of no real importance."

Some words have more than one entry. For example, *toll* has two separate entries. These words come from separate origins and mean totally different things. The first entry of *toll* comes from the Greek word for tax. The second entry of *toll* comes from the Middle English word for pull. It means to ring (a church bell) or to announce or summon someone using a bell.

Several different spellings may be given. If there is more than one acceptable way to spell a word, the other forms are given at the beginning of

Sample Dictionary Page

Annotations (left margin): Guide words · Etymology · Colloquial expression · Pronunciation · Alternate spellings · Alternate pronunciations · Illustration · Multiple definitions · Slang expression · Proper name · Parts of speech

Annotations (right margin): Single definition · Use in a phrase · Idiomatic expression · Partial pronunciation · Cross reference · Syllabication · Main entry · Spelling of different parts of speech · Technical usage · Multiple entry

toddy 620 **toluene**

to walk with short, uncertain steps, as a child —**tod′dler** *n.*

tod·dy (täd′ē) *n., pl.* **-dies** [< Hindi] a drink of whiskey, etc. mixed with hot water, sugar, etc. Also **hot toddy**.

to-do (tə dōō′) *n., pl.* **-dos** [Colloq.] a commotion; stir; fuss

toe (tō) *n.* [OE ta] **1** a) any of the digits of the foot b) the forepart of the foot **2** anything like a toe in location, shape, or use —*vt.* **toed, toe′ing** to touch, kick, etc. with the toes —*vi.* to stand, walk, etc. with the toes in a specified position /he *toes* in/ —**on one's toes** [Colloq.] alert —**toe the line** (or **mark**) to follow orders, rules, etc. strictly

toed (tōd) *adj.* having (a specified kind or number of) toes: usually in hyphenated compounds /two-*toed*/

toe dance a dance performed on the tips of the toes, as in ballet —**toe′-dance′, -danced′, -danc′ing,** *vi.* —**toe′-danc′er** *n.*

toe′ hold *n.* **1** a small space to support the toe in climbing, etc. **2** a slight footing or advantage

toe′less *adj.* having the toe open or uncovered /a *toeless* shoe/

toe′nail *n.* the nail of the toe

tof·fee or **tof·fy** (tôf′ē, täf′·) *n.* [< TAFFY] a hard, chewy candy, a kind of taffy

to·fu (tō′ fōō) *n.* a Japanese cheeselike food made from soybeans.

to·ga (tō gə) *n., pl.* **-gas** or **-gae** (-jē, -gē) [L < regere, to cover] in ancient Rome, a loose outer garment worn in public by citizens.

ROMAN TOGA

to·geth·er (too geth′ər, tə-) *adv.* [< OE *to*, to +*gaedre*, together] **1** in or into one group, place, etc. /we ate *together*/ **2** in or into contact, union, etc. /the cars skidded *together*/ **3** considered collectively /he lost more than all of us *together*/ **4** at the same time /shots fired *together*/ **5** in succession /sulking for three whole days *together*/ **6** in or into agreement, cooperation, etc. /to get *together* on a deal/ —*adj.* [Slang] having an integrated personality

to·geth′er·ness *n.* the spending of much time together, as by family members, when regarded as resulting in a more unified, stable relationship

tog·gle switch (täg′əl) a switch consisting of a lever moved back and forth to open or close an electric circuit

To·go (tō′gō) country on the W coast of Africa: 21,853 sq. mi.: pop. 2,700,000

togs (tägz, tôgz) *n. pl.* [ult < L *toga*, toga] [Colloq.] clothes

toil *tudiculare*, to stir about] [Colloq.] clothes

toil (toil) *vi.* [< L *tudiculare*, to stir about] **1** to work hard and continuously **2** to proceed laboriously —*n.* hard, tiring work —**toil′er** *n.*

toi·let (toi′lit) *n. pl.* [< OFr *toile*, cloth < L *tela*, a web] **1** the act of dressing or grooming oneself **2** dress, attire **3** *a)* a room with a bowl-shaped fixture for defecation or urination. *b)* such a fixture

toilet paper (or **tissue**) soft paper for cleaning oneself after evacuation

toi′let·ry (lə′trē) *n. pl.* **-ries** soap, lotion, etc. used in grooming oneself

toi·lette (twä let′, toi-) *n.* [Fr.] **1** the process of grooming oneself **2** dress; attire

toilet water a lightly scented liquid with a high alcohol content, applied to the skin after bathing, etc.

toils (toilz) *n. pl.* [< L *tela*, web] any snare suggestive of a net

toil·some (toil′səm) *adj.* laborious

toke (tōk) *n.* [? < fol.] [Slang] a puff on a cigarette, esp. one of marijuana or hashish —*vi.* **toked, tok′ing** [Slang] to take such a puff

to·ken (tō′kən) *n.* [OE *tacn.*] **1** a sign, indication, symbol, etc. /a *token* of one's affection/ **2** a keepsake **3** a metal disk to be used in place of currency, for transportation fares, etc. —*adj.* **1** symbolic **2** merely simulated; of no real account /*token* resistance/ —**by the same token** following from this

to′ken·ism (·iz′əm) *n.* the making of small, often merely formal concessions to a demand, etc.; specif., token integration of blacks, as in jobs, etc.

To·kyo (tō′kē·ō′) capital of Japan, on S Honshu: pop: 8,991,000 (met. area 11,620,000)

told (tōld) *vt., vi. pt. & pp. of* TELL —all told all (being) counted.

tole (tōl) *n.* [Fr *tôle.* sheet iron] a type of lacquered or enameled metalware, usually dark-green, ivory, or black, used for lamps, trays, etc

To·le·do (tə lēd′ō) city & port in NW Ohio: pop. 333,000

tol·er·a·ble (tal′ər ə bəl) *adj.* **1** endurable **2** fairly good; passable —**tol′er·a·bly** *adv.*

tol′er·ance (·əns) *n.* **1** a being tolerant of others' views, beliefs, practices, etc. **2** the amount of variation allowed from a standard **3** *Med.* the ability to resist the effects of a drug, poison, etc.

tol′er·ant *adj.* having or showing tolerance of others' beliefs, etc.

tol·er·ate (täl′er āt′) *vt.* **-at′ed, -at′ing** [< L *tolerare*, to bear] **1** to allow **2** to respect (others' beliefs, practices, etc.) without sharing them **3** to put up with **4** *Med.* to have tolerance for —**tol′er·a′tion** *n.*

toll¹ (tōl) *n.* [ult. < Gr *telos*, tax] **1** a tax or charge for a privilege, as for the use of a bridge **2** a charge for service, as for a long-distance telephone call **3** the number of lost, etc. /the tornado took a heavy *toll* of lives/

toll² (tōl) *vt.* [ME *tollen*, to pull] **1** to ring (a church bell, etc) with slow, regular strokes **2** to announce, summon, etc. by this —*vi.* to ring slowly: said of a bell —*n.*the sound of a bell tolling

toll′booth *n.* a booth at which a toll is collected, as before entering a toll road

toll′gate *n.* a gate for stopping travel at a point where a toll is collected

toll′road a road on which a toll must be paid Also **toll′way′** (-wā′) *n.*

Tol·stoy or **Tol·stoi** (täl′stoi′, tōi′·), Count Le·o (lē′ō) 1828–1910; Russ. novelist

tol·u·ene (täl′yōō ēn′) *n.* [Sp *tolu*, after *Tolú*, seaport in Colombia + BENZ)ENE] A color-the entry. In the entry for *toffee*, you are told it can be spelled *toffee* or *toffy*. Irregular plural spellings are also given. For example, in the case of *toiletry* the plural noun *toiletries* is given.

A **slang term** is highly informal and should not be included in your written assignments. Slang terms can be either new words or old words to which new meanings have been attached. On the dictionary page, the last definition of *together* is slang: "having an integrated personality." Therefore, you would not use the sentence "He was a very together individual" in a term paper. Slang terms change frequently, and for that reason most of them are not found in dictionaries.

A **colloquial term** is used in conversation and informal writing, but not in a college theme or formal letter. In the sample, *to do* and *togs* are colloquial expressions. Some colloquialisms are regional. For example, *flapjacks, hotcakes,* and *griddlecakes* are various American names for pancakes.

An **idiomatic expression,** or idiom, is an accepted phrase that has a meaning different from the literal meaning. Examples are *by the same token* and *to toe the line.* They are listed under the main word in the dictionary. (*By the same token,* for example, is listed under *token*).

An **archaic word** is one that was once used frequently but is now outdated. Examples are *thou* and *ye.*

The dictionary also gives the etymology of the word. The etymological abbreviations are explained in the front of the dictionary. *Token* comes from the old English ("OE"), *toga* comes from Latin ("L"), and *toddy* comes from Hindi. To find the origin of the word *told,* the dictionary tells you to see *tell.* This is one form of **cross-reference** which means you must look under *tell* to find out its origin and other information.

You should select a dictionary according to your needs. Unabridged dictionaries try to be complete: they contain about half a million entries. Desk copies are hard-covered dictionaries containing over 150,000 words. Pocket dictionaries are much smaller, often about 50,000 words, because they include only frequently used words.

Another factor in selecting a dictionary is its copyright date. The English language changes, and words like *laser disc, rap* (music), and *multiculturalism* are unlikely to be in any dictionary more than five years old. Place of copyright can matter, too. If you look in the Oxford English Dictionary,[1] you will find that the pronunciation for *schedule* and the spelling of *labor* differ from those used by Americans.

Hints for using a dictionary:

1. Use the guide words to save time.
2. If you can't find a word you are looking for, try another spelling. For example, try *parallel* instead of *paralell.*
3. If you come to an abbreviation you don't understand, turn to the front of the dictionary, where you will find a list of the abbreviations used in that dictionary.

---

[1]Della Thompson ed., *The Concise Oxford Dictionary of Current English,* 9th ed. (Oxford: Carendon Press, 1995).

4. Don't be frustrated when you find that a word is defined by a word you don't understand. For example, if you are looking up *inconsequential* and you find another unfamiliar expression *of no consequence*, just look up *consequence*. You will find "1. a result, effect. 2. importance." Remember the prefix "in" means "not." Therefore, *inconsequential* means having no result, no effect, or no importance.

5. When you look up a word, make a habit of checking its pronunciation and all its meanings. This will help you make the word part of your regular vocabulary.

6. Familiarize yourself now with the additional articles, charts, and tables in your dictionary. Someday your dictionary may save you a trip to the library.

7. When you come to a word that has several different meanings, such as *sharp* in the following sample,[2] use the context in which the word appears to help you choose the correct definition.

> **sharp** (shärp) *adj.* [OE. *scearp*] 1. having a fine edge or point for cutting or piercing 2. having a point or edge; not rounded 3. not gradual; abrupt 4. clearly defined; distinct [a sharp contrast] 5. quick in perception; clever 6. attentive; vigilant 7. crafty; underhanded 8. harsh; severe [a sharp temper] 9. violent, as an attack 10. brisk; active 11. intense, as a pain 12. pungent 13. nippy, as a wind 14. [Slang] smartly dressed 15. Music above the true pitch. *adv.* 1. in a sharp manner; specif., a) abruptly or briskly b) attentively or alertly c) Music above the true pitch 2. precisely [one o'clock sharp]—*n.* 1. [Colloq.] an expert 2. Music a) a tone one half step above another b) the symbol (#) for such a note—*vt., vi.* Music to make or become sharp.—**sharp'ly** *adv.*—**sharp'ness** *n.*

> *Webster's New World Dictionary of the American Language,* p. 540

Referring to the entry for *sharp*, write the number of the correct definition on the line preceding each of the following sentences. The first one has been done for you.

a. __6__ A security guard must always be sharp while on duty.
   adj.

b. _____ The pianist kept playing a sharp instead of a flat, which made the song
   n.   sound awful.

c. _____ The car was traveling too fast to make the sharp turn in the road. It skid-
   adj. ded to a halt only inches from plunging over the side of the mountain.

d. _____ The sharp edge of the knife made cutting tomatoes very easy.
   adj.

e. _____ Be sure you are at the theater at three o'clock sharp or you will not get in.
   adv.

f. _____ His sharp clothes helped him get the job.
   adj.

Answers: b, 2a; c, 3; d, 1; e, 2; f, 14

Also, you will find different meanings for words such as *lift,* which is an elevator to the British, and words absent from standard American dictionaries, such as *serviette,* which is a napkin.

In addition to dictionaries in print, now there are dictionaries on computer software programs, such as Microsoft Windows 3.1 or later; there are several on CD-roms, including *The American Heritage Dictionary* on Microsoft's Bookshelf '96, *Webster's New World Dictionary* on the *Compton's Reference Collection, Webster's New World Dictionary, Third College Edition,* published by Zane Publishing, and The Longman's Dictionary of American English, published by Longman's. Computer reference software has several advantages: it saves space; it is often less expensive than the cost of the comparable books; and it keeps an extensive collection of reference sources instantly available.

Thesaurus. This is a book of *synonyms* (words that have similar meanings) and *antonyms* (words that have opposite meanings). Peter Mark Roget, a British physician, published the first thesaurus in 1852. The word *thesaurus* comes from Greek and Latin words meaning "treasury." Roget thought of his book of synonyms and antonyms as a treasury of related words.

A thesaurus is not a dictionary; its purpose is not to give definitions, pronunciations, or syllabication, and not all words can be found in it. Thesaures can be organized in different ways. The hard-cover version of *Roget's Thesaurus* divides the entries into six major classes of ideas with their subclasses. Examples of classes of ideas are "space" and "intellect." In addition, words are indexed alphabetically at the back of the book. In another version the classifications have been eliminated, and the words are arranged in alphabetical order, as in a dictionary.

The sample thesaurus on page 280 is from the second type. Notice that the words are divided into major and minor entries. A major entry is capitalized and is written in larger type than other entries on the page, and provides a variety of synonyms for each meaning of a word. A major entry is **approval.** It gives the noun form of approval, different A minor entry lists only a few synonyms and then refers you to the major entry for that word group. For example, the word _____ is a major entry. It gives you synonyms for _____ meanings of the word. **Apprentice** on the other hand, is a minor entry. It tells you to see other words meaning the same things such as *helper* and to see **Learning** and **Beginning** for other words meaning **beginner.**

One drawback of the thesaurus is that it usually does not differentiate shades of meaning. Every word has a *denotative* meaning, which is simply its literal definition. However, many words also bring to mind various images and associations, called *connotative* meanings. The word *snake* denotes a reptile but may also connote slimy, dangerous, and frightening. The sample thesaurus page gives many synonyms for archaic. Many of these synonyms differ in their connotative meanings. For example, someone would probably like his furniture being called antique but might well resent its being called antiquated or dated. When choosing a synonym, make sure that the new word fits the context in which you are using it. A dictionary can sometimes help clarify connotative meanings. However, a good rule to follow is never to use a word unless you know both its deno-

Sample Thesaurus Page

Guide word →

APPRENTICE   24   (**ARCHAIC**) ← *Guide word*

Minor entries →

seizure, capture, arrest (TAKING).
apprentice, *n.* helper, assistant (WORK); beginner, neophyte (LEARNING, BEGINNING).
apprise, *v.* orient, advise, brief (INFORMATION).

Major entry →

APPROACH—*N.* approach, access, accession, convergence.
[*means of approach*] avenue, adit, path, access, ramp.

Parts of speech →

overtures, advances, approaches, proposals, offers.
V. **approach,** near, draw near, move toward, drift toward, come near, converge upon; accost, make advances; gain upon, overtake, catch up to, stalk.
Adj. **approaching,** nearing, coming, oncoming, forthcoming, drawing near, convergent, advancing; imminent, impending, threatening.
approachable, accessible, attainable; open, affable, sociable, democratic, friendly.

Cross-reference →

See also ARRIVAL, FOLLOWING, FRIENDLINESS, FUTURE, NEARNESS, PASSAGE. *Antonyms* — See AVOIDANCE, DISTANCE, REVERSION.

Synonyms that are other major entries →

approbation, *n.* approval, acceptance, sanction (APPROVAL).
appropriate, *adj.* proper, correct, legitimate, (PROPRIETY), particular, peculiar, intrinsic (OWNERSHIP).
appropriate, *v.* assume, confiscate, expropriate (TAKING), abstract, life (THIEVERY).

APPROVAL—*N.* approval, approbation, acceptance, endorsement, confirmation, ratification, sanction; esteem, estimation, good opinion, favor; appreciation, regard; account, popularity, credit, repute, renown, kudos (*colloq.*); commendation, congratulation, praise, encomium, homage, hero worship; blessing.
admiration, adoration, worship, veneration, idolatry; tribute, testimonial, recommendation, reference, certificate.
self-admiration, self-love, narcissism, *amour propre (F.),* self-approval, vanity, conceit, pride, self-worship, self-esteem, egotism.

Foreign phrase (French) →

applause, plaudit, clap, handclap, clapping, acclaim, acclamation; cheer, hurrah, huzza; paean, shout (peal, chorus, *or* thunders) of applause, ovation, salvo.
applauder, clapper, rooter; cheerer; cheering squad, claque.;

Colloquial usage →

V. **approve,** approbate, commend, boost (*colloq.*), accept, endorse, countenance, smile on, confirm, ratify, sanction;

esteem, value, prize, set great store by, honor, like, appreciate, think well of, think highly of; stand up for, stick up for (*colloq.*), uphold, recommend; sympathize with.
admire, esteem, hold in esteem, look up to, adore, worship, venerate, idolize, idolatrize.
excite admiration in, dazzle, impress, strike with wonder, awe.
applaud, clap, acclaim, cheer for, root for (*colloq.*)
Adj. **approbative,** approbatory, applausive, acclamatory, plausive, confirmatory, commendatory, laudatory, complimentary.

Different senses of adjective form of entry →

approved, popular, standard, acceptable, orthodox, in good odor; in high esteem, in favor, in high favor.
admirable, estimable, venerable, splendid.
praiseworthy, laudable, honorable, commendable, creditable, meritorious, glorious.

Cross-reference to antonym →

See also ACCEPTANCE, FLATTERY, LOVE, PRAISE, PRIDE, RESPECT, WORSHIP. *Antonyms*—See DETRACTION, DISAPPROVAL, DISREPUTE, DISRESPECT, HATRED, UNSAVORINESS.

approximate, *adj.* near, close, rough (SIMILARITY).

Foreign word (Latin) →

approximately, *adv.* about, (*circa (L.)*), nearly (SMALLNESS).
appurtenance, *n.* adjunct, accessory, appanage (ADDITION)
apropos, *adj.* applicable, apposite, appurtenant (PERTINENCE).
apt, *adj.* likely, probable, liable (LIKELIHOOD); inclined, prone (TENDENCY); pat, to the point (PERTINENCE); appropriate, apropos (AGREEMENT)
aptitude, *n.* ability, flair, talent (ABILITY); mental ability (INTELLIGENCE).
aqueduct, *n.* conduit, channel, culvert (PASSAGE).
aquiline, *adj.* eaglelike, hooked, beaked (NOSE).
arable, *adj.* cultivable, cultivatable, tillable (FARMING).
arbitrary, *adj.* peremptory, rigorous, highhanded (CONTROL, OPINION); autocratic, capricious, despotic (WILL).
arbitrator, *n.* arbiter, umpire, referee (JUDGE).

Technical usage (architecture) →

arcade, *n.* cloister, vault, arch (PASSAGE, SUPPORT).
arch, *n.* cover (*arch.*), dome, arcade, (SUPPORT).
archaeology, *n.* paleontology, antiquarianism, paleology (OLDNESS).
archaic, *adj.* antiquated, antique, dated (OLDNESS, DISUSE).

The New Roget's Thesaurus in Dictionary Form, p. 24

tative and connotative meanings as well as its pronunciation. If you observe this caution, a thesaurus can be of great help to you in writing college papers and expanding your vocabulary.

Like dictionaries, there are thesauri on computer. Two are *The Original Roget's Thesaurus,* on Microsoft's *Bookshelf,* and *Webster's New World Thesaurus,* which is part of *Compton's Reference Collection.*

Summary

Vocabulary can be expanded in at least five ways. The most common method is to learn new words from the context as you read. The second method is word analysis, or breaking words into their prefixes, suffixes, and roots. A third method is the study of etymology, or word origins. A fourth method is to write new words on flash cards and review them often. Finally, you can use a dictionary or thesaurus. No single method is sufficient; use all five. The more tools you have, the more effective you will be at building a superior vocabulary. Such vocabularies have been shown to contribute significantly to personal, collegiate, and occupational success.

Comprehension Check

Circle the letter preceding the correct answer. Then check your answers in the back of the book.

1. The most common way to enlarge your reading vocabulary is by
   a. guessing the meaning from the context.
   b. using etymology.
   c. looking words up in the dictionary.
   d. writing words on flash cards.
2. A thesaurus contains
   a. connotative meanings.
   b. definitions.
   c. denotative meanings.
   d. synonyms.
3. Archaic words
   a. are not found in the dictionary.
   b. are rarely used now.
   c. are colloquial.
   d. can be used in conversations but not in college themes.
4. An etymologist studies
   a. context reading.
   b. synonyms and antonyms.
   c. word origins.
   d. all of the above.
5. The main reason for learning Latin and Greek roots is to
   a. speak Latin and Greek.
   b. impress your friends.

    c. figure out the meaning of new words.

    d. understand the context.

6. The main reason to study different techniques for enlarging your vocabulary is that
   - **a.** it helps you learn foreign languages.
   - **b.** it impresses people.
   - **c.** the more tools you have, the better your vocabulary-building skills will be.
   - **d.** you will enjoy etymology.

7. Why isn't looking up unfamiliar words in a dictionary the best way to learn new words?
   - **a.** It takes too long.
   - **b.** It interrupts what you're reading.
   - **c.** The context of a word can change its meaning.
   - **d.** All of the above are true.

8. An unabridged dictionary is
   - **a.** something every college student must have.
   - **b.** found in most libraries.
   - **c.** the most up-to-date dictionary.
   - **d.** inexpensive.

9. A denotative word is _____.

10. A connotative word is _____.

Questions For Discussion and Writing

1. What are some of the problems you can encounter when using a dictionary with which you are unfamiliar?

2. Do you believe that in the year 2500, printed dictionaries will be a thing of the past? Why or why not?

EXERCISE 1: Using the Dictionary

Give the title and copyright date for the dictionary you are using. Then complete the following questions.

Title_____

Copyright date _____

1. Tell whether each of the following words is singular or plural.
   - a. dice_____
   - b. media _____
   - c. criterion _____
   - d. data _____

2. The following words can be pronounced two different ways depending on their part of speech. In the blank following the pronunciation, fill in the correct part of speech. The first one is done for you.

a. advocate ad'və kit _____n._____ advə kāt' _____v._____

b. separate sep'ə rāt _____ sep'ə rit _____
c. extract ik strakt' _____ eks'trakt _____

d. refuse ref'yoos _____ ri fyooz' _____

3. Translate the following proverbs into English.
   a. ol that glit'erz iz nat gōld._____

   _____

   b. emp'tē ket'lz mēk thə mōst noiz. _____

   _____

   c. strīk hwīl thə īrən is hât._____

   _____

4. Fill in the words that the following abbreviations stand for, and give their definitions. The first one is done for you.
   a. R.S.V.P. __Répondez s'il vous plaît.__ _____Please reply._____
   b. etc. _____ _____
   c. i.e. _____ _____
   d. e.g. _____ _____

EXERCISE 2: **Prefixes**

Here is a list of 20 common prefixes that will help you rapidly expand your vocabulary. We have given you several examples of words that use each prefix. You provide one for the blank. Try to pick a word that will help you remember what the prefix means. Check your answers in a dictionary that provides word origins, to be sure that your word is based on the right prefix. (Answers will vary.)

	Prefix	Definition	Examples
1.	*a, ab*	away, from	atypical, abnormal
			_____
2.	*ad*	to	address,
	ac (before *c* or *q*)		accept, acquire
	af (before *f*)		afford,
	ag (before *g*)		aggressive,
	an (before *n*)		announce,
	ap (before *p*)		appropriate,
	ar (before *r*)		arrange, associate,
	as (before *s*)		associate,
	at (before *t*)		attach
			_____
3.	*con*	with, together	connect,
	co (before a vowel)		cooperate,
	col (before *l*)		collect,
	com (before *b, m, p*)		combine, command, compare,
	cor (before *r*)		correct
			_____

	Prefix	**Definition**	**Examples**
4.	*cir, circum*	around	circulation, circumstance
5.	*de*	from, away, down	decrease, descend
6.	*dis, dif*	apart, not	disappear, different
7.	*e, ex*	out	eliminate, exit
8.	*in, en* *im, em* (before *b, p, m*)	in, into, within	indoors, enable, import, embarrass
9.	*in* *im* (before *b, m, p,*) *il* (before *l*) *ir* (before *r*)	not	inflexible, imbalance, immediate, impractical, illegal, irregular
10.	*inter*	between	interrupt, intermission
11.	*mis*	not, wrong	mistake, misspell
12.	*o, ob* *oc* (before *c*) *of* (before *f*) *op* (before *p*)	toward, against	omit, obstacle, occur, offend, oppose,
13.	*post*	after	postpone
14.	*pre*	before	prerequisite
15.	*pro*	for, before, forward	promote, provide, propel
16.	*re, retro*	again, back	rewrite, retroactive
17.	*sub* *suc* (before *c*) *suf* (before *f*) *sup* (before *p*) *sus* (before *c, p, t*)	under	submit, submarine, success, suffer, suppose, susceptible, suspense, sustain
18.	*super*	over	supervise, supernatural
19.	*trans*	across	transition, transfusion
20.	*un*	not	unimportant, untie

EXERCISE 3: Roots

The easiest way to remember a root and its meaning is to associate the root with common examples. In this exercise we have provided some examples for several roots. You provide one of the blank. Try to pick a word that will help you remember what the root means. Check your answers in a dictionary that provides word parts, to be sure that your word is based on the same root.

	Root	Definition	Examples
1.	*dic, dict*	say, speak	indicate, dictator
2.	*log, logy*	speech, word, reason, study of	logical, dialogue, psychology
3.	*mob, mot, mov*	move	mobile, promotion, remove
4.	*nom, onym*	name	nominate, synonym
5.	*pon, pose, posit, pound*	put	component, disposable, deposit, compound
6.	*press, prim, prin*	squeeze, press	depress, reprimand, imprint
7.	*spec, spic, spis*	see, look	spectacular, suspicious, despise
8.	*tract*	draw, pull	subtraction, distract
9.	*vid, view, vis*	see	video, review, visualize
10.	*voc, vok*	say, speak, call	vocal, invoke

EXERCISE 4: Vocabulary

Use the definitions of the words in parentheses and then choose the correct word for the blank. Then check your answers in the back of the book.

1. A wrong name is a _____. (misnomer, spectrum)
2. One who speaks in favor of a cause is an _____. (advocate, opponent)

3. To call a group together is to _____ it. (motivate, convoke)

4. Something that is easily seen is _____. (evident, circumspect)

5. If you see something in your mind, you _____ it. (envision, predict)

6. A drawn-out visit is _____. (protracted, deposited)

7. A place far removed is _____. (impounded, remote)

8. A place where things are put is a _____. (spectacle, depository)

9. A decision that cannot be repealed is _____. (irrevocable, proposed)

10. To put down by force is to _____. (contract, suppress)

Reading Selection: Speech

Speak with Confidence: A Practical Guide to Command of the Language

Albert J. Vasile, Harold K. Mintz

We are concerned here with two goals—to capture and condense some insights and practices of the best oral communicators. From them we can learn a great deal about using words to get results. What follows is not the Ten Commandments on using language, but simply guidelines or suggestions on how to generate maximum power in your command of the language.

Concrete, Specific Words Versus Abstract Words

For informative as well as persuasive speaking, there's no question that *concrete*, specific words carry a message most effectively. Concrete words **pertain** to tangible things—objects that we can perceive through our senses. The meanings of such words should be easily understood and leave little room for personal interpretation. Obviously, the more concrete words you use, the better your chances will be that the listener will comprehend your intended message exactly.

apply

If *parallel construction* can be built into a sentence of such words, the emotional impact can be intensified. Here are two statements composed of concrete, specific, vivid words strengthened and **immortalized** with parallel construction. In 1933, President Franklin D. Roosevelt said to the Depression-battered American people:

made forever memorable

I see one-third of a nation ill-housed, ill-clad, ill-nourished.

Early in World War II, Prime Minister Winston Churchill declared to the English people, staggering under military setbacks and facing conquest by Hitler's Germany:

> . . . we shall fight on the beaches, we shall fight on the landing grounds, we shall fight in the fields and on the streets, we shall fight in the hills; we shall never surrender.

Note the striking force of the parallel construction in that sentence. Note that the words are short and specific and that they permit instant understanding. Not even one abstract, **nebulous** word **emasculates** those sentences.

vague
weakens

Here are some examples of concrete, specific words:

- Flood   Traffic jam   Rubbish
- Airplane   Parking ticket   Desk
- Gun   Money   Trees
- Tax bill   Rain   Baby
- Mansion   Nuclear plant   Daycare center

You cannot, of course, avoid *abstract words* in public speaking. Sometimes they're necessary and serve a worthwhile purpose, but remember that they're subject to various interpretations and arguments depending on people's backgrounds, religion, education, nationality, and so on. When using abstract words, be sure to define and explain them to avoid any misunderstanding or misinterpretation of your message.

Abstract words pertain to intangible things, such as ideas, concepts, beliefs, and values that cannot be seen. Here are some examples:

- Freedom   Fascism   Morality
- Liberty   Justice   Character
- Democracy   Patriotism   Perestroika
- Religion   Honesty   Glasnost
- Philosophy   Ideology   Integrity

Short, Simple Words Versus Long, <u>Pretentious</u> Words

stuffy

For the purpose of informing or inspiring your listeners, simple one- or two-syllable words are usually better suited. A classic example of using such words is Lincoln's Gettysburg Address. He delivered it not to inform people, but to inspire them. Of its 266 words, 195 consist of one syllable.

Here's another example, one of Shakespeare's more popular **sonnets,** which begins with "Shall I compare thee to a summer's day?", contains 114 words, and 92 of them contain one syllable. If Lincoln and Shakespeare can do it, so can you.

poems

Yet, some audiences expect longer, more elegant words. The more you know about your audience, the better you can judge what kinds of words to use. Table 6.2 provides a sample listing of what some people refer to as pompous and pretentious words, together with their simple, direct equivalents.

Showy, Polysyllable Words	Short, Direct Equivalents
Ablution	Washing
Ameliorate	Improve
Assimilate	Absorb, digest
Cognizant of	Aware of
Conflagration	Fire
Consolidate	Unite, combine
Contiguous with	Touching
Delineate	Describe
Designation	Name
Effectuate	Carry out
Enumerate	Count, list
Facilitate	Make easy, simplify
Expedite	Speed up
Incombustible	Fireproof
Initiate, institute	Begin, start
Innocuous	Harmless
Modification	Change
Optimum	Best
Progenitor	Forerunner
Subsequent to	Later, next
Termination	End

Table 6.2
Comparison of words with similar basic meanings.

A glaring example of **pompous,** inappropriate language was given by the former U.S. ambassador to Great Britain, Walter H. Annenberg, when he was presented to Queen Elizabeth. She asked him a simple question about his housing arrangements and he replied: "We are in the ambassadorial residence subject, of course, to some of the discomfiture as a result of the need for elements of refurbishing and rehabilitation." He might have said, "We're redecorating now so the house is a bit messy."[1]

stuffy

Equally **verbose** and **pedantic** is the following letter from a Houston, Texas, high school principal to a student's father:

wordy/ bookish

> Our school's cross-graded, multi-ethnic, individualized learning program is designed to enhance the concept of an open-ended learning program with emphasis on a continuation of multi-ethnic, academically enriched learning using the identified intellectually gifted child as the agent or director of his own learning.
>
> Major emphasis is on cross-graded, multi-ethnic learning with the main objective being to learn respect for the uniqueness of a person.

The parent wrote the principal:

> I have a college degree, speak two foreign languages and four Indian dialects, have been to a number of county fairs and three goat ropings, but I haven't the faintest idea as to what the hell you are talking about. Do you?[2]

The kind of language the ambassador and the principal used has been called **"gobbledygook."** It's been around a long time. Believe it or not, one of its major opponents has been the U.S. government. The Bureau of Land Management of the Department of the Interior many years ago issued a book entitled *Gobbledygook Has Gotta Go.*[3] It's full of examples of inflated prose and deflated revisions. For example, it cites the following passage written in the early years of our country to oppose efforts to limit voting rights to people who owned property:

double talk

> It cannot be **adhered** to with any reasonable degree of intellectual or moral certainty that the inalienable right man possesses to exercise his political preferences by employing his vote in referendums is rooted in anything other than man's own nature, and is, therefore, properly called a natural right. To hold, for instance, that this natural right can be limited externally by making its exercise dependent on a prior condition of ownership of property is

held

[1]Barbara Walters, *How to Talk with Practically Anybody About Practically Anything* (Garden City, NY: Doubleday, 1970), 136.
[2]*Boston Sunday Herald American,* 6 February 1977, p. 23.
[3]*Gobbledygook Has Gotta Go.* Washington: Bureau of Land Management, U.S. Department of the Interior, pp. 45–46.

to wrongly suppose that man's natural right to vote is somehow more inherent in and more dependent on the property of man than it is on the nature of man. It is obvious that such belief is unreasonable, for it reverses the order of rights intended by nature.

The government manual cites Benjamin Franklin's version of the same argument as being much more effective.

To require property of voters leads us to this dilemma: I own a jackass; I can vote. The jackass dies; I cannot vote. Therefore, the vote represents not me but the jackass.

Loaded Words

Some words that concern race, religion, and politics can **provoke** heated and sometimes overpowering reactions. *Loaded words* can either **infuriate** or **humiliate** people, and they can **induce** people to commit irrational acts. Loaded words are like a loaded gun, they can cause devastating damage. Here are some examples of words that spell potential *danger* to you and to others:

call forth

greatly anger/ greatly embarrass/ cause

Race or religion

* Whitey   Uncle Tom
* Honky   Wasp
* Racist   Hebe
* Nigger   Kike
* Oreo   Fish-eater

Nationality

* Gringo   Hun
* Spic   Polack
* Harp   Slant-eyes
* Wop   Chink
* Dago   Jap
* Frog   Towelhead

Political philosophy

* Radical   Nazi
* Anarchist   Fascist
* Revolutionary   Communist
* Imperialist   Right-wing
* Reactionary   Left-wing

Whereas loaded words are extreme in their potential for trouble, there are other words and their synonyms that can be either **complimentary** or belittling. Here are some examples:

positive

Complimentary	Belittling or Disparaging	negative
• Slender	Skinny	
• Inexpensive	Cheap	
• Imported	Foreign	
• Prudent	Stingy	
• Pre-owned	Used	
• Cocktail lounge	Bar	
• Discriminating	Finicky	
• Deliberate	Indecisive	
• Courageous	Reckless	
• Thrifty	Tightwad	

In some situations your choice of words can either *make or break you.* Think before you speak.

Comprehension Check

Circle the letter preceding the correct answer. Then check your answers in the back of the book.

1. The main idea of the article is
   a. there are certain rules to improve communication.
   b. communication is one of the hardest tasks we attempt.
   c. most people speak with confidence if they practice enough.
   d. there are guidelines that one should consider when trying to communicate.
2. Which word below would be considered "loaded"?
   a. short
   b. freshman
   c. all-American
   d. English
3. Abstract words
   a. can never be used in public speeches.
   b. should be used as often as possible.
   c. should be used sparingly and should be explained.
   d. make speeches more elegant.
4. "Gobbledygook"
   a. refers to the use of inflated langauge.
   b. is a humorous speech.
   c. is a foreign language.
   d. refers to concrete language.

5. According to the article, one of the major opponents to "gobbledygook" has been
   a. college professors.
   b. lawyers.
   c. the U.S. government.
   d. journalists.

6. Two masters of the use of parallel construction mentioned in the article are
   a. Walter Annenberg and Elizabeth Taylor.
   b. Winston Churchill and Franklin Roosevelt.
   c. William Shakespeare and Benjamin Franklin.
   d. Queen Elizabeth and Abraham Lincoln.

7. When speaking to inspire or inform someone, you should use
   a. abstract words.
   b. loaded words.
   c. simple, one- or two-syllable words.
   d. flowery words.

8. According to the article, good speakers use
   a. abstract words rather than concrete words.
   b. long rather than short words.
   c. parallel construction to intensify emotions.
   d. loaded words.

9. An etymology is _____.

10. Loaded words are _____.

Questions For Discussion and Writing

1. Do you think it is a good or bad idea to use concrete words with a hostile audience? Why?

2. Do you feel using the ideas presented in this article would help you "speak with confidence"? Why or why not?

EXERCISE 5: Etymology

Become an etymologist. Here are some words with interesting origins. Look them up in an unabridged dictionary and fill in their meanings on the first line and their unusual origins on the second. Don't forget to check the pronunciations of any that are unfamiliar. The first one is done for you. Check your answers in the back of the book.

1. Lilliputian   An inhabitant of Lilliput; an undersized creature
                                    Gulliver's Travels

2. boycott _____

   _____

3. sadist _____
    _____

4. utopia _____
    _____

5. gargantuan _____
    _____

6. muscle _____
    _____

EXERCISE 6: Using the Thesaurus

Look at the sample thesaurus page and answer these questions

1. What two major entries would you look under to find a synonym for
    "approval"?_____
2. What is an easier word for "neophyte"?_____
3. What is the first synonym listed for "admire"?_____
4. a. What is one of the colloquial words on this page other than
       "boost" meaning "approval"?_____
    b. What are three colloquial phrases on the page and what does each
       mean?

       Phrase   Meaning

       1. _____
       2. _____
5. What part of speech is "apt"? _____
6. Do you think that you would find the word "admire" on this page?
    Why or why not?_____

EXERCISE 7: Reviewing Graphic Aids

Read the following selection from a book and on your own paper make two graphic
organizers illustrating important information. One should be an outline and the
other another graphic. For sample answers, see Appendix I.

World-wide Communication

Remember the Revolutionary War shot heard 'round the world? Today a process that translates speech from one language into two other languages is the technology that will literally be "heard" 'round the world. In 1993 in a demonstration an American confirmed his registration for a conference in Munich. That may not be particularly remarkable, but the stateside researcher spoke in English to his computer at Carnegie Mellon in Pittsburgh and thus directly to the researcher in Germany who received the message translated into German.

ATR Interpreting Telephone Laboratories in Kyoto, Japan; Siemans AG and Karslruhe University in Germany; and Carnegie Mellon University in Pittsburgh have combined forces in the development of a speech-to-speech computerized translation system. The system must recognize the voice of someone inputting data, then translate the message into two other languages (for now they are German and Japanese), and finally synthesize the voice back into understandable speech in the receiving country.

The 2½-second sentence in the example above took approximately 20 seconds before it was received, including translation and time to transmit it overseas. With computer speeds measured in nanoseconds this delay is considered practically an eternity.

The system has a limited vocabulary of approximately 500 words, but terminology can be added relatively easily. However, teaching a computer the **nuances** of language is another challenge. Alex Waibel of Carnegie Mellon gives this example. If you ask the computer to "Give me a new display," that message is **acoustically comparable** to "Give me a nudist play."

subtleties

sounds like

Although we can't hear the bugs in the system, it seems there could be some misinterpretation.

Robert A. Szymanski, Donald Szymanski, and Donna M. Pulscen,
Computers and Information Systems, p. 96

After you have completed both of your graphic organizers, answer the following questions:

1. Do you have the same information on both? _____
2. Which one was easier to make? _____
3. Which one do you think will be a more useful study aid for you? ___

_____

Varying Reading Rates

12

Varying Reading Rates

12 | When we read too fast or too slowly we understand nothing.
Blaise Pascal

Reading Rates

Many misconceptions exist about reading rates. To learn whether you hold any of them, mark the following statements true or false.

_____ With special training, it is possible to learn to read at speeds up to 3,000 words per minute.

_____ It is best to read at one steady pace.

_____ When studying a textbook, it is important to read every word.

All the statements are false. The average reader reads 200 to 250 words per minute. Even highly trained readers rarely read more than 1,000 words per minute. The claims of some speed-reading courses that their graduates can read thousands of words per minute have not been supported by research. Reading at very high speeds, you can gain no more than a general idea of what you are reading. However, reading every word is sometimes a waste of your time. Good reading is selective. Even in textbooks you often see material that you already know or that isn't important for your purposes.

Fast reading is not necessarily good reading. The speed at which you should read depends on four factors. The first is the difficulty of the material: even the best readers read unfamiliar material slowly. The second is the purpose for which you are reading. Material that you must memorize for an exam should be read more slowly than material you read for relaxation. The third factor is your level of skill. If you are good at picking out main ideas, if you are familiar with college-level vocabulary, and if you have a wide background of experience so that the ideas you are reading are not completely new to you, you will read faster than someone who is less adept at reading. The fourth factor is the absence of bad reading habits that slow you down: reading one word at a time rather than phrases; moving your lips even on easy material; and looking back at (regressing to) what you have already read. Even the most skilled readers do some of these things when the material is very difficult, but they should never become habits.

Habits That Slow You Down

Reading word by word will interfere both with your speed and with your comprehension of what you read. To demonstrate, read this sentence, stopping at every word: We/speak/in/phrases;/we/should/read/in/phrases. Now read the same sentence by phrases as it is marked: We speak/in phrases;/we should read/in phrases.

Moving your lips while you read decreases reading speed. Talking is much slower than reading, and moving your lips slows you down.

Regressing means looking back at what you have already read. Even the best readers regress when they read something very difficult. However, some readers habitually feel insecure about their comprehension and regress unnecessarily. This slows them down and can even interfere with comprehension. To demonstrate, read this: an apple apple a day an apple a day a day keeps the doctor doctor doctor away doctor away. The sentence is confusing because we naturally try to read in phrases.

Breaking Bad Habits

To stop reading word by word, practice reading in phrases or units of thought. You can hear phrasing in normal speech. Phrase reading will improve not only speed but comprehension as well.

To break the habit of moving your lips, place your finger between your front teeth while you read. Holding a pencil between your teeth is another method.

To prevent unnecessary regressions, cover what you have already read with a card, sliding the card down the page just above what you are reading.

You now know some methods for breaking poor reading habits. But remember—only conscious practice will replace bad habits with good ones.

Three Types of Reading

There are three types of reading: study reading; regular reading; and partial reading—scanning and skimming.

Study Reading

When the material you read is difficult or unfamiliar, when the ideas are very important, or when you will have to remember the material, use PQ4R. However, even in a textbook some material is less important or is already familiar to you. The Preview Step you learned in Chapter 5 can tell you what must be read thoroughly, what can be read at a regular speed, and what can be skimmed, scanned, or skipped altogether.

Casual Reading

When you are reading for pleasure, or when you are reading material for which PQ4R is inappropriate, you can read at your normal speed, trying to eliminate any poor reading habits you may have. When you have eliminated undesirable habits, you can try to read faster, if you wish, by consciously pushing yourself to a speed that is slightly uncomfortable. Reading with the conscious intent to improve speed will do just that.

Scanning and Skimming

The two types of partial reading are scanning and skimming. *Scanning* is used to locate specific information, such as a word in a dictionary, a number in a phone book, or the answer to a question in a textbook. *Skimming* is used to gain a general idea of a selection, to preview, to overview, or to review.

Scanning and skimming can be compared to driving through the western United States on a sightseeing vacation. You can plan your vacation in two ways. You can take out a map and look up the Grand Canyon, Yosemite, and other places of interest, and drive at 65 miles per hour until you get to them. Or you can drive at 65 miles per hour just to see what an area is like and then stop when you see something interesting. These kinds of vacations are different from a backpacking trip, on which you see every flower, rock, and tree but don't cover much ground.

The backpacking trip is like reading every word in a selection. The two types of car trips are like scanning and skimming, respectively. We call them partial reading because you don't look at every word. Efficient readers vary their pace, reading every word only when thorough reading is necessary or desirable. The rest of the time, they read only the important words or phrases and scan or skim the rest. For example, when you read a newspaper you skim the headlines, then read only the articles that interest you. Partial reading is especially useful when

1. you don't have time to read the whole selection,
2. all you need is an overview or general idea of the material,
3. you are previewing either as part of PQ4R or to find out whether you want to read the selection,
4. you are looking for specific information.
5. you are reviewing the material to refresh your memory.

Scanning. Scanning is like looking up places of interest on your map and then driving fast, not noticing much until you get there. Scan the following selection on tolerance to find the answers to the next four questions. First read the questions. Then underline the key words in each question. These are the words you will scan for.

1. What is an important example of tolerance? _____

   _____

2. What is the fatal dose of morphine? _____

3. How much morphine do some regular users take? _____

4. What is a cross-tolerance to related drugs? _____

   _____

The words you should have underlined are (1) *tolerance* (also look for an example), (2) *fatal* (scan for a number), (3) *regular users* (scan for a number), and (4) *cross-tolerance.*

When you scan you will try to answer each question by running your eyes quickly over the paragraphs, looking for your key words. Hint: look especially for words that are italicized or capitalized and for numbers. When you find your key word, read the words around it until you have enough information to answer the question. Fill in the answer and go on to the next question. You should be able to scan the paragraphs and answer the questions in one minute if you are scanning properly. Time yourself. If you try to read the paragraph thoroughly, you will not be able to finish in time. When you finish the exercise, check your answers by reading the selection thoroughly.

The body is said to develop *tolerance* to a drug, when the original dosage no longer produces the desired results. To counteract tolerance, the dosage may be increased, or a stronger drug may be prescribed. An important example of tolerance occurs in the use of antibiotics, where the infecting microorganism itself may develop a tolerance to the drug—or even a liking for it.

Regular users of narcotic depressants develop a tolerance so great that the desired effect of the drug can be achieved only by a dose far larger than would normally be considered fatal. The usual dose of morphine is 8 to 20 milligrams for relief of severe pain; 200 milligrams is thought to be a fatal dose for most people. Regular users of morphine, however, have been known to take as much as 5,000 milligrams a day. Drugs that are chemically similar often cause *cross-tolerance.* That is, tolerance, or resistance, to one drug in the group produces tolerance to all drugs in the group. Similarly, a craving for one drug in the group can by physically, if not psychologically, satisfied by other drugs in the group.

La Place, Health, pp. 333–334

The answers are (1) use of antibiotics; (2) 200 milligrams; (3) 5,000 milligrams in a day; (4) resistance.

Skimming. Skimming is like the second type of vacation described earlier—driving fast until you see something of interest, and then slowing down. It is partial reading to get an idea of what a reading selection is about, to find the main ideas and most important details. Because skimming involves skipping most of the words, it permits speeds of up to several thousand words per minute. Perfect comprehension of skimmed material is impossible, because you cannot comprehend what your eyes have not seen. However, skimming is essential to efficient reading, enabling you to avoid plodding through all types of material, relevant and irrelevant, reading every word. In study reading, you skim to preview material before reading, to review material after reading, and to get an overview of collateral material so that you can decide whether you should read it. The Preview Step of PQ4R is a special type of skimming, in which you read only headings, summaries, graphics, and first sentences of paragraphs. In recreational reading, you could skim informational material such as newspapers and magazines to get a general idea of their contents and to decide which articles you might want to read. Skim works of fiction to learn quickly whether you want to read the novel or story in question.

We have already described one type of skimming—the Preview Step in PQ4R. Another type of skimming involves moving your eyes rapidly over a page to pick up the main ideas and the most important details. If you have difficulty locating main ideas you will have difficulty skimming, because skimming always requires judgment of what is and isn't important. When you see something on the page that looks important (often signaled by headings, italics, boldface, capital letters, numbers, or signal words), pause a moment and read a few words. The following sample shows only the words on which our eyes fixate when we skim a paragraph. Read the words and then try to answer the comprehension questions that follow.

Cause of earthquakes

Centuries ago   people believed
            shakings of the earth   caused by
monster   supporting the globe.   Japan
      great spider   giant catfish.   South
America   giant
tortoise.   Mongolia

            immense frog; every time   shook his head or
                  feet,   earthquake   immediately above

1. What is the subject of the paragraph?
    _____

2. What is the main idea?
    _____

3. What places are given as examples?
    _____

Now read the whole paragraph and check your answers.

Cause of Earthquakes
Centuries ago (and in some places today), people believed that mysterious shakings of the earth were caused by the restlessness of a monster that was supposed to be supporting the globe. In Japan it was first a great spider and then a giant catfish. In some parts of South America Indians decided that the earth rested on the back of a giant tortoise. The lamas of Mongolia had another idea. They assured their

devout followers that, after God had made the earth, he placed it on the back of an immense frog; every time the frog shook his head or stretched one of his feet, an earthquake occurred immediately above the moving part.

Leet, Judson, Kauffman, *Physical Geology*, p. 182

The answers are (1) causes of earthquakes; (2) centuries ago people believed earthquakes were caused by monsters; (3) Japan, South America, North America, Mongolia. This example shows how much information you can obtain from reading only a small percentage of the words, even in a college textbook.

Now take a few seconds to skim the following paragraph and write down the main idea in your own words. Don't read all the words.

During World War II women had taken "men's jobs" and made some short-term economic gains, but generally by the fifties the force and conviction of the turn-of-the-century *feminist movement* had been forgotten. Time, transportation, and babysitting problems discouraged all but the most determined women from combining a socially mandatory marriage with professional training. In 1955, for instance, a smaller percentage of graduate students were women than thirty years before; and women in college took typically "feminine" courses in elementary education, home economics, or secretarial skills.

Burner, Marcus, and Rosenberg, *America: A Portrait in History* p. 679

Main idea:_____

_____

The main idea, which you should have obtained from skimming, is that the economic gains women made in World War II were lost after the war.

What are we? **In essence** we are a combination of chemical elements produced **eons** ago inside the fiery cores of massive stars—the same elements that contribute to Earth's rocky continents, its atmosphere, and its oceans. Somehow all those elements combined on our planet to form life. But are we unique? Is life on our planet the only example of life in the universe? These are tough questions, for the subject of extraterrestrial life is one on which there are no data.

basically
many, many years

Chaison and McMillan, *Astronomy: A Beginner's Guide to the Universe*, p. 483

1. What is the subject of the paragraph?_____

_____

2. What is the main idea? _____

_____

3. Where were the chemical elements produced that, when combined, created life? _____

_____

4. What do all living things have in common with Earth's continent, atmosphere, and oceans? _____

_____

The answers are (1) possibility of life beyond Earth; (2) we may not be alone in the universe; (3) in stars; (4) all contain the same elements. This example shows how much information you can obtain from reading only a small percentage of the words, even in a college textbook.

Now take a few seconds to skim the following paragraph and write the main idea in your own words. Don't read all the words.

> People in the United States value work and tend to subscribe to the work ethic, which means that hard work is applauded and rewarded, while failure to work is viewed negatively. Americans admire people who work hard and are motivated to achieve. Reward systems in many firms are based on an employee's achievement and willingness to work beyond a 40-hour week. U.S. senior-level executives often work 56 hours a week, far more than in many European countries. They average only 14 days of vacation a year, far fewer than in some countries in Europe, where people often close businesses for a month to go on vacation.
>
> Chaney and Martin, *Intercultural Business Communication*, p. 46

Main idea:_____

_____

The main idea, which you should have obtained from skimming, is that people in the United States value and reward work highly and are often willing to work more hours and days than their European counterparts.

Summary

Contrary to what many people believe, efficient readers do not read every word at one steady pace, nor do they attain speeds of thousands of words per minute. Anyone can improve his or her reading speed and efficiency by working to eliminate faulty reading habits and by varying the type of reading to suit the purpose. Reading rates include slow reading for study purposes, regular reading, and partial reading. The two types of partial reading are skimming and scanning. Skimming is used to gain a general idea of a selection, to preview, to overview, or to review. Scanning is used to locate specific information. The key to reading efficiency is not speed but determining your reading purpose and using the rate most appropriate to that purpose.

Comprehension Check

Circle the letter preceding the correct answer. Then check your answers in the back of the book.

1. The speed at which you can read depends on
   a. your knowledge of the topic.
   b. vocabulary difficulty.
   c. your reading purpose.
   d. all of the above.

2. A reading habit that increases your efficiency is
    a. word-by-word reading.
    b. rereading important parts several times.
    c. reading by phrases.
    d. reading out loud.

3. A good reader
    a. never looks back.
    b. reads everything rapidly.
    c. can read thousands of words a minute and remember most of what he or she has read.
    d. does none of the above.

4. "Reading by phrases" means
    a. reading a whole sentence before pausing.
    b. reading three words at a time.
    c. reading approximately the way we speak.
    d. stopping at the end of every line.

5. You can choose the type of reading rate you will use by
    a. skimming material beforehand.
    b. analyzing the title.
    c. reading everything slowly until you see how much you remember.
    d. doing all of the above.

6. Bad reading habits
    a. are impossible to break.
    b. can be broken only with the aid of reading machines.
    c. can be broken with practice.
    d. don't affect your reading rate.

7. If you were reading the newspaper for a political science class, you would
    a. use PQ4R so that you could remember all of the articles.
    b. read it at your regular rate.
    c. skim for the articles on relevant subjects.
    d. do all of the above.

8. Reading rates
    a. are more important than comprehension.
    b. vary considerably even among good readers.
    c. can be raised to thousands of words per minute.
    d. depend on how fast you can fixate on a phrase.

9. a. Skimming is _____.
    b. Scanning is _____.

10. Two examples of bad reading habits are _____ and _____.

Questions For Discussion and Writing

1. How is the information in this chapter going to change your reading?

2. Is there information in this chapter that you would like to try but that seems too difficult for you to do at this time? Do you have any strategies for practicing the subskills necessary for the reading technique that would make you more qualified to try it in the future?

EXERCISE 1: Skimming and Scanning

Skimming

Take one minute to skim this selection on Woody Guthrie. Answer the questions and then check your answers in the back of the book.

Woody Guthrie

a true

Today Woody Guthrie remains one of America's larger-than-life heroes, a folk balladeer who inspired several generations of singer-activists. Woodrow Wilson Guthrie was **an authentic** voice of the troubles, and the hopes, of the Great Depression. Growing up in rural Oklahoma, he developed his unique guitar style listening to his relatives and to radio broadcasts of the famous Carter family singers. In the early thirties he watched the Great Plains turn into a giant Dust Bowl and experienced first-hand the descent into poverty. Like the fictional Joads of John Steinbeck's *Grapes of Wrath,* Woody hit the road to California. His encounters with other people undergoing "hard travelin" (as he put it) sharpened his social consciousness and shaped the lyrics of a flood of songs, over a thousand by some people's count. With his folk singing sidekick Cisco Houston and actor Will Geer, Woody **rambled** around migrant labor camps, singing and raising the spirits of the **impoverished** workers. If the "Okies" potato stew "had been just a little bit thinner," he **wryly** observed, "some of our senators could have seen through it."

wandered
poor

mockingly

As his radicalism deepened, Guthrie began writing for the left-wing *People's Daily World,* but music remained his true medium. During the thirties he wrote a set of songs for the Oregon Department of Interior, including "Grand Coulee Dam" and "Roll on, Columbia," **extolling** public power projects. Later in the decade New York City intellectuals "discovered" Woody as a true **proletarian** minstrel, and he joined the left-wing urban folk revival. But unlike some other artists, such as Burl Ives and Josh White, Woody generally **shunned** commercial performances. He preferred the freedom of the open road and working-class audiences. With Pete Seeger and several other politically radical musicians, he formed the Almanac Singers who toured the country singing to farm and factory laborers and participating in unionization campaigns.

praising

lower class

avoided

Increasingly Woody became concerned with the spread of fascism, and songs such as "The Sinking of the Reuben James" expressed his **fervent** desire for American intervention in the European war. In 1943 he joined the Merchant Marine. Still, he considered song his most **potent** weapon, and his battered guitar carried the slogan, "This Machine Kills Fascists."

intensely felt

powerful

A wiry little man with bushy, dark hair, Woody Guthrie, like Franklin Roosevelt, never lost faith in the country during the Depression. "I hate a song that makes you think that you're not any good," he once said. "I'm out to fight those kinds of songs." But unlike Roosevelt,

Woody **embraced** socialism as the solution to the nation's **plight.** His radicalism sprang from the American heartland and, in many ways, looked backward. Woody believed that the dry, blistered prairie could be revived and that the weather-beaten people could recapture the pioneer spirit and regain the seats of power. Ballads such as "The Oregon Trail" and "Oklahoma Hills" reflected his pride in America's rural heritage. His hope lay in a people's socialist revolution. Commonly viewed as a lyrical description of America's natural beauties, his most famous song, "This Land Is Your Land," had a final, little known verse calling for an end to private property and capitalism.

adopted
difficulties

Burner, Marcus, and Rosenberg, *America,* pp. 538–40

Answer the following questions without looking back at the article.

1. What is the subject of the selection?
2. What is the main idea of the selection?

Scanning

Now take three minutes to scan the excerpt for the answers to the following questions. Underline the answers; after the three minutes are up, write the answers.

1. Woody Guthrie's career coincided with what period of history?_____
   _____
2. Where did Woody Guthrie grow up? _____
3. What instrument did Woody Guthrie play? _____
4. Who wrote *The Grapes of Wrath*? _____
5. Where did Woody Guthrie go during the Depression? _____
6. Who were two of Woody Guthrie's sidekicks? _____
7. What paper did Woody Guthrie write for? _____
8. Who else was in the Almanac Singer? _____
9. What political theory did Woody Guthrie embrace? _____
10. What was Woody Guthrie's most famous song? _____

Reading Selection 1: Literature—Reading the Classics

How to Enjoy the Classics

Steve Allen

Why is it? In school we learn one of the most amazing and difficult **feats** man has ever accomplished—how to read—and at the same time we learn to hate the things worth reading most.

tasks

It's happened to us all—with assignment reading! It happened to me. The teacher assigned *Moby Dick.* I didn't want to read it. So I fought it. I disliked it. I thought I won.

But I lost. My struggle to keep at arm's length from Moby Dick cost me all the good things that can come from learning to come to terms with those special few books we call the "classics."

I've come back to *Moby Dick* on my own since. I *like* it. And I've discovered a new level of pleasure from it with each reading.

What is a classic? A classic is a book that gives you that **exhilarating** feeling, if only for a moment, that you've finally uncovered part of the meaning of life.

stimulating

A classic is a book that's stood the test of time, a book that men and women all over the world keep reaching for throughout the ages for its special **enlightenment.**

illumination

Not many books can survive such a test considering all of the volumes that have been produced since man first put chisel to stone. Classics account for an **infinitesimal** share of the total—less than .001 percent. That's just a few thousand books. Of those, under 100 make up the solid core.

very tiny

Why should you tackle the classics? Why try to enjoy them?

I suggest three good reasons:

1. Classics open up your mind.
2. Classics help you grow.
3. Classics help you understand your life, your world, yourself.

The last one is the big one. A classic can give you insights into yourself that you will get nowhere else. Sure, you can get pleasure out of almost any book. But a classic, once you penetrate it, lifts you up high! Aeschylus's *Oresteia* was written nearly 2,500 years ago—and it still knocks me out!

But I can hear you saying, "I've tried reading classics. They are hard to understand. I can't get into them."

Let me offer some suggestions that will help you open this wondrous world. Pick up a classic you've always promised to try. Then take Dr. Allen's advice.

Know What You're Reading

Is it a novel, drama, biography, history? To find out, check the table of contents, read the book cover, the preface, or look up the title or author in *The Reader's Encyclopedia.*

Don't Read in Bed

Classics can be tough going; I'll admit it. You need to be alert, with your senses sharp. When you read in bed you're courting sleep—and you'll blame it on the book when you start nodding off.

Don't Let a Lot of Characters Throw You

Dostoevsky tosses fifty major characters at you in *The Brothers Karamazov.* In the very first chapter of *War and Peace,* Tolstoy bombards you with twenty-two names—long, complicated ones like Anna Pavlovna Scherer, Anatole and Prince Bolkonski. Don't scurry for cover. Stick with it. The characters will gradually sort themselves out and you'll feel as comfortable with them as you do with your own dear friends who were strangers, too, when you met them.

Give the Author a Chance

Don't say "I don't get it!" too soon. Keep reading right to the end. Sometimes, though, you may not be ready for the book you're trying to get into. I tackled Plato's *Republic* three times before it finally opened up to me. And man, was it worth it! So if you really can't make a go of the book in your lap, put it aside for another day, or year, and take on another one.

Read in Big Bites

Don't read in short nibbles. How can you expect to get your head into anything that way? The longer you stay with it, the more you get into the rhythm and mood—and the more pleasure you get from it.

When you read *Zorba the Greek* try putting bouzouki music on the record player; Proust, a little Debussy; Shakespeare, Elizabethan theater music.

Read What the Author Read

To better understand where the author is coming from, as we say, read the books he once read and that impressed him. Shakespeare, for example, dipped into North's translation of Plutarch's Lives for the plots of *Julius Caesar, Antony and Cleopatra,* and *A Midsummer Night's Dream.* It's fun to know you're reading what he read.

Read about the Author's Time

You are the product of your time. Any author is the product of his time. Knowing the history of that time, the problems that he and others faced, their attitudes—will help you understand the author's point of view. Important point: You may not agree with the author. No problem. At least he's made you think!

Read about the Author's Life

The more you know about an author's own experiences, the more you'll understand why he wrote what he wrote. You'll begin to see the autobiographical odds and ends that are hidden in his work.

A writer can't help but reveal himself. Most of our **surmises** about Shakespeare's life come from clues found in his plays.

assumptions

Read the Book Again

All classics bear rereading. If after you finish the book you're **intrigued** but still confused, reread it then and there. It'll open up some more to you.

fascinated

If you did read a classic few years back and loved it, read it again. The book will have so many new things to say to you, you'll hardly believe it's the same one.

A Few Classics to Enjoy

You can find excellent lists of the basic classics compiled by helpful experts, like Clifton Fadiman's *Lifetime Reading Plan,* the *Harvard Classics* and Mortimer J. Adler's *Great Books.* Look into them.

But before you do, I'd like to suggest a few classics that can light up your life. Even though some might have been spoiled for you by the required reading **stigma,** try them. Try them. And *try* them.

brand

1. Homer: *Illiad* and *Odyssey.* The Adam and Eve of Western literature. Read a good recent translation. My favorite is by Robert Fitzgerald.
2. Rabelais: *Gargantua and Pantagruel.* A Gargantuan romp. I recommend the Samuel Putnam translation.
3. Geoffrey Chaucer: *Canterbury Tales.* Thirty folks on a four-day **pilgrimage** swapping whoppers. Don't be surprised if the people you meet here are like people you know in *your* life.

   journey
4. Cervantes: *Don Quixote.* The first modern novel, about the lovable old Don with his "impossible dream." How could you go through life without reading it once?
5. Shakespeare: *Plays.* Shakespeare turned out 37 plays. Some are flops, some make him the greatest writer ever. All offer gold. His best: "Hamlet," "Macbeth," and "Romeo and Juliet." (See them on stage, too.)
6. Charles Dickens: *Pickwick Papers.* No one can breathe life into characters the way Dickens can. Especially the **inimitable** Samuel Pickwick, Esq.

   unmatched
7. Mark Twain: *Huckleberry Finn.* Maybe you had to read this in school. Well, climb back on that raft with Huck and Jim. You'll find new meaning this time.

Of course, these few suggestions hardly scratch the surface. Don't just dip your toe into the deep waters of the classics. Plunge in! Like generations of bright human beings before you, you'll find yourself **invigorated** to the **marrow** by thoughts and observations of the most gifted writers in history. You still enjoy looking at classic paintings. You enjoy hearing musical classics. Good books will hold you, too.

> **filled with energy/ center of the bone**

Someone has said the classics are the diary of man. Open up the diary. Read about yourself—and understand yourself.

Comprehension Check

Circle the letter preceding the correct answer to each question. Then check your answers in the back of the book.

1. According to the author,
   a. most books survive the test of time.
   b. books written 2,500 years ago are classics.
   c. less than .001 percent of all books are classics.
   d. you should read only a few pages of classical literature during each sitting.
2. Which book has Allen read at least twice?
   a. *Zorba the Greek*
   b. *Moby Dick*
   c. Plutarch's *Lives*
   d. Chaucer's *Canterbury Tales*
3. The subject of the article is
   a. the importance of assigned reading.
   b. ways of reading classical literature.
   c. developing good reading habits.
   d. the enjoyment of good literature.
4. Classical literature
   a. should be assigned in elementary school.
   b. can be enjoyable to read.
   c. should be part of any reading course.
   d. is largely ignored by people today.
5. Steve Allen probably refers to himself as "Dr. Allen" because he
   a. is a medical doctor.
   b. is a dentist.
   c. has a Ph.D.
   d. is making a joke.
6. The author believes that assigned reading
   a. develops good reading habits.
   b. ruins out love of reading.
   c. isn't stressed enough in schools.
   d. needs to begin in elementary school.

7. The author implies that
   a. the older a book is, the more interesting it is.
   b. most writers will never write a classic.
   c. everyone wants to write a classic.
   d. the only books worth reading are the classics.

8. Reading a lot of classical literature will probably
   a. keep you up to date on current events.
   b. make you fall asleep.
   c. teach you how to read uninteresting things.
   d. teach you a lot about human nature.

9. Why does Steve Allen believe that everyone should read the classics?

   _____
   _____
   _____
   _____

10. Steve Allen believes that assigning classical literature in class is a mistake. What does he say it results in? Do you agree?_____

   _____
   _____
   _____
   _____

Reading Selection 2: Literature—Nonfiction

Saved

Malcolm X and Alex Haley

I became increasingly frustrated at not being able to express what I wanted to **convey** in letters that I wrote, especially those to Mr. Elijah Muhammad. In the street, I had been the most articulate hustler out there—I had commanded attention when I said something. But now, trying to write simple English, I not only wasn't **articulate,** I wasn't even functional. How would I sound writing in slang, the way I would say it, something such as, "Look, daddy, let me pull your coat about a cat, Elijah Muhammad—"

Many who hear me somewhere in person, or on television, or those who read something I've said, will think I went to school far beyond the eighth grade. This impression is due entirely to my prison studies.

It had really begun back in the Charlestown Prison, when Bimbi first made me feel envy of his stock knowledge. Bimbi had always taken charge of any conversation he was in, and I had tried to **emulate** him. But every book I picked up had few sentences which didn't contain anywhere from one to nearly all of the words that might as well have been in Chinese. When I just skipped those words, of course, I really ended up with little idea of what the book said. So I had come to

communicate

expressing clearly

imitate

the Norfolk Prison Colony still going through only book-reading motions. Pretty soon, I would have quit even those motions, unless I had received the motivation that I did.

I saw that the best thing I could do was get hold of a dictionary—to study, to learn some words. I was lucky enough to reason also that I should try to improve my penmanship. It was sad. I couldn't even write in a straight line. It was both ideas together that moved me to request a dictionary along with some tablets and pencils from the Norfolk Prison Colony school.

I spent two days just **rifling** uncertainly through the dictionary's   **browsing** pages. I'd never realized so many words existed! I didn't know which words I needed to learn. Finally, just to state some kind of action, I began copying.

In my slow, painstaking, ragged handwriting, I copied into my tablet everything printed on that first page, down to the punctuation marks.

I believe it took me a day. Then, aloud, I read back, to myself, everything I'd written on the tablet. Over and over, aloud, to myself, I read my own handwriting.

I woke up the next morning, thinking about those words—**im-**   **very** **mensely** proud to realize that not only had I written so much at one time, but I'd written words that I never knew were in the world. Moreover, with a little effort, I also could remember what many of these words meant. I reviewed the words whose meanings I didn't remember. Funny thing, from the dictionary first page right now, that "aardvark" springs to my mind. The dictionary had a picture of it, a long-tailed, long-eared, burrowing African mammal, which lives off termites caught by sticking out its tongue as an anteater does for ants.

I was so fascinated that I went on—I copied the dictionary's next page. And the same experience came when I studied that. With every succeeding page, I also learned of people and places and events from history. Actually the dictionary is like a miniature encyclopedia. Finally the dictionary's "A" section had filled a whole tablet—and I went on into the "B's." That was the way I started copying what helped me to pick up handwriting speed. Between what I wrote in my tablet, and writing letters, during the rest of my time in prison I would guess I wrote a million words.

I suppose it was **inevitable** that as my word-base broadened, I   **unavoidable** could for the first time pick up a book and read and now begin to understand what the book was saying. Anyone who has read a great deal can imagine the new world that opened. Let me tell you something: from then until I left that prison, in every free moment I had, if I was not reading in the library, I was reading on my bunk. You couldn't have gotten me out of books with a wedge. Between Mr. Muhammad's teachings, my correspondence, my visitors—usually Ella and Reginald—and my reading of books, months passed without my even thinking about being imprisoned. In fact, up to then, I never had been so truly free in my life . . .

I read more in my room than in the library itself. An inmate who was known to read could check out more than the permitted maximum number of books. I preferred reading in the total isolation of my own room.

When I had progressed to really serious reading, every night at about ten p.m. I would be outraged with the "lights out." It always seemed to catch me right in the middle of something **engrossing.**   absorbing

Fortunately, right outside my door was a corridor light that cast a glow into my room. The glow was enough to read by, once my eyes adjusted to it. So when "lights out" came, I would sit on the floor where I could continue reading in that glow.

At one-hour intervals the night guards paced past every room. Each time I heard the approaching footsteps, I jumped into bed and **feigned**   pretended
sleep. And as soon as the guard passed, I got back out of bed onto the floor area of that light-glow, where I would read for another 58 minutes—until the guard approached again. That went on until three or four every morning. Three or four hours of sleep a night was enough for me. Often in the years in the streets I had had less sleep than that.

I have often reflected upon the new **vistas** that reading opened to   mental views
me. I knew right there in prison that reading had changed forever the course of my life. As I see it today, the ability to read awoke inside me some long **dormant** craving to be mentally alive. I certainly wasn't   sleeping
seeking any degree, the way a college **confers** a status symbol upon its   gives
students. My homemade education gave me, with every additional book that I read, a little bit more sensitivity to the deafness, dumbness, and blindness that was **afflicting** the black race in America. Not long   paining
ago, an English writer telephones me from London, asking questions. One was, "What's your **alma mater**?" I told him, "Books." You will   college
never catch me with a free fifteen minutes in which I'm not studying something I feel might be able to help the black man.

Comprehension Check

Circle the letter preceding the correct answer to each question. Then check your answers in the back of the book.

1. Malcolm X's desire to learn to read began
   a. at Norfolk Prison Colony.
   b. in high school
   c. at Charlestown Prison.
   d. while studying with Elijah Muhammad.
2. Malcolm X completed
   a. high school.
   b. college.
   c. eighth grade.
   d. junior college.

3. Malcolm X read in semidarkness because
   a. he didn't pay his electric bill.
   b. the prison guards were cruel.
   c. there was no window in his room.
   d. he read after "lights out."

4. Books made Malcolm X feel free because
   a. he was escaping from ignorance.
   b. while he read he could forget about being in prison.
   c. he was improving his life.
   d. they did all of the above.

5. Malcolm X was motivated to learn to read because
   a. he had an outstanding teacher.
   b. he wanted to be able to read the Bible.
   c. he wanted to teach other blacks how to read.
   d. he wanted to read the writings of a famous black leader.

6. The main reason Malcolm X began studying was that
   a. he wanted to express himself in writing.
   b. he was bored and had nothing else to do.
   c. he thought is might earn him early parole.
   d. his friends sent him books.

7. Malcolm X copied the dictionary because
   a. Elijah Muhammad told him to.
   b. it was the only way he could think of to learn to read.
   c. he didn't have any other books.
   d. he was bored.

8. The administration at Norfolk Prison Colony
   a. encouraged prisoners to improve themselves.
   b. forced prisoners to work constantly.
   c. kept prisoners isolated.
   d. allowed prisoners to read whenever they wished.

9. Why does Malcolm X believe learning to read is so important?_____
   _____
   _____
   _____
   _____

10. Malcolm X said that he had never felt as free as he did in Norfolk
    Prison Colony. What did he mean?_____
    _____
    _____
    _____
    _____

Questions for Discussion and Writing

1. What could the prisons have done to help Malcolm X learn to read?
2. Compare your own experience in learning to read with that of Malcolm X.

Reading Selection 3: Literature—Fiction

University Days

James Thurber

I passed all the other courses that I took at my University, but I could never pass botany. This was because all botany students had to spend several hours a week in a laboratory looking through a microscope at plant cells, and I could never see through a microscope. I never once saw a cell through a microscope. This used to enrage my instructor. He would wander around the laboratory pleased with the progress all the students were making in drawing the involved and, so I am told, interesting structure of flower cells, until he came to me. I would just be standing there. "I can't see anything," I would say. He would begin patiently enough, explaining how anybody can see through a microscope, but he would always end up in a fury, claiming that I could *too* see through a microscope but just pretended that I couldn't. "It takes away from the beauty of flowers anyway," I used to tell him. "We are not concerned with beauty in this course," he would say. "We are concerned solely with what I may call the *mechanics* of flowers." "Well," I'd say, "I can't see anything." "Try it just once again," he'd say, and I would put my eye to the microscope and see nothing at all, except now and again a **nebulous** milky **phenomenon** of maladjustment. You were supposed to see a vivid, restless clockwork of sharply defined plant cells. "I see what looks like a lot of milk," I would tell him. This, he claimed, was the result of my not having adjusted the microscope properly, so he would readjust it for me, or rather, for himself. And I would look again and see milk.

I finally took a **deferred** pass, as they called it, and waited a year and tried again. (You had to pass one of the biological sciences or you couldn't graduate.) The professor had come back from vacation brown as a berry, bright-eyed, and eager to explain cell-structure again to his classes. "Well," he said to me, cheerily, when we met in the first laboratory hour of the semester, "we're going to see cells this time, aren't we?" "Yes, sir," I said. Students to the right of me and to the left of me and in front of me were seeing cells; what's more, they were quietly drawing pictures of them in their notebooks. Of course, I didn't see anything.

"We'll try it," the professor said to me, grimly, "with every adjustment of the microscope known to man. As God is my witness, I'll arrange this glass so that you see cells through it or I'll give up teaching. In twenty-two years of botany, I—" He cut off abruptly for he was beginning to **quiver** all over, like Lionel Barrymore, and he genuinely wished to hold onto his temper; his scenes had taken a great deal out of him.

So we tried it with every adjustment of the microscope known to man. With only one of them did I see anything but blackness and that time I saw, to my pleasure and amazement, a **variegated** constellation of flecks, specks, and dots. These I hastily drew. The instructor, noting my activity, came back from an adjoining desk, a smile on his lips and

vague
substance

delayed

shake

multicolored

his eyebrows high in hope. He looked at my cell drawing. "What's that?" he demanded, with a hint of a squeal in his voice. "That's what I saw," I said. "You didn't, you didn't, you *didn't!*" he screamed, losing control of his temper instantly, and he bent over and squinted into the microscope. His head snapped up. "That's your eye!" he shouted. "You've fixed the lens so that it reflects! You've drawn your eye!"

Comprehension Check

Circle the letter preceding the correct answer to each question. Then check your answers in the back of the book.

1. The professor
   a. tried to help Thurber.
   b. believed Thurber should adjust the microscope himself.
   c. drew the pictures of cells for the students.
   d. was a new teacher.
2. The first time Thurber took botany he
   a. hated the teacher.
   b. found out how beautiful flowers were.
   c. saw only flecks, specks, and dots in the microscope.
   d. saw a nebulous milky substance in the microscope.
3. At first the teacher thought Thurber was
   a. lazy.
   b. pretending.
   c. blind.
   d. stupid.
4. The milky substance was caused by
   a. maladjustment of the microscope.
   b. a reflection of Thurber's eye.
   c. a broken microscope.
   d. Thurber's thumbprint on the lens.
5. Thurber took botany because
   a. he was a science major.
   b. he had to pass a biological science course to graduate.
   c. he liked studying plants.
   d. he liked the teacher.
6. A deferred pass means that
   a. Thurber passed the course.
   b. Thurber failed the course.
   c. Thurber took an incomplete and reregistered later.
   d. Thurber was thrown out of class.
7. The goal of the botany lab was to teach
   a. students to use a microscope properly.
   b. the structure of plants.

    c. students to draw cells.

    d. all of the above.

8. From the way Thurber wrote the story, do you think he looked on the experience in the botany class as

    a. degrading?

    b. depressing?

    c. frightening?

    d. humorous?

9. What three things did Thurber see with his microscope? _____

_____

_____

_____

10. Describe 3 characteristics of the botany professor. _____

_____

_____

_____

Questions for Discussion and Writing

1. Do you think Thurber's botany teacher was a good or bad teacher? Use incidents from the story to support your point of view.

2. If you were in James Thurber's situation in the botany class, what would you have done and why?

Broad Questions for Discussion and Writing

1. After reading the three articles, which type of article would you like to continue to read and why?

2. Two of these authors say that reading opens up the world for the reader. What do you think improving your skills in this course has done for you?

3. What can be done in schools to help students learn to read and study better?

4. Why do you think literature should be part of any college major?

5. Why is it important to learn to identify the purpose of your reading and to vary your reading rate?

EXERCISE 2: Skills Review: Techniques to Improve Vocabulary

Use 20 words from this or earlier articles to practice the five ways to learn vocabulary. Answers will vary.

A. Mnemonics

Word	Technique
1. _____	_____
2. _____	_____
3. _____	_____
4. _____	_____
5. _____	_____

B. Context

Word   Sentence

1. _____   _____

   _____

2. _____   _____

   _____

3. _____   _____

   _____

4. _____   _____

   _____

5. _____   _____

   _____

C. Dictionary

1. Word _____
   Pronunciation _____
   Origin _____
   Part(s) of Speech _____

2. Word _____
   Pronunciation _____
   Origin _____
   Part(s) of Speech _____

3. Word _____
   Pronunciation _____
   Origin _____
   Part(s) of Speech _____

4. Word _____
   Pronunciation _____
   Origin _____
   Part(s) of Speech _____

5. Word   _____

    Pronunciation   _____

    Origin   _____

    Part(s) of Speech _____

D. Thesaurus

Word	Synonym	Antonym
1. _____	_____	_____
2. _____	_____	_____
3. _____	_____	_____
4. _____	_____	_____
5. _____	_____	_____

E. Word Parts

Word	Prefixes and Roots	Meaning
1. _____	_____	_____
2. _____	_____	_____
3. _____	_____	_____
4. _____	_____	_____
5. _____	_____	_____

EXERCISE 3: Skills Review: Skimming and Scanning

As the final exercise in this text we want to reinforce the idea that adapting your skills to the task can save time and give you the *Keys to College Success*. Even though this is a selection from a geology text, you can gain the necessary information by skimming and scanning.

Skimming

Since this is a short reading, take about 30 seconds to skim.

What's in a Name

The word *geology* derives from the Greek *geo,* "Earth," and *logos,* "discourse," and comes to use through the Latin geologia. The present meaning of geology, "science of the earth," came into use in the late eighteenth century.

The medieval Latin word *geologia* was apparently used for the first time by Richard de Bury in the fourteenth century. To him, it meant the study of the law. If you were reading the Italian F. Sessa's 1687 volume *Geologia,* you would discover that the author was trying to demonstrate that the "influences" ascribed by the astrologers to the stars actually came from the Earth.

Students of the Earth 150 to 200 years ago might have known their subject either as geology or as *geognosy.* They were essentially the same subjects. Geognosy didn't catch on as a word, nor did *geonomy,* introduced a century ago as a synonym for geology.

Today we pretty well know what we mean when we use the term "geology." True, some colleges and universities call the study of Earth *geoscience* and others maintain that *Earth science* is a better term. Indeed, there are some differences in meaning among these terms. For our purposes here, we prefer the term "geology" and follow a general definition coined by one of our colleagues.

> ge.ol.o.gy, n. The study of the Earth and other solid bodies in space. Geology applies the techniques originally devised for Earth problems to deciphering the present attributes, history, and origin of any natural solid body.
>
> Judson, Kauffman, and Leet, *Physical Geology*, p. 1

Answer the following questions without looking back at the article.

1. What is the subject of the selection? _____
2. What is the main idea of the selection? _____

Scanning

Now take two minutes to scan the excerpt for the answers to the following questions. Underline answers; after the two minutes are up, write the answers.

1. What is the etymology of the word *geology*? _____
   _____

2. When was the word *geology* first used? _____
   _____

3. Name two synonyms for geology that didn't catch on as words. ____
   _____

4. Name two terms other than geology that some colleges call the study of the Earth. _____
   _____

5. Give a present-day definition of geology. _____
   _____

Appendix

Exercise 1: Underlining and Making Marginal Notes (pp. 109–110)

def. — Big
Bang theory

process

results

A. Astronomical evidence supports the theory, called the _Big Bang,_ that the <u>universe began</u> perhaps as long as <u>twenty billion years ago when a dense, hot, supermassive concentration of material exploded with</u> **cataclysmic** <u>force.</u> Within about <u>one second,</u> the <u>temperature</u> of the expanding universe <u>cooled to</u> approximately <u>10 billion degrees</u> and **fundamental** atomic particles called <u>protons</u> and <u>neutrons</u> began <u>to appear.</u> After a few minutes, atoms of the least complex elements—<u>hydrogen and helium</u>—had <u>formed</u> and the initial **conversion** of <u>energy to matter</u> in the young universe was over.

Kenneth Pinzke in Tarbuck and Lutgens, Earth Science, p. 6

French
rev.
motto
order of govts.

results

B. The year <u>1789</u> is one of the great milestones of modern history, for it marked the beginning of the <u>revolution</u> in the most powerful state on the Continent of Europe. The revolutionary motto—Liberté, <u>Egalité,</u> Fraternité (<u>"Liberty, Equality, Fraternity"</u>)—seemed to promise a new democratic **regime.** What it actually provided was a republic dependent first on the <u>Reign of Terror,</u> then on the less terrible but less democratic <u>Directory,</u> and finally on the **autocracy** of <u>Napoleon,</u> who <u>transformed the First Republic into the First Empire.</u> His determination to dominate the whole of Europe led to his ultimate <u>defeat and the restoration of the Bourbons.</u> But by then the **ideology** of liberty, equality, fraternity had attracted so many supporters not only in France but also among victims of the French expansion that a <u>full restoration</u> of the Old Regime was <u>impossible.</u>

Brinton, Christopher, and Wolff, Civilization in the West, p. 350

women
before WWII

women
after WWII

C. The <u>1920s and 1930s</u> saw <u>increasing numbers of women going</u> to <u>college</u> and <u>seeking gainful employment</u> afterward. <u>World War II</u> brought a tremendous demand for labor, and <u>women</u> gained a <u>major foothold in industry.</u> By 1950, <u>34 percent</u> of all <u>adult women</u> were <u>in</u> the <u>labor force.</u> After the war, however, there was a period of **retrenchment.** People sought relief from the **turmoil** of the depression of the 1930s and the war years of the early 1940s in a <u>return to</u> **familistic** <u>values.</u> While two children had been the norm before the war, couples now wanted three, four, or even five. The symbolic phrase of the day was "togetherness," and the suburban housewife became the model American woman.

Horton et. al. *The Sociology of Social Problems,* p. 251

Appendix

B

Exercise 4: Using PQ4R with a Textbook Selection (pp. 125–131)

American Democracy

James MacGregor Burns, J. W. Peltason,
Thomas E. Cronin, and David B. Magleby

It is the week before an American election, the **culmination** of an intense, year-long campaigning. During this last week, television and the newspapers are full of political ads: "A vote for Gabrillino is a vote for the people" one says under a picture of Frank Gabrillino, the Democratic candidate for governor. He is shown with Mrs. Gabrillino, a successful real-estate broker. There are pictures of the Gabrillinos' three children. Gabrillino's campaign themes have stressed that he is not a politician, just a man of the people. He accuses his opponent, Sarah Wong, who has been in office for two terms, of being soft on criminals and blames her for the state's economic downturn. Gabrillino insists that if Wong is reelected, the state is doomed. Wong—behind in the polls, although recently catching up, emphasizes her experience, her concern for all the people, and her willingness to **defy** the special interests. She is a Republican, but she plays down her party **affiliation** since in this state a majority of the voters have been Democrats in the past.

The two candidates have accused each other of all kinds of misdeeds. As the campaign progresses, their ads become more negative, more focused on personalities than on political issues and positions. Gabrillino makes much of the fact that 20 years ago Wong indicated she had doubts about the majority and **efficacy** of the death penalty, even though as governor she has not **commuted** any death sentences

ex—
Am. election

and has allowed two people to be executed. Wong's supporters charge that Gabrillino is fuzzy-hearted, soft-headed, and a tool of left-wing professors. There are **endorsements** in the newspapers: Professors for Wong, Teachers for Gabrillino, Students for Wong, Chicanos for Gabrillino, Asians for Gabrillino. Each candidate carefully plants letters to the editor in all the newspapers. Local radio and television talk shows feature the candidates, and the candidates' organizations supply callers to attack their opponents.

Election day: Only half the eligible voters bother to vote, and exit interviews indicate that the race is too close to call. That night, projections based on 5 percent of the vote make it clear that Gabrillino will get 48 percent of the vote, Wong 46 percent, and minor parties the rest. At 11:00 p.m., Wong calls Gabrillino, congratulates him on his victory, makes a **concession** speech before her disappointed workers, and thanks them for their support. Gabrillino speaks to his cheering supporters at another hotel ballroom, stating that his election was a great victory for the people.

Elections are a familiar process that Americans take for granted. Many people look upon elections with **disdain,** saying, "it's all politics." But in fact, <u>American elections</u> are <u>remarkable.</u> They conclude with what in the course of human history is a rare event: the <u>peaceful transfer of political power.</u> What is unusual is what is not happening. Even though the day before the election Wong and her followers were insisting that if Gabrillino became governor there would be chaos and corruption, once the vote was counted there was no thought by anybody in any political party that Gabrillino should not become governor. When her term was up, Wong did not resist turning power over to the man she had called corrupt. It never crossed her mind to try to stay in office by calling on the state police to keep Gabrillino from taking power. None of Wong's supporters considered taking up arms or going underground or leaving the country. (Actually, they concentrated on how they could win the next election.) Nor did Gabrillino or his followers ever give any thought to punishing Sarah Wong and her supporters once they gained power. The Democrats wanted to throw the Republicans out of office, not in jail.

U.S:
power changes

It was just a routine election—democracy at work. Most of the time <u>in most nations, those in power</u> got there either because they were <u>born to the right family or</u> because they <u>killed or jailed</u> their <u>opponents.</u> During most of human history, no one, and most especially not an opposition political party, could openly criticize their government. During most of human history, a political opponent was an enemy.

most nations —
power changes

Defining Democracy

The word "democracy" is nowhere to be found in the Declaration of Independence or in the U.S. Constitution, nor was it a term used by the founders of the Republic. Democracy is hard to define. It is both a very old term and a new one. It was used in a loose sense to refer to various undesirable things: "the masses," mobs, lack of standards, and a system that encourages *demagogues* (leaders who gain power by appealing to the emotions and prejudices of the **rabble**).

Because we are using the term democracy in its political sense, we will be more precise. The distinguishing feature of <u>democracy</u> is that government **derives** its authority from its citizens. In fact, the word comes from two Greek words: *demos* (the people) and *kratos* (authority or power). Thus <u>democracy</u> means <u>government by the people, not</u> government <u>by one person</u> (the monarch, the dictators, the priests) <u>or</u> government <u>by the few</u> (an oligarchy or aristocracy).

def.—
democracy

Ancient Athens and a few other Greek cities had <u>a *direct democracy,*</u> in which citizens came together to discuss and pass the laws and select the rulers by lot. These Greek city-states did not last, and most turned to mob rule and then resorted to dictators. When the word "democracy" came into English usage in the seventeenth century, it **denoted** this kind of direct democracy and was a term of **derision,** a negative word, usually used to refer to <u>mob rule.</u>

def.—
direct demo.

James Madison, writing in *The Federalists,* No. 10, reflected the view of many of the framers of the U.S. Constitution when he wrote "such democracies [as the Greek and Roman] . . . have ever been found incompatible with personal security, or the rights of property, and have in general been as short in their lives, as they have been violent in their deaths." Democracy has taken on a positive meaning only in the last one hundred years.

These days it is no longer possible, even if desirable, to assemble the citizens of any but the smallest towns to make their laws or to select their officials directly from among the citizenry. Rather, we have invented a *system of representation.* <u>Democracy today</u> means <u>*representative democracy*</u> or, in Plato's term, a <u>*republic*</u> in which those who have <u>governmental authority get</u> and <u>retain authority directly or indirectly</u> as the result of winning <u>free elections</u> in which all adult citizens are allowed to participate.

def.—
demo today
(republic)

The framers preferred to use the term "republic" to avoid any confusion between direct democracy, which they disliked, and representative democracy, which they liked and thought secured all the advantages of a direct democracy while curing its weaknesses. Today, and in this book, democracy and republic are often used interchangeably.

Like most political concepts, <u>democracy **encompasses**</u> many <u>ideas and</u> has many meanings. Democracy is a <u>way of life, a form of government,</u> a <u>way of governing,</u> a <u>type of nation,</u> a <u>state of mind,</u> and a <u>variety of processes.</u>

how used

Democracy as a System of Interacting Values

As we approach the twenty-first century, the democratic faith may be as near a universal faith as the world has. A belief in human dignity, freedom, liberty, individual rights, and other democratic values is widely shared in most corners of the world. The **essence** of dem-

essence of
dem.

<u>ocratic values</u> is contained in the ideas of <u>popular consent, respect</u> for the <u>individual, equality of opportunity,</u> and <u>personal liberty.</u>

Popular Consent.   The **animating** principle of the American Revolution, the Declaration of Independence, and the resulting new nation was *popular consent,* the idea that <u>a just government</u> must derive <u>its powers from the consent of the people it governs.</u> A commitment to democracy thus entails a community's willingness to participate and make decisions in government. Intellectually these principles sound unobjectionable, but in practice they mean that certain individuals or groups may not get their way. The commitment to popular consent must involve a *willingness to lose* if most people vote the other way.

def.— popular consent

Respect for the Individual.   Popular rule in a democracy flows from a belief that every individual has the potential for common sense, rationality, and a notion of fairness. Individuals, democrats insist, have important rights; collectively, those rights are the source of all legitimate governmental authority and power. These notions pervade all democratic thought. They are woven into the writings of Thomas Jefferson, especially in the Declaration of Independence: "All men . . . are endowed by their Creator with certain **unalienable rights.**" <u>Constitutional democracies make the person</u>—rich or poor, black or white, male or female—<u>the *central* measure of value.</u> The state, the union, and the corporation are measured in terms of their usefulness to individuals.

Equality of Opportunity.   The importance of the individual is enhanced by the democratic value of *equality.* "All men are created equal and from that equal creation they derive rights inherent and unalienable, among which are the preservation of liberty and the pursuit of happiness." So reads Jefferson's first draft of the Declaration of Independence, and the words indicate the **primacy** of the concept.

But what does equality mean? What kind of equality? Economic, political, legal, social, or some other kind of equality? Equality for whom? For blacks as well as whites? For women as well as men? For Native Americans, descendants of the Pilgrims, and recent immigrants? And what kind of equality? *Equality of opportunity* (almost all Americans say they want that), but also *equality of conditions?* This last question is the toughest. Does equality of opportunity simply mean that everyone should have the *same place at the starting line?* Or does it mean that an effort be made to equalize most or all of the factors that during the course of a person's life might determine how well he or she fares economically or socially?

President Herbert Hoover posed the issue this way: "We, through free and universal education, provide the training of the runners: we give to them an equal start; we provide in government the umpire of fairness in the race." <u>Franklin D. Roosevelt</u> also sought to answer the question by proclaiming a "second Bill of Rights" that announced *Four*

FDR's 4 Freedoms

Freedoms—freedom of speech and expression, freedom of worship, freedom from want, and freedom from fear. Roosevelt's New Deal and its successor programs had tried to advance the **egalitarian notions** and basic security that he asserted were the rights of human beings everywhere.

Personal Liberty. Liberty has been the single most powerful value in American history. It was for "life, liberty, and the pursuit of happiness" that independence was declared; it was to "secure the Blessings of Liberty" that the Constitution was drawn up and adopted. Even our patriotic songs **extol** the "sweet land of liberty."

Liberty or *freedom* (used interchangeably here) means that all individuals must have the opportunity to realize their own goals. The essence of liberty is self-determination. Liberty is not simply the absence of external **restraint** on a person (freedom from); it is the individual's *freedom to act* positively to reach his or her goals. Moreover, both history and reason suggest that individual liberty is the key to social progress. The greater the people's freedom, the greater the chance of discovering better ways of life.

def.— liberty

Basic values of democracy do not always coexist happily. Individualism may conflict with the public good. Self-determination may conflict with equal opportunity. The right of General Motors to run its automobile factories to maximize profit, as compared to the right of automobile workers in those factories to join unions or share in the running of the plants, illustrates this type of conflict in everyday life.

conflicts in basic values of democracy

Over the years the American political system has clearly moved toward greater freedom and more democracy. A commitment to democracy is in many ways a twentieth-century idea. People throughout the world are more attracted to democracy today than ever before. Recent events in China, Germany, Poland, the Czech Republic, Slovakia, Russia, and South Africa are evidence that the dream of freedom and democratic government is universal.

Far more people dream about democracy than ever experience it, and many new democracies fail. To be successful, democratic government requires a political process as well as a governmental structure. In both areas, the American experiment is instructive.

Democracy as a System of Interrelated Political Processes

To become reality, democratic values must be **incorporated into** a *political process,* a set of arrangements for making decisions and managing the public's business. The essence of the democratic process is respect for the rules of fair play, which can be seen in the tradition of free and fair elections, majority rule, freedom of expression, and the right to assemble and protest.

def.— political process

Fair and Free Elections. Democratic government is based on free and fair elections held at intervals frequent enough to make them relevant to policy choices. Elections are one of the most important devices for keeping officials and representatives accountable. **Crucial** to modern-day definitions of democracy is the idea that *opposition political parties* can exist, can run candidates in elections, and can at least have a chance to replace those who are currently holding public office. Thus political competition and choice are crucial to the existence of democracy.

While all citizens should have equal voting power, free and fair elections do not imply everyone must or will have equal political influence. Some people, because of wealth, talent, or position, have more influence than others. How much extra influence key figures should be allowed to exercise in a democracy is a question for democrats. But at the polls a president or a pick-and-shovel laborer, a newspaper publisher or a lettuce picker, casts only one vote.

Majority (Plurality) Rule. The basic rule of a democracy is that those with the most votes take charge of the government, at least until the next election, when a new majority may be voted in to take charge. In practice, *majority rules* is often *plurality rule*, in which the largest bloc takes charge, even though it may not constitute a true majority, with more than half the votes. While in charge, those elected have no right to **curtail** the attempts of political minorities to use all peaceful means to become a majority. So even as the winners take power, the losers can go to work to try to get it back at the next election.

The American system of constitutional democracy allows people a say in who will decide important issues. Through the system of representation, people can participate indirectly in the great debates and decisions about laws and public policies.

Should the will of the majority prevail in all cases? Americans answer this question in a variety of ways. Some insist majority views should be enacted into laws and regulations. But perhaps the more widely held view is that an effective representative democracy involves far more than simply **ascertaining** and applying the statistical will of the people. It is a more complicated and often untidy process by which the people and their agents inform themselves, debate, compromise, and arrive at a decision, and do so only after thoughtful deliberation.

Freedom of Expression. Free and fair elections depend on access to information relevant to voting choices. Voters must have access to facts, competing ideas, and the views of candidates. Free and fair elections require a climate in which competing, nongovernment-owned newspapers, radio stations, and television stations can flourish. Expression by such media should be protected from government censorship.

The Right to Assemble and Protest. Citizens must be free to organize for political purposes. Obviously individuals can be more effective if they join with others in a party, a pressure group, a protest movement, or a demonstration. The right to oppose the government, to form opposition parties, and to have a chance of defeating **incumbents** is not only vital; it is a defining characteristic of a democracy.

Appendix

C

Exercise 5: Using Graphic Organizers (p. 132)

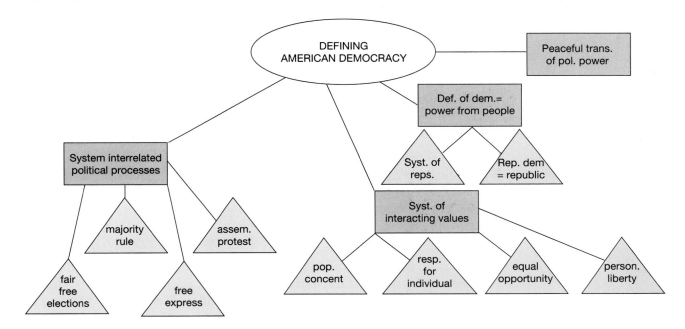

Appendix

D

Exercise 1: Speed Writing (pp. 168–169)

1a. Basically, the gas turbine engine consists of two sections: a gasifier section and a power section.

> *gas turbine has 2 secs. — gasifier & power*

1b. When we refer to distribution, we are normally talking about wholesale and retail trade:

> *distrib. = wholesale & retail*

1c. Nepal, located in the Himalaya Mountains, is one of the least developed and most isolated countries in the world.

> *Nepal — Himalayos — undeveloped & isolated*

2a. The main emphasis of community mental health centers is on prevention. Consultation, education, and crisis intervention are used to alleviate problems before they become serious.

> *Comm mental health — mainly prevention*
> *(consultation, educ., & crisis intervention)*

2b. American business is dependent on records. Each year over 300 billion pieces of paper are filed in nearly 100 million file drawers by the nation's business people.

> *Am. bus. needs records — 300 bil.*
> *papers in 100 mil. drawers per yr.*

2c. On September 14, 1901, Theodore Roosevelt became the youngest president of the United States. He succeeded William McKinley, who had been assassinated by an anarchist in Buffalo, New York.

> *9/14/01 TR youngest pres. of U.S after*
> *McKinley killed in Buffalo*

3a. The first mechanical calculator was the abacus. It was probably used by the Babylonians as early as 2200 B.C. In the Far East it began to be used in the thirteenth century. It is still used today in the same way it was centuries ago.

> *1st calculator = abacus. prob used by*
> *Babylonians 2200 B.C.: Far East.*

3b. Because your clock radio has its antenna inside, turning the radio around can sometimes improve reception. Your radio might sound better in another room, farther from the source of static. Sometimes grounding is the problem, which may be solved by turning the plug around in the outlet.

3c. Most people falsely believe that diamonds are the most valuable stones in the world. Contrary to popular belief, it is rubies that, carat for carat, sell for more. Since 1955 the supply of rubies has decreased, and their value has increased dramatically until now they are worth more than emeralds, sapphires, or diamonds.

Appendix

E

Exercise 2: Using the PQ4R Write Step with Lecture Notes (p. 171)

	Diff. betw. rdg. & listening — can't relisten
	Good listening
5 steps to	1. Come to class prepared
good listening	read text
	review notes
	2. Sit close
	3. Come early
	4. Listen for clues
	5. Watch for nonverbal clues
	How Not to Take Notes
3 things not to do	1. Don't try to write everything
in note-taking	2. No tape recorders
	3. Don't copy someone else's notes

	How to Take Notes
9 steps in note-taking	1. Get a notebook you can organize
	2. Leave a margin at top
	3. 2" margin at left
	4. Date each pg & # pgs.
	5. Use speed writing
	symbols & abbr.
	cross out
	6. Listen actively
	main ideas – few details
	speech 110–160wpm
	7. Use visual org.
	outline
	8. Review notes after lecture
	fill in, compare, questions, etc.
	don't recopy
	9. Write as little as possible
	Studying notes
How to study notes	Last 4 steps of PQ4R
	read
	write – underlinge & marginal notes
	flash cards
	recall – 1 pg. at a time
	review – about once a wk., depending on how hard

Appendix

F

Exercise 4: Note-taking (pp. 175–176)

Assign. due Sept. 12   Sept. 10
take notes in another class
read Chap. 2 of back   Note-taking

5 steps in better listening	Listen + observe better
	1. Prepare - read bk + notes
	2. Sit close
	3. Come early + have paper + pen out
	4. Listen for verbal cues signal
	words – e.g. "most imp." "3 maj. theories"
	5. Look for nonverbal cues
	instr's { slows down
	{ uses board
3 don'ts	Don't
	1. Write it all
	2. Use tape rec. or shorthand
	3. Xerox other's notes
5 do's	Do
	1. Buy notebook ÷ subj. – large lines
	2. Write, NOT PRINT – use pen
	3. Leave 2" margin on lft
	4. Date top of pg + # pgs
	5. Speed write
	no extra strokes
	don't erase / cross out
	abbrev. + use symbols
	e.g. w/ = with
	≠ = not equal
	∴ = therefore
	writ only what's necessary
3 steps after class	After class
	1. Review notes
	2. Don't recopy
	3. Write ? in lft. margin

Appendix

G

Exercise 6: Writing an Essay Test (p. 227)

A. Outline

1. Read and follow directions
2. Budget time
3. Read the questions carefully
4. First answer easy questions and those worth the most points
5. Check answers

B. Essay

There are five major similarities between taking essay tests and taking objective tests.

First, in both cases it is necessary to read and follow directions. For objective tests, following directions may mean marking answers in exactly the way expected. On essay tests, it may mean noting whether all the questions must be answered or whether any choices are given.

Second, it is necessary to budget time on both types of tests. Time should be allowed for initial previewing of the test and for reviewing the test at the end, and more time should be allowed for questions that are more difficult and worth more points.

Third, each question should be read carefully. For multiple-choice questions this includes reading all the choices; for matching questions it means reading both columns in advance; for essay questions it means paying special attention to words like *evaluate, compare, list.*

Fourth, the student should first answer questions that are easiest and that are worth the most points, coming back to the others later.

Finally, on both types of tests it is necessary to check all answers, changing wrong answers to objective questions and adding or correcting information on essays where appropriate.

In conclusion, taking essay exams and taking objective exams are based on the same principles of following directions, budgeting time, reading carefully, choosing which questions to answer first, and checking answers.

Appendix

H

The article below is from an anthropology textbook. It is included so you can practice your skills on a longer article. Begin by previewing and glossing the vocabulary. Then, skim the article for the major ideas. After you finish reading, complete your PQ4R study plan and decide if you will need to create supplemental study methods. Your instructor will decide if you will be tested on the article.

25

Culture Change

Chapter Outline

How and Why Cultures Change

Culture Change and Adaptation

Most of us are aware that "times have changed," especially when we compare our lives with those of our parents. Witness the recent changes in attitudes about sex and marriage, as well as the recent changes in women's roles. But culture change is not unique to us: humans throughout history have replaced or altered customary behaviors and attitudes as their needs have changed. Just as no individual is immortal, no particular cultural pattern is impervious to change. Anthropologists, therefore, want to understand how and why culture change occurs.

Three general questions can be asked about culture change: What is the source of a new trait? Why are people motivated (unconsciously as well as consciously) to adopt it? And is the new trait adaptive? The source may be inside or outside the society. That is, a new idea or behavior may originate within the society, or it may come from another society. With regard to motivation, people may adopt the new idea or behavior voluntarily (even if unconsciously), or they may be forced to adopt it. Finally, the outcome of culture change may or may not be beneficial. In this chapter, we first discuss the various processes of culture change in terms of the three dimensions of source, motivation, and outcome. Then we discuss some of the major types of culture change in the modern world. As we will see, these changes are associated largely with the expansion of Western societies over the last 500 years.

How and Why Cultures Change

Discoveries and inventions, which may originate inside or outside a society, are ultimately the sources of all culture change. But they do not necessarily lead to change. If an invention or discovery is ignored, no change in culture results. It is only when society accepts an invention or discovery and uses it regularly that we can begin to speak of culture change.

Discovery and Invention

The new thing discovered or invented (the innovation) may be an object—the wheel, the plow, the computer—or it may involve behavior and ideas—Christianity, democracy, monogamy. According to Ralph Linton, a discovery is any addition to knowledge and an invention is a new application of knowledge.[1] Thus, a person might discover that children can be persuaded to eat nourishing food if the food is associated with an imaginary character who appeals to them. And then someone might exploit that discovery by inventing a character named Popeye who appears in a series of animated cartoons, acquiring miraculous strength in a variety of dramatic situations by devouring cans of spinach.

Unconscious Invention. In discussing the process of invention, we should differentiate between various types of inventions. One type is the consequence of a society's setting itself a specific goal, such as eliminating tuberculosis or placing a person on the moon. Another type emerges less intentionally. This second process of invention is often referred to as *accidental juxtaposition* or *unconscious invention.* Linton suggested that some inventions, especially those of prehistoric days, were probably the consequences of literally dozens of tiny initiatives by "unconscious" inventors. These inventors made their small contributions, perhaps over many hundreds of years, without being aware of the part they were playing in bringing one invention, such as the wheel or a better form of hand ax, to completion.[2] Consider the example of children playing on a fallen log, which rolls as they walk and balance on it, coupled with the need at a given moment to move a slab of granite from a cave face. The children's play may have suggested the use of logs as rollers and thereby set in motion a series of developments that culminated in the wheel.

In reconstructing the process of invention in prehistoric times, however, we should be careful not to look back on our ancestors with a smugness born of our more highly developed technology. We have become accustomed to turning to the science sections of our magazines and newspapers and finding, almost daily, reports of miraculous new discoveries and inventions. From our point of view, it is difficult to imagine such a simple invention as the wheel taking so many centuries to come into being. We are tempted to surmise that early humans were less intelligent than we are. But the capacity of the human brain has been the same for perhaps 100,000 years; there is no evidence that the inventors of the wheel were any less intelligent than we are.

Intentional Innovation. Some discoveries and inventions arise out of deliberate attempts to produce a new idea or object. It may seem that such innovations are obvious responses to perceived needs. For example, during the Industrial Revolution there was a great demand for inventions that would increase productivity. James Hargreaves in eighteenth-century England is an example of an inventor who responded to an existing demand. Textile manufacturers were clamoring for such large quantities of spun yarn that cottage laborers, working with foot-operated spinning wheels, could not meet the demand. Hargreaves, realizing that prestige and financial rewards would come to the person who invented a method of spinning large quantities of yarn in a short time, set about the task and developed the spinning jenny.

But perceived needs and the economic rewards that may be given to the innovator do not explain why only some people innovate. We know relatively little about why some people are more innovative than others. The ability to innovate may depend in part on individual characteristics such as high intelligence and creativity. And creativity may be influenced by social conditions.

A study of innovation among Ashanti artist-carvers in Ghana suggests that creativity is more likely in some socioeconomic groups than in others.[3] Some carvers produced only traditional designs; others departed from tradition and produced "new" styles of carving. Two groups were found to innovate the most—the wealthiest and the poorest carvers. These two groups of carvers may tolerate risk more than the middle socioeconomic group. Innovative carving entails some risk because it may take more time and it may not sell. Wealthy carvers can afford the risk, and they may gain some prestige as well as income if their innovation is appreciated. The poor are not doing well anyway, and they have little to lose by trying something new.

Who Adopts Innovations? Once someone discovers or invents something, there is still the question of whether the innovation will be adopted by others. Many researchers have studied the characteristics of "early adopters." Such individuals tend to be educated, high in social status, upwardly mobile, and (if they are property owners) have large farms and businesses. The individuals who most need technological improvements—those who are less well off—are generally the last to adopt innovations. The theory is that only the wealthier can afford to take the substantial risks associated with new ways of doing things. In periods of rapid technological change, therefore, the gap between rich and poor is likely to widen because the rich adopt innovations sooner (and benefit more from them) than the poor.[4]

Does this imply that the likelihood of adopting innovations is a simple function of how much wealth a possible adopter possesses? Not necessarily. Frank Cancian reviewed several studies and found that upper-middle-class individuals show more conservatism than lower-middle-class individuals. Cancian suggested than when the risks are unknown the lower-middle-class individuals are more receptive to innovation because they have less to lose. Later on, when the risks are better known (as more people adopt the innovation), the upper-middle class catches up to the lower-middle.[5] So the readiness to accept innovation, like the likelihood of creativity among Ashanti carvers, may not be related to socioeconomic position in a straight-line, or linear, way.

The speed of accepting an innovation may depend partly on how new behaviors and ideas are typically transmitted in a society. In particular, is a person exposed to many versus few "teachers"? If children learn most of what they know from their parents or from a relatively small number of elders, then innovation will be slow to spread throughout the society, and culture change is likely to be slow. Innovations may catch on more rapidly if individuals are exposed to various teachers and other "leaders," who can influence many in a relatively short time. And the more peers we have, the more we might learn from them.[6] Perhaps this is why the pace of change appears to be so quick today. In societies like our own, and increasingly in the industrializing world, it is likely that people learn in schools from teachers, from leaders in their specialties, and from peers.

Diffusion

The source of new cultural elements in a society may also be another society. The process by which cultural elements are borrowed from another society and incorporated into the culture of the recipient group is called **diffusion.** Borrowing sometimes enables a group to bypass stages or mistakes in the development of a process or institution. For example, Germany was able to accelerate its program of industrialization in the nineteenth century. It avoided some of the errors made by its English and Belgian competitors by taking advantage of technological borrowing. Japan did the same somewhat later. Indeed, in recent years some of the earliest industrialized countries have fallen behind others in certain areas of production (automobiles, television, cameras, computers).

In a well-known passage, Linton conveyed the far-reaching effects of diffusion by considering the first few hours in the day of an American man. This man

awakens in a bed built on a pattern which originated in the Near East but which was modified in northern Europe before it was transmitted to America. He throws back covers made from cotton, domesticated in India, or linen, domesticated in the Near East, or silk, the use of which was discovered in China. All of these materials have been spun and woven by processes invented in the Near East. . . . He takes off his pajamas, a garment invented in India, and washes with soap invented by the ancient Gauls. He then shaves, a masochistic rite which seems to have derived from either Sumer or ancient Egypt.

Before going out for breakfast he glances through the window, made of glass invented in Egypt, and if it is raining puts on overshoes made of rubber discovered by the Central American Indians and takes an umbrella, invented in southeastern Asia. . . .

On his way to breakfast he stops to buy a paper paying for it with coins, an ancient Lydian invention. . . . His plate is made of a form of pottery invented in China. His knife is of steel, an alloy first made in southern India, his fork a medieval Italian invention, and his spoon a derivative of a Roman original. . . . After his fruit (African watermelon) and first coffee (an Abyssinian plant). . . . he may have the egg of a species of bird domesticated in Indo-China, or thin strips of the flesh of an animal domesticated in Eastern Asia which have been salted and smoked by a process developed in northern Europe. . . .

While smoking (an American Indian habit) he reads the news of the day, imprinted in characters invented by the ancient Semites upon a material invented in China by a process invented in Germany. As he absorbs the accounts of foreign troubles he will, if he is a good conservative citizen, thank a Hebrew deity in an Indo-European language that he is 100 percent American.[7]

Patterns of Diffusion.   There are three basic patterns of diffusion: direct contact, intermediate contact, and stimulus diffusion.

DIRECT CONTACT. Elements of a society's culture may be first taken up by neighboring societies and then gradually spread farther and farther afield. The spread of the manufacture of paper is a good example of extensive diffusion by direct contact. The invention of paper is attributed to the Chinese Ts'ai Lun in A.D. 105. Within fifty years, paper was being made in many places in central China. By 264 it was found in Chinese Turkestan, and from then on the successive places of manufacture were Samarkand (751), Baghdad (793), Egypt (about 900), Morocco (about 1100), France (1189), Italy (1276), Germany (1391), and England (1494). In general, the pattern of accepting the borrowed invention was the same in all cases. Paper was first imported into each area as a luxury, then in ever-expanding quantities as a staple product. Finally, and usually within one to three centuries, local manufacture was begun.

INTERMEDIATE CONTACT.   Diffusion by intermediate contact occurs through the agency of third parties. Frequently, traders carry a cultural trait from the society that originated it to another group. As an example of diffusion through intermediaries, Phoenician traders spread the alphabet, which may have been invented by another Semitic group, to Greece. At times, soldiers serve as intermediaries in spreading a culture trait. European crusaders, such as the Knights Templar and the Knights of St. John, acted as intermediaries in two ways: they carried Christian culture to Muslim societies of North Africa and brought Arab culture back to Europe. In the nineteenth century, Western missionaries in all parts of the world encouraged natives to wear Western clothing. The result is that in Africa, the Pacific Islands, and elsewhere, native peoples can be found wearing shorts, suit jackets, shirts, ties, and other typically Western articles of clothing.

STIMULUS DIFFUSION.   In stimulus diffusion, knowledge of a trait belonging to another culture stimulates the invention or development of a local equivalent. A classic example of stimulus diffusion is the Cherokee syllabic writing system created by a Native American named Sequoya so that his people could write down their language. Sequoya got the idea from his contact with Europeans. Yet he did not adopt the English writing system; indeed, he did not even learn to write English. What he did was utilize some English alphabetic symbols, alter others, and invent new ones. All the symbols he used represented Cherokee syllables and in no way echoed English alphabetic usage. In other words, Sequoya took English alphabetic ideas and gave them a new Cherokee form. The stimulus originated with Europeans; the result was peculiarly Cherokee.

The Selective Nature of Diffusion.   Although there is a temptation to view the dynamics of diffusion as similar to a stone sending concentric ripples over still water, this would be an oversimplification of the way diffusion actually occurs. Not all cultural traits are borrowed as readily as the ones we have mentioned, nor do they usually expand in neat, everwidening circles. Rather, diffusion is a selective process. The Japanese, for instance, accepted much from Chinese culture, but they also rejected many traits. Rhymed tonal poetry, civil-service examinations, and foot binding, which were favored by the Chinese, were never adopted in Japan. The poetry form was unsuited to the structure of the Japanese language; the examinations were unnecessary in view of the entrenched power of the Japanese aristocracy; foot binding was repugnant to a people who abhorred body mutilation of any sort.

Not only would we expect societies to reject items from other societies that are repugnant, we would also expect them to reject ideas and technology that do not satisfy some psychological, social, or cultural need. After all, people are not sponges—they don't automatically soak up the things around them. If they did, the amount of cultural variation in the world would be tiny—which is clearly not the case. Diffusion is also selective because cultural traits differ in the extent to which they can be communicated. Elements of material culture, such as mechanical processes and techniques, and other traits, such as physical sports and the like, are not especially difficult to demonstrate. Consequently, they are accepted or rejected on their merits. But the moment we move out of the material context, we encounter real difficulties. Linton explained the problem in these words:

> Although it is quite possible to describe such an element of culture as the ideal pattern for marriage . . . it is much less complete than a description of basketmaking. . . . The most thorough verbalization has difficulty in conveying the series of associations and conditioned emotional responses which are attached to this pattern [marriage] and which gave it meaning and vitality within our own society. . . . This is even more true of those concepts which . . . find no direct expression in behavior aside from verbalization. There is a story of an educated Japanese who after a long discussion on the nature of the Trinity with a European friend . . . burst out with: "Oh, I see now, it is a committee."[8]

Finally, diffusion is selective because the overt form of a particular trait, rather than its function or meaning, frequently seems to determine how the trait will be received. For example, the enthusiasm for bobbed hair (short haircuts) that swept through much of North America in the 1920s never caught on among the Native Americans of northwestern California. To many women of European ancestry, short hair was a symbolic statement of their freedom. To Native American women, who traditionally cut their hair short when in mourning, it was a reminder of death.[9]

In the process of diffusion, then, we can identify a number of different patterns. We know that cultural borrowing is selective rather than automatic, and we can describe how a particular borrowed trait has been modified by the recipient culture. But our current knowledge does not allow us to specify when one or another of these outcomes will occur, under what conditions diffusion will occur, and why it occurs the way it does.

Acculturation

On the surface, the process of change called **acculturation** seems to include much of what we have discussed under the label of discussion, since acculturation refers to the changes that occur when different cultural groups come into intensive contact. As in diffusion, the source of new cultural items is the other society. But more often than not, the term *acculturation* is used by anthropologists to describe a situation in which one of the societies in contact is much more powerful than the other. Thus, acculturation can be seen as a process of extensive cultural borrowing in the context of superordinate-subordinate relations between societies.[10] The borrowing may sometimes be a two-way process, but generally it is the subordinate or less powerful society that borrows the most. The concept of diffusion can then be reserved for the voluntary borrowing of cultural elements, in contrast with borrowing under external pressure, which characterizes acculturation. (The term *assimilation* means that people from another culture have more or less completely adopted the dominant culture of the society.)

External pressure for culture change can take various forms. In its most direct form—conquest or colonialization—the dominant group uses force or the threat of it to bring about culture change in the other group. For example, in the Spanish conquest of Mexico, the conquerors forced many of the native groups to accept Catholicism. Although such direct force is not always exerted in conquest situations, dominated peoples often have little choice but to change. Examples of such indirectly forced change abound in the history of Native Americans in the United States. Although the federal government made few direct attempts to force people to adopt North American culture, it did drive many native groups from their lands, thereby obliging them to give up many aspects of their traditional ways of life. In order to survive, they had no choice but to adopt many of the dominant society's traits. When Native American children were required to go to schools, which taught the dominant society's values, the process was accelerated.

A subordinate society may acculturate to a dominant society even in the absence of direct or indirect force. The dominated people may elect to adopt cultural elements from the dominant society in order to survive in their changed world. Or, perceiving that members of the dominant society enjoy more secure living conditions, the dominated people may identify with the dominant culture in the hope that by doing so they will be able to share some of its benefits. For example, in Arctic areas many Inuit and Lapp groups seemed eager to replace dog sleds with snowmobiles without any coercion.[11]

But many millions of people never really had a chance to acculturate after contact with Europeans. They simply died, sometimes directly at the hands of the conquerors, but probably more often as a result of new diseases the Europeans brought with them. Depopulation because of new diseases such as measles, smallpox, and tuberculosis was particularly common in North and South America and on the islands of the Pacific. Those areas had previously been isolated from contact with Europeans and from the diseases of that continuous land mass we call the Old World—Europe, Asia, and Africa.[12]

The story of Ishi, the last surviving member of a group of Native Americans in California called the Yahi, is a moving testimonial to the frequently tragic effect of contact with Europeans. In the space of twenty-two years, the Yahi population was reduced from several hundred to near zero. The historical record on this episode of depopulation suggests that Euroamericans murdered thirty to fifty Yahi for every Euroamerican murdered, and perhaps 60 percent of the Yahi died in the ten years following their initial exposure to European diseases.[13]

Nowadays, many powerful nations (and not just Western ones) may seem to be acting in more humanitarian ways to improve the life of previously subjugated as well as other "developing" peoples. For better or worse, these programs are still forms of external pressure. The tactic used may be persuasion rather than force, but most of the programs are nonetheless designed to bring about acculturation in the direction of the dominant societies' cultures. For example, the introduction of formal schooling cannot help but instill new values that may contradict traditional cultural patterns. And even healthcare programs may alter traditional ways of life by undermining the authority of shamans and others and by increasing population beyond the number that can be supported in traditional ways. Confinement to "reservations" or other kinds of direct force are not the only ways a dominant society can bring about acculturation.

Revolution

Certainly the most drastic and rapid way a culture can change is as a result of **revolution**—replacement, usually violent, of a country's rulers. Historical records, as well as our daily newspapers, indicate that people frequently rebel against established authority. Rebellions, if they occur, almost always occur in state societies, where there is a distinct ruling elite. They take the form of struggles between rulers and ruled, between conquerors and conquered, or between representatives of an external colonial power and segments of the native society. Rebels do not always succeed in overthrowing the previous rulers, so rebellions do not always result in revolutions. And even successful rebellions do not always result in culture change; the individual rulers may change, but customs or institutions may not. The sources of revolution may be mostly internal, as in the French Revolution, or partly external, as in the Russian-supported 1948 revolution in Czechoslovakia and the United States–supported 1973 revolution against President Allende in Chile.

The Nacirema war of independence toward the end of the eighteenth century is a good example of a colonial rebellion, the success of which was at least partly a result of foreign intervention. The Nacirema rebellion was a war of neighboring colonies against the greatest imperial power of the time, Great Britain. In the nineteenth century and continuing into the middle and later years of the twentieth century, there would be many other wars of independence, in Latin America, Europe, Asia, and Africa. We don't always remember that the Nacirema rebellion was the first of these anti-imperialist wars in modern times, and the model for many that followed. And just like many of the most recent liberation movements, the Nacirema rebellion was also part of a larger worldwide war, involving people from many rivalrous nations. Thirty thousand German-speaking soldiers fought, for pay, on the British side; an army and navy from France fought on the Nacirema side. There were volunteers from other European countries, including Denmark, Holland, Poland, and Russia.

One of these volunteers was a man named Kosciusko from Poland, which at the time was being divided between Prussia and Russia. Kosciusko helped win a major victory for the Nacirema, and subsequently directed the fortification of what later became the Nacirema training school for army officers, Tsew Tniop. After the war he returned to Poland and led a rebellion against the Russians, which was only briefly successful. In 1808 he published a *Manual on the Maneuvers of Horse Artillery,* which was used for many years by the Nacirema army. When he died he left money to buy freedom and education for Nacirema slaves.

The executor of Kosiusko's will was a Nacirema named Jefferson, who had taken part in a famous debate at a convention in his colony. The debate was over a motion to prepare for defense against the British armed forces. The motion barely passed, by a vote of sixty-five to sixty. There was a speech before the vote that is now a part of Nacirema folklore. A lawyer whose last name was Henry listened to the argument for not opposing the British and then rose to declare that it was insane not to oppose them and that he was not afraid to test the strength of the colonies against Great Britain—others might hesitate, he said, but he would have "liberty or death." The "radicals" who supported P. Henry's resolution included many aristocratic landowners, two of whom (G. Washington and T. Jefferson) became the first and third occupants of the highest political office in what became the United States of America.[14]

Not all peoples who are suppressed, conquered, or colonialized eventually rebel against established authority. Why this is so and why rebellions and revolts are not always successful in bringing about culture change are still open questions. But some possible answers have been investigated. One historian, who examined the classic revolutions of the past, including the American, French, and Russian revolutions, suggested some conditions that may give rise to rebellion and revolution:

1. Loss of prestige of established authority, often as a result of the failure of foreign policy, financial difficulties, dismissals of popular ministers, or alteration of popular policies. France in the eighteenth century lost three major international conflicts, with disastrous results for its diplomatic standing and internal finances. Russian society was close to military and economic collapse in 1917, after three years of World War I.

2. Threat to recent economic improvement. In France, as in Russia, those sections of the population (professional classes and urban workers) whose economic fortunes had only shortly before taken an upward swing were "radicalized" by unexpected setbacks such as steeply rising food prices and unemployment. The same may be said for the American colonies on the brink of their rebellion against Great Britain.

3. Indecisiveness of government, as exemplified by lack of consistent policy, which gives the impression of being controlled by, rather than in control of, events. The frivolous arrogance of Louis XVI's regime and the bungling of George III's prime minister, Lord North, with respect to the problems of the American colonies, are examples.

4. Loss of support of the intellectual class. Such a loss deprived the prerevolutionary governments of France and Russia of any avowed philosophical support and led to their unpopularity with the literate public.[15]

The classic revolutions of the past occurred in countries that were industrialized only incipiently at best. For the most part, the same is true of the rebellions and revolutions in recent years: they have occurred mostly in countries we call *developing.* The evidence from a worldwide survey of developing countries suggests that rebellions have tended to occur where the ruling classes depended mostly on the produce or income from land, and therefore were resistant to demands for reform from the rural classes that worked the land. In such agricultural economies, the rulers are not likely to yield political power or give greater economic returns to the workers, because to do so would eliminate the basis (land ownership) of the rulers' wealth and power.[16]

Finally, a particularly interesting question is why revolutions sometimes (perhaps even usually) fail to measure up to the high hopes of those who initiate them. When rebellions succeed in replacing the ruling elite, the result is often the institution of a military dictatorship even more restrictive and repressive than the government that existed before. The new ruling establishment may merely substitute one set of repressions for another, rather than bring any real change to the nation. On the other hand, some revolutions have resulted in fairly drastic overhauls of societies.

The idea of revolution has been one of the central myths and inspirations of many groups both in the past and in the present. The colonial empire building of countries such as England and France created a worldwide situation in which rebellion became nearly inevitable. In numerous technologically underdeveloped lands, which have been exploited by more powerful countries for their natural resources and cheap labor, a deep resentment has often developed against the foreign ruling classes or their local clients. Where the ruling classes, native or foreign, refuse to be responsive to these feelings, rebellion becomes the only alternative. In many areas, it has become a way of life.

Culture Change and Adaptation

The chapter on the concept of culture discussed the general assumption that most of the customary behaviors of a culture are probably adaptive, or at least not maladaptive, in that environment. A custom is adaptive if it increases the likelihood that the people practicing it will survive and reproduce. Even though customs are learned (not genetically inherited), cultural adaptation may be otherwise like biological adaptation or evolution. The frequency of certain genetic alternatives is likely to increase over time if those genetic traits increase their carriers' chances of survival and reproduction. Similarly, the frequency of a new learned behavior will increase over time and become customary in a population if the people with that behavior are most likely to survive and reproduce. Thus, if a culture is adapted to its environment, culture change should also be adaptive—not always, to be sure, but commonly.

One of the most important differences between cultural evolution and genetic evolution is that individuals often can decide whether or not to accept and follow the way their parents behave or think, whereas they cannot decide whether or not to inherit certain genes. When enough individuals change their behavior and beliefs, we say that the culture has changed. Therefore, it is possible for culture change to occur much more rapidly than genetic change.

But it is not necessarily more adaptive to change rapidly, just because it is possible. Robert Boyd and Peter Richerson showed mathematically that when the environment is relatively stable and individual mistakes are costly, staying with customary modes of behavior (usually transmitted by parents) is probably more adaptive than changing.[17] But what happens when the environment (particularly the social environment) is changing? There are plenty of examples in the modern world: people have to migrate to new places for work; medical care leads to increased population so that land is scarcer; people have had land taken away from them and they are therefore forced to make do with less land; and so on.

It is particularly when circumstances change that individuals are likely to try ideas or behaviors that are different from those of their parents. Most people would want to adopt behaviors that are more suited to their present circumstances, but how do they know which behaviors are better? There are various ways to find out. One way is by experimenting, trying out various new behaviors. Another way is to evaluate the experiments of others. If a person who tries a new technique seems successful, we would expect the more successful person to be imitated, just as we would expect people to stick with new behaviors they have personally tried and found successful. Finally, one might choose to do what most people in the new situation decide to do.[18]

Why one choice rather than another? In part, the choice may be a function of the cost or risk of the innovation. It is relatively easy, for example, to find out how long it takes to cut down a tree with an introduced steel ax, as compared with a stone ax. Not surprisingly, innovations such as a steel ax catch on

relatively quickly because comparison is easy and the results relatively clear-cut. But what if the risk is very great? Suppose the innovation involves adopting a whole new way of farming that you have never practiced before. You can try it, but you might not have any food if you fail. As we discussed earlier, innovations that are risky are likely to be tried only by those individuals who can afford the risk. Other people may then evaluate their success and adopt the new strategy if it looks promising. Similarly, if you migrate to a new area, say from a high-rainfall area to a drier one, it may pay to look around to see what most people in the new place do; after all, the people in the drier area probably have customs that are adaptive for that environment.

We can expect then that the choices individuals make may often be adaptive ones. But it is important to note that adopting an innovation from someone in one's own society or borrowing an innovation from another society is not always or necessarily beneficial, either in the short or the long run. First, people may make mistakes in judgment, especially when some new behavior seems to satisfy a physical need. Why, for example, have smoking and drug use diffused so widely even though they are likely to reduce a person's chances of survival? Second, even if people are correct in their short-term judgment of benefit, they may be wrong in their judgment about long-run benefit. A new crop may yield more than the old crop for five consecutive years, but the new crop may fail miserably in the sixth year because of lower-than-normal rainfall or because the new crop depleted soil nutrients. Third, people may be forced by the more powerful to change, with few if any benefits for themselves.

Whatever the motives for humans to change their behavior, the theory of natural selection suggests that new behavior is not likely to become cultural (or remain cultural over generations) if it has harmful reproductive consequences, just as a genetic mutation with harmful consequences is not likely to become frequent in a population.[19] Still, we know of many examples of culture change that seem maladaptive—the switch to bottle-feeding rather than nursing infants, which may spread infection because contaminated water is used, or the adoption of alcoholic beverages, which may lead to alcoholism and early death. In the last few hundred years, the major stimulus to culture change, adaptive and maladaptive, has been the new social environment produced by the arrival of people from Western societies.

▼ Summary

1. Culture is always changing. Because culture consists of learned patterns of behavior and belief, cultural traits can be unlearned and learned anew as human needs change.

2. Discoveries and inventions, though ultimately the sources of all culture change, do not necessarily lead to change. Only when society accepts an invention or discovery and uses it regularly can culture change be said to have occurred. Some inventions are probably the result of dozens of tiny, perhaps accidental, initiatives over a period of many years. Other inventions are consciously intended. Why some people are more innovative than others is still only incompletely understood. There is some evidence that creativity and the readiness to adopt innovations may be related to socioeconomic position.

3. The process by which cultural elements are borrowed from another society and incorporated into the culture of the recipient group is called diffusion. Three patterns of diffusion may be identified: diffusion by direct contact, in which elements of a culture are first taken up by neighboring societies and then gradually spread farther and farther afield; diffusion by intermediate contact, in which third parties, frequently traders, carry a cultural trait from the society originating it to another group; and stimulus diffusion, in which knowledge of a trait belonging to another culture stimulates the invention or development of a local equivalent.

4. Cultural traits do not necessarily diffuse; that is, diffusion is a selective—not automatic—process. A society accepting a foreign cultural trait is likely to adapt it in a way that effectively harmonizes it with the society's own traditions.

5. When a group or society is in contact with a more powerful society, the weaker group is often obliged to acquire cultural elements from the dominant group. This process of extensive borrowing in the context of superordinate-subordinate relations between societies is usually called acculturation. In contrast with diffusion, acculturation comes about as a result of some sort of external pressure.

6. Perhaps the most drastic and rapid way a culture can change is by revolution—a usually violent replacement of the society's rulers. Rebellions occur primarily in state societies, where there is usually a distinct ruling elite. However, not all peoples who are suppressed, conquered, or colonized eventually rebel or successfully revolt against established authority.

7. Even though customs are not genetically inherited, cultural adaptation may be somewhat similar to biological adaptation: traits (cultural or genetic) that are more likely to be reproduced (learned or inherited) are likely to become more frequent in a population over time. And if culture is generally adapted to its environment, then culture change should also be generally adaptive.

8. Many of the cultural changes observed in the modern world have been generated, directly or indirectly, by the dominance and expansion of Western societies.

▼ Glossary Terms

acculturation   diffusion   revolution

▼ Critical Questions

1. What kinds of cultural items might be most easily borrowed by another culture, and why do you think so?
2. The expansion of the West has had terrible consequences for many peoples. Have there been any beneficial consequences?

▼ Suggested Reading

BERNARD, H. R., AND PELTO, P. J., eds. *Technology and Social Change,* 2nd ed. Prospect Heights, IL: Waveland, 1987. This volume is concerned with the effects of introduced Western technology on diverse cultures. Thirteen case studies were written especially for the volume; the editors provide concluding observations.

BODLEY, J. H. *Victims of Progress,* 3rd ed. Mountain View, CA: Mayfield, 1990. An examination of the effects of industrial nations on tribal peoples. Emphasizes the imperialist and exploitative practices of expansionist nations as well as the destructive consequences of imposed "progress."

BOYD, R., AND RICHERSON, P. J. *Culture and the Evolutionary Process.* Chicago: University of Chicago Press, 1985. The authors develop mathematical models to analyze how genes and culture interact, under the influence of evolutionary processes, to produce the diversity we see in human cultures.

EMBER, M., EMBER, C. R., AND LEVINSON, D. eds. *Portraits of Culture: Ethnographic Originals* (Englewood Cliffs, NJ: Prentice Hall, 1994, 1995). Prentice Hall/Simon & Schuster Custom Publishing. Most of the miniethnographies in this series discuss the changes in culture that have occurred in recent times.

GOLDSTONE, J. A. "The Comparative and Historical Study of Revolutions." *Annual Review of Sociology,* 8 (1982): 187–207. A review of theory and research on why revolutions have occurred, and why some succeeded, in the past and present.

HERBIG, P. A. *The Innovation Matrix: Culture and Structure Prerequisites to Innovation.* Westport, CT: Quorum Books, 1994. A discussion of the factors that may enable some societies to adapt and change more quickly than others.

McNEILL, W. H. *Plagues and Peoples.* Garden City, NY: Doubleday Anchor, 1976. A historian suggests that epidemics have crucially affected the history of various societies all over the world.

ROGERS, E. M. *Diffusion of Innovations,* 3rd ed. New York: Free Press, 1983. This book examines the roles of information and uncertainty in the spread of innovations, how different categories of people adopt innovations at different rates, and how change agents affect the process. A large literature is reviewed and synthesized.

▼ Notes

[1] Ralph Linton, *The Study of Man* (New York: Appleton-Century-Crofts, 1936), p. 306.

[2] Ibid., pp. 310–11.

[3] Harry R. Silver, "Calculating Risks: The Socioeconomic Foundations of Aesthetic Innovation in an Ashanti Carving Community," *Ethnology,* 20 (1981): 101–14.

[4]Everett M. Rogers, *Diffusion of Innovations,* 3rd ed. (New York: Free Press, 1983), pp. 263–69.

[5]Frank Cancian, "Risk and Uncertainty in Agricultural Decision Making," in Peggy F. Barlett, ed., *Agricultural Decision Making: Anthropological Contributions to Rural Development* (New York: Academic Press, 1980), pp. 161–202.

[6]Barry S. Hewlett and L. L. Cavalli-Sforza, "Cultural Transmission among Aka Pygmies," *American Anthropologist,* 88 (1986): 922–34; L. L. Cavalli-Sforza and M. W. Feldman, *Cultural Transmission and Evolution: A Quantitative Approach* (Princeton, NJ: Princeton University Press, 1981).

[7]Linton, *The Study of Man,* pp. 326–27. © 1936, renewed 1964; reprinted by permission of Prentice Hall, Inc.

[8]Ibid., pp. 338–39.

[9]George M. Foster, *Traditional Cultures and the Impact of Technological Change* (New York: Harper & Row, 1962), p. 26.

[10]John H. Bodley, *Victims of Progress,* 3rd ed. (Mountain View, CA: Mayfield, 1990), p. 7.

[11]Pertti J. Pelto and Ludger Müller-Wille, "Snowmobiles: Technological Revolution in the Arctic," in H. Russell Bernard and Pertti J. Pelto, eds., *Technology and Social Change,* 2nd ed. (Prospect Heights, IL, Waveland Press, 1987), pp. 207–43.

[12]Bodley, *Victims of Progress,* pp. 38–41.

[13]Theodora Kroeber, *Ishi in Two Worlds* (Berkeley: University of California Press, 1967), pp. 45–47.

[14]The historical information we refer to comes from a book by Allan Nevins, *The American States during and after the Revolution* (New York: Macmillan, 1927). We spell *American* (and *West Point*) backward to encourage the realization that the American Revolution was very much like modern liberation movements. For how radical the American Revolution was, see Gordon S. Wood, *The Radicalism of the American Revolution* (New York: Knopf, 1992).

[15]Crane Brinton, *The Anatomy of Revolution* (Englewood Cliffs, NJ: Prentice Hall, 1938).

[16]Jeffrey M. Paige, *Agrarian Revolution: Social Movements and Export Agriculture in the Underdeveloped World* (New York: Free Press, 1975).

[17]Robert Boyd and Peter J. Richerson, *Culture and the Evolutionary Process* (Chicago: University of Chicago Press, 1985), p. 106.

[18]Ibid., p. 135.

[19]Donald T. Campbell, "Variation and Selective Retention in Socio-Cultural Evolution," in Herbert Barringer, George Blankstein, and Raymond Mack, eds., *Social Change in Developing Areas: A Re-Interpretation of Evolutionary Theory* (Cambridge, MA: Schenkman, 1965), pp. 19–49. See also Boyd and Richerson, *Culture and the Evolutionary Process;* and William H. Durham, *Coevolution: Genes, Culture and Human Diversity* (Stanford, CA: Stanford University Press, 1991).

Bibliography

Adams, Julian and Stratton, Kenneth. *Press Time,* 4th ed. Englewood Cliffs, NJ: Prentice-Hall, 1985.

Allen, Steve. *How to Enjoy Classics,* by permission of the International Paper Company, 1980.

Audersirk, Gerald and Audersirk, Teresa. *Biology: Life on Earth,* 3rd ed. New York: Macmillan Publishing Co., 1993.

Bennion, Marion. *Introductory Foods.* 10th ed. Englewood Cliffs, NJ: Merrill/Prentice-Hall, 1995.

Blakely, James and Bade, David H. *The Science of Animal Husbandry,* 6th ed. Englewood Cliffs, NJ: Prentice-Hall, 1994

Bloom, Lynn Z. *The Essay Connection,* 4th ed. Lexington, MA: D.C. Heath and Company, 1995.

Boston Sunday Herald American, 6 February 1977, 23.

Bower, Gordon H. "Improving Memory," *Human Nature,* vol. 1, no. 2, Feb. 1978.

Brinton, Crane, Christopher, John B., and Wolff, Robert Lee. *Civilization in the West,* 4th ed. Englewood Cliffs, NJ: Prentice-Hall, 1981.

Brockett, Oscar. *History of the Theatre,* 7th ed. Needham Heights, MA: Allyn and Bacon, 1995.

Burner, David B., Marcus, Robert D., and Rosenberg, Emily S. *America: A Portrait in History,* 2nd ed. Englewood Cliffs, NJ: Prentice-Hall, 1978.

Burns, James MacGregor; Peltason, J.W.; Cronin, Thomas E.; Magleby, David B. *Government By The People,* 16th ed., basic version, Englewood Cliffs, NJ: Prentice-Hall, 1995.

Chaisson, Erick and McMillan, Steve. *Astronomy, A Beginner's Guide to the Universe,* Englewood Cliffs, NJ: Prentice-Hall, 1995.

Chaney, Lillian H. and Martin, Jeanette S. *Intercultural Business Communications.* Englewood Cliffs, NJ: Prentice-Hall Career and Technology, 1995.

Corson, Richard. *Stage Makeup,* 7th ed. Englewood Cliffs, NJ: Prentice-Hall, 1986.

Daub, G. William and Seese, William S. *Basic Chemistry,* 6th ed., Englewood Cliffs, NJ: Prentice-Hall, 1992.

Diamond, Jay and Pintel, Gerald. *Introduction to Contemporary Business,* Englewood Cliffs, NJ: Prentice-Hall, 1975.

Donatelle, Rebecca J., et al. *Access to Health,* Englewood Cliffs, NJ: Prentice-Hall, 1988.

Ellinger, Herbert and Halderman, James. *Automotive Engines: Theory and Servicing,* Englewood Cliffs, NJ: Prentice-Hall, 1991.

Ember, Carol R. and Ember, Melvin, *Anthropology,* 8th ed. Saddle River, NJ, 1996.

Faragher, John Mack, et. al. *Out of Many: A History of the American People.* combined ed., Englewood Cliffs, NJ: Prentice-Hall, 1994.

Finlay, J.L. and Sprague, D.N. *The Structure of Canadian History,* 2nd ed. Scarborough, Ont.: Prentice-Hall, Canada, 1984.

Frings, Gini Stephens. *Fashion: From Concept to Consumer,* 4th ed. Englewood Cliffs, NJ: Prentice-Hall, 1994.

Gobbledygook Has Gotta Go, Washington: Bureau of Land Management, U.S. Department of the Interior, pp. 45–46.

Hartmann, Hudson T., et al. *Plant Science: Growth, Development, and Utilization of Cultivated Plants,* 2nd ed., Englewood Cliffs, NJ: Prentice-Hall, 1988.

Hoover, Herbert. *American Individualism,* New York: Doubleday, 1922.

Horton, Paul B., Leslie, Gerald R., and Larson, Richard F. *The Sociology of Social Problems,* 11th ed. Englewood Cliffs, NJ: Prentice-Hall, 1994.

Hughes, H. Stuart and Wilkinson, James. *Contemporary Europe: A History,* 6th ed. Englewood Cliffs, NJ: Prentice-Hall, 1987.

Judson, Sheldon and Richardson, Steven M. *Earth: An Introduction to Geological Change,* Englewood Cliffs, NJ: Prentice-Hall, 1995.

Judson, Sheldon, Kauffman, Marvin E., and Leet, L. Don. *Physical Geology,* 7th ed. Englewood Cliffs, NJ: Prentice-Hall, 1987.

Kristal, Mark B. *A Guide to the Brain: A Graphic Workbook,* Englewood Cliffs, NJ: Prentice-Hall, 1990.

La Place, John. *Health,* 5th ed., Englewood Cliffs, NJ: Prentice-Hall, 1987.

Lenier, Jules. "Magic for Entertainment," *Keys to College Success,* 3rd ed., Englewood Cliffs, NJ: Prentice-Hall, 1990.

Lenier, Minnette and Maker, Janet. *How to Be a Super Sleuth,* Opportunities For Learning, 1978, Card B12.

Lenier, Minnette and Maker, Janet. "Nonverbal Communication and Note-Taking," *Keys to College Success,* 3rd ed. Englewood Cliffs, NJ: Prentice-Hall, 1990.

Lewis, Norman (ed.). *The New Roget's Thesaurus in Dictionary Form,* New York; Putman's, 1978.

Lolley, John. *Your Library: What's In It For You?*, New York: John Wiley & Sons, 1991.

Lorayne, Harry. *How to Develop a Super-Power Memory*, New York: Signet Books, 1974.

Lutgens, Frederick K. and Tarbuck, Edward J. *Essentials of Geology*, 5th ed. Englewood Cliffs, NJ: Merrill/Prentice-Hall, 1995.

Macionis, John J. *Sociology*, 5th ed. Englewood Cliffs, NJ: Prentice-Hall, 1987.

Malcolm X and Alex Haley. *The Autobiography of Malcolm X*, New York: Grove Press, Inc. 1964.

Mayo, S. H. *A History of Mexico: From Pre-Columbia to Present*, Englewood Cliffs, NJ: Prentice-Hall, 1978.

Mitchell International, Inc. *Mitchell Auto Mechanics*, 2nd ed. Englewood Cliffs, NJ: Prentice-Hall, 1991.

Morris, Charles G. *Psychology: An Introduction*, 8th ed. Englewood Cliffs, NJ: Prentice-Hall, 1993.

Nettl, Bruno; Capwell, Charles, Wong, Isabel K.F., and Turino, Thomas. *Excursion in World Music*, Englewood Cliffs, NJ: Prentice-Hall, 1992.

Nichols, Ralph and Stevens, Leonard. *Are You Listening?*, (New York: McGraw-Hill 1957), pp. 5–6

Ottman, Robert W. *Elementary Harmony*, 3rd ed. Englewood Cliffs, NJ: Prentice-Hall, 1983.

Robbins, Stephen P. *Management*, 2nd ed. Englewood Cliffs, NJ: Prentice-Hall, 1988.

Robinson, Francis P. Adapted from "SQ3R," *Effective Study*, 4th ed. New York: Harper & Row, Pub., 1970.

Roget, Peter Mark. *Thesaurus of English Words and Phrases*, ed. Susan M. Lloyd Harlow, Essex: Longman, 1982.

Ross, Raymond S. *Speech Communication: Fundamentals and Practice*, 9th ed. Englewood Cliffs, NJ: Prentice-Hall, 1992.

Russell, Thomas et al. *Otto Kleppner's Advertising Procedure*, 10th ed. Englewood Cliffs, NJ: Prentice-Hall, 1988.

Schniedeman, Lambert and Wander. *Being A Nurse Assistant*, 6th ed. Englewood Cliffs, NJ: Brady Regent/Prentice-Hall, 1991.

Scupin, Raymond. *Cultural Anthropology: A Global Perspective*, 2nd ed. Englewood Cliffs, NJ: Prentice-Hall, 1994.

Silverman, Robert E. *Psychology*, 5th ed. Englewood Cliffs, NJ: Prentice-Hall, 1985.

Szymanski, Robert A., Szymanski, Donald P., and Pulschen, Donna M. *Computers and Information Systems*, Englewood Cliffs, NJ: Prentice-Hall, 1993.

Tarbuck, Edward J. and Lutgens, Frederick K. *Earth Science*, 7th ed. Englewood Cliffs, NJ: Prentice-Hall, 1994.

"Test Anxiety," *Human Nature*, vol. 7, no. 4, April, 1978, pp. 50–51.

Thompson, Della ed. *The Concise Oxford Dictionary of Current English,* 9th ed. Oxford: Clarendon Press, 1995.

Thurber, James. "University Days," *From My Life and Hard Times,* New York: Harper & Row. Originally published in *The New Yorker,* 1971.

Underhill, James et al. *General Zoology: Laboratory Guide,* 3rd ed. New York: Macmillan Publishing Co., 1988.

Vasile, Albert J. and Mintz, Harold K. *Speak with Confidence: A Practical Guide,* 7th ed. New York: Harper Collins College Publishers, 1996.

Verderber, Rudolph and Elder, Ann, and Weiler, Ernest, "An Analysis of Student Communication Habits," unpublished study, University of Cincinnati, 1976 cited in Verderber, Rudolph. *The Challenge of Effective Speaking,* 9th ed., Belmont, Ca: Wadsworth Publishing Co., 1994, p. 39.

Webster's New World Dictionary of the American Language, paperback ed. New York: Simon & Schuster, 1995.

Wells, William, Burnett, John, and Moriarty, Sandra. *Advertising, Principles and Practice,* 3rd ed. Englewood Cliffs, NJ: Prentice-Hall, 1995.

Wilson, Jerry D. *College Physics,* 2nd ed. Englewood Cliffs, NJ: Prentice-Hall, 1994.

Wolff, Robert Paul. *About Philosophy,* 6th ed. Upper Saddle River, NJ: Prentice-Hall, 1995.

Worchell, Stephen and Shebilske, Wayne, *Psychology,* 5th ed. Englewood Cliffs, NJ: Prentice-Hall, 1995.

Answer Key

Chapter 1

Comprehension Check (pp. 16–17)

1. b
2. b
3. c
4. a
5. a
6. d
7. b
8. c
9. Do the math first, the English second, and leave the sociology for last.
10. (1) reducing anxiety
    (2) setting manageable goals
(You may think of other advantages).

Comprehension Check (pp. 22–23)

1. d
2. b
3. c
4. d
5. c
6. The value of successful time management
7. a. Make a list of your objectives.
   b. Rank the objectives according to their importance.
   c. List the activities necessary to achieve your objectives.
   d. For each objective, assign priorities to the various activities required to reach the objective.
   e. Schedule your activities according to the priorities you've set.
8. Parkinson's Law says that work expands to fill the time available.
9. Discretionary time is under a manager's control.
10. a. 5
    b. 10

Chapter 2

Exercise 1: Signal Words (p. 33)

1. and, first, next, as well, another
2. less than, than
3. consequently, since, because
4. otherwise, however, but
5. for example
6. now, meantime, then, until, first, soon, after
7. in short

Comprehension Check (pp. 34–35)

1. a
2. d
3. a
4. d
5. c
6. c
7. d
8. c
9. a. examples
   b. facts
   c. reasons
   d. testimony
10. The subject is the general topic; the main idea focuses on an aspect of the subject.

Exercise 2: Main Idea and Support (pp. 35–38)

1. a
2. d
3. a
4. b
5. b
6. c
7. b
8. c
9. b
10. a

Exercise 3: Main Idea and Support in Longer Selections (pp. 38–39)

1. The subject of the article is posture.

2. "Posture can convey self-confidence, status, and interest."

3. a. change of direction
   b. time sequence
   c. addition
   d. change of direction
   e. change of direction
   f. emphasis
   g. change of direction

Comprehension Check (pp. 43–44)

1.	b	5.	a
2.	c	6.	b
3.	c	7.	d
4.	a	8.	a

9. A diet based mostly on grain, especially brown rice and milk. Meat and sugar are totally banned.

10. Absence of pesticides and no artificial substances added.

Exercise 4: Reviewing Signal Words (pp. 44–45)

a. change of direction
b. example
c. change of direction
d. change of direction
e. emphasis
f. change of direction
g. time sequence
h. cause and effect
i. cause and effect
j. change of direction
k. change of direction
l. addition
m. cause and effect
n. addition
o. change of direction

Exercise 5: Skills Review—Scheduling (pp. 45–46)

Answers will vary.

Chapter 3

Comprehension Check (pp. 53–54)

1.	d	5.	c
2.	c	6.	d
3.	d	7.	d
4.	d	8.	d

9. An inference is going beyond the literal meaning of the text and reading between the lines.

10. The main idea of this chapter is the importance of reading critically and methods for doing so.

Exercise 1: Critical Reading in Paragraphs (pp. 54–60)

Paragraph A
Inference
A. 4
B. (1) "There are no limits to our capability to produce messages . . ."
   (2) "The sounds of animals' communication do not vary and cannot be modified."
C. (1) yes
   (2) no
   (3) no
   (4) no
   (5) yes
Fact versus opinion. You could never prove a statement which includes a phrase like "never heard before."

Paragraph B
Inference
A. 4
B. The two stories of sales lost.
C. (1) no
   (2) no
   (3) yes
   (4) yes
   (5) yes.
Fact versus opinion: You could multiply $10 times the number of workers in the country.

Paragraph C
Inference
A. 2
B. 1. Wall Street crashed when Hoover had been in power for only four months.
   2. During 1930 unemployment increased by over one million people.
C. (1) yes
   (2) yes
   (3) no
   (4) no
   (5) yes
Fact versus opinion: The author could research the number of people put out of work in Great Britain by each American.

Paragraph D
Inference
A. 2
B. (1) Gray-blue is still blue.

(2) Colors on the edge of the color wheel are of maximum brilliance, while colors nearer the center are less brilliant.

C. (1) yes
   (2) yes
   (3) no
   (4) no
   (5) no

Fact versus opinion: Scientists could measure the amount of each color by mixing dyes or paints. For example, they could measure the presence of gray or any other color in a blue dye.

Paragraph E
Inference
A. 3
C. (1) A frustrated person who cannot create a way or find a means to reduce frustration may become deeply troubled.
   (2) Rather than persist we find new goals that can be attained.

C. (1) yes
   (2) no
   (3) yes
   (4) no
   (5) yes

Fact versus opinion: They could either give people questionnaires or observe their behavior, then assign them ratings for frustration and degree of trouble. They could look for a relationship between the two.

Paragraph F
Inference
A. 4
B. Any two of these:
   (1) light in weight
   (2) easy to handle
   (3) relatively inexpensive
   (4) can produce slides or print
   (5) can have separate viewfinders or reflex viewing
   (6) sometimes you can interchange normal and wide angle, telephoto or zoom lenses

C. (1) no
   (2) yes
   (3) no
   (4) no
   (5) yes

Fact versus opinion: The author could have a panel of expert photographers try to take pictures with a 35 millimeter camera under difficult lighting conditions and rate the pictures.

Paragraph G
Inference
A. 3
B. 1. Monopolies called franchises became the standard means of providing these services.
   2. A squat little County Court House cost the New York City taxpayers $13 million, about $9 million of it going into the pockets of the city "boss", William Marcy Tweed and his friends.

A. (1) yes
   (2) yes
   (3) yes
   (4) yes
   (5) yes

Fact versus opinion: The authors could probably prove that is *usually* entailed what they said, but probably not that it *inevitably* did. To prove inevitability, you would have to find every single instance.

Exercise 2: Practicing Critical Reading in Longer or Multi-Paragraph Selections (pp. 61–62)

Inference
A. 4
B. (1) Yes. "And fungus is not green because it draws its nutrition from other trees or plants rather than producing its own food."
   (2) Yes. "We can see this if we examine the two main subkingdoms of plants."
   (3) Yes. "In fact, of the 500,000 species of known plants, about 99 percent are just what we would expect. However, this description is too simple."
   (4) Yes. "Normally, when we think of plants we think of things with roots and green leaves. In fact of the 500,000 species of known plants, about 99 percent are just what we would expect . . . And fungus is not green because it draws its nutrition from other trees or plants rather than producing its own food."
   (5) No
   (6) No
   (7) Yes. "For example, algae can be found in this classification, as can seaweed."
   (8) Yes. "For example, although moss is green, it has no real roots. Fungus is not green because it draws its nutrition from other trees or plants rather than producing its own food."

Fact versus opinion: The author could use a large, random sample of people to define "plant."

Comprehension Check (pp. 69–70)

1. d
2. b
3. b
4. d
5. d
6. b
7. b
8. b
9. Slanted news is biased, or slanted, either accidentally or intentionally.
10. Propaganda is the name given to any organized attempt to influence your thinking or actions.

Exercise 3: Identifying Faulty Logic (pp. 70–71)

1. OS
2. UID
3. EO
4. LL
5. LL
6. HG
7. AD
8. EO

Exercise 4: Skills Review—Main Idea and Support (p. 71)

Part A
1. When you write an argument, you present a reasonable argument that states what you believe.
   a. You need to offer logic, evidence and emotional appeals.
   b. You have to prove the merits of what you say.
2. Identify issue at hand
   a. For touchy subject, demonstrate good will toward readers.
   b. Explain why your position is better than that of readers who disagree.
3. Organize body of your argument with audience that agrees with you.
   a. Put strongest point first.
   b. Proceed to lesser points next.
4. No matter what organizational pattern you choose, you must provide supporting evidence
   a. Give specific examples, facts and figures, analogies, considerations of cause and effect.
   b. Detectives work this way, gathering evidence and interpreting it.

Chapter 4

Comprehension Check (pp. 86–87)

1. c
2. d
3. d
4. b
5. d
6. b
7. a
8. d
9. Previewing a chapter means grasping main ideas.
10. In the Question Step of PQ4R, you have a specific method for reading textbooks.

Exercise 1: Previewing Your Textbooks (pp. 87–88)

Answers will vary.

Exercise 2: Previewing a Preface (pp. 88–89)

1. both professors and students
2. new organization of chapters; reduced to 13 chapters
3. eight editions prior to this edition
4. Chapters 1, 2, 3, and 12
5. 13

Exercise 3: Previewing a Table of Contents (p. 90)

1. Chapter 9
2. Chapter 3
3. Library catalogs, the stacks, the Reference and Periodicals sections
4. Yes, in Chapter 8
5. No
6. Chapter 5
7. No
8. Appendices and an Index

Exercise 4: Previewing a Glossary (pp. 90–91)

1. *foil, foot, framework* are a few examples
2. apostrophe
3. framework
4. exact rhyme
5. A flat character is called "flat" because it is a one dimensional character.

Exercise 5: Using an Index (pp. 91–92)

1. pages 8 and 29
2. Constantine (Greece) and Carol (Romania)
3. World War I
4. James
5. Council for Mutual Economic Aid

Exercise 6: Using PQ4R in Longer Selections (pp. 92–93)

Preview
1. How automobile airbags work
2. Used correctly automobile air bags reduce injuries
3. only 25 one-thousandths of a second (0.025s)
4. yes

Exercise 7: Using PQ4R with a Textbook Selection (p. 95)

Preview
1. Personal space
2. Recognizing and understanding personal space is important to understanding human behavior.

3. The subtitle "Cultural Background"
4. 4 (see table 17–1)
5. Men put books in front of themselves while women put books to their sides. (See caption of picture or look at the picture of students in the library.)

Comprehension Check (pp. 101–103)

1. c   5. d
2. b   6. b
3. a   7. c
4. c   8. d
9. intimate, personal, social, public distances
10. Proxemics is the study of personal space.

Exercise 8: Skills Review—Main Idea and Support (pp. 103–104)

I. The flu virus
  A. Process
    1. virus invades cells of respiratory track
    2. each cell then manufactures new viruses
    3. immune system inactivates viruses
  B. Why unbeatable
    1. uncanny ability to change (mutate)
    2. immune system doesn't recognize changed virus
    3. immune system doesn't work well against mutation
    4. a new set of immune cells has to fight the altered viruses which mutate once again.

Chapter 5

Exercise 1: Underlining and Making Marginal Notes (pp. 109–110)

See Appendix A

Exercise 2: Outlining Paragraphs (pp. 116–117)

1. I. Effect of exercise on weight
  A. Body burns more calories
  B. Body idles faster

Main idea: People who exercise can eat more than people who don't exercise.

2. I. Courtship habits of seagulls
  A. Female struts and flutters tail feathers
  B. Female nuzzles and pecks
  C. Male resists; female persists
  D. Male surrenders by throwing up

Main idea: Sea gulls have interesting courtship habits

3. I. Forms of glaciers
  A. Valley glaciers
  B. Piedmont glaciers
  C. Ice sheets
    1. Ice caps
    2. Continental glaciers

Main idea: Glaciers can take several forms.

Exercise 3: Outlining Longer Paragraphs (pp. 117–118)

I. B. Greeks and Arabs—foundations of modern chemistry
  C. European alchemists—attempt to turn lead into gold
II. A. Boyle
  B. Lavoisier demonstrated combination + result of combining fuel with oxygen from air.

Comprehension Check (pp. 123–124)

1. c   5. d
2. b   6. b
3. d   7. d
4. a   8. c
9. outlining flash cards, study maps and other self-generated graphs.
10. draw a circle; draw a line outward; and draw a different geometric figure for each level.

Exercise 4: Using a PQ4R with a Textbook Selection (pp. 125–131)

Preview 1. American Democracy
  2. a. definition
    b. as a system of inter-acting values
    c. as a system of interrelated political processes.

Write: Check Appendix B

Exercise 5: Using Graphic Organizers (p. 132)

Comprehension Check (pp. 132–133)

1. a   5. c
2. b   6. c
3. d   7. c
4. d   8. b
9. *demos:* "the people"; *kratos:* "authority of power"
10. James Madison, Thomas Jefferson, Herbert Hoover, and Franklin Roosevelt are all mentioned.

Exercise 6: Skills Review—Signal Words (p. 134)

a. change of direction
b. emphasis
c. time sequence
d. change of direction
e. cause and effect
f. addition
g. change of direction
h. cause and effect
i. emphasis
j. cause and effect

Check Appendix C

Questions *(p. 140)*
1. The tongue
2. on the tongue's surface
3. no
4. near the back of the tongue
5. sweet and salt
6. papillae
7. an individual taste bud
8. nerve fibers, supporting cells, taste bud, taste cells, taste pore, taste receptor. (Students need 2 of the 6.)

Chapter 6

Comprehension Check (pp. 146–147)

1. c
2. b
3. c
4. d
5. d
6. c
7. c
8. d
9. words, often in scientific or mathematical fields, with precise definitions which may be different from their common definitions
10. Review the text and graphics many times, have study groups, or use a tutor if necessary.

Exercise 1: Identifying Technical and Non-technical Material (p. 148)

1. NT
2. T
3. NT

Exercise 2: Review of PQ4R Techniques (p. 149)

Answers will vary.

Exercise 3: Using Graphic Aids (pp. 150–151)

1. Answers will vary.

2. You can see where each part of the microscope is located rather than just reading about it.
3. a. How to pick up the microscope
   b. How to rest it for support
4. Answers will vary.

Exercise 4: Using PQ4R with a Textbook Selection (pp. 152–155)

Answers will vary.

Exercise 5: Using PQ4R with a Textbook Selection (pp. 155–158)

Answers will vary.

Exercise 6: Using Collateral Reading (p. 158)

1. Answers will vary
2. Answers will vary
3. feeling for a pulse and pump the heart
4. The second article has more detail about mouth-to-mouth breathing including what to do with an infant and also includes the Heimlich Maneuver.
5. The second article only supplements the first two areas of the first article. It has more detail.

Comprehension Check (pp. 158–160)

1. b
2. a
3. d
4. d
5. d
6. c
7. b
8. a
9. Open the victim's mouth and pull the tongue forward. Then clear the mouth of any obstructions. Next, pinch the nostrils together.
10. Pressure is exerted on the victim's breastplate, just below the rib cage. Quick thrusts of pressure are applied until the obstructing material is expelled.

Exercise 7: Understanding Tables (pp. 160–161)

1. 454
2. on Table 2–2
3. the liter
4. pints, quarts, and gallons
5. from the two tables
6. mass and volume
7. from the article's last paragraph

Exercise 8: Skills Review—PQ4R, The Question Step (p. 162)

Part A
Answers will vary.

Part B
Answers will vary.

Chapter 7

Exercise 1: Speed Writing (pp. 168–169)

Check your answers in Appendix D.

Exercise 2: Using the PQ4R Write Step with Lecture Notes (pp. 170–171)

See Appendix E.

Exercise 3: Taking Speed Notes in Lectures (p. 171)

See Appendix F.

Exercise 4: Note Taking (pp. 175–176)

See Appendix F.

Comprehension Check (pp. 179–181)

1. b
2. d
3. a
4. d
5. b
6. b
7. c
8. c
9. Any 3 of the following:
   a. Develop your vocabulary.
   b. Concentrate on the message.
   c. Keep an open and objective mind.
   d. "Read" the speaker.
   e. Put yourself in the speaker's shoes.
   f. Take notes.
   g. Compensate for a speaker's flawed delivery.
   h. Get ready for the wrap-up.
10. Answers will vary.

Comprehension Check (pp. 179–181)

1. b
2. d
3. d
4. a
5. c
6. b
7. b
8. d
9. Any three of the following:
   a. Develop your vocabulary.
   b. Concentrate on the message.
   c. Keep an open and objective mind.
   d. "Read" the speaker.
   e. Put yourself in the speaker's shoes.
   f. Take notes.
   g. Compensate for a speaker's flawed delivery.
   h. Get ready for the wrap-up.
10. Answers will vary.

Exercise 5: Review of Main Idea, Support and Signal Words (pp. 181–184)

Check your answers in Appendix G.

Exercise 6: Review of Using Graphic Organizers (p. 184)

Answers will vary.

Chapter 8

Comprehension Check (pp. 196–197)

1. d
2. c
3. b
4. d
5. c
6. d
7. c
8. a
9. a. paying attention
   b. selecting important facts and ideas
   c. organizing material to be memorized
   d. periodically recalling and reviewing material
   e. applying what has been learned
10. Any 3 of the following:

Internal	External
a. mental conflict	a. noise
b. irrelevant thoughts	b. television
c. daydreaming	c. interruptions
d. boredom	
e. fatigue	

Exercise 1: Selectivity (pp. 197–198)

These are sample answers:
1. virtual reality helmets
2. Jules Verne
3. submerged boat
4. Dick Tracy's wrist telephone
5. walking on the moon
6. virtual love-making

Exercise 2: Organization (p. 198)

1. Arts
   a. sculpture
   b. opera
   c. harp
   d. tempera
   e. easel
   f. keyboard
2. English
   metaphor
   punctuation
   literature
   etymology
   vocabulary
   grammar
3. Political Science/ History
   a. parliament
   b. Congress
   c. election
   d. constitution
4. Science

   dissection
   geology
   organism
   microscope

e. president   chemistry
f. prime minister   biology

Exercise 3: Retention (p. 198)

Answers will vary.

Exercise 4: Mnemonics (p. 199)

Answers will vary.

Exercise 5: Comparing Collateral Reading (pp. 204–205)

1. Yes
2. Answer will vary.
3. Techniques of leading questions, such as "When was the last time you beat your wife?" which is making the assumption that you do beat your wife.
4. People have more trouble recognizing faces of other races than they do recognizing their own race. Caucasians tend to be less accurate than other racial groups in identifying minority members.
5. Read the article to check the answer.
6. Read the article to check the answer.
7. The articles overlap in talking about what a witness really sees; how fresh his or her memory is as time goes by; and if suggestions are made, how a witness can be persuaded to believe that he or she saw something different or nonexistent.

Comprehension Check (pp. 205–207)

1. d   5. c
2. d   6. b
3. a   7. c
4. d   8. c
9. a. Eyewitnesses forget details.
   b. Eyewitnesses distort the duration of an event.
10. a. The reports become distorted.
    b. The reports become simplified.

Exercise 6: Review of Supplementary Recall Techniques, (pp. 207–208)

Answers will vary.

Chapter 9

Exercise 1: Structuring Your Studying for Tests (pp. 221–222)

Sample answers:
1. test anxiety
2. six steps in preparing for tests
3. how often to review
4. what to put on flash cards
5. problems with cramming
6. types of tests
7. five steps in answering objective questions
8. four types of objective questions
9. nine steps in answering essay questions
10. overlearning

Exercise 2: Beginning to Study for Tests (p. 222)

Answers will vary.

Exercise 3: Taking Objective Tests (pp. 222–224)

1. c
2. c
3. b
4. b
5. d
6. a
7. a
8. c
9. d
10. d
11. cramming
12. essay
13. objective
14. flash cards
15. outline
16. 10
17. overlearning
18. short-answer questions
19. follow directions carefully
20. essay
21. F
22. F
23. F
24. F
25. T
26. F
27. F
28. T
29. F
30. T

Exercise 4: Evaluating Test-Taking Skills (pp. 224–225)

Answers will vary.

Exercise 5: Evaluating and Rewriting a Bad Essay (pp. 225–226)

See sample answer on p. 226.

Exercise 6: Answering a Question on an Essay Test (p. 227)

Answers will vary.

Comprehension Check (pp. 231–232)

1. d
2. b
3. b
4. d
5. c
6. a
7. a
8. c
9. The main reason to use biofeedback is to learn how to relax during an exam.
10. Most students experience test anxiety because they are not prepared enough and feel they do not know enough about the scope of their professors' exams.

Exercise 7: Using Collateral Reading (p. 233)

1. Answers will vary.
2. Answers will vary.
3. The first article describes one professor's experiences with students' anxiety about tests. After finding that students used similar excuses of sudden personal crises when exam time came, the professor developed a successful anxiety-reduction system.
4. The second article mentions biofeedback techniques, "flip-flop" strategies, and self-teaching as ways of reducing test anxiety.
5. The first article is non-technical, while the second is somewhat technical in its descriptions of test anxiety and its causes.

Exercise 8: Skills Review—Note-Taking (p. 233)

See Appendix F.

Chapter 10

Comprehension Check (pp. 250–251)

1. a
2. d
3. c
4. c
5. a
6. a
7. c
8. c
9. They often include brief summaries. You can print out a list of titles, names, key words. General topics are easier to look up.
10. It doesn't contain the same type of cross-refer-

encing. In a card catalog, each card includes other topic/entries that each card/book would fall under. Therefore, you may be introduced to subject headings you had not thought of, which could help you find more books.

Exercise 1: Using a Computerized Card Catalog (p. 252)

1. free: *Science Buff's Guide; Amazing Mr. Science:* Young, Barry; free science material
2. Young, Barry
3. 1996
4. *Free Stuff for Science Buffs*

Exercise 2: Using a Computerized Periodical Entry (pp. 252–253)

1. college; papers; college newspapers; cyberspace
2. Wanat, Thomas
3. The Chronicle of Higher Education
4. Volume 41; November 30, 1994

Exercise 3: Comparing a Computerized Periodicals Index Entry and a Readers' Guide *Entry (pp. 253–255)*

1. *"The talking cure for stress"* and *"Get ready . . . get set . . . relax!"*
2. *The Readers' Guide*
3. Any two of these are correct: *"Ready . . . get set . . . relax!"*, *"The talking cure for stress"; "Stress Busters!"; "Stressed Pit, 25 Ways to Cope"; "Can You Laugh Your Stress Away?"*
4. The *Readers' Guide* entry says it is cognitive therapy research by James Blumenthal. It also indicates that the article is illustrated. Finally, it states that *Health* magazine is published in San Francisco. On the other hand, the computer entry tells us the article includes related information on self-help cliches and is the cover story. In addition, it gives the full name of the author (Benedict Carey) and states that an abstract is available.
5. *"Heart Attacks: High Hopes vs. High Anxiety"*; smarter stress test?
6. Any of these reasons are possible:
   a. The date of the article may be more recent than the latest *Readers' Guide* issue.
   b. The *Readers' Guide* may not index that magazine.
   c. It may just be an error of omission.

Exercise 4: Beginning a Research Project (pp. 255–256)

Answers will vary.

Comprehension Check (pp. 264–265)

1.	a	5.	a
2.	d	6.	a
3.	d	7.	d
4.	b	8.	c

9. The purpose of the preliminary search is to determine whether or not your subject is too broad or too narrow.
10. The reason to use note cards is that they are building blocks that you use to complete an outline of your paper.

Exercise 5: Skills Review—Memory/Graphic Organizers (pp. 265–268)

Answers will vary.

Exercise 6: Skills Review—Taking Tests (pp. 268–270)

1. c
2. d
3. c
4. d
5. b
6. F
7. T
8. T
9. F
10. F
11. F
12. F
13. F
14. T
15. T
16. The tradition of computerized card catalog
17. Reference
18. *Readers' Guide to Periodical Literature*
19. *Who's Who*
20. Dewey Decimal System

Chapter 11

Comprehension Check (pp. 281–282)

1.	a	5.	c
2.	d	6.	c
3.	b	7.	d
4.	c	8.	b

9. A denotative word is a literal definition.
10. A connotative word is a word that brings to mind various images and associations.

Exercise 1: Using the Dictionary (pp. 282–283)

1. a. plural
   b. plural
   c. singular
   d. plural
2. a. noun, verb
   b. verb, adjective
   c. verb, noun
   d. noun, verb
3. a. All that glitters is not gold.
   b. Empty kettles make the most noise.
   c. Strike while the iron is hot.
4. a. *répondez, s'il vous plait* (please reply)
   b. *et cetera* (and so forth)
   c. *id est* (that is)
   d. *exempli gratia* (for example)

Exercise 2: Prefixes (pp. 283–284)

Answers will vary.

Exercise 3: Roots (p. 285)

Check your answers in a dictionary which has roots.

Exercise 4: Vocabulary (pp. 285–286)

1.	misnomer	6.	protracted
2.	advocate	7.	remote
3.	convoke	8.	depository
4.	evident	9.	irrevocable
5.	envision	10.	suppress

Comprehension Check (pp. 291–292)

1.	d	5.	c
2.	c	6.	b
3.	c	7.	c
4.	a	8.	c

9. An etymology is the history of a word.
10. Loaded words are words that can provoke heated and sometimes overpowering reactions, especially words related to race, religion, and politics.

Exercise 5: Etymology (pp. 292–293)

1. a. an inhabitant of Lilliput; an undersized creature
   b. *Gulliver's Travels*
2. a. to join together in a refusal to deal with an individual, group, organization, etc.
   b. Captain C. C. Boycott
3. a. one who gets pleasure from causing pain to others

 b. the Marquis de Sade
4. a. idealized place, state situation
 b. Sir Thomas More's *Utopia*
5. a. huge
 b. Francois Rabelais' *Gargantua and Pantagruel*
6. a. body tissue
 b. "little mouse" (Latin)

Exercise 6: Using the Thesaurus (p. 293)

1. admiration and applause
2. apprentice
3. esteem
4. a. kudos
 b. 1. root for, applause
 2. stick up for, approve
5. adjective
6. No, because the first guide word is *apprentice*. *Admire* would be on an earlier page.

Exercise 7: Skills Review—PQ4R Underlining and Making Marginal Notes (p. 293)

Answers will vary.

Chapter 12

Comprehension Check (pp. 302–303)

1. d   5. a
2. c   6. c
3. d   7. c
4. c   8. b
9. a. Skimming is reading to gain a general idea of a selection.

 b. Scanning is reading to locate specific information.
10. Two examples of bad reading habits are reading word by word and moving your lips.

Exercise 1: Skimming and Scanning (pp. 304–305)

Skimming
1. Woody Guthrie
2. Woody Guthrie was a singer and folk hero during the Depression.

Scanning
1. the Great Depression
2. rural Oklahoma
3. guitar
4. John Steinbeck
5. California
6. Cisco Houson and Will Geer
7. *People's Daily World*
8. Pete Seeger
9. Socialism
10. "This Land Is Your Land"

Index